33

Eritrea,
a Pawn in World Politics

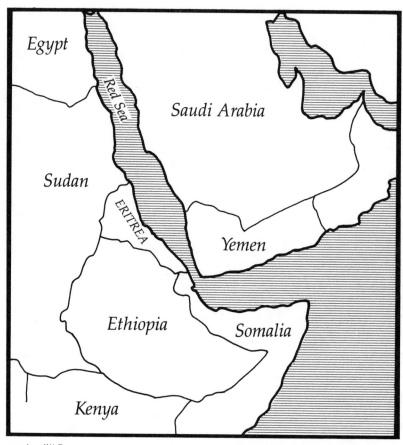

map by Jill Dygert

Eritrea,
a Pawn in World Politics

Okbazghi Yohannes

University of Florida Press / Gainesville

The University of Florida Press is a member of
University Presses of Florida, the scholarly publishing
agency of the State University System of Florida. Books
are selected for publication by faculty editorial committees
at each of Florida's nine public universities: Florida A&M
University (Tallahassee), Florida Atlantic University (Boca
Raton), Florida International University (Miami), Florida
State University (Tallahassee), University of Central Florida
(Orlando), University of Florida (Gainesville), University
of North Florida (Jacksonville), University of South Florida
(Tampa), University of West Florida (Pensacola).

Orders for books published by all member presses should be
addressed to University Presses of Florida, 15 NW 15th St.,
Gainesville, FL 32611.

Library of Congress Cataloging-in-Publication Data

Okbazghi Yohannes.
    Eritrea : a pawn in world politics / Okbazghi Yohannes.
    p.   cm.
    Includes bibliographical references and index.
    ISBN 0–8130–1044–6
    1. Eritrea (Ethiopia)—Politics and government—1941–1942.
2. Eritrea (Ethiopia)—Politics and government—1952–1962.
3. Eritrea (Ethiopia)—Politics and government—1962– 4. Eritrea
(Ethiopia)—Foreign relations—1889–1974. 5. Eritrea (Ethiopia)—
Foreign relations—1974– I. Title.
DT395.3.038 1991   90–44256
963'.506—dc20   CIP

In memory of my father, Yohannes Mirach,
murdered by Ethiopian soldiers in his village inside Eritrea
on March 19, 1989. He taught me the art of perseverance
and the science of struggle.

Contents

Preface

THIS BOOK IS A product of both personal and professional interest. As a student of nationalism, I have been fascinated by the tenacity of Eritrean nationalism as much as by its tragic human dimensions. In this regard, the evolution of my thinking has significantly been influenced by the poignant question raised by Basil Davidson: namely why Eritrea was held hostage to the caprice of international power politics while all other colonial territories which had passed through colonial experiences similar to Eritrea's were, without exception, permitted to exercise their universal right to self-determination. The question has been intellectually so fascinating and politically so perplexing that I chose to concentrate on the external dimensions of the Eritrean problem.

I began my intellectual inquiry into the complexities surrounding this problem six years ago. In the process I discovered that the Ethio-Eritrean conflict was essentially a function of exogenous forces that had harnessed the future of the former Italian colony to the vicissitudes of power politics; hence this book. The primary purpose of the book is, therefore, to describe and to increase the understanding of the external dimensions of the Eritrean problem. To be sure, this book is a history of imperialism and of postwar power politics in Eritrea. The narrations pertaining to the genesis and evolution of Eritrean nationalism are peripheral in relation to the larger issue and are intended to provide the reader with a general frame of reference.

In preparing this book, I have immensely benefited from the assistance of many organizations and individuals. I would like to express my deep appreciation to the British Public Record Office for their generous assistance in making their primary documents available. I am also indebted to the Research and Information Center on Eritrea for providing other valuable documents. Equal gratitude extends to Recording for the Blind, without whose continuous support in providing taped materials and books the conclusion of this project would have been impossible.

I am very grateful to Timothy Fernyhough who read the manuscript twice and provided me with valuable suggestions. His constructive criticisms have certainly contributed to the reduction of many stylistic delinquencies and substantive deficiencies. I remain indebted to John McCamant, George Shepherd, and Bob Schulzinger who also offered constructive criticism that nurtured the production of new ideas.

Special thanks go to my longtime friend and reader, Carolyn Garner, who taped innumerable documents and books. Her anecdotes and remarks were always insightful.

I am also grateful to my mother-in-law, Mary Ann Rombold, for her encouragement and moral support, especially during the hectic days in London.

I owe a special debt of appreciation to my wife, Tamara, who gave me constant support, encouragement, and advice when I needed them most. Ever since the beginning of this project, Tamara served as my personal secretary, adviser, editor, co-researcher, co-traveller, and most of all, faithful companion. Without her editing talents, constant encouragement and support, the book would never have been completed.

The arrival of our little daughter, Keren, during the final stage of the production of this book gave new momentum to my work. Her cries and laughter kept me company and her rosey smell gave me faith in the future.

1

From Colonialism to Nationalism

LIKE MOST COLONIAL formations in Africa, Eritrea is the creation
of modern colonialism. Between 1885 and 1890 the Italians forged
the colony by piecing together different historical units. But unlike
other colonial formations, Eritrea has not been adequately researched
and consequently is the least understood colony on the entire continent. Three fundamental features distinguish Eritrea from other colonies: it is the only former colony never allowed independence; its
armed resistance is the longest war of liberation in contemporary Africa; and the Eritrean question is perhaps the only contemporary
issue of international relations on which the two superpowers col-
luded by taking turns supporting Ethiopia's claim over Eritrea.

If the nonresolution of Eritrea's colonial status was the direct cause
of the insurrectionary process in Eritrea, the recurrent pattern of
intervention by external powers provided the context for the continuation of the Eritrean problem. The purpose of this study is, therefore,
to provide a comprehensive analysis of the genesis and evolution of
Eritrean nationalism from its diplomatic dimensions. I have drawn
a theoretical distinction between what Chabal calls the context and
the process of revolution. Chabal defines the context of a revolution
as the structural determinations that precipitate the revolution in the
first place, whereas the process of a revolution involves the actual
implementation of revolutionary programs that challenge the existing
state of affairs.[1]

1

Consistent with this definition, I have presupposed in this work that the Eritrean problem was exogenously determined when the United Nations created a federal structure that linked the territory to Ethiopia. Since this approach accords primacy to the exogenous factors that have not been attended to in other writings, a comprehensive study of Eritrean nationalism seems warranted. Granted that my heterodox thesis may be biased, a clarification of the theoretical and methodological apparatus of this work is in order.

Despite divergence in emphasis, students of comparative nationalism concur that nationalism is a self-defining ethnophenomenon that develops in reaction to real or perceived oppression by an out-group.[2] Even though the definition of nationalism usually contains such objective factors as language, culture, religion, politics, and ethnic distinction, it also encapsulates important ethnopsychological components such as sentiments, feelings, and myths. Shafer, for example, enumerates ten factors that could go into the definition of nationalism. They include demarcated territoriality, commonality of culture and language, shared belief in a common history and destiny which can be real or imagined, a desire for statehood, veneration of fellow nationals, shared animosity toward others, and so on.[3]

Implicit in this definition is that nationalism is dynamic. The contents and forms, the extent and intensity of national sentiments, and loyalties vary over time and space. They are sociohistorically and contextually determined and are continually conditioned.[4] In the words of Ernest Renan, the nineteenth-century French writer, "The existence of a nation is a plebiscite of everyday, as the existence of the individual is a perpetual affirmation of life."[5]

According to some experts in the field, the idea of modern nationalism is codeterministic with the rise and development of capitalism. Hans Kohn, for example, sees a parallelism in the emergence of industrialism, democracy, and nationalism mediated by the dynamic process of economic exchange and the attendant intensification of communication and acculturation, elements that trigger the emergence and development of a common psychological makeup.[6] For Kohn, nationalism is more than anything else a "state of mind"; it is how the people concerned define themselves, rather than how others define them. He observes: "Although objective factors are of great importance for the formation of nationalities, the most essential element is a living and active corporate will. It is this will which we call nationalism, a state of mind inspiring the large majority of a people and claiming to inspire all its members."[7]

The development of capitalism and the bourgeois revolutions in Europe lend credence to Kohn's analysis. Thus, if capitalism provided the context for the emergence of nationalism in Europe, the implantation of capitalism in the colonial formations likewise provided the context for anticolonial nationalism. As Shafer observed, colonial capitalism created monetized economies, new methods of production and consumption, centralized state administration, communication networks, and territorial delimitations often containing disparate ethnic groups, and it introduced modern education and capitalist values that included the ideas of democracy, freedom, and social equality.[8] Thus, the implantation of colonial capitalism not only destroyed the traditional mode of existence, but also created a new consciousness on the part of the native populace who learned through experience of the differential access to the benefits of colonial capitalism.

To put it differently, colonialism provided both the context and the basis of anticolonial nationalism. It is this context and basis that Eritrean nationalism shares with all anticolonial nationalisms in Africa and elsewhere. Eritrean nationalism is not, thus, an a priori reflection of a single ethnic crystallization. It is a historical reflection of a larger reality whose explanation must be sought in the implantation of colonial capitalism into Eritrea. In other words, Eritrea is a multinational country which emerged as a result of modern capitalist colonization.

The impregnation of the territory with capitalism gave rise to the emergence of Eritrean nationalism under which nine ethnic groups found common expression. Consequently, the Eritrean nationalists developed over time the political urge to create an Eritrean state. This political urge was explicitly articulated as early as 1946, for example, by one nationalist group which argued that "the territorial unity of Eritrea, as it was prior to 1935, be maintained, and that it is recognised as an indivisible unity from the geographical, political and economic point of view; in conformity with the right of self-determination granted to peoples, that a guarantee be given that she will be free to express herself and defend her natural rights; and therefore she does not accept nor adhere to any decision aiming to

partition Eritrea in any form whatever, in so much as the UNO charter does not contemplate placing a country under the sovereignty
of another against the wish of the people."[9]

Three years later, an American envoy to the Eritrean capital
grudgingly admitted that Eritrean nationalists were insistent about
their aspiration for national independence when he communicated
his assessment to the Department of State in these terms: "Fixed platform of Independence Bloc has four planks: immediate independence, democratic government, territorial integrity within present
boundaries, and no partition."[10]

As we shall see later, this basic nationalist orientation was at odds
with the plans that the major external actors had for Eritrea. In view
of their strategic interest in the area, Anglo-American policymakers
viewed Eritrea as an expendable entity. When they considered the
restoration of the colony to Italy, for example, one British official
bluntly put the matter in these terms: "The return would, of course,
be widely detested, but owing to the comparative lack of weapons,
organisation and leadership the native Eritreans on their own are
not capable, in my opinion, of expressing their resentment effectively
against European troops."[11] It was on the basis of this orientation
that the major external actors preempted Eritrean independence in
favor of its "association" with Ethiopia as a way of assuring their long-
term interest in the area. Herein lies the genesis of the Eritrean problem. The progressive obliteration of the insignia of Eritrea's separate
identity and of its political and cultural institutions, which culminated
in the formal abolition of the Eritrean government by Ethiopia in
1962, simply reinforced the contextual dimensions of Eritrean nationalism and the determination of the nationalists in their quest for independence.

The elements of my thesis here, then, crystallize around two fundamental propositions. First, the existing state of affairs in Eritrea today
is the natural consequence of the imposition of external authority
on Eritrea in the form of federation. The absence of any external
restraining or countervailing power in the federal structure presented an unbounded opportunity for Ethiopia to upturn the UN-
created status quo in its favor. The refusal of the United Nations,
as the author of the Federal Act, to intervene in the interest of preserving the federation when Ethiopia annulled the act unilaterally
in 1962 has been the logical consequence of its prior inability to imple-

ment the principle of self-determination with respect to Eritrea. Second, the elements of competition between the major powers of the United Nations in the 1940s were decisive in the production of the type of solution imposed on Eritrea. Subsequent developments associated with the recurrent pattern of external involvement in the Ethio-Eritrean conflict are eloquent demonstrations of the persistence of these same elements of competition which have continued to be responsible for the protraction and unpredictability of the conflict today.

To be sure, the thesis holds that the Ethio-Eritrean conflict was exogenously determined and continues today to be externally conditioned, if not determined. By providing a comprehensive study of the historical context and international environment of the Eritrean question, I hope to make a modest contribution to the understanding of the question under study.

The Land and the People

Eritrea occupies a land area of about 50,000 square miles in the Horn of Africa. It is bounded by the Red Sea on the east, Djibouti on the southeast, Ethiopia on the south, and the Sudan on the west and north. Its strategic importance depends on its geographical location, stretching for 1,000 kilometers on the western shores of the Red Sea. The Eritrean ports of Massawa and Assab are to be found here. Furthermore, over 100 tiny islands, most of which have only military significance, squat within its territorial waters. Its strategic location gives Eritrea a dominant position to command both the strait of Bab El Mandeb on the southern tip of the Red Sea, serving as a gateway to the Indian Ocean, and the Suez Canal, leading to the Mediterranean on the north. Eritrea looks across the Red Sea and the Gulf of Aden to the oil-rich Arabian peninsula. All commercial liners bound for Europe and the Mediterranean region from the Persian Gulf, east Africa, Asia, and the Far East must pass through the Red Sea. Thus, all kinds of activities are intimately connected with the strategic utility of the Red Sea region in which Eritrea plays a dominant role. For reasons of strategic consideration, anything that happens in Eritrea inevitably heightens the perception and interest of regional as well as international actors.

Eritrea is divided into four topographic regions. The central plateau region, 6,000 to 8,000 feet above sea level, comprises the three provinces of Akkele Guzai, Hamasien, and Serae. The three rivers, Barka, Anseba, and Mareb or Gash, which flow into the Sudan through western Eritrea, have their sources in this plateau. The annual rainfall averages between sixteen and twenty-four inches, and vegetation is sparse. With Asmara as its center, the plateau region comprises 20 percent of Eritrea's territory and almost half of its population.

The core of the northern highlands, or the Rora region, is the province of Senhit, with Keren at its center. Sections of Sahel and Barka provinces are also part of this region. The altitude ranges between 2,500 and 4,500 feet above sea level. Vegetation and rainfall are highly varied, although the average annual rainfall is about sixteen inches. This region covers about one-third of Eritrea's territory.

The western lowlands region is composed of the broad plains lying west and southwest of the Barka River and north of the Setit River. The river basins are generally endowed with rich vegetation. Annual rainfall for the plains north of the Gash River varies between twelve and fourteen inches while the average rainfall in the Gash-Setit lowlands ranges between twenty and twenty-five inches.

The eastern coastal plains extend from the Sudan border in the north to the border of Djibouti in the south. The region includes the provinces of Dankalia in the south, Semhar in the center, and parts of Sahel province in the north. It is a semidesert area, and the annual average rainfall is below ten inches.

The social morphology of the Eritrean people corresponds roughly to the physical configuration of the country. Eritrea is a mosaic of nine nationalities belonging to the Semitic, Cushitic, and Nilo-Saharan language families.

The Tigrinya speakers inhabit the plateau region of Eritrea. They are either Semitic or an admixture of Semitic and Cushitic in origin. There are about 1.5 million Tigrinya speakers who profess Coptic Christianity. The Jeberti, who profess Islam, are also Tigrinya speakers found in this region.

The Sahos are a "lowland east" Cushitic-speaking ethnic group inhabiting the coastal depression of Eritrea between Massawa and the province of Akkele Guzai. The Sahos, who according to a 1976 estimate number about 120,000, are Muslims by confession.[12] Their seasonal migration takes them up to the Eritrean plateau and even far beyond the Mereb River into the Ethiopian province of Tigrai. They migrate into these areas during the summer months and stay in the coastal areas during the months of winter. This constant migration over the centuries has brought them into contact with the Tigrinya-speaking people in the plateau, with the result that some of them have become permanent settlers.

The Afars are also a "lowland east" Cushitic-speaking ethnic group inhabiting the entire Eritrean province of Dankalia. They are so closely related to the Sahos that their languages are mutually intelligible. The Afars are estimated at about 150,000. They are nomadic Moslems.

The Bilen are a central Cushitic-speaking ethnic group who forced their way into the Rora region of Eritrea in the thirteenth century when the Agaw dynasty at Lasta collapsed under Amhara pressure. The Bilen are now found in and around Keren in the province of Senhit. They are estimated to number over 40,000.[13] About three-quarters of the Bilen are Moslem; the remainder profess Roman Catholicism. The Bilen are generally bilingual, speaking Bilen and Tigre, and many are even trilingual, adding either Tigrinya or Arabic. However, their own language is at the point of extinction and is now used only for private conversation at home.

The Beja, or Beni Amer, are a "north" Cushitic-speaking ethnic group contained in the lowland triangle of the Barka Valley and the Gash area in western Eritrea, bordering the Sudan. In 1976, they were estimated to stand at 100,000.[14] They are increasingly intermarrying with the Tigres, with the result that most of them now speak Tigre. The Beja are nomadic or seminomadic with the exception of a small portion who are settled agriculturalists. They are also predominantly Moslems.

Tigre is another ethnic group found in western and northern Eritrea. Tigre is a term that can mean either the common people, as distinct from the nobility, or the language itself, which the speakers themselves refer to as Tigrayit. Today, there are over 200,000 Tigre speakers. Although both Tigrinya and Tigre have a 70 percent basic lexicon resemblance to Giiz, they are not mutually intelligible.[15]

The Kunama are a Nilo-Saharan ethnic community living between the Gash and Setit rivers in southwestern Eritrea. Said to number about 70,000, they are remnants of the ancient inhabitants of the region.[16] Originally, the Kunama were animists, and their conversion _n and Protestantism is of recent history. They are agricultural-ists organized into villages.

The Nera or Barya are another remnant of the Nilo-Saharan com-munity of people. Their presence in southwestern Eritrea was first mentioned in King Ezana's inscription of the fourth century A.D. Al-though the scholarly assumption is that they might have migrated from the Sudan to Eritrea under pressure of invaders, their own tra-dition suggests that they once lived near Keren. Numbering about 25,000, the Nera today live north and west of Barentu. Most of them are bilingual, speaking Nera Bana and Tigre, the latter being their second language.[17] Even though both the Kunama and the Nera are Nilo-Saharan in origin, they speak different languages which are not mutually intelligible.

The Rashaida are a small minority of Arabic-speaking people who live in northern Eritrea along the Red Sea coast. They represent the most recent immigrants from Arabia. They confess Islam exclusively, and their culture and language are still Arabic.

The Impact of European Colonization on Eritrean Society

The underlying economic motivation of Italian colonialism was spurred by the demand for commercial expansion and maritime trade. Burgeoning problems precipitated by declining agrarian pro-duction and rural overpopulation were also additional considerations for Italy's colonial orientation.[18] It was thus in anticipation that Eri-trea would contribute to Italy's commercial development and to the alleviation of its agrarian crisis that the territory was colonized.

Italy's primary objectives in Eritrea were to develop settler colonies for Italian peasants, exploit natural resources, recruit colonial sol-diers for the further expansion and consolidation of the Italian over-seas empire, and make use of Eritrea for industrial and commercial purposes.[19]

To achieve these ends in the creation of settlement colonies, Italy sent a commission of inquiry to Eritrea in 1891 to study agricultural prospects. The commission commented favorably on the agrarian via-bility of the territory and on the presumed "docility" of Eritreans toward Italian agrarian colonization. Accordingly, between the beginning of 1893 and the middle of 1895, 400,000 hectares of land were expropriated by the colonial state for distribution to Italian immigrants.[20]

Nonetheless, the initial attempts to settle Italian immigrants in the region did not meet with success. The Italian project failed, first, because the Eritrean plateau was not suitable for European-type agricultural development which was based on mechanization, extensive utilization of fertilizers, irrigation schemes, and prior development of infrastructural facilities. Second, the Italian government was halfheartedly committed to expenditures on infrastructural development in Eritrea. Third, there were fundamental practical difficulties complicated by the underdevelopment of Eritrea. Fourth, the Italians failed to appreciate the relationship between land and the Eritrean social forces that tilled the land.[21]

The most crucial element that contributed to the failure of Italy's expropriation policy was, however, the growing discontent on the part of the Eritreans over the policy. It was manifested in an open revolt against the Italians in December 1894 under the leadership of Bahta Hagos. Bahta was a local chief in Akkele Guzai who rose to prominence through his resistance, first to the Abyssinian presence in his region and later to the Italian policy of land confiscation.[22] On 14 December 1894, Bahta called upon the Eritrean peasantry to revolt against the Italian policy. As he poised his 2,000-man army for an assault on the Italian presence in Eritrea, he arrested the Italian secretary at Segeneiti, along with two Italian telegraph workers. The colonial governor of Eritrea, General Baratieri, however, dispatched over 3,000 troops from Massawa and Asmara to reinforce the Italian contingent in the area. By 19 December the Eritrean uprising was crushed and Bahta Hagos was killed.[23]

Despite this early suppression of the Eritrean uprising, the December revolt was crucial insofar as it marked the beginning of Eritrean nationalism, which had to be reckoned with. Even Governor Baratieri acknowledged that the uprising was a manifestation of a growing "national sentiment" in Eritrea.[24] At any rate, Italy's policy of land expropriation was discontinued by mid-1895. Nonetheless, during the period of Martini's governorship (1897–1907) an unofficial policy of land confiscation was under way. Between 1899 and 1907, for example, close to 70,000 hectares of land were expropriated in highland

Eritrea alone. To put it differently, by 1906 the colonial state had about 482,000 hectares of land at its disposal for distribution to Italian settlers.[25]

In 1926 the Italian government issued revised decrees in such a manner as to encourage Italian farmers to participate actively in the development of commercial farms along the lines of capitalism. The Italian government established credit facilities to benefit these farmers, and financial incentives such as tax credits and custom-free importation of agricultural equipment were made available to all Italian farmers.[26] In economic terms, these steps were of immense significance in the sense that privatization and commercialization of Eritrean agriculture on an extensive capitalist scale were made possible with the result that Eritrean peasants were evicted and detached from the land.

In their final attempt to complete the privatization of land in Eritrea, the Italians turned against the established institution of the Eritrean Coptic Church. The church was the most powerful economic and social force in Eritrea, by virtue of its possession of large tracts of arable land and its influence on the populace. Thus, both for economic and political reasons, the colonial government confiscated the fiefs of the church and converted them into crown land, thereby reducing the church to relative economic and political impotence.[27] The inevitable result was that the peasants who had been working on the church's fiefs were evicted and thus swelled the reservoir of landless peasants. In addition, violent seizures of land for construction and infrastructural development created more and more landless peasants and accentuated the depeasantization process in Eritrea.

In summary, the agricultural policy of the Italian government in Eritrea produced two important factors that were crucial for the total economic as well as sociopolitical configuration of the territory. In the first instance, the ferocious expropriation of land, which resulted in the alienation of land as the basis of a natural economy for Eritrean peasants, and its conversion into crown land facilitated the capitalist penetration of rural Eritrea and hence the eventual incorporation of Eritrea into the world capitalist structure. Second, the privatization and commercialization of agriculture in Eritrea destroyed the means of subsistence for Eritrean peasants, resulting in tens of thousands of landless peasants. This continuous process of expropriation, privatization, and commercialization of Eritrean agriculture thus forced the peasants either to flock to the newly emergent colonial centers in pursuit of menial occupations or to join the commercial farms of the Italians in the countryside where they could sell their labor power. Those who were hired in commercial agriculture thus constituted the incipient rural proletariat in Eritrea, and it was in the rural areas that the first process of commodification of labor started. Now rural Eritrea became an appendage to the city in a capitalist fashion.

The political significance of this economic process was that the affected peasants from all nationalities, for the first time, began to work together and were subjected to the same kinds of exploitation, oppression, and discrimination in big plantations owned by foreign entrepreneurs. Under such conditions, it was inevitable that the rural proletariat would develop some sense of solidarity within itself which, over time, would translate into national awakening and political activism.

Italy's long-term objective was the creation of an Italian empire in east Africa, encompassing the entire region of the Horn, which might eventually extend from the Mediterranean shores in the north to the western tip of the Indian Ocean. In strategic terms, Eritrea was seen as merely a springboard for further expansion, and military programs within Eritrea itself, such as the building of military installations, bases, depots, warehouses, and military airports, were developed. This expansion, in turn, required the availability of cheap labor which was to be found in the reservoir of landless Eritrean peasants. Some of the landless peasants were hired to work in military installations, infrastructural developments, and military-related facilities.

More important, however, the landless peasants were militarily crucial in the sense that they formed the backbone of the Italian colonial army, which was to be engaged in Italian conquest of other territories. For example, thousands of Eritreans were sent to Libya and Somalia to fight Italy's colonial wars there.[28] Moreover, in 1935 alone the Italians conscripted 65,000 Eritreans for their colonial war in Ethiopia.[29] A 1938 study even suggested that up to 70,000 Eritreans were conscripted for use in Ethiopia.[30]

The significance of the militarization process, from the point of view of class configuration, was that a sizable portion of the landless Eritrean peasants were absorbed into the colonial army and military structure, whereby they were transformed into an incipient class of the petit bourgeoisie, oriented toward modern technology and ideas. Again, the military sector was an important meeting ground for thousands of Eritreans who came from different ethnic and sociocultural backgrounds.

The capitalist agricultural ventures and the military projects in Eritrea triggered the necessity of creating centers of control on which the various linkage areas converged. The development of commercial farms required centers for distribution of imported goods as well as of agricultural products destined for Italy. In addition, the militarization process stimulated the development of urban housing where soldiers and their families could live. In reaction to these demands, housing projects flourished. The spin-off effects of this development were that, in order to meet the needs of the emerging urban population, shopping centers, repair shops, cottage industries, and the like were established. In this way, a number of towns and cities sprang up, including the Eritrean capital of Asmara.

The 1930s saw tremendous growth in and a flourishing of the urban centers owing to Italy's feverish preparation for invading Ethiopia. Hundreds of millions of Italian lire poured into Eritrea for the construction of roads and railways and the expansion of seaports and military installations. The port of Massawa was enlarged to a daily capacity of 1,500 tons. Furthermore, the port was linked to Asmara by one of the world's longest cableways, with a daily capacity of 500 tons. A railway was built linking Massawa on the east coast, Asmara at the center, Keren in the northern plateau, and Agordat in the west, serving about two-thirds of Eritrea. In addition, 1,176 kilometers of new asphalt roads were built connecting the various centers of Eritrea.[31] The airports of Asmara and Guraa were rebuilt and modernized.[32]

To meet the growing needs of the urban population, many public utility establishments were also set up. By 1939, there were twenty-five post offices and fifty-seven telegraph lines, and seventeen localities were receiving telephone services. Many electric power stations were set up with the capacity of reaching 15 million kilowatt hours.[33]

Alongside the development of urban centers, urban populations grew tremendously. Prior to 1930 there had been only 5,000 Italians in Eritrea; in 1935 the figure reached 50,000, and, by 1941, 70,000.[34]

On the Eritrean side of the ledger, 20 percent of the total population was urbanized by 1941. Before 1935, for example, the city of Asmara had had only 15,000 natives, but by 1941 it housed 120,000 Eritreans.[35]

In sum, the creation of commercial agricultural concessions, the militarization process involving the engagement of tens of thousands of Eritreans in the construction and elaboration of communication networks, the development of water resources and mineral prospects, and the creation of modern towns and cities had unprecedented implications for Eritrean society. All these required the displacement and transformation of the Eritrean peasants and their labor. Now the various regions of Eritrea inhabited by different nationalities were linked by roads and railways. Members of all nationalities flocked to the urban centers and were represented in the colonial army. These processes of communication and commodification of labor inevitably led to contacts, exchange of ideas, and sharing of common experience transcending ethnic loyalties and identities among native Eritreans. These objective processes were of particular importance to the secularization of Eritreans as a force.

The pressure from urban population growth triggered the need for the establishment of industrial and commercial firms geared to the production and distribution of consumer commodities to satisfy the new wants created within Eritrea. Initially Italy had no interest in the industrialization of its colony since one of its purposes had been to use Eritrea as a dumping ground for finished Italian goods. However, in the 1930s, on the eve of Italy's invasion of Ethiopia, the availability of finished commodities at hand was so important, in view of the growing local demands and the urgency of war preparations, that the industrialization of Eritrea proceeded, albeit in restricted form.

Before 1930, there had been only 56 industrial firms in Eritrea. But now, motivated by the war efforts of the Italian government, many Italian entrepreneurs began to pour their capital into Eritrea. Consequently, in 1939, there were 2,198 industrial firms with operating capital of close to 2,200 million lire and another 2,690 commercial firms with total capital of 486 million lire.[36] The industrial firms produced a wide variety of consumer goods, including leather goods, cement, boots and shoes, boot polish, hand tools, buttons, matches, lampshades, canned food, fish meal, fish oil, pickles, flour, seed oil, tomato sauce, pottery, paints, alcoholic beverages, sodas, and refractory bricks.[37]

This industrialization process, started by the Italians, was continued in the 1940s by the British. Now Eritrea, under British occupation since 1941, had to supply the whole Middle East, which was cut off from Europe by the war. The war contributed immensely to the industrial prosperity of Eritrea. This assertion is borne out by the fact that, when the British dismantled the Italian war projects in Eritrea in 1942, the fourteen thousand workers who were attached to the war projects were quickly absorbed by the flourishing local industrial firms. In addition, as a result of heavy British investment in Eritrea for the purpose of meeting wartime requirements, three hundred industrial firms were created in less than three years before the end of the war.[38] Of special importance among these firms were the aircraft assembly plant, an aircraft repair base, and the repair and maintenance facilities in Asmara and Guraa.[39] This new industrial boom in Eritrea was highlighted by the December 1943 industrial exhibition in which over four hundred industrial firms participated to display their products to attract the Middle Eastern market.[40]

The social and political significance of this industrialization process was that a strong Eritrean working class emerged. The greater portion of the previously landless Eritrean peasants came to constitute the Eritrean industrial army. Since the depeasantization process affected almost every ethnic group in Eritrea to some degree, this industrial army emerged as a multinational force. Since the members of the working class came to work under one roof or in the same plantation for the foreign colonists, they shared a common experience of exploitation, subjugation, and victimization. But that process of working together helped them to develop their own means of communication. Ethnic and linguistic barriers began to crumble, and new modes of existence and expression were asserted. Changes in the structural determinations necessarily entailed changes in the modes of expressing ideas, views, conceptions, or, in one word, consciousness, reflecting the condition of the workers' material existence and social relations.

The relative political maturity of the Eritrean working class was borne out by its agitational and organizational strength which, in December 1952, formed the General Union of Eritrean Labour Syndicates, one of the first of its kind in Africa. Furthermore, the leader of the Eritrean labor movement, Wolde-ab Woldemariam, who escaped five Ethiopian assassination attempts prior to April 1950, was one of the founding fathers of the proindependence Eritrean Liberal Progressive Party and later of the Eritrean Liberation Front.

The introduction and development of colonial capitalism in Eritrea initiated and promoted a new equilibrium in social and human relations among the various nationalities in Eritrea without the understanding of which it becomes impossible to comprehend Eritrean nationalism. As the result of the four processes of depeasantization, militarization, urbanization, and proletarianization, the regional seclusion and self-sufficiency of the nationalities were shattered and free migration and movement from one region to another were made possible. In place of the old attachment to the land, a good portion of the peasants became wage earners. Quite apart from the negative aspect of colonialism, the development of colonial capitalism gave rise to colonial consciousness and hence to Eritrean nationalism. The caveat here is that the significance of the capitalist penetration of Eritrea lies not in its magnitude but in its qualitative determinations.

Colonial capitalism brought not only the mechanics of oppression but also the means of liberation. It did this in three ways.

First, colonial capitalism virtually destroyed all modes of precapitalist existence, and consequently old forms of social relations and classes were replaced by new ones. In addition to the rural and industrial proletariat, a strong class of the petit bourgeoisie emerged. The emergence of Eritrean "half-castes" of mixed Italian and Eritrean marriages also had a significant bearing on the multinational configuration of the Eritrean population. This segment, which numbered 25,000 in 1950, was allowed to obtain higher education and skill by attending Italian schools. The group became politically conscious, economically well off, and technically advanced commensurate with its commitment to the cause of capitalist development.

Second, colonial capitalism provided an elaborate network of communications along which ideas, information, and directives could flow. In this regard, the fragmented cosmopolitan towns of Eritrea played an important role as loci for the diffusion of ideas and information. In fact, it was precisely in the towns that the Eritrean social forces took shape and received their training to fight for national liberation, due, more than anything else, to the fact that the most compact strata of the Eritrean population were to be found in the towns. This social compactness laid the material conditions for universal interaction and internalization of capitalist values and the development of social solidarity, which later came to be translated into political activism on a national scale. No wonder, therefore, in view of their material and spiritual way of life, that the urban populations assumed the guiding role in the shaping of Eritrean consciousness.

Third, the exposure of Eritreans to modern education, albeit in a restricted fashion, was an important catalyst in the development of Eritrean national consciousness. Between 1894 and 1948, about 20,000 Eritreans received Western education in primary schools in native languages. In the 1940s, the British colonial administration gave a push to the educational process. Consequently, fifty-nine primary schools, one middle school, and one teachers' training college were set up.[41] Textbooks in Tigrinya and Arabic began to be published, which acted as a catalyst for these two languages to become the official languages of Eritrea. This stride in educational development added a new dimension to the growth of national bourgeois and proletarian classes. In short, the capitalization process in Eritrea was responsible for the emergence of multinational classes, which at the same time fostered the growth of Eritrean consciousness.

2

The Making of History

AS FAADIA TOUVAL noted, "Historical facts are sometimes less important than popular belief in shaping the attitudes of people."[1] This holds true because political groups, in their quest for historical and moral justifications to their claims, are apt to dwell upon mythological arguments and hence are capable of distorting facts, thereby significantly shaping the orientations of the masses of people. That process may perhaps be acceptable to a degree insofar as the rights and claims of other peoples are not affected by any mythical components of an argument. But here we are entertaining the doubt that the United Nations had made adequate examination of the historical facts presented to it when considering the disposition of Eritrea and that therefore it was influenced by the mythical components of the Ethiopian view. The purpose here, then, is to familiarize the reader with the competing historical views of Eritreans and Ethiopians and to present a brief account of some precolonial history of Eritrea.

Conflicting Views of History

Since 1941, the foreign policy of Ethiopia has been dominated by the struggle to acquire and maintain Eritrea. Ethiopia based its claims on ethnic and historical considerations. For example, an official memorandum of the imperial Ethiopian government submitted to the Council of Foreign Ministers of the Four Powers in 1945 stated:

17

It is noted that a general proposal has been made to place the Italian colonies under trusteeship. Whatever may be the considerations which lead to such a proposal for other territories, a matter on which the Imperial Ethiopian Government does not now express an opinion, it is their desire to make known their convictions in regard to the application of such proposals to territories wrested from Ethiopia by Italian aggression. Of the colonies under discussion, Eritrea must be distinguished from the others by the fact that for three thousand years it has formed an integral part of a nation from which it was detached by Italian aggression and with which its culture, language, religion, and race have been identified since the beginning of history in this area. It is in Eritrea that is spoken the most ancient language of the Empire of Ethiopia and are harboured venerated shrines and traditions of the Empire.[2]

The same historical theme was expounded by the Ethiopian foreign minister in 1949 to the United Nations Commission on Eritrea in similar terms: "In the course of your travels in Eritrea and Ethiopia you have been able to note for yourselves the complete identity of territories and peoples which for thousands of years have been identified under the name of Ethiopia. Notwithstanding fifty years of Italian regime in Eritrea you have seen the same peoples. . . . Why, gentlemen? . . . For 4,000 years Eritrea and Ethiopia have been identical, identical in their origins, identical in their historical development, identical in their defence of the Ethiopian and Eritrean region."[3]

This imperial version of the historical argument presupposes the continuity of an Ethiopian state over a definite geographical area and common peoples. In fact, it denotes an unequivocal claim to boundaries fixed by an a priori ordinance immune to the vicissitudes of history. Given this thesis, a particularly important factor in advancing the claim to territories in the Horn of Africa has been the identity of peoples in their race, culture, language, and religion. This importance was amplified in a memorandum communicated to President Roosevelt by Emperor Haile Selassie of Ethiopia: "It is as easy for the inhabitants of Addis Ababa to converse with the inhabitants of Asmara as with any peasants in the vicinity of Addis Ababa for the inhabitants of Addis Ababa and Asmara speak dialects of identical origin."[4]

Internally, however, the imperial regime presented the situation differently. The diversity of ethnic composition and languages was emphasized to preempt demand for any degree of devolution of authority. In 1967, for example, when the question of granting even limited self-administration to the various districts in the country was debated, Haile Selassie's imperial parliament rejected the idea on grounds that, "while it is clear that Ethiopia has existed for the last 3,000 years, . . . it is also known that Ethiopia is comprised of different tribal groups which were far from regarding one another as members of the same nation, viewing each other as outsiders, having different outlooks and with no free intermingling: and to create separate and autonomous *awrajas* [districts] before the people know one another . . . would be encouraging separatist tendencies."[5] What is not clear is why these peoples did not regard themselves as belonging to the same nation if they had lived together for three thousand years.

These contradictory statements show only that the imperial government had two policies, one for international consumption and another for domestic use. The truth of the matter is that there are more than seventy languages belonging to four different language phyla spoken in Ethiopia.[6] Ethiopian rulers have manipulated their data in an apparent effort to justify contradictory positions.

The preceding historical and sociological arguments of the Ethiopian monarchs are shared by the present military regime of Ethiopia with no significant variations in overtones and substance. Paradoxically enough, one is able to see a striking symmetry between the policies of the present regime and its predecessors regarding this question, in spite of the former's profession of "scientific socialism" and its subsequent rejection of all policy orientations pursued by the latter. In fact, one of the only things that has never been overturned or condemned in "socialist" terms has been Haile Selassie's policy on Eritrea. From the historical perspective of the military regime (the Dergue), Eritrea was an artificial creation "carved out" of Ethiopia and temporarily colonized by Italy. Like its predecessor, the Dergue emphasizes the continuity of the Ethiopian state for three or four thousand years during which time Eritrea is claimed to have been an integral part of Ethiopia. This contention has been expounded clearly in an important document, "The Ethiopian Revolution and the Problem in Eritrea," promulgated by the military government: "History attests that the northern part of Ethiopia, especially the region now called Eritrea, has been the cradle of Ethiopian civilization. When the Axumite civilization reached its apogee from the fourth to the eighth century A.D., the Eritrean region was an integral part of Ethiopia. They played a leading role in maintaining the cohesion of the country. Hence up and until the second half of the 19th century, the strong link between the Eritrean region and the central government has never been severed."[7]

Thus the historical justifications of the Dergue in refusing to recognize Eritrea as a separate political entity replicate exactly the historical arguments adduced by the previous regime. The only significant shift in the Dergue's argument has been its admission of the existence of multinationalities in Eritrea. But that admission is diluted by a twisted ad hoc logic that asserts that the very fact that Eritrea is a multiethnic entity disqualifies her to be eligible for self-determination as a nation. This theme is unequivocally made clear in a statement by Colonel Mengistu: "The designation Eritrea and the regional colonialist name of Eritrea was given only after the Italian colonists, who had been harbouring such ambitions over northern Ethiopia, seized those parts of Ethiopia in 1889, and by this memory various nationalities were wrested there from the rest of the country, creating an artificial Italian-made entity. Prior to that, there never was and history knows nothing of a region separate from Ethiopia and known as Eritrea. The mere fact that there are no less than eight nationalities in the region of Eritrea belies the claim of the separatists that Eritrea is a nation" (translation mine).[8]

Both the official document and the colonel's speech are in sharp contradiction to previously held imperialist views. In fact, they represent a marked departure from the earlier ipso facto explanations. However, they are presented in a more self-defeating and self-refuting manner. First, the admission that "there are not less than eight nationalities" in Eritrea, "each characterized by its own cultural and linguistic identity," shatters the Ethiopian claim that the peoples of Eritrea and Ethiopia belong to the same race and cultural identity and speak the same language. Unless one assumes that these nationalities were direct transplantations of Italian colonialism in Eritrea or the subsequent outgrowth of it, it becomes objectively impossible to deny the fact that these nationalities have for thousands of years maintained their own ethnolinguistic and cultural identities. If, even after successful colonial capitalist penetration of Eritrea, these nationalities still maintain their separate identities, the more glaring become the ethnic and sociocultural differences and historical experiences.

Second, the argument that Eritrea is not a qualified candidate for nationhood, and by extension for self-determination and independence, by virtue of the presence of multinationalities has a boomerang effect on the Ethiopian effort to follow it as a logical policy. Ethiopia, like Eritrea, has many ethnic groups within its borders, with more than seventy distinct nationalities having their own cultural and linguistic identities. If the presence of a single nationality is the criterion for determining the right of a nation to self-determination and independence, then Ethiopia would be the first and most disqualified candidate for independence. It seems that this departure from the imperial regime's policy on the part of the military regime has been inadvertent, and the regime is probably unaware of its theoretical and policy implications.

Third, in order to comprehend correctly the essence and problem of polyethnicity in the region, one has to take the above argument one step further. Despite the presence of nine nationalities, the Eritrean experience of the last ninety years has been sufficient to demonstrate the prevalence of a high degree of cohesion in professing a faith in secular nationalism or Eritreanism. The various political parties and organizations during the 1940s attested to this position when they unanimously and vehemently objected to the proposal of partitioning Eritrea along ethnic and religious lines. Subsequent political developments also showed that the centripetal forces in Eritrea have been sufficiently in control of the historical process. By contrast, Ethiopia is lacking in any degree of political cohesion and unified secular nationalism requisite for the erection of a democratic multinational state. It has recently become self-evident that Ethiopia is torn asunder by centrifugal forces represented by such political organizations as the Western Somali Liberation Front and the Oromo Liberation Front, which are avowed to the realization of their right to self-determination and the formation of their own separate states.

As we saw in chapter 1, the relative cohesion of Eritrean nationalism is intelligible only in relation to an objective historical process initiated and stimulated by the colonization and incorporation of Eritrea into the capitalist structure on a world scale, which subsequently opened up the avenues for wider interaction between the nationalities in Eritrea as subject peoples sharing common experience

under Italian colonialism. The significance of this capitalist incorporation of Eritrea into the global structure and its subsequent implications for Eritrean society is, according to Richard Leonard, that there
is "a heritage Eritrea shares with virtually all African states. . . . [T]his
common heritage which Eritrea shares with other former European
colonies is the historical fact that the territorial extent and consequently the ethnic composition of European colonies was determined
almost exclusively by the balance of power between colonizing countries and other considerations germane only to the colonial power.
As a result, . . . all African states, Ethiopia included, are multinational and are defined by externally fixed borders which take almost no account of local ethnic, geographical or economic realities."[9]

In its advisory opinion on Eritrea, the Permanent Peoples Tribunal
also turned down the Ethiopian argument based on the artificiality
of Eritrea and concurred with Leonard's assessment:

> [T]he multi-national character of Eritreans does not necessarily
> prohibit them from forming a people. Indeed, a human commu-
> nity can be considered as forming a people even if it is made
> up of a number of groups having various ethnic, linguistic, and
> religious characteristics. What is important, is that these groups
> have evolved within the framework of a distinct entity as a result
> of historical, social, economic and political factors which differ-
> entiate this entity as such. . . .
>
> Italian colonial domination and the British administration
> which followed, brought about radical changes in social condi-
> tions in Eritrea. Despite contradictions occasioned by external
> domination, the social transformations provoked by the Italians
> and the British unquestionably favored the birth of a national
> consciousness.[10]

In fact, in advancing their views of history, Eritreans have capital-
ized on these political and legal analyses. Eritreans refute the claim
that Eritrea has always been part of Ethiopia prior to colonization
of the territory by Italy. From their point of view, the crux of the
matter is, first, that Ethiopia itself has never before been a historically
constituted territorial and political entity in its present form nor has
it been the extension or succession of the Axumite and Abyssinian

empires. As Eritreans for Liberation in North America (EFLNA) have pointed out, "All available documentary evidence about the Axumite kingdom shows that Axum did not comprise all of present day Eritrea. Nor is it true that the Abyssinian kingdom is an 'expansion,' 'extension,' 'growth' or 'evolution' of the Axumite kingdom. The two kingdoms occupied different territories at different periods of time."[11]

According to the Eritrean description, then, the Axumite empire was brought to its historical end by the beginning of the seventh century A.D. Due to internal decay and external pressures and incursions, Axum could not expand or even survive as an independent empire.[12] Eritreans admit that part of Eritrea had been part of the Axumite empire. But the second level of their historical argument suggests that the link that southern Eritrea had with Axum ended with the collapse and disintegration of the empire. Furthermore, the concept of discontinuity is an important element in the Eritrean argument. As the historians present it, there is a gap of seven centuries between the disappearance of Axum as an empire and the emergence of the Abyssinian kingdom, which is the predecessor of present-day Ethiopia. Finally, in terms of geography, Axum and Abyssinia occupied different areas at different times. Therefore, since the downfall of Axum, Ethiopia and Eritrea have had their own independent historical evolutions, which led to their present geographical and sociopolitical distinctions.

At the third level of their historical presentation, Eritreans place the emphasis on the socioeconomic transformations of Eritrean society provoked by subsequent colonial penetration of the territory. For Eritreans, the Italian period of colonization is of particular importance because at that time Eritrea emerged for the first time as a unified political entity comprising four different regions with different historical experiences. This theme was amplified in a joint memorandum of the Eritrean Liberation Front (ELF) and the Eritrean Peoples Liberation Front (EPLF) submitted to the Permanent Peoples Tribunal in Milan, Italy: "It will be sufficient for us to state here that Eritrea and Ethiopia, like most of the other Afro-Asian countries took on their present territorial and political shapes with the advent of European colonialism. Since a nation, as a historical phenomenon, comes about with the rise of capitalism, that is, out of the dialectical

process of the collapse of feudalism and the development of capitalism, it cannot be said that there was a nation or a centralized state
in Africa before the advent of colonialism."[13]

The Eritrean presentation of the case seems consistent with independent historical analysis. True, as we shall see, Yohannes of Ethiopia had conquered part of Eritrea in the nineteenth century. But
Yohannes's conquest of part of Eritrea does not entitle present-day
Ethiopia to assert any claim over the whole of Eritrea. More important, mere conquest does not bestow upon the conquerer an irrevocable right of perpetual occupation over the conquered.

The Axumite and Amhara Kingdoms

The Axumite kingdom arose toward the end of the second millenium
B.C. in the northern parts of modern-day Tigrai and southern Eritrea. The original inhabitants of this region are presumed to have
been Nilo-Saharans. In the course of history, the inhabitants of the
area gradually lost their distinct racial characteristics as a result of
intermarriages, first with Cushitic invaders from northern Africa and
later with Semitic immigrants from across the Red Sea. The constant
immigration of Semitic tribes had cardinal significance, not only in
the racial evolution of the peoples but also in the emergence of a
peculiarly sophisticated civilization, including a complex state organization, a commercial network, and an elaborate military structure.
The immigration process was so overwhelming that Semitization of
the peoples of the region in terms of language, religion, and civilization was complete between 1000 and 400 B.C. Thus, Axum became
par excellence the creation of Semitic invaders from southern Arabia.
Having built a "noble and distinctive civilization," the Semitic immigrants "provided the present forebearers of the Tigre people" in the
province of Tigrai in Ethiopia and in southern Eritrea.[14]

During the period of Hellenic expansion, the Ptolemaic Greeks
occupied the western shores of the Red Sea, from which they pushed
the Semitic immigrants into the interior. Some historians argue that
the rise of the port city of Adulis might have been connected with
the Hellenic colonization of the coastal areas of the Red Sea. In fact,
the name "Erythraea," which means "red" in Greek, was given to
this body of water and was later given to the territory west of the
Red Sea colonized by the Italians.[15] Another historical hypothesis sug-

gests that Adulis was founded by Egyptian slaves earlier than the Ptolemaic colonization of the area. It follows that the Egyptians might have previously occupied the area and thus founded the port city.[16] But it is equally valid to argue that when Egypt itself fell under the Ptolemies, the western shores of the Red Sea might also have fallen to them. At any rate, Adulis came to be the command post for the rising Axumite empire throughout the first six centuries A.D. Although it is not clear what role the Ptolemies played in Axum, there is sufficient evidence that Hellenic influences on Axum were so great that virtually all inscriptions until the early fourth century A.D. were made in Greek.[17]

Many historians agree that Axum arose as a result of a process of amalgamation of various city-states, such as Materea, Adulis, Kohito, and Tokondao in present-day Eritrea and Axum and Yeha in present-day Tigrai. This amalgamation was facilitated by the fact that the city-states that were forged into the Axumite empire shared more or less the same culture, language, and religion. Subsequent expansions of the empire into neighboring areas were a result of conquest, not of amalgamation. The power and wealth of the empire were based on trade and taxation of subject peoples. As Greenfield has stated: "It is known of the city-state of Aksum, that the organization which its ruler set up came to *dominate* other cities and a considerable area of north-eastern Africa—a fact perhaps not determined by, but far from unrelated to, the very considerable extent of trade in the area at the beginning of the first Christian millenium. Evidence for the reconstruction of this commercial activity can be drawn from the inscriptions of ancient Egypt and Persia, from numismatics and from other archaeological discoveries in Arabia as well as Eritrea, Ethiopia, and the Nile Valley."[18]

Greenfield also suggests that the fact that the Axumite ruler took the title "king of kings" indicates that there were states incorporated into Axum by conquest for the purpose of exacting tributes. This thesis is borne out by an inscription by one Axumite king of kings: "Some expeditions were conducted by myself in person and ended in victory (!) and the others I entrusted to my officers."[19] Greenfield interprets this inscription as the "story of conquest, 'pacification' and economic reorientation: in fact, typical colonialism. What was created was acknowledged to the greater credit and power of the king of kings and his nationals, by other rulers of the world—such as the

Emperor Constantine who compared Aksumites to Romans; another imperial race."[20]

This thesis is given credence by another inscription written in the early fourth century A.D. and found in Adulis. The author of the inscription stated that, "Having commanded peoples closest to my kingdom, to preserve the peace I bravely waged war and subjugated in battles the following peoples," and then enumerated the conquered.[21]

At the zenith of its expansionism, Axum extended as far as Meroe around the vicinity of modern-day Khartoum in the west and of southern Arabia in the east. However, since its expansion was based on conquest, the territories over which Axum had control were subject to constant fluctuations. Many of the kingdoms held in tributary relationships were frequently in rebellion. For example, Ezana II's inscription of the second half of the fifth century bears witness to the prevalence of rebelliousness among the subject peoples. The inscription reads: "[P]eoples of the Noba rebelled and were proud. . . . They attacked the peoples of Mangurto and Hasa and Baria and everyone else. And twice and thrice they broke their vows and killed their neighbors without compunction."[22] In another inscription, Ezana II also said: "And I fought with them on the Tekezze at the Kemalke ford. Here I put them to flight. And I, not pausing, chased those who were fleeing for 23 days, killing, taking prisoners and taking spoils."[23]

Given such a historical description of Axum, some conclusions can be drawn. First, the Axumite empire arose as a result of the amalgamation of a number of city-states in northern Tigrai and southern Eritrea. Second, the westward and eastward expansion of Axum did not represent a cohesive evolutionary growth of the empire but a ferocious incorporation of independent kingdoms and tribes for the purpose of exacting tributes and maintaining Axum's supremacy in trade and commerce, a course of action that is explainable in terms of primitive forms of colonization. This viewpoint is born out by the fact that the Axumite empire was constantly plagued by unrest and rebellion among its peoples throughout its imperial existence. As Kobishchanov accurately observed, "Even on the outskirts of the Tigre plateau the authority of the Axumite king was unstable. The king could feel confident only in Axum itself. As happened not infrequently in the Axumite kingdom (let us recall the Adulis inscription), the beginning of Ezana II's reign was marked by an increase of anarchy and separatism, by defection of dependent tribes and 'kingdoms,' even those closest to Axum."[24]

Third, there are no material records that show that Axum extended southward to what is today the habitat of the Amharas in northern Ethiopia. Contrary to the Ethiopian claim, the limited available evidence shows that the history of Axum, more than anything else, is the history of southern Eritrea and northern Tigrai. Furthermore, there is no historical indication of any kind that the Amharas were part of the Axumite empire. Even if a concession were given that the Amharas were part of the empire, Ethiopia could lay a claim only to southern Eritrea, since only that area was part of Axum. In respect to areas that constitute western, northern, and southeastern Eritrea, there is no evidence that those parts were ever under Axum.

The period between the seventh and the thirteenth centuries A.D. is described by historians as the Dark Ages, in view of the absence of corroboratory evidence of what was going on in the Horn of Africa. By the end of the seventh century, the Axumite empire had already disintegrated. In fact, by the beginning of the seventh century, the empire was on the point of extinction for a number of interrelated reasons. First, Axum overextended itself to areas over which it could not possibly exercise any effective control. Consequently, the dependent kingdoms and tribes were often able to carry out rebellions against Axum. Axum thus consumed itself by waging constant wars against its subject peoples. Therefore, one explanation for its downfall is to be found in the internal process of decay, mainly due to the raids and counterraids of peoples within the empire. This process enormously weakened Axum as a trading imperial state. Second, the internal decay of Axum was accompanied by two interrelated external factors: the Beja invasion from the north and the penetration of Islam from the east.[25]

The Beja were a Cushitic people who had been active in disrupting trade routes in northern and northeastern Africa since the time of Herodotus. Their historical habitat was located in northern Sudan and southern Egypt. They were constantly moving southward, and by the third century A.D. they were located in central and eastern Sudan, close to the Axumite empire.[26]

The relationship of the Beja to the Axumite kingdom was one of raids and counterraids. By the middle of the sixth century, the Beja had overrun the Eritrean plateau, dealing a severe blow to the core of the Axumite civilization. The Beja incursions were accompanied by another contemporary development: the rise of Islam. In 640 A.D., there were naval skirmishes between Axum and Moslem Arabs. Though Axum temporarily emerged victorious, in 683 the Moslems from Mecca took the offensive against Axum and destroyed its maritime supremacy on the Red Sea. Consequently the Moslems established commercial centers in the Dahlak archipelago, which served as the center for the diffusion of Islam into the Horn of Africa.[27] Now cut off from the outside world, Axum began to disintegrate, and it quickly faded as a trading empire.

The intrusion of the Beja and Moslem elements into the Horn of Africa had significant implications for subsequent historical developments in the region. Between the seventh and thirteenth centuries, some Axumite elements moved southward, where they intermingled with other Cushitic peoples and developed a new civilization through a process of assimilation and adaptation.[28]

With the collapse of Axum, the Beja were able to establish themselves in an area extending from the Red Sea coast to the eastern parts of the Sudan. They set up five independent kingdoms encompassing eastern Sudan and all of present-day Eritrea, with the exception of Dankalia. Combining agriculture with mining, the Beja developed a prosperous confederacy.[29] Although this loose federation of Beja kingdoms lasted until the fourteenth century, it began to decay and crumble owing mainly to internecine warfare among the kingdoms.

As the Beja occupation and Islamization of the northern half and eastern fringes of the Axumite empire continued, its southern half was also on the point of extinction. Constant pressure and rebellions by such Cushitic peoples as the Falashas and the Agaws also contributed to the disintegration of Axum. Under the legendary queen Judith, the Falashas rebelled against Axum from the south, destroying Christian churches, persecuting Christians, and devastating the region. In fact, they were able to establish their own Judaic state in what is now northern Ethiopia. The underlying motivation of the Falasha rebellion is said to have been the desire to revivify the older Judaic indigenous cult and religious practice.[30]

The Falasha uprising was accompanied by another rebellion by the Agaw, who also created their own imperial state.[31] Before the end of the tenth century, the Agaw had firmly established their rule over an area whose geographical extent is unknown. The locus of the Agaw power was around the mountainous fortress of Lasta. The Zagwe dynasty of the Agaw, as it came to be called, had developed an elaborate genealogy which traced itself to the Israelite nobility to justify its claim to rule. One of the ironies in the period is that, despite being Cushitic, the Zagwe rulers claimed to be Semitic in origin, probably in order to legitimize their rule and to win the acceptance of the Semitic populace, who were otherwise known as Axumites.[32] The Zagwe rulers attempted to revive Christianity and Semitic literature and established contacts with Egypt and Jerusalem. At any rate, the Agaw state survived until 1270, when it was overthrown by a new Amhara dynasty.

No historian has ever been able to trace precisely the true origin of the Amharas; the hypothesis is that Axumite elements intermarried with the Agaw, as the result of which the Amhara emerged as a distinct ethnic group.[33] Nonetheless, since the thirteenth century, the Amharas have been the most active and dominant makers of history in the region and have certainly made tremendous contributions to both its civilization and its problems. Though their language is highly influenced by Semitic phonologies and characteristics, it contains non-semitic ingredients, reflective of its being a product of Cushitic and Semitic admixtures. The same can be said about their cultural attributes. Like the Agaw, the Amharas quickly "accepted the semitized civilization of the north and became its militant exponents."[34]

The first Amhara king known to history was Yukuno Amlak, who overthrew the Zagwe dynasty in 1270. Yukuno Amlak proclaimed himself after he killed the last Zagwe king, who had taken refuge in a church.[35] The Amharic version of the matter is, however, different. The legend states that the Zagwe king voluntarily transferred power to the "legal" owner of the throne through the mediation of a certain monk, Tekle Haymanot. According to the legend the Zagwe period was a temporary interruption of the Solomonic line so that the enthronement of Yukuno Amlak represented the restoration of the Solomonic dynasty created by Menilek, son of Solomon of Jerusalem and the Queen of Sheba of Axum.[36]

The significance of this Amharic legend lies not only in Yukuno Amlak's use of it to justify his claim as a "rightful" heir to the throne but also in its frequent usage by subsequent Amhara rulers for the same purpose. In fact, even the well-known Ethiopian historian Tadesse Tamrat contends that the Zagwe period represented the continuity rather than the interruption of the Axumite political order.[37] There are six factors that militate against the Amharic legend, however.

First, the territory that Yukuno Amlak inherited from the Zagwe rulers was limited to the province of Lasta and the Amhara-inhabited regions. Although little is known about the fate of other peoples in the vicinity of Lasta, the whole of Eritrea was still under the Beja confederacy at that time.[38]

Second, the six and a half centuries that elapsed between the final collapse of Axum and the emergence of Abyssinia in 1270 were marked by a cyclical pattern of withdrawals and supersessions of one group of people by another. It is hardly possible even to conjecture that the Axumites would survive as a state controlled by people other than themselves.

Third, Yukuno Amlak's immediate action in sending an envoy to Egypt to solicit the assistance of the Egyptian sultan in obtaining a Coptic bishop for Abyssinia is a good indicator that he was badly in need of the church's support in establishing his authority.[39] Fourth, the conflict that ensued between Tigraians and Amharas over the accession of Yukuno Amlak to the throne also indicates that the former never accepted the Amhara claim to the Solomonic dynasty nor to its Axumite origin.[40]

Fifth, the geographical location of the new Amhara kingdom, or Abyssinia, was quite different from that of Axum. Sixth, the relationship of the Amhara to the Zagwe rulers has never been historically clear. Amharic chronicles and genealogies cannot be demonstrated to be accurate. As Greenfield noted: "Unfortunately, as has been argued, Ethiopian history has too long been represented merely as a catalogue of kings, and that interpretation of the story of the Zagwe rulers fits into such a chronological framework almost too readily. *The truth is that we know very little about Lasta and the Zagwe.* Roha . . . was the capital and in the late sixties archaeologists discovered it to have been a walled city—walled against whom? We have little or no idea of the extent of the rulers' authority beyond those walls and hence do not know how many other foci and national loyalties existed in north-eastern Africa one thousand years ago."[41]

Thus all available evidence, albeit scanty, indicates that the Amhara kingdom, otherwise known as Abyssinia, did not represent the continuity of the Axumite state nor were the Tigraians ready to accept the Amharic claim. As Abir noted, the Tigraians, who were the direct descendants of the Axumites both by virtue of geographical location and cultural traits, were held in subjection by the Amharas by means of force, although the subjection was later transformed into an entirely different relationship.

The point here is that the descriptions of the period are essentially based on hagiographical and legendary stories that cannot be factually demonstrated. Therefore these historical descriptions should not be extended beyond their literary significance to any relevance in understanding the problems of the area today.

The Scramble for Eritrea

The precolonial history of Eritrea[42] is a history of four fragmented regions, each with its own unique experience. It is also the history of external forces "scrambling" for the control and domination of these fragmented regions.

The plateau region of Eritrea developed into a distinct political entity beginning in the fifteenth century. In the seventeenth century Portuguese visitors identified this entity as Medri-Bahri (or Land of the Sea) and its rulers as Bahre-Nagassi (or Kings of the Sea). In 1770 the Scottish traveler James Bruce also reported that Medri-Bahri and Abyssinia were two distinctly separate political entities constantly at war with each other.[43]

For reasons of geopolitics, the international relations of the Bahre-Nagassi were marked by diplomatic ambivalence. When their cultural survival was at stake, they allied themselves with the Christian rulers of Abyssinia. For example, Bahre-Nagassi Issak made a significant military contribution to the defeat of Ahmed Gragn in the sixteenth century. As we shall see, at this time the Eritrean Christians and the Eritrean Afars were religious enemies. On the other hand, when the political survival of Medri-Bahri was threatened by Abyssinia, the Bahre-Nagassi allied themselves with their Moslem neighbors and the Turks. In 1572, for example, the king proposed to the Adalite states and the Turks that they form a common front against Abyssinia.[44]

Another important element in Medri-Bahri during the sixteenth century was the coming of the Turks. Following the footsteps of

Islam, Ottoman Turkey made several advances into the Red Sea area. By the year 1517, the Turks had occupied the whole northeastern part of modern-day Eritrea extending from Massawa to Swakin in the Sudan. They had even conquered Medri-Bahri and occupied it for twenty years until they were driven out during the last quarter of the sixteenth century. Nevertheless, the Turks were in firm control of the coastal areas for three hundred years until the advent of Italian colonialism.[45]

The impact of the Turkish presence in the coastal fringes on the historical configuration of the region was immense. In the first place, by virtue of their proximity to the local actors, the Turks were able to give immediate moral, political, and material support to the petty Moslem states in the Horn in their campaigns against the Christian kingdoms of Tigrai and Amhara; this support precipitated the involvement of Christian Portugal in the conflict on the side of the Christian kingdoms. As a matter of fact, Turkish and Portuguese contention in the area as "defenders" of their respective allies was essentially the precursor of modern imperialist rivalry and intervention. The underlying motivation for the rivalry between those two major powers was the desire to establish hegemony over the commercial veins around the Red Sea region.

In view of the predominance of this external element in the affairs of the Horn since the sixteenth century, the texture of the historico-political development of the region has been so complex that spontaneous development in a direction toward political homogeneity and cohesion has been impossible. Second, the Turkish presence in northeastern Eritrea was a major factor in the consolidation of Islam there and the development of a distinct people and culture which contributed to the rise of the Eritrean identity.[46]

Another salient element in the regional configuration in the sixteenth century was the rise of Ahmed Gragn, Somali by blood, a popular military commander who organized a huge army from among the Danakils and Somalis for the purpose of liquidating Christian Abyssinia and spreading Islam. Between 1529 and 1542, the Danakil/Somali forces under Ahmed made several attacks. They destroyed Abyssinian churches and monasteries and devastated the Christian kingdom. According to chroniclers of the times, nine-tenths of the Christians were converted to Islam.[47]

In the meantime, 400 Portuguese soldiers arrived in Eritrea to reinforce the beleaguered Abyssinian army. In 1542, Ahmed was wounded but managed to escape. For the moment, the balance of forces seemed to change in favor of the Abyssinians, and Ahmed was compelled to solicit Turkish military assistance. He received 900 Turkish musketeers along with ten cannons. Reinforced, Ahmed undertook a seemingly decisive offensive against the Abyssinian/Medri-Bahrian/Portuguese alliance. Deluded by this victory, Ahmed committed a serious military blunder before the war was over. He sent back the Turkish contingent and returned to his headquarters. This move gave the Abyssinians and their allies a breathing space to regroup and launch a counteroffensive. In October 1542 they launched a final assault on Ahmed's forces. Ahmed was killed and his demoralized army disintegrated.[48]

Portuguese intervention in the war not only helped in the resurrection of the Abyssinian kingdom but also saved Christianity from total liquidation. It survived to serve as a contending ideology in the region. Christianity was to prove an important vehicle for Abyssinia to establish and maintain links with Europe. Another important concomitant result of this Euro-Abyssinian relation was that the Abyssinian point of view was given uncritical and generous reception in European historiography. From the sixteenth century onward, the history of the Horn of Africa was to be described as the history of Abyssinia, of its expansions and contractions as the manifestations of a monocausal process. That orientation persists even to this day, despite the fact that the various Moslem petty states and sultanates have had a "glorious" history of their own, marked by a similar process of expansion and shrinkage subject to shifts in the balance of forces in the region. After the defeat of Ahmed Gragn, the petty Moslem states and sultanates in the eastern and coastal regions of the Horn were still flourishing independently, making their own history. Among them, the sultanate of Dankalia, today comprising the southeastern province of Eritrea and eastern Wello province, resisted all forms of aggression and maintained its independence.

While the Eritrean political formations in the plateau and in Dankalia were evolving into distinct entities, the Funj empire in the Sudan expanded eastward and conquered what is today western and northern Eritrea. The peoples inhabiting the Barka lowland and in the northern hills paid regular or periodic tribute to the Funj rulers.[49]

The second half of the nineteenth century was the most important period in Eritrean history. The country was hemmed in by external contending forces. Egyptian advances in Eritrea were made possible by the collapse of the Funj empire by the beginning of the nineteenth century. Egypt's southward drive coincided with its revival as a major power under Khedive Ismail. Two main factors motivated this Egyptian expansion. First, the khedive wanted to control the sources of the Nile River in the Abyssinian plateau and the equator, a reflection of Egyptian interest in the hydrographic reality. Second, the geopolitical transformation of the Red Sea as an important waterway heightened the ambition of the khedive to play an hegemonic role in controlling the trade routes to and from the Persian Gulf and the Far East.[50]

In 1840 the advancing Egyptian expedition founded Kassala as the capital of Taka province in the Sudan, and from there the Egyptians organized many raids against the Eritrean Bilen in the fertile valley of Keren. In 1852 the Egyptian army erected a fort at Kufit, midway between Asmara and Kassala. From Kufit the Egyptians made advances into western Eritrea and invaded the land of the Kunama.[51]

In January 1854 the governor of Taka province launched a major invasion against the Eritrean province of Bogos (or Senhit), burned the village of Mogara, and took 350 Eritrean women and children plus 1,800 head of cattle to Kassala.[52] This Egyptian invasion perturbed the head of the Catholic mission, Giovanni Stella, who contended that the Eritreans of Bogos and Mensa were independent people who deserved protection against external assaults. Consequently, under strong Catholic objection and British intercession, the Eritrean captives were returned to their country.[53]

While Egyptian forces continued to annex parts of Eritrea in the west and north, other Egyptian forces were placed in strategic locations along the Eritrean Red Sea coast. The consolidation of Egyptian positions in eastern Eritrea was facilitated by the decline of Ottoman power there. In 1865 Turkey handed over the administration of Massawa and other tributary enclaves to the Egyptians. In 1871 Egypt obtained the services of Munzinger, a Swiss national who was head of the French consulate at Massawa and an articulate spokesman for the Catholic interest in Eritrea until he officially traded his consular position for an Egyptian governorship of Massawa. In the summer of 1872 Munzinger led an Egyptian expedition from Massawa and occupied the Bogos. He built a strategic bridgehead between Massawa and the Egyptian Sudan.[54]

Weakened by incessant external incursions, the fragmented Eritrean political formations were no match for the highly coordinated Egyptian offensives. The only formidable threat to Egyptian advances came from the resurgent imperial state of Abyssinia under Yohannes IV. In the late 1860s Yohannes had obtained the submissions of various minor chiefs in Tigrai and later he reduced his Amhara rivals in the south, including Menelik of Shewa, to vassalage. Having established Tigraian ascendancy in Abyssinia, Yohannes's main preoccupation became pushing his empire northward into Eritrea. He had enough arms and ammunition, which he had received from the British expedition under Lord Napier for his collaboration in the defeat of Tewodros in 1868. Yohannes's northern drive brought him on a collision course with the Egyptians over Eritrea. In addition, though fragmented, the Eritrean chiefs were still a major menace to Yohannes's advances. Ras Welde-Mikael of Hamasien, Dejach Bahta Hagos of Akkele Guzai, Fitewrari Kiflu of Seraye, and Kentiba Hamid of Habab were among the dominant figures committed to making Eritrea ungovernable by imperial Abyssinia.

The third force that Yohannes had to reckon with in Eritrea was the Catholic church. The Catholic church in Eritrea was founded in the eighteenth century by an Italian Lazarist, Giusteino De Jacobis, who engineered an indigenous ministry as a way of ensuring Catholic permanence in Eritrea. He advocated the blending of indigenous Eritrean liturgy with strict observance of Catholic canons. Thus, the Eritrean Catholic church, with its indigenous liturgy, bishops, and see at Asmara, began to flourish[55] and in the early 1870s there were close to 28,000 Catholics in highland Eritrea.[56] But for Eritrean rulers the political presence and overtures of the church were more important than the number of its members.

In the wake of their growing influence in highland Eritrea, the missionaries felt that the growth of Catholicism could be nurtured only when the political destiny of the Catholic communities in Eritrea was protected against Abyssinian invasions. For this reason, in the early 1870s missionary activities in Eritrea were highly politicized in an apparent effort to place the Catholic portions of Eritrea under European protection, preferably French.[57] For reasons of practical politics, the Eritrean rulers, too, saw the growth of Catholicism as a positive force serving as a countervailing power to both Egyptian and Abyssinian hegemony. Even the non-Catholic rulers welcomed this development and at times used the good offices of the church to establish diplomatic connections with Europe as well as Egypt. It was under such political circumstances that relations between Munzinger and Ras Welde-Mikael developed. In 1869 Ras Welde-Mikael, the Hamasien chief, sent a diplomatic dispatch to Napoleon III in an effort to establish relations.[58]

Having seen the possible solidification of political relations between the Eritrean rulers and the Catholic church, Yohannes launched a series of assaults on both forces in Eritrea. Though he was able to incarcerate Welde-Mikael and to obtain the submission of Haylu, Welde-Mikael's rival in Hamasien, he was far from completely quelling Eritrean resistance to his expansionism. For example, in October 1871 in the face of fierce resistance by Golja's forces, Yohannes was compelled to send a strong army of 6,000 men under three generals to the Eritrean highland. What followed was a protracted guerilla warfare-type engagement.[59]

Under the pretext that the Catholic church was behind this Eritrean resistance, Yohannes sent another contingent to Akkele Guzai. His troops immediately proceeded to burn churches, homes of priests, and villages. The people who could not escape were chained and carried away.[60] The Abyssinian persecution of the Catholic church now posed a grave danger to its survival. This shift prompted the Catholics to drift politically toward Egypt in an apparent effort to avert their total liquidation by Yohannes. It was under these circumstances that Munzinger resigned his consular post and joined the Egyptian services. In sum, by the mid-1870s the political presence of the Catholic church in Eritrea was reduced to a trifling significance. In light of Yohannes's imperial acquisitiveness, combined with his Coptic fanaticism and anti-Catholic posture, the Catholic church found it politically expedient to shift its anti-Egyptian policy of the 1850s into one of tacit collaboration with Egypt in the 1870s.

Nonetheless, both the Catholic church and the Eritrean rulers forgot that Egypt had its own imperial ambition that brought it into direct confrontation with Abyssinia. Between 1872 and 1875 Ethio-Egyptian relations in Eritrea were marked by raids and counterraids into their possessions. Their confrontation over Eritrea reached its climax in the fall of 1875, when Egypt decided to launch a three-pronged offensive to occupy the entire Horn of Africa.

One expeditionary force under Mohammed Rauf proceeded from Zeila into the interior of the Horn and occupied Harrar. Another expedition, under Munzinger, proceeded from Tajura to conquer the Eritrean Danakils and establish a caravan route between Assab and Shewa as relations between Egypt and King Menelik grew more cordial. But in mid-November 1875 Munzinger's expedition was decisively defeated by the Afars. Munzinger was killed and only 150 of his 400 men returned to Tajura.[61]

While this was happening, Egypt undertook feverish preparations at Massawa to dispatch a third expedition to occupy highland Eritrea. In the summer of 1875 Aladin Bey, the Egyptian governor of Taka, informed his government that Abyssinian forces had already entered Seraye and Hamasien. The khedive reacted quickly by dispatching two battalions to Massawa to reinforce the Egyptian garrison there. In September he named a Danish colonel in the Egyptian services, Aren Drup, as commander of the Egyptian army at Massawa and Senhit. Aren Drup was advised to proceed cautiously into highland Eritrea until the entire plateau region was "liberated" from Abyssinian occupation. In the meantime the Egyptian government debated the future status of Eritrea. The khedive had proposed to Arakil Bey, the Egyptian governor of Massawa, to organize highland Eritrea either as a vassalage or as an independent entity under Egyptian protection to serve as a buffer zone between Egyptian Eritrea and Abyssinia. Arakil, however, advised the khedive that it was in Egypt's best interest to exercise direct Egyptian rule over highland Eritrea. Thus the idea of independence was precluded.[62]

With this in mind, Aren Drup invaded highland Eritrea. By 6 November one column of his expeditionary force reached Gundet in southern Seraye just 40 kilometers from Yohannes's capital, Adowa. Aren Drup's forces were well entrenched in strategic positions and communication lines with Massawa were in place. In the wake of this imminent threat to his empire, Yohannes was able quickly to mobilize between 50,000 and 70,000 men to meet the 3,000 strong Egyptian army. In mid-November a fierce battle for the control of highland Eritrea began. The Abyssinians encircled Aren Drup's forces at Gundet and launched a surprise attack. The Egyptian strategy collapsed and Aren Drup himself was killed. The Abyssinians killed 800 Egyp-

tians and trapped another 1,300. This victory represented a milestone
not only in Yohannes' northward push but also in the acquisition
of new arms captured from the Egyptians with which he was to continue his contention for Eritrea. The Abyssinians took up to 2,500
Remington rifles and 16 cannons and rockets along with huge quantities of ammunition.[63]

The Ethio-Egyptian confrontation over Eritrea was by no means
finished, however. The khedive became even more determined not
only to acquire Eritrea, but also to restore his credibility and the international image of Egypt. Thus, no sooner had the wounds of Gundet
been healed than the khedive began feverish preparations for yet
another military showdown. By early 1876 he assembled 15,000 men,
one cavalry, 1,058 horses, and 1,224 mules, and placed them under
the leadership of Ratib Pasha, aided by the khedive's own son and
General Loring of America, a Civil War veteran.[64]

Yohannes assembled 60,000 men. The two forces met at Gura some
40 kilometers southeast of Asmara. As the battle began on 7 March
1876, the Abyssinians scored an initial success so quickly that the
balance of forces tilted disastrously against the Egyptians. As at
Gundet, the Egyptians lost the war. Of the 6,000 Egyptians engaged
in the battle, 5,100 were either killed, captured, or wounded by the
Abyssinians.[65]

The Egyptian khedive was now convinced that his original purpose
in occupying Eritrea was unobtainable by military means. He showed
his readiness to return to the status quo ante and to conclude a peace
treaty with Yohannes by sending an envoy to Yohannes. Egypt's terms
of peace included the restitution of arms lost by Egypt to Abyssinia
in the two wars, repatriation of Egyptian prisoners of war, and free
commerce between the two countries. Yohannes, however, while accepting the first two Egyptian conditions, demanded the cession of
the Eritrean province of Bogos to Abyssinia.[66]

In the meantime, the Eritreans began their own armed resistance
against Abyssinia. This new upsurge of Eritrean peasant resistance
found leadership in Ras Welde-Mikael. But his rival, Haylu, remained
loyal to Yohannes and refused to join forces against Abyssinian occupation. As a first step to the complete liberation of highland Eritrea,
in July 1876 Welde-Mikael launched an attack on Haylu near Asmara.
Haylu was killed in the fierce and bloody battle, and Ras Welde-Mikael
lost his own son.[67]

In the wake of this peasant insurrection in highland Eritrea, Yohannes broke off the peace negotiations with Egypt, and in September he personally led an expedition against the Eritrean peasant army. In the ensuing encounters he scored successive victories and the Eritrean forces retired into the Bogos. Then Yohannes appointed General Alula governor of highland Eritrea, thus formally annexing it into his empire.[68]

As the Eritrean peasant insurrection compounded the tensions that were building between Egypt and Abyssinia, the British legation in Cairo proposed British mediation, and so General George Gordon was chosen to undertake negotiations with Abyssinia on behalf of Egypt. He arrived in Eritrea in February 1877 and immediately proposed the following conditions for peace between the two belligerent nations: granting general amnesty to Welde-Mikael and his peasant army pending the conclusion of peace; returning to the status quo ante; establishing freedom of commerce between Egypt and Abyssinia; extending Yohannes the right to import limited amounts of arms through Massawa free of duties; and taking measures to disarm Welde-Mikael and to demobilize the Eritrean peasant army.[69]

However, Gordon soon learned that no comprehensive peace plan could succeed without neutralizing Welde-Mikael, who was said to have a 7,000 strong army equipped with 700 Remington rifles. The Eritrean army's use of the Bogos as a springboard against Abyssinian occupation became of concern to Egypt lest Yohannes use it as a pretext to attack Egypt.[70]

Gordon soon was convinced that for peace to have a chance to succeed, the Eritrean question had to be settled first. He acknowledged the fact that the conclusion of two treaties of peace, one with Yohannes and the other with the Eritrean leader, was of paramount importance.[71] With the hope of neutralizing the Eritrean peasant unrest, in March 1877 Gordon held talks with Welde-Mikael at Keren and proposed that Welde-Mikael make peace with Abyssinia on condition that the latter would return Welde-Mikael's governorship of Hamasien. Alternatively, Gordon would carve out a territory for Welde-Mikael in Egyptian Eritrea, stretching from Massawa to Kassala.[72] The Eritrean leader rejected the offer and reaffirmed his determination to continue the struggle against Abyssinian occupation.

Gordon was taken aback when Welde-Mikael struck in May 1877 against the Abyssinian forces, killing one of Yohannes's generals.

Yohannes was infuriated and became more insistent in his imperial acquisitiveness. The net result was that Gordon's peace mission ended in complete failure.

When Gordon resumed his peace efforts in October 1878, he found Welde-Mikael in the Bogos still in command of his 7,000 strong army. He pleaded with Welde-Mikael to make peace with Yohannes. He even offered him 1,000 pounds per month on condition that he would refrain from attacking Abyssinian forces in highland Eritrea. Welde-Mikael, however, rejected the offer. Instead, he overran the Eritrean provinces of Hamasien and Seraye.[73]

Despite its relative success against Abyssinian occupation, the Eritrean peasant army could not sustain the liberation of Eritrea. First, protraction of the war was to the peasants' disadvantage. Yohannes could amass a large army and dispatch his troops in a continuous wave against the Eritreans. In the face of limited resources and manpower, this was too much for Welde-Mikael to withstand. Second, in view of the repeated retributive onslaughts on the population, highland Eritrea was laid waste and had reached a point at which it could no longer sustain a continuation of the war. Third, Gordon and Egypt mounted pressures against Welde-Mikael that made it increasingly difficult for him to obtain arms and ammunition to continue the war of liberation. The Egyptian threat to expel the Eritrean forces from the Bogos became crucial in the last analysis. Thus, diplomatically isolated and militarily encircled, Welde-Mikael was eventually forced to accept the peace offer with the condition that his governorship of Hamasien be restored. In January 1879 the Ethio-Eritrean conflict came to an end, and highland Eritrea was relatively pacified after three years of protracted warfare.

But the so-called reconciliation between Yohannes and Welde-Mikael soon proved an Abyssinian ploy to disarm the Eritrean peasant uprising both politically and militarily. Once in his home country, Welde-Mikael's popularity among his people grew, and the strength of his followers reached a threatening proportion. Having seen this and at Yohannes's order, Governor Alula quickly seized Welde-Mikael on the pretext that he was preparing to retire into the Bogos with his strong army to resume fighting. Hence, the Eritrean leader was sent to prison on a mountain where he starved to death. His son, Mitson, was also imprisoned and followed the fate of his father.[74]

There is every reason to believe that Alula took this action against

Welde-Mikael at Gordon's instigation in order to facilitate his mediation efforts between Egypt and Yohannes. Gordon had always entertained the idea that internal Eritrean formations were expendable
in the interest of appeasing Yohannes and restoring Egyptian hegemony in Eritrea. He wrote prior to resuming his second peace mission,
"I now hope in my interview with Alula . . . simply to ask him to
keep Waled-el-Michel and his Chiefs in prison, and to let Egypt work
her will on his troops in the Bogos; this will not cause much trouble,
for they will be as sheep without a shepherd."[75]

At any rate, with the incarceration and death of Welde-Mikael,
the Eritrean peasant uprising temporarily receded, but the effect of
the war was lasting. According to eyewitness reports, highland Eritrea
was devastated, villages were turned into ashes, and most of the population centers lost nine-tenths of their residents. A British diplomat
then visiting Eritrea, for example, gave the following moving description:

> The famine was caused by the many years of war mostly, but
> helped by a bad season, and from all accounts the misery was
> something awful. On the road I travelled by human skulls were
> by no means rare, some isolated, others in batches of two or
> three, around the usual camping-places they were more plenti-
> ful. Evidently the people had assembled there on the chances
> of getting taken to Massowah or into the interior by charitable
> travellers; what they must have been before the hyenas and jack-
> als dragged the corpses into the brushwood on each side of the
> road is a mere conjecture. The French Consul also informed
> me that on the Halai road it was the same, he brought with
> him three perfectly fresh skulls of females that he found on
> the roadside.[76]

With the elimination of Welde-Mikael, Gordon returned to Massawa in the fall of 1879 to give his peace effort another try. Yohannes,
too, seemed ready to enter into peace negotiations with Egypt. In
the meantime, to ensure the consolidation of his possessions in Eritrea, Yohannes began to orchestrate the complete "Europeanization"
of Abyssinia. While Gordon was on his way to meet him, Yohannes
wrote to Queen Victoria, "I have now another mother and another
protector among the European kings and people: only believe En-

gland as my country: if my country is fair in the religion and love of our Lord Jesus Christ we are one and near. I cannot believe that your Majesty shall separate me from your children."[77]

Yohannes's manipulative praise certainly captured the minds of many British diplomats with the exception of Gordon, who was unfavorably disposed to Abyssinian claims in Eritrea. The British Foreign Office began to consider seriously Yohannes's letter to the queen. W. H. Wylde prepared a minute outlining a British response to the Abyssinian plea. He argued that in addition to the development of free commerce in the Red Sea and in the interior of Abyssinia, it was in British interest to avert another outbreak of war between Egypt and Abyssinia. War with Abyssinia would be disastrous, not only for Egypt, but also indirectly for Britain. Egypt had already lost about 30,000 men, 1 million pounds, 30 pieces of artillery, and an enormous amount of war material. If another war were to break out, Britain would have to subsidize the Egyptian war effort in order to protect British communication lines. In Wylde's view, there was also a high probability that Yohannes might have been in communication with other European powers that might obtain influence with him and thus destabilize the Eritrean coast. Finally, Wylde suggested that a careful study should be made of Yohannes's claim of territory in Eritrea with a view to ascertaining whether there were any expendable territories that could be ceded to Abyssinia.[78]

A. B. Wylde concurred with the idea of mediating between Egypt and Abyssinia. Like most British diplomats, he was of the opinion that Abyssinia should receive highland Eritrea with the exception of the Bogos, Habab, and the coastal regions. Furthermore, he cautioned against Abyssinian acquisition of the coastal lines "as the country is not in a fit state nor will be to manage a seaport and be ready to deal with vexing questions in dealing with other nations."[79]

In A. B. Wylde's view, Abyssinia's weakness in guarding the coast would invite France, Italy, and Russia to establish trading posts in Eritrea, which might eventually lead to the invasion of Abyssinia herself, thereby disrupting British commerce and communication lines. Thus, he argued that with the support of Britain, Egypt should be able to retain the entire coastal regions of Eritrea, Senhit, and Abab. In addition, the presence of a European colony dependent on tobacco cultivation militated against the cession of Senhit to Abyssinia. In furthering his argument, Wylde was encouraged by Alula's statement that Abyssinians "never claimed the coast but wished to force upon Egypt the necessity of allowing them to trade through Massawa."[80] Wylde saw this as an opportune moment for resuming a peace negotiation to resolve the Ethio-Egyptian scramble for Eritrea.

Thus, in the fall of 1879 a new British consensus emerged that another diplomatic endeavor should be undertaken to smooth over the tensions in Eritrea, and it was under this seemingly favorable climate that Gordon arrived in Eritrea. In November 1879 he met with Yohannes and reiterated his previous points for a comprehensive peace. Emboldened by successive defeats of the Egyptians, Yohannes became overly demanding in his claims to Eritrea. Now he demanded the immediate cession of the ports of Zula and Anfila in addition to a war endemnity of two million pounds. Alternatively, if the khedive was unable to pay cash, Yohannes requested the cession of Massawa and the Bogos.[81] In the enormity of Yohannes's demands, the talks with Gordon quickly collapsed. Gordon returned empty-handed and the state of belligerency between Egypt and Abyssinia over Eritrea continued.

For the next four years, Abyssinian forces made many incursions into Egyptian Eritrea, looting, pillaging, and collecting tributes from Eritrean tribes. As these incursions increased, in both scale and frequency, Egypt needed peace more than Abyssinia did. About 51 percent of Egypt's total military budget for the entire Sudan was spent to maintain its garrison in Massawa.[82]

The deterioration of peace in Eritrea was further complicated by other burgeoning problems both at home and in the Sudan. Egypt's decline in Eritrea was the result not only of her war with Abyssinia, but also of her association with European powers. As early as 1854 Egypt had granted concessions to European interests in order to construct the Suez Canal, which made Egypt heavily indebted to the European powers.[83]

The by-product of Egypt's economic dependence on Europe was that the opening and the operation of the canal immensely heightened European strategic interest in Egypt herself. In view of Egypt's growing strategic importance, Britain and France in particular were generous in extending loans to the khedive to obtain his political subservience. But when in 1878 the khedive was unable to continue payment on treasury bills, he suspended all payments to Britain and France. His creditors reacted quickly by creating an international body representing both his shareholders and creditors in order to supervise the khedive's own finances. When Ismail resisted, Britain and France replaced him with Towfik. The European powers now created a system of dual control consisting of two appointed commissioners, one from France and the other from Britain, to serve as agents for the International Debt Commission.[84]

Resentful of European domination, patriotic Egyptians launched an insurrection in 1881 and gained control of most of the country, abolished the Anglo-French system of dual control, and deposed the pliant Khedive Towfik. Consequently, Britain proposed a joint Anglo-French military action. The French parliament, however, refused on economic grounds to grant credit for the proposed French expedition to restore the international character of Egypt. Britain then went on her own and crushed the insurgents, reinstated Towfik to power, and established effective unilateral control of Egypt.[85]

British protectorate over Egypt had two consequences on future developments in the area, including Eritrea. First, the nonparticipation of France in quelling the rebels in Egypt and its eventual eviction from there, accentuated Anglo-French rivalry in the Horn, which in the last analysis was beneficial to Abyssinia. Second, Britain came to assume Egypt's diplomatic responsibility insofar as the administration or disposition of all Egypt's dependent territories including those in Eritrea was concerned. It was during this time that a religious movement known as Mahdism, dedicated to the liquidation of Egyptian and European interests in the region, surged in the Sudan. In the wake of this religious upsurge, Egyptian garrisons supported by British forces were on the verge of total destruction. Thus, the conclusion of peace between Abyssinia and Egypt became a strategic necessity, not only for Egypt but also for Britain. In fact, the situation was so grave that Britain had to solicit the assistance and cooperation of Yohannes in relieving the trapped garrisons.

Britain saw this new development in the Sudan as having wider implications for general British interest. British maintenance of Indian security depended on Britain's ability to preserve the stability of Egypt and its neighbors and to maintain her naval predominance in the Red Sea region. Thus, a major British preoccupation was to prevent any possibility that might contribute to the establishment and consolidation of a hostile European power on the coastal fringes of Eritrea, which could threaten her sea communication lines to India.

Egypt's ability to defend her possessions in Eritrea became increasingly precarious. In the early 1880s, Abyssinian forays into Senhit and Sahel increased while Egyptian forces showed no resistance. Camels were killed in the thousands and herds of cattle were carried away to feed Abyssinian marauders. Isolated Egyptian forts in highland Eritrea were frequently attacked and some Egyptians were even kidnapped by Abyssinian forces.[86] Thus, the continued deterioration in morale of the Egyptian army and the financial drainage of the Egyptian economy, coupled with the rise of Mahdism in the Sudan, dramatically changed the strategic configuration of forces in the area, which precipitated active British intervention in the international sphere of diplomacy.

For this purpose, Britain designated Sir Admiral William Hewett to negotiate and conclude a peace treaty with Abyssinia on behalf of Egypt. In June 1884 he was able to conclude a treaty with Yohannes that formally ended the Ethio-Egyptian scramble for Eritrea. The terms of the treaty included free passage of all goods destined for Abyssinia through Massawa, the cession of the Bogos to Abyssinia, Abyssinian assistance in facilitating the evacuation of Egyptian troops from the Sudan to Massawa through Abyssinian territory, and extradition of dissident elements.[87]

For concluding the Hewett Treaty Yohannes was generously rewarded with Eritrean land, but at great future cost. The European powers and Abyssinian rulers shared the same imperial metaphysics. To both Europeans and Abyssinians, the Eritrean regions were expendable on the basis of suitable quid pro quo arrangements. At any rate, Yohannes's new collaborationism with Britain pushed the Europeanization of Abyssinia further. In return for pieces of land he obtained in Eritrea, Yohannes purchased a new enemy, that of Mahdist Sudan. After the conclusion of the Hewett Treaty, Eritrea became the prime target of the Mahdist offensive. The Eritreans not only became the object of this new retributive onslaught, but they also were used as cannon fodder by both the British and the Abyssinians in their counteroffensive to halt Mahdist advances into Eritrea. As Haggai Erlich perceptively observed, the Hewett Treaty not only improved Abyssinia's relations with Europe but also opened a new confrontation with the Mahdist state.[88]

Toward the end of 1884 the military situation in the Sudan completely deteriorated, and Britain had to act. Although he had the option to use Abyssinian forces to relieve the trapped Egyptian garrisons, the British governor of Massawa, Governor Colonel Chermside, advised against sending Christian Abyssinian troops to the Moslem-inhabited parts of Eritrea so as not to provoke anti-Abyssinian feelings among Moslem Eritreans. He thus decided to organize Moslem Eritreans who belonged to the Orthodox Islamic sect of Mirghaniyya, based in eastern Sudan and western Eritrea. Shaykh Uthman al Mirghani, head of the Mirghaniyya sect, was to supply the spiritual leadership to the British plan by appealing to the chiefs of the Beni Amir to provide the needed military force. But in January 1885 the Eritrean Beni Amir fighters were heavily defeated. Thus Chermside's policy to fight radical Islam with orthodox Mirghaniyya collapsed and he was compelled to ask Abyssinia to do the job.[89]

Meanwhile, in the summer of 1885 the military situation in the Sudan worsened and the people in western Eritrea became ungovernable, further weakening the Anglo-Egyptian position in the region. To avert a complete disaster the British now pleaded with Ras Alula, soliciting his cooperation in relieving the trapped Egyptian garrisons in Kassala and the Bogos. In August, the British gave Alula 50,000 talers and about 1,000 rifles and promised him an additional 300,000 talers to cover his future expenses should he agree to dispatch an expedition to the threatened areas.[90]

Thus, in September the British were able to assemble an Abyssinian-Eritrean alliance in which the Beni Amir played a dominant role. Having received information about these military preparations, the Mahdist leader in eastern Sudan, Uthman Diqna, collected between 6,000 and 12,000 men and entrenched them around Kufit waiting for the Abyssinian-Eritrean forces, which were estimated at 10,000 and 20,000 men and were constantly reinforced on the way to Kufit. On September 22 the first military engagement between these two forces occurred. Despite initial military successes, the Mahdist forces were annihilated on September 23, 1885, ending the Mahdist threat against Eritrea.[91]

Though the Mahdists were defeated, the scramble for Eritrea among external forces was not yet over, for Italian imperialism was looming on the horizon. As early as 1869 the Rubattino shipping company had purchased a harbor at Assab from a local sultan to serve as a calling station for its commercial vessels. With the transformation of the Red Sea as a strategic waterway, the interest of the Italian government heightened, and it decided to buy out the Rubattino shipping company; in 1882, the Italian government took over the harbor at Assab. Italy soon developed the harbor into a flourishing port. Fearful of the French and the Russians, Italy quickly occupied hundreds of miles of territory along the Eritrean coast. On 5 February 1885, with British acquiescence, the Italians occupied Massawa, but as the Italians began expanding their holdings into highland Eritrea, they came into direct confrontation with Yohannes. An Italian contingent occupied Sahati, a gateway to highland Eritrea halfway between Massawa and Asmara. Although the Hewett Treaty of June 1884 was silent on matters of boundary delineations, the Abyssinians contended that it had been verbally agreed that Sahati would be placed within their territory. The Italian occupation of this town gave Alula a pretext to attack. As part of his campaign in January 1887, Alula's forces encircled an Italian contingent at Dogale, some 18 kilometers from Massawa, and destroyed the Italians.[92]

The Dogale massacre, as it was called, sent a shock wave throughout Europe. The Italian parliament reacted to the episode by allocating 5 million lire to strengthen Italian forces at Massawa.[93] The Italian government, now determined to colonize Eritrea by a piecemeal strategy, began to construct elaborate military structures to ensure swift mobility of Italian contingents in the event of likely military engagements with Abyssinia. In March 1888 Italy completed a 27-kilometer-long railway from Massawa to Sahati, at a cost of 3 million lire.[94] To avoid a repetition of the Dogale incident, the Italians built impenetrable fortresses and effective communication lines.

On the diplomatic front, Italy was able to obtain full British support for her policy in Eritrea. The British even charged that the Abyssinian attack on Italian forces was unwarranted. The British preference of Italy over Abyssinia in the struggle for Eritrea was explained in a number of ways. First, as a member of the Triple Alliance, Italy already had the sympathy and blessing of Germany, which was preoccupied with establishing influence in east Africa. In the eyes of the British, therefore, it became expedient to offer a counterbribe to Italy by way of supporting her in Eritrea with a view to enticing the Italian government into softening its relations with the Triple Alliance. Second, since Italy was the weaker participant in the scramble for the Horn, it seemed in the interest of Britain to encourage Italy in the Horn just as she was encouraging Portugal against French and German expansion in western and southern Africa. In particular, fearful that France might gain Abyssinia and use it as a base of operation against vital British interests in the Sudan, it was in Britain's interest to encourage Italy to participate actively in the partition of the Horn.[95] Third, when Britain established unilateral control over Egypt in 1882, the Italian consul in Cairo was the only European diplomat who gave continuous and unqualified support to Britain and did so much to the disappointment of France. Britain had thus to express her gratitude by supporting Italy in Eritrea.

In addition, the growing antagonism between France and Britain was an important factor in encouraging Italian expansion in Eritrea. Since 1884 French moves in Abyssinia had alarmed Britain. Hewett had reported that the French consul at Massawa was actively seeking to establish French influence with King Yohannes. In fact, in November 1884 the French consul in Khartoum was charged with the task of leading a mission to Yohannes to establish diplomatic relations between the two countries and to solicit Yohannes's acceptance of permanent French representation at Adowa.[96]

Another aspect of Italian diplomacy was to isolate Yohannes from his vassal kings. For this purpose Petro Antonelli was working on King Menelik of Shewa to obtain his alliance, or at least his neutrality, in an Italo-Abyssinian conflict over Eritrea. Italy and Menelik were both dedicated to the liquidation of Yohannes's empire, though for different reasons. Italo-Shewa relations had begun in the 1870s and culminated in several treaties of commerce and amity. As a result a trade route linking Assab to Shewa was established, and in April 1883 Menelik received two thousand Remington rifles from Italy.[97] In a treaty of November 1884 Italy agreed to provide Shewa fifty thousand rifles over a period of ten years.[98] Further, in October 1887 Menelik signed a secret treaty with Italy in which he received five thousand rifles on condition that he remain neutral in the Italo-Abyssinian conflict over Eritrea.[99]

Diplomatically isolated, Yohannes now made a critical decision to dislodge the Italians from Eritrea by military means. He mobilized 200,000 men to achieve this goal. As tensions mounted, the Italian government dispatched 20,000 additional troops to Eritrea and the Italian commander was authorized to determine strategy and tactics to defend and expand the Italian gains in Eritrea. Toward the end of March 1888 Yohannes reached Sahati with his peasant army. But the Italians refused to come out into the open fields and meet the Abyssinian army, knowing well their numerical inferiority and the strategic superiority of their fortifications. A standoff ensued. Under the scorching heat, the Abyssinians ran out of provisions and water, and many of the soldiers fell ill. Yohannes had to order a rapid demobilization of his forces and return to Adowa.[100]

This retreat from Sahati was a humiliating defeat for Yohannes both psychologically and politically. Encouraged by the Sahati fiasco, Yohannes's vassal kings in Shewa and Gojjam were engaged in conspiracy against him, though they later repudiated this and pledged their allegiance.[101] Internationally isolated and abandoned by his vassal kings, Yohannes now pleaded with the Mahdist forces for peace and for a common front against European powers. It was too late for Yohannes, however, to convince the Mahdists. While campaigning in March 1889 against the Mahdists in the western fringes of his empire, Yohannes was killed and his forces demoralized and disintegrated.[102]

Yohannes's defeat by the Mahdists at Matamah ended Tigraian ascendancy in Abyssinian politics. Both Menelik and Italy welcomed the Mahdist victory and on 2 May 1889, Italy and Shewa signed the Wichale (or Ucciale) Treaty. Under the terms of this treaty Menelik recognized Italian sovereignty over Eritrea, and Italy accepted Menelik as the sole emperor of Ethiopia. Thus, in the summer and fall of 1889 the Italians occupied highland Eritrea and joined it to the other regions of what was to become Eritrea. In January 1890 the Italian government officially named its newly acquired colony Eritrea.

Italian colonialism breathed new life into the hitherto disconnected Eritrean ethnic groups and allowed Eritrea to become a new political entity unto itself. Eritrea became a new synthesis of nine nationalities, and it is precisely here that the modern history of Eritrea begins. But, as opposed to the case with all other African states, Italian colonialism did not entitle Eritrea to exercise the same right to national self-determination that other former colonies enjoyed. Instead, Italian colonialism was a mere interlude in the long drama of a human tragedy.

3

The Eritrean Question in the Postwar Power Balance

THE ERITREAN QUESTION was only one part of the postwar readjustment in international diplomacy at the close of World War II. Although new ways of disposing of non-self-governing territories were enunciated in the charter of the United Nations and the Atlantic Charter, based on the respect for the principle of self-determination, Eritrea was offered up for grabs by the victors. Needless to say, the Allied powers had nothing against Eritrea in particular; they were merely guided by the dictates of their own national interests in the cold war that became the characteristic feature of the new world order.

Two important factors mitigated against any favorable disposition of Eritrea. First, by historical coincidence, Eritrea happened to be a colony of a defeated country, Italy, which had to forfeit all titles to her former colonies. Consequently, the particular conflict that had existed between Eritrea as subject colonial state and metropolitan Italy was transformed into a general one as the victors soon laid claim to Eritrea, and thus her disposition had to be carried out in accordance with what they regarded as their respective national interests. In other words, unlike other colonial questions that were dealt with between the subject states and metropolitan "mothers," the internationalization of the Eritrean question became crucial in determining the destiny of the territory. Second, the alliance of the East and the West against Fascism was a temporary marriage of convenience. With the elimination of fascism as the primary opponent, both camps began to move toward a bipolar international political configuration. Consequently, the Eritrean question came to be viewed in the light of cold war politics. The fundamentals of the cold war and the clashing economic and strategic needs of the major powers more than anything else determined the Eritrean question.

In this chapter we shall be concerned with the important factors that intervened increasingly to set the course of Eritrea's future. We shall identify the major forces, the articulation of interests, and the evolution of policy options and how they shaped the Eritrean question.

The Internal Setting

In April 1941, as part of the general drive of Axis forces out of Africa, British forces "liberated" Eritrea from Italian occupation. The British thus set up what was to be called the British Military Administration (BMA) in Eritrea in place of the fascist Italian regime. Under the prescription of the Hague convention, Britain was obligated as an occupying power to restore order in Eritrea, to maintain its economic and social life, to minimize disruptions of indigenous values, to respect the organization and administration of the territory, and to assist the inhabitants in the utilization of their services.[1] Nonetheless, despite the rules of this convention, Britain developed two overriding objectives in Eritrea, one immediate and the other long-range.

From the point of view of political expediency, it was essential for Britain to maintain the Italian Fascist administration in Eritrea intact. The availability of cheap Italian administrators and the shortage of British administrative officers induced the British to maintain the previous administration in its entirety. In practical terms the British retained Italians in office and strengthened their land and property holdings in Eritrea. In addition, much to the disappointment of Eritreans, the British expropriated 10,000 acres of land owned by Eritrean peasants for distribution among Italians.[2] This alienation of land occurred at a time when the Italian colonial army was demobilized and, consequently, thousands of soldiers were flocking to the countryside seeking means of livelihood. At the same time, thousands of workers and functionaries thrown out of jobs were moving to the villages because of the economic distress. What was most vexatious to Eritreans was that preferential treatment was always given to Italians with regard to applications for business licenses for the exploitation of woodland and mineral resources and for retail shops.[3]

In the administration of justice, land and civil disputes between Eritreans and Italians continued to be litigated before Italian judges who applied the colonial law, which was from its inception prejudicial to Eritrean interests. In sum, the colonial disposition of Eritreans continued under Britain, and Italians were still well entrenched in their power. As Tom J. Farer observed, "Faced with an enthusiastically Fascist settler community, the British, determined to maintain control with a minimum commitment of men and resources and eager to use the colony as an entrepot and arsenal for their North African campaign, simulated the snail more than the hare in altering the structure of Italian ascendancy."[4]

In so doing, however, the British not only aided in continuing the antagonism between Eritreans and Italians, but also aggravated the conflict between Eritreans and themselves by the measures they undertook to gain short-term results. Some British officials had been aware of the consequences of such a policy in Eritrea. A British memorandum of June 1941, for example, had made the following prognosis:

> An important political problem the Italians create lies in the irritation . . . they cause the native populace, coupled with the necessity for our recognising Italian sovereignty, temporarily in abeyance, in a country in which Italian prestige has suffered severely in the eyes of the native population, which vastly outnumbers the Italians. . . .
>
> Since the Italians are to a large extent dependent on the native for supplies, and since the Italians have the lion's share of capital and commerce, relations between the two races must not be allowed to become too bad. As time passes their relationship may improve of itself, but as long as Italians continue to exercise executive authority over natives, or until the natives see that the British are going to adopt more sympathetic administrative measures, with which intention they are credited, this improvement will be uncertain in many parts of the country.[5]

Despite this political prognosis, however, British officials in Eritrea opted to continue their policy of appeasement with the Italians. In rebuffing native interests, one official even went so far as to suggest that British policy in Eritrea should be guided merely by political expediency and British interest:

> It is the duty of the British administration in Eritrea to adminis-ter the country with the minimum demands for military assist-ance and shipping, and to exercise a prudent expenditure of sterling. At present soldiers are far more valuable than money in the Middle East.
>
> Our leniency towards the Italians must be dictated by our own interests, and we are not here to strive after a native Utopia, although our administration should not be so open to criticism that it adversely affects British prestige in neighbouring coun-tries."[6]

The reaction of Eritreans to the British measures was predictable. The economic and political alienation of Eritreans grew to such an extent that they increasingly questioned British intent and purpose. As one member of the British administration in Eritrea observed: "Under the nagging ache of poverty and unredressed grievances the sophisticated Eritreans began to suspect the British of favouring their enemies. . . . They were puzzled and angered by the contrast between British treatment of Eritreans in Asmara and elsewhere."[7]

In addition to her short-term interest in Eritrea, Britain had a long-term objective. Since Britain could not remain in Eritrea indefi-nitely as an occupying power, as we shall see, her strategists had been entertaining the idea of partitioning Eritrea, with the western region going to the Sudan, a British colony. With this in mind, they started preparation by focusing on politicizing Eritrean society on the basis of sectarianism and devitalizing the Eritrean economy by physically dismantling certain key manufacturing plants or by allowing the eco-nomic process to deteriorate.

Politically, in an endeavor to promote British interest in Eritrea, British military administrators began to give special attention to west-ern Eritrea by encouraging Islam and the learning of Arabic and even by bringing books from Egypt for this purpose.[8] On the other hand, they fomented Tigraian nationalism in the highland region of

Eritrea by stressing the ethnic and religious connections between the highlanders and those people living in the Ethiopian province of Tigrai, and they even considered the idea of creating a Tigraian entity federated with Ethiopia.[9] Obviously the main purpose of British preoccupation with sectarian politics was to weaken the secular Eritrean nationalism that was militating against long-term British interest in the area.

On the economic front, retrogression of the Eritrean economy was consistent with the long-term British interest. First, as we shall see, in order to bring to fruition the idea of partitioning Eritrea, the British had to be able to demonstrate factually the economic nonviability of Eritrea. This claim was to constitute the core of the British argument against the independence of Eritrea. Second, it was expedient for Britain to recover its prewar Middle Eastern markets which had become dependent on Eritrea during the war for their supply of consumer goods.

For these purposes, the British destroyed the U.S.-built airport at Guraa, 40 kilometers southeast of Asmara, and dismantled the railroad that branched from the Eritrean town of Agordat to Kassala in the Sudan and to Gondar in Ethiopia and sold it to the Sudan for scrap. The floating dry dock at Massawa was sold to Pakistan and sixteen harbor boats were sold to private Italians and Arabs.[10]

According to the report of the Four Power Commission for Eritrea, between 1941 and 1947 Great Britain had taken from Eritrea industrial equipment worth 85 million pounds sterling while the corresponding figure for Somalia was only 1.4 million pounds sterling.[11] According to a report of the UN Commission for Eritrea, the dismantling of enterprises and plantations in Eritrea was a matter of deliberate British policy. Cotton, tobacco, and coffee plantations were abandoned and the gold mines were destroyed. For example, by 1949 the production of coffee in Eritrea was one-third that of 1940. Likewise, in 1940 the annual yield of gold had reached a steady level of 17,000 ounces with a prospect for further increase, while in 1949 the annual yield was only 2,800 ounces. The deliberate lopsidedness of British budgetary allocation illustrates these changes. While police and prison budgets amounted to about 400,000 pounds annually, education and agriculture received only 107,000 and 56,000 pounds, respectively.[12] The net result of this British policy was that the territory was thrown into economic disarray and political chaos, which precipitated the internal politicization of Eritrean forces and a recurrent pattern of external involvement.

Like the British, the Italians had a stake in Eritrean affairs. While Eritrea was an Italian colony, the Italian government had promulgated racist laws, deprived Eritreans of their land, and taken measures that amounted to attempted cultural extinction. As we have seen in chapter 1, most of the fertile land was declared crown land. That process of expropriation had continued even under the British administration with the net result that 40 percent of Eritrea's arable land was crown land. In addition, local Italian administrators had allocated to their compatriots land that had not been declared state property.

In matters of culture and politics, Italian policy had been one of blocking any incipient growth of Eritrean national consciousness. Initially, the Italians denied the natives access to Western education to avoid the unintended liberating consequences of education that might lead to the emergence of a distinct Eritrean psychological makeup or a challenge to the raison d'être of colonialism.[13] Even later, when the colonial administration had changed its policy toward native education, the curricula were developed in such manner as to establish a symmetry between native schooling and Italian colonial needs in Eritrea. In addition, the duration of native education was restricted to four years of elementary schooling. For example, in a confidential directive the Italian director of education in Eritrea communicated to all school headmasters: "By the end of his fourth year, . . . the Eritrean student should be able to speak our language moderately well: he should know the four arithmetical operations within normal limits; he should be a convinced propagandist of the principles of hygiene; and of history he should know only the names of those who have made Italy great."[14]

Despite such efforts to control the Eritrean mind, however, the differential access to education between natives and Italians and the policy of rigid separation between the races were in themselves sufficient to evoke a sense of separate Eritrean identity and hence resulted in the development of deep anti-Italian hostility.

This antagonism was sharpened by the retention of Italian economic and administrative ascendancy. However, it did not take long for the settlers and the Italian government to assess the implications of that hostility on Italy's hope to return to Eritrea. Recognizing that restoration of colonial status was unattainable, Italy pressed for trusteeship or independence for Eritrea, hoping that they would be able to perpetuate their status by creating neocolonial institutions in Eritrea. To this end, they had to obtain an internal social base which they found in thousands of demobilized Eritrean soldiers who had claims to pensions, gratuities, and unpaid checks.[15] Thus on the pretext of seeking social rectification collectively from the Italian government, the Eritrean War Veterans Association was organized to give cover to a pro-Italy party that was covertly controlled and financed by Italians. While one of the association's goals was to press Italy to honor its international obligation and reward Eritreans for their military services, another was to prevent anyone from making claims outside the organization as a way of consolidating the association in its pro-Italy position.[16]

Thus, in April 1947, the Eritrean War Veterans Association, with a membership of 35,000, was officially registered with the British administration. While the association covertly advocated Italian trusteeship for Eritrea, in September 1947, the Pro-Italia party was also officially registered on the platform of Eritrean unity and Italian trusteeship leading to independence.[17]

Like Britain and Italy, Ethiopia also had to create suitable conditions in Eritrea that could lend support to her claim. Although such conditions were initially nonexistent, the emperor Haile Selassie spared no effort in looking for a constituency in Eritrea; he found it in the Eritrean Coptic Church which had a stake in a new marriage between Eritrea and Ethiopia. Under Italian rule, the church had been reduced to virtual impotence in view of the fact that all its fiefs were declared state land and thus its social influence on Eritrean society was almost completely eliminated. In addition, every petition by the abuna (bishop) to the British administration for the return of its confiscated land had been rejected. Consequently, the priests in the Eritrean church hierarchy were convinced that restoration of the church's past could be effected only by the unconditional unification of Eritrea with Ethiopia. The church thus became the most active political institution fanning the Ethiopian cause in Eritrea. As Trevaskis recorded, "By 1942 every priest had become a propagandist in the Ethiopian cause, every village church had become a centre of Ethiopian nationalism, and popular religious feast days such as 'Maskal' (the Feast of the Cross) had become occasions for open displays for Ethiopian patriotism. The cathedral, monasteries, and village churches would be festooned with Ethiopian flags and the sermons and prayers would be delivered in unequivocal political language."[18]

An excellent example of the church's support of Ethiopia was the bishop's speech of January 1942, in which he presented his political views in this metaphorical way: "A male child . . . is brought into the Church forty days after it has been born and a female child is brought eighty days after birth. Names are then given to them. When the child cries, its mother gives it milk and it stops crying as soon as she lifts it to her breast. But you my people, have you a name? Yes, you have a mother and you must come to know her as she already knows you."[19]

In view of the church's growing political meddling through its religious processions and sermons while the secular forces were prohibited from staging any political demonstrations because of the war situation, the British administration became increasingly concerned about the bishop's behavior. It was under these circumstances that the British administration officially reprimanded the bishop in February 1943 and told him to confine his activities to confessional matters only.

Another important constituency for Haile Selassie was the segment of feudal and urban notables who had lost their land holdings and prestigious positions in Eritrean society. These notables were desperate for the restoration of their aristocratic positions, which could only be hoped for under a union of Eritrea and Ethiopia.[20] Cognizant of this fact, the emperor held out bounteous promises of reward to members of this aristocratic segment in return for their opportunistic collaboration. Since they were at variance with the rising Eritrean national bourgeoisie and petit bourgeoisie, the notables came to realize that their interests would be best served by the union of Eritrea with Ethiopia in the light of the emperor's promises for the restitution of their feudal privileges and lands.

Having thus identified the elements of his constituency in Eritrea, the emperor was able to smuggle many Ethiopians into Eritrea for the purpose of infiltration and agitation in the newly organized Mahber Fekri Hager (Association of Love for Country) which had come into being immediately after the British occupation of Eritrea. Aided by ecclesiastics and notables, the Ethiopians began religious and xenophobic agitation against native Moslems and foreigners. Thus, together with Mahber Fekri Hager, as Trevaskis recorded, they began agitating Christians against Arabs, Moslems, and Italians by pointing out that Christians were masters in Ethiopia while the Moslem tribesmen were their inferiors.[21]

The emperor's Minister of Pen, Woldegiorgis, formed an organization in 1944 dedicated to the unification of Eritrea and Ethiopia. His society provided millions of dollars for the unionists in Eritrea.[22] Moreover, in 1945, another Eritrean henchman to the emperor, Gabre-Maskal Habtemariam, a middle-level official in the Ethiopian government, was placed in charge of campaigns of the unionist movement in Eritrea and Ethiopia, and in September of the same year he led a large procession to the British legation in Addis Ababa to "dramatize Ethiopia's determination" to acquire Eritrea.[23] In March 1946, the British administration also allowed Ethiopia to have a liaison officer in Asmara on the proviso that he would not meddle in Eritrean politics. For this purpose, the emperor appointed Col. Negga Haile Selassie who immediately assumed leadership of the unionist movement.

Out of this well-coordinated movement emerged the Unionist party of Eritrea in April 1946. Its platform was unconditional union of Eritrea with Ethiopia, absolute opposition to Italy's return to power, and total rejection of foreign trusteeship. Much to the disappointment and frustration of Ethiopian authorities, however, the Unionist party did not attract as many Eritreans as expected, despite Ethiopia's pouring millions of dollars into bribery. Consequently, the party increasingly resorted to its ultimate weapons, terrorism and intimidation, by exploiting racial and religious differences in Eritrea. The net result was that, in April 1946, Christian hooligans began attacking foreigners and Moslems in Massawa and Keren, destroying their property. During other xenophobic activities within Ethiopia itself between June and July 1946, the Ethiopian government expelled 275 Arabs and 92 Italians and dumped them into Eritrea after confiscating their property.[24] In addition, in August 1946, some Sudanese members of the British colonial army were stormed by a Christian mob at the Asmara marketplace and one Sudanese soldier was stoned to death. In reaction, 70 Sudanese soldiers came out of their barracks and ransacked the marketplace from their armored vehicle, killing 46 Christians and wounding another 60.[25]

The purpose of such campaigns was, of course, to increase the sense of alienation and separation of Eritrean Christians from Moslem Eritreans; the Sudanese were considered part of the Eritrean Moslem community by virtue of their shared religion. Therefore, such sectarian tensions were calculated to weaken the proindependence movement by fomenting ethnic and religious tensions. Many Eritrean supporters of proindependence were murdered.

Despite such articulation of external interests in Eritrea, the inhabitants of the territory were equally determined to assert their political views and aspirations. British policy in Eritrea contributed immensely to the political awakening of the inhabitants. Its economic policy was particularly important in this respect. During the British administration, the rate of inflation increased by 611 percent while the salaries increased by only 60 percent.[26]

The economic stress led to the political awakening of the Eritrean working class, which began to unionize. The unionization and politicization process within the working class opened avenues for the Eritrean intelligentsia to establish political linkages with the working-class constituency. The progressive members of the nascent Eritrean bourgeoisie increasingly came to embrace the working class as a way of countering Ethiopian influence in Eritrea. Consequently, a secular nationalist movement dominated by liberal Christians sprang up in highland Eritrea, and, in February 1947, the Liberal Progressive party of Eritrea, with a membership in 53,500, came into being.[27] The party's platform was based on preservation of Eritrean unity, categorical opposition to union with Ethiopia, and progressive independence of Eritrea, under U.S. trusteeship if necessary.

In the lowland areas of Eritrea, peasant revolt had been under way ever since the British occupation began. This emancipation process, in which nine-tenths of the Tigre-speaking serfs participated, was directed against the remnants of aristocratic feudalism. By raising the political consciousness, the peasant revolt enabled the progressive Moslem segment of the Eritrean intelligentsia to establish connections with the peasant constituency. Consequently, while the Moslem aristocrats began drifting toward Ethiopia through the Unionist party, Ibrahim Sultan Ali, the most outspoken leader of the emancipation movement, organized a general meeting of all Moslem groups to consider the future of Eritrea. From this meeting emerged, in December 1946, a strong organization, the Moslem League of Eritrea.

The league's program was based on total rejection of union with Ethiopia, defense of Eritrean unity, and independence for Eritrea.[28] In addition, the National Moslem party of Massawa, with its consituency in the Red Sea area, was officially registered in April 1947 with a similar party program.[29]

The politicization, polarization, and organization of Eritrean society continued throughout the 1940s. At one point the number of political parties reached well over a dozen. All but the Unionist party supported the ultimate independence of Eritrea.

The International Setting

By the end of the war, the traditional competition among Western capitalist powers in northern Africa was still much in evidence. The British were most favorably placed in the competitive process by virtue of their "liberation" of the former Italian colonies of Eritrea, Libya, and Italian Somaliland, which had occupied strategic locations in the Mediterranean and Red Sea regions. Consequently, British strategists felt that the inclusion of these territories into the British empire in one form or another would enable Britain not only to maintain her colossal empire, but also to shape a new world order in her favor. Accordingly, the British Foreign and Colonial offices mobilized their respective research departments to make comprehensive studies and recommendations on what direction British policy should take in the former Italian colonies, including Eritrea.

In 1941, the British had established a sphere of influence in Ethiopia. Thus, in the eyes of British strategists, the disposition of Eritrea and Italian Somaliland had to be carried out in conformity with their interest in Ethiopia.

A Foreign Office subcommittee had given its first tentative recommendation on Eritrea in December 1942. While strongly opposing the restitution of Eritrea to Italy, the subcommittee suggested that Eritrea be given to Ethiopia with an international base being retained at Massawa.[30] This idea was later refined during the interdepartmental debates.

Robert Howe, the British minister in Ethiopia, had advised his government in 1943 of the importance of retaining Ethiopia within the British sphere of influence to safeguard the flow of the Blue Nile, which was crucial for the Gezzira cotton plantation in the Sudan, and to expand trade and maintain tranquility along the Ethiopian borders adjoining the Sudan and Kenya. In Howe's view, in addition to obtaining border rectifications in the form of ceding some Ethiopian territories to Kenya and the Sudan, "[t]he maintenance of British influence in Ethiopia" had to be of paramount importance for the Foreign Office. Moreover, he advised that putting pressure on Haile Selassie to accede to the "[d]isposal of Eritrea and ex-Italian Somaliland in such a way as to safeguard our imperial interests" should be given equal consideration in the formulation of a general policy.[31] As a way of consolidating the British hold in the Horn, Howe recommended the creation of "greater Somalia" by incorporating the various Somali territories held by different powers including Ethiopia. Howe was mindful of the political utility of the idea of greater Somalia insofar as it would be used as a bargaining chip in connection with the disposal of Eritrea. For Howe, in striking a deal with Ethiopia time was of the essence so as to capitalize on Ethiopia's gratitude for British "liberation" of the country and British economic assistance.

The BMA in Eritrea, for its part, undertook a study of the precolonial history of Eritrea with the purpose of breaking the territory along its traditional lines. In July 1943 it produced a document entitled "Eritrea and Her Neighbours," which claimed that strategic and political necessities required a new reallocation of Eritrea, with its different parts going to Ethiopia and the Sudan. According to this analysis, western and northern Eritrea had been severed from the Sudan arbitrarily. The political prescription was then to cede this region back to the Sudan.[32]

In regard to the Red Sea region, the authors argued that this part of Eritrea was inhabited by "self-contained" and "independent-minded" people whose historical relationships with Ethiopia were antagonistic. They further argued that this historical "self-containedness" would certainly "clash . . . in the future, with the political ambitions of Ethiopia." Despite this assessment, however, the document recommended that the Red Sea region be ceded to Ethiopia since its separate identity would not conform with the British requirement of territorial adjustment.[33]

According to "Eritrea and Her Neighbours," the political mapping of highland Eritrea was confusing. First, the fifty years of Italian colonization had brought about profound changes in this plateau region of Eritrea. The Italians had established modern administration and had imparted a capitalist orientation to the rising Eritrean middle and working classes, in sharp contrast to the "precarious regime in Ethiopia." Second, the historical connection of highland Eritrea was with Tigrai, not with Ethiopia as a whole. To the author of the document, however, despite the profound economic and administrative transformation of this region, the ethnic affinity and economic interdependence with Tigrai would offset any future inconvenience should this part of Eritrea and Ethiopia merge. Taking cognizance of this argument, they concluded that the plateau region should be annexed to Ethiopia.[34]

Based on the BMA's analysis, Steven Longrigg, the chief military administrator in Eritrea, presented his strategic plans to the Foreign Office for the dismemberment of Eritrea. His plans included three key elements: first, retention of strategic areas and communication lines; second, setting up a regime reflecting a "permanent ethnographical and economic reality" to ensure the governability of Eritrea; and third, minimization of the cost of administering Eritrea.[35]

Retention of strategic areas and communication lines was supposed to ensure "free communications" with the Sudan. Longrigg saw the second desideratum as a precondition for the reconstitution of "greater Tigrai," with Asmara as its capital, which would solidify British interest in the region. Once instituted, greater Tigrai would be under effective British control with nominal Ethiopian sovereignty. To compensate the Ethiopian emperor for the loss of his right to direct administration over Tigrai, Longrigg proposed the cession of Dankalia in its entirety along with the port of Assab to Ethiopia. The rest of Eritrea would be annexed to the Sudan. If the plan to create greater Tigrai under British control were to materialize, Massawa and Keren were to be added to it. Conversely, should the Ethiopian emperor oppose such formation, Massawa and Keren were to be attached to the part of Eritrea that would be annexed to the Sudan.[36]

A British committee on Ethiopia in Cairo, chaired by Lord Moyne, expressed similar views and its anxiety that Ethiopia might slip out of British hands. The committee suggested that, since "there are signs that the Ethiopians are seeking political support in other than British quarters," immediate negotiations should start on the basis of the following quid pro quo: cession of southern Eritrea, including the port of Assab, to Ethiopia and retention of highland Christian Eritrea as well as the acquisition of the Ethiopian province of Tigrai to create a united greater Tigrai under British protection; and putting maximum pressures on Ethiopia to concede to the creation of greater Somalia by ceding the Ogaden region peopled by Somalis and to give wells in southwestern Ethiopia to Kenya and the Baro River area to the Sudan.[37]

On the home front, the British Foreign Office had specifically asked its research department to undertake an in-depth historical analysis on the Eritrean question and to provide the office with concrete recommendations. The tentative report stated that Eritrea lacked ethnic and economic cohesion and did not have the necessary political makings to be a viable state. The alternative was, according to the report, either a wholesale absorption of Eritrea into Ethiopia or the Sudan, or "its dismemberment along the natural lines of cleavage."[38] The department, however, cautioned that the final proposal on the dismemberment of Eritrea should depend to a large measure on the decision taken to create greater Somalia and frontier rectifications along the Ethiopia/Sudan/Kenya border: "If it were decided to ask the Emperor to relinquish the whole province of Ogaden with parts of Harar and Bale, a strip of territory along the Kenya frontier near Moyale, and the Baro triangle in the west, it might be thought necessary to offer him in full sovereignty all those parts of Eritrea to which he will attach particular importance—the Tigrinya-speaking area, the Danakil country and Massawa. If strategic considerations were to preclude the offer of Massawa, it might be necessary to lighten the other side of the scales correspondingly."[39]

In June 1943 the Foreign Office research department gave its definitive conclusions, recommending that Britain ask Ethiopia to cede the Ogaden for the purpose of creating greater Somalia as well as certain pieces of land to the Sudan in return for certain portions of Eritrea including an outlet to the sea. It enunciated three policy proposals: (1) partition of Eritrea with the west going to the Sudan and the remainder to Ethiopia; (2) retention of the Massawa and Asmara areas within the British sphere; and, (3) if the first two were unacceptable to Ethiopia, cession of a large portion or the whole of Eritrea, subject to obtaining a suitable quid pro quo arrangement.[40]

Early on the research department had added a new dimension to the Eritrean problem by suggesting that Britain support Jewish settlement in Eritrea. The primary purpose of creating a Jewish colony in Eritrea was to divert Jewish immigration from Palestine and thereby to relax tensions in the British dominion in Palestine itself. In support of their recommendation, the authors of these findings argued that Eritrea had a suitable climate and sufficient unexploited land to be used for Jewish colonization.[41] This reasoning belies the department's previous argument that Eritrea was economically unviable as a state. At any rate, the Foreign Office soon found obstacles to the realization of a Jewish colony in Eritrea. First, the Jewish settlement might come into conflict with the Europeans who were already entrenched in the agrocommercial and technical sectors of Eritrea. Second, Jewish settlement would certainly clash with the interests of the local population, thus necessitating a European or international protection of the Jewish colony. Furthermore, it was doubtful whether any Jewish organization would be willing to undertake such colonization without explicit protection from a European power, the United States, or an international body. Third, if Eritrea were given to Ethiopia in return for frontier rectifications, the idea of a Jewish colony in Eritrea would be resisted by the Ethiopian emperor. Fourth, although Eritrea met the requirement of being a non-Arab territory, to avoid a strain in Anglo-Arab relations, its geostrategic position was still thought to make it an unhappy choice from the same Anglo-Arab perspective.[42] For these reasons, the idea of a Jewish colony in Eritrea was eventually dropped.

In its evolution, British foreign policy in Eritrea made no mention of the rights of the Eritreans to the principle of self-determination. The overriding British objective was to prevent other powers, in particular Russia, from establishing any foothold in the region. In so doing, however, British interests clashed with those of her allies. France was particularly apprehensive of British intentions since she had been the most victimized by Nazi aggression, and thus her political and diplomatic image had significantly diminished. Consequently, France, rather than acceding to British policy, opted to pursue a conscientious policy that might lead to the recreation of the status quo ante, including undiminished French colonial possessions. France was concerned that any change in the status of the former Italian colonies leading to independence might serve as a catalyst to nationalist awakening in French colonial Africa, particularly in the Maghrib region encompassing Algeria, Morocco, and Tunisia. Thus, as a policy, France insisted upon the return of the former colonies to Italy as a way of re-creating the status quo ante and maintaining French interest.

Italy, too, reappeared on the scene, claiming territorial possession of Eritrea and her other colonies on the argument that she had participated in the war against Germany as a cobelligerent power, an act that entitled her to the restoration of her colonial holdings. Italy was mainly motivated by considerations of domestic politics (since all political parties in Italy supported the return of the colonies), the desire to regain international prestige and power status, and the need to provide protection to her nationals and her investment in the colonies.[43] Thus Italian ambition, in conjunction with the French objection to the consolidation of British hegemony in Eritrea and elsewhere, posed an immediate problem to the realization of British objectives.

Another component of this difficulty was the appearance of the United States on the global scene and its inevitable clash with British overall policy on the substance of the colonial system. The British mind was conditioned by the Churchillian doctrine premised upon the metaphysics of nineteenth-century empire building. For the British, the frame of reference on the colonial question was the handbook of nineteenth-century imperialism. As W. R. Louis perceptively noted, Churchill still believed that the destiny of the world was based "on the power, prosperity, and prestige of the British empire."[44]

This British mind-set clashed with the visionary American mind-set. American policymakers advocated a new world order on the basis of American self-extension that was antithetical to the nineteenth-century metaphysics. To give way to this self-extension, the colonial system would have had to be entirely transformed from one of total dependency on European powers to one of controlled independence with the United States playing the hegemonic role. True, by self-extension American visionaries meant not the extension of the American system of government, but, just like their Latin American backyard, making the former colonies open for multilateral competition. The British saw the substance of this philosophical thrust as a dangerous force looming on the horizon, bound to destroy the colonial network. American self-extension meant British self-negation and the liquidation of the colonial system.

This basic contradiction between the two countries was exemplified by their respective attitudes toward the substance of the Eritrean question. The British were in favor of strengthening their colonial holdings by dismembering Eritrea in conformity with the strategic requirements of the British empire while the United States favored United Nations collective trusteeship. Beneath the surface of this political contradiction were concealed real economic interests, which could be translated in international, regional, and local terms.

In international terms, despite being allies during the war and sharing a common ideology and system of economics, the capitalist powers of the West never emerged as a monolithic bloc. They were attuned to the traditional forms of competition to ensure a flow of raw material, foreign markets, and areas for investment. Predictably, the international political process corresponded to the international process of economic configuration. Many scholars argue that the intra-West rivalry emanated from the essence of capital itself since capital always possesses a distinctive nationality. In the presence of another primary opponent, such as Soviet so-called Marxism, capitalist competition manifests only the peaceful process of elimination of foreign competitors for domestic or international markets. Domestically, foreigners are excluded from national markets by appropriate measures of taxation, protectionism, or special expenditure policies. On the international scene, unequal treaties may be forced on weaker states, or additional territories may be acquired by means of conquest, annexation, or penetration: "Under these circumstances, it is impossible to speak of capital as qualitatively homogeneous: its power and profitability are functions, not only of its magnitude but also of other specific characteristics among which nationality occupies an extremely important position. . . . It follows that to exist capital must have nationality."[45]

This assessment is supported by the fact that the policy differences among Western powers toward Eritrea seem to have stemmed from their particular national interests in the area. For that reason, the disposition of Eritrea dragged on for such a long time until the United States' global hegemony had been securely established by the process of economic and diplomatic penetration of western Europe itself and by taking control over the economic channels developed by metropolitan Europe in its previous relations with the colonial dependencies.

An important dimension in assessing the significance of the Anglo-American contradiction is the correlation between the expansion of the United States' economy and the political transformation of the

United States from a continental imperialist power into a global hegemonic power. As a result of World War II both the dynamics of U.S. foreign relations and its economy were globalized. In 1939 the U.S. economy employed 46 million persons, and by 1945 this figure rose to 53 million. The American armed forces increased from 370,000 to 11.4 million persons, and government purchases of goods and services rose from $11 billion to $117 billion during the same period. Civilian domestic consumption also rose from $137 billion to $171 billion during this time.[46] The U.S. gross national product expanded from $90.5 billion in 1939 to $211.9 in 1945.[47] U.S. investment abroad also increased from $11.3 billion in 1940 to $13.7 billion in 1945, while commercial export expanded from $4 billion to $10.5 billion over the same period.[48]

American policymakers were exuberant over the significance of this economic globalization. Early on Dean Acheson told a congressional committee, "We have gotten to see that what the country produces is used and sold under financial arrangement to make its production possible." Acheson hastened to add that the government "must look to foreign markets."[49] Taking cognizance of this fact, Christopher Eastwood of the British Colonial Office openly acknowledged in the early 1940s that: "independence is a political catchword which has no real meaning apart from economics. The Americans are quite ready to make their dependencies politically 'independent' while economically bound hand and foot to them and see no inconsistency in this."[50]

In regional terms, U.S. commercial activities were expanding to the Middle East and the Horn during World War II. More important, the U.S. Department of State was keenly interested in restoring relations with Ethiopia for both political and economic reasons; it did so in 1942. Politically, since Ethiopia was the first nation to be liberated from Axis occupation, resumption of relations with Ethiopia would be counted as a demonstration of American interest in contributing to the rehabilitation and reconstruction of previously Axis-occupied countries. It would thereby create an international image of the United States as a nation committed to her tradition of anti-colonialism, the principle of self-determination, and democracy. In economic terms, the United States was interested in ensuring that American products would have unhampered access to postwar markets and, in particular, that Pan-American Airlines would obtain landing rights in Ethiopia on its way to the Far East and India. In addition, the American Sinclair Oil Company had already won concessions from the Ethiopian government to explore for petroleum in the Ethiopian-held Ogaden region.[51] In view of these newly established relations, the United States indicated early on to the emperor its willingness to support Ethiopia in getting an outlet to the sea through the Eritrean port of Assab. But at this point, the United States was not committed to the complete incorporation of Eritrea into Ethiopia.

In regard to the Middle East, which was traditionally the bastion of British hegemonism, Great Britain was unable to feed the populace of the region during the war while it was cut off from Europe. That need opened the door for American merchant ships to cruise along the Red Sea and supply the inhabitants of the region with consumer goods. Much to the chagrin of the British, the result was that American exports in 1942 soared to twice the 1938 figure and by the end of the war American business establishments had taken a commanding lead over British trade in the area.[52] In a nutshell, American penetration into the area not only deprived Britain and the other European powers of their monopoly of the region, but also heralded the emergence of America as a world power and the decline of European hegemony in the area.

Locally, in Eritrea, the strategic location of the colony squarely fit into the long-term U.S. objective. World War II provided the opportunity for the United States to develop Eritrea into a military outpost. In 1942 the U.S. Army Signal Corps entered Eritrea and took possession of the Italian-built communications center at Asmara. Soon thereafter, Eritrea became a focus of United States military attention. Seventy-seven American officers, aided by another 259 enlisted men, embarked upon a military project to enlarge existing installations and facilities and to add new ones. The project employed 2,829 American civilians, 5,611 Italians, 7,384 Eritreans, and 22 Arabs.[53] It was thus clear that the United States' interest in Eritrea was as important as, if not more important than, any other power's and it proved to be decisive in the last analysis in determining the future of the colony.

Despite the contradictory outlooks of Britain and the United States on the colonial question, the United States certainly emerged triumphant on matters pertaining to the colonial question. Its dominance thus determined the direction of international relations, which the British had to accept, albeit grudgingly.

One important catalyst in aiding the coalescence process was what Harry Magdoff called the emergence of the Bolshevik element as one of the dominant features of international relations. In Magdoff's view, two interrelated factors contributed to the emergence of the West as a unified bloc. The first was the shift of the main emphasis from rivalry in carving up the world to the struggle against the contraction of the imperial system. The struggle among the capitalist powers prior to World War II was to redivide the globe among themselves into colonies and spheres of influence. After the war, however, with the introduction of the Bolshevik element into the competitive struggle, the West came to be preoccupied with the urge to reconquer those parts already under socialism and to prevent other parts from leaving the imperial network. The second factor was the emergence of the United States as the organizer and leader of the new postwar imperial system.[54]

For Magdoff, the new economic and politico-military strength of the United States and its assumption of leadership of the entire imperial network were more significant. In consequence of its maturing economic and military strength and the war ravages inflicted on its postwar Western rivals, the United States came to possess enormous capacity and opportunity to organize and lead the imperial system. According to Magdoff, this process of organizing a postwar world order proceeded through U.S. leadership of such international organizations as the United Nations, the World Bank, the IMF, UNRRA, the Marshall Plan, and other military and economic programs.[55]

In summary, the policy variations adopted by the nations of the West toward Eritrea can be explained in the context of the distinct stages of the coalescence process during the second half of the 1940s. In the final analysis, the perception of the specter of communism had a preponderant impact on these evolving policies and consequently on the disposition of Eritrea.

Like the West, the Soviet Union had developed a keen interest in the former Italian colonies. In fact, as early as the Potsdam conference in the summer of 1945, the USSR had formally demanded one of the colonies, preferably Libya, for herself while leaving the other two to the decision of Britain and the United States. The Soviet Union's foreign policy put primary emphasis on the disposition of the colonies since she was eager to break out of "capitalist encirclement" and isolation by establishing some foothold on the African continent and on the shores of the Mediterranean.

The USSR's policy toward the Italian colonies emanated from the general orientation of Soviet practical politics and ideology at the close of the war. In Joseph Stalin's view, World War II was a direct product of the development of world economic and political forces on the basis of monopoly capitalism, suggesting that the capitalist world economy concealed within it the elements of general crisis and military clashes. Thus, since the war was not an accident but a result of the dominant urge among the capitalist powers to redivide the world in their favor by means of armed force, future patterns in international relations would inevitably follow the same line.[56]

In the parlance of Soviet theoreticians, socialism, being a new stage of the objective historical process geared toward the eventual elimination of capitalism, was the determinate negation of capitalism on both domestic and international scales. Consequently for them, all elements of international relations, whether economic or political, must be analyzed and understood in light of the ultimate goals of socialism, which were to be understood in terms of the subordination of interests of other states to the immediate policy objectives of the Soviet Union, the objective representation of socialism against which the economic and political forces of monopoly capitalism were mobilized. As Herbert Marcuse perceptively summarized, the fundamental points of Soviet analysis of contemporary capitalism during the 1940s and 1950s were: (1) the triumph of monopoly capitalism over the surviving elements of free capitalism is now complete; (2) the organization of monopoly capitalism on the international scale on the basis of a permanent war economy with growing tendencies toward state capitalism has assumed colossal proportions; (3) economic and political subjugation of the weaker capitalist powers by the stronger ones, with the United States the strongest, and consequently the creation of a large intercontinental area of exploitation has come about; (4) total mobilization of all human, material, and technical resources for the struggle against communism has become rampant; (5) restriction or outright abolition of the democratic process, of civil and political liberties, and of liberal and humanitarian ideologies has begun in earnest; (6) containment of the force and corruption of the revolutionary potential within the capitalist system has become the dominant policy objective of the bourgeoisie; and (7) global political and social division of the world into imperialist and socialist camps is now complete.[57]

Although providing detailed critical analysis of each of these elements is beyond the scope of this work, the net result of this Soviet theorization has been the production of rationalizing justifications for Soviet foreign policy in which all the elements have been squeezed into one dominant contradiction which is said to exist between capitalism and socialism. In plain terms, every postwar adjustment in the international system was viewed in the light of whether or not that adjustment would facilitate the expansion of the socialist camp or the immediate contraction of the imperialist network. The practical implication of this theory for Soviet foreign policy was made manifestly clear early on by the recurrent oscillations of the Soviet position in the international forum when the disposition of Eritrea and the other Italian colonies was being considered. For four years, until 1949, Russia never invoked the principle of national self-determination for Eritrea or the other colonies. Instead, she incessantly emphasized the need for the redivision of the spoils of war among the victors, laying claims on Libya for herself.

Looking at the process of capitalist unification and reconsolidation after the war from the Soviet point of view, Kremlin strategists might have had legitimate grounds for obsession with that threatening process. The salience of this argument lies in the fact that the Soviet Marxist notion about the inevitability of the interimperialist conflict and war was shattered when the capitalist powers gradually came to close ranks to form a united front against the specter of world communism, evidenced by the intense military and diplomatic movements in the West, apparently directed against the East. Good examples are Churchill's speech about the "iron curtain," the formulation of the Truman Doctrine and the Marshall Plan, and the creation of NATO in 1949 while the Eritrean question was still on the UN floor.

In a nutshell, the reconsolidation of capitalism on an international scale, the relative stability of capitalism, and the formation of one imperialist camp seem to have convinced Soviet strategists of the importance of pursuing a crude foreign policy pursuant to the requirements of readjustment politics. That orientation was carried on in

Zhdanov's report to the Cominform in 1947 in which he underlined the rise of "a new alignment of political forces" on the basis of the coming together of Western, Far Eastern, and Middle Eastern countries.[58]

Furthermore, at the founding of the Cominform, Zhdanov acknowledged the importance of the shift in Soviet foreign policy in favor of some sort of accommodation in light of the growing strength of the West. He reported "Soviet foreign policy proceeds from the fact of the coexistence for a long period of the two systems—capitalism and socialism. From this it follows that cooperation between the USSR and countries with other systems is possible provided that the principle of reciprocity is observed and that obligations once assumed are honoured."[59]

Translated into practical terms, "coexistence" and "reciprocity" came to mean readjustment of a new world order in accordance with the actual division of the world into imperialist and socialist camps with obvious exclusion of forces that occupied the intermediate zones, especially the colonial and semicolonial countries. This interpretation seems consistent with Soviet political behavior as manifested at various conferences when the Eritrean question was being considered.

It was precisely for this reason that the Soviet position on the Italian colonies was marked by oscillation in strategy and tactics. But the Soviet position clearly reflected Soviet desire for the partition of the colonies among the victors on the basis of quid pro quo. Initially, Soviet consideration focused on Eritrea and Libya. At one point, the USSR had even openly expressed concern that Eritrea should not fall into enemy hands.[60] Just as negotiations on the colonies became acrimonious, the Soviets dropped their demand for Eritrea and focused on the acquisition of the Libyan region of Tripolitania and the Dodecanese Islands in the Aegean Sea, leaving Eritrea and Somaliland to Britain and the United States. Again, when they failed in this endeavor, the Soviets offered to abandon any claims to Tripolitania and the Dodecanese if it were agreed that Trieste, with its 500,000 Italians, would be handed over to Yugoslavia.[61] However, the Soviet plan was once again emphatically rejected by the West, and particularly by Britain.

This Soviet behavior reveals the fact that the Soviet Union, like the West, in practice repudiated the principles of the Atlantic Charter which recognized the equality and right of all nations to self-determination. Thus the postwar Soviet international posture represented a marked deviation from the thesis of the Third International on the colonial and national questions.

The other two countries that claimed to have direct interest in Eritrea were Ethiopia and Egypt. Ethiopia based its contention on historical and ethnic arguments, which were refined in due course with the addition of other arguments based on economics and justice in the form of reparation for Italian aggression in the 1930s. On 18 April 1942 Ethiopia formally demanded that Britain return Eritrea to Ethiopia. The Ethiopian communication noted that Eritrea was linked to Ethiopia racially, legally, and historically.[62] Consequently, the British Foreign Office instructed its legation in Ethiopia to study the claim by taking note of the alleged historical and legal links between Eritrea and Ethiopia. Having made comprehensive studies of the questions involved, the British legation in Addis Ababa produced a memorandum in which two facts were indicated. First, the legation noted that throughout its history Eritrea had changed hands many times and that portions of what is today Eritrea had been ruled by Arabs, Turks, Egyptians, and Italians. Second, the Ethiopian emperor had signed two important legal treaties with Italy affirming Italian sovereignty over Eritrea. Therefore, Ethiopia could not justify her claim to Eritrea because the legal significance of the two treaties "lies in the incontrovertible fact that they were freely negotiated by Menilik, the undoubted master of united Ethiopia, in his hour of triumph. In them were fixed the frontiers between Eritrea and Ethiopia and these frontiers stood the Italo-Ethiopian war of 1935–36. It follows, therefore, that on treaty or judicial grounds the Emperor Menilik's successors can have no claim to Eritrea."[63]

One of these two treaties, the Uccialli Treaty, was specific about the separate political character of Eritrea. Articles 2 and 3, for example, read:

Art. 2. King Menilik recognizes the sovereignty of the King of Italy over the colony known as "Italian possession of the Red Sea."

Art. 3. The present convention is binding not only on the present Ethiopian emperor, but also on its direct heirs and successors to the suzerainty over all the territory under the sovereignty of King Menilik.[64]

These articles were reaffirmed in the Addis Ababa peace treaty signed between Menelik and Italy after the defeat of the latter at Adowa in 1896. This treaty especially, and others signed after Ethiopia's victory over Italy, were concluded under conditions in which Ethiopian supremacy was assured. The Foreign Office research department even acknowledged that Ethiopia's claim had a "juridical weakness in that approximately the present frontier was first conceded to Italy by the Emperor Menilik at a time when he had defeated an Italian army in the field and could therefore not plead that he was signing the treaty of peace under duress."[65] Therefore, the claim that Italy's occupation of Eritrea represented an "illegal usurpation" of Ethiopia's territory is no less than absurd. The documents available to us indicate that Menelik had no territorial claim on Eritrea since he had never ruled any part of Eritrea prior to the coming of the Italians. Moreover, even if he had had any territorial claim to any portion of Eritrea, he had willingly renounced it by virtue of recognizing Italian sovereignty over all portions of Eritrea by signing treaties to this effect, which were also binding on all his successors.

From the point of view of practical diplomacy, however, the Ethiopian position was not hopeless. A memorandum of the British legation recommended, for example, that even though no historical and legal arguments could be made, other facts should be sought. The memorandum urged that "the Ethiopian claim to Eritrea cannot be settled now, though it will have to be faced one day. Tricky questions of geography, race, religion, culture, economic and higher politics, which have hardly been touched upon in this note will then have to be most carefully weighed."[66]

The Ethiopian emperor and his advisors spared no time in availing themselves of the British recommendations upon which they began to stress racial, religious, and cultural linkages. To their previously held arguments, they now added questions of economics, security, and justice. They argued that Eritrea and Ethiopia were interdependent, and stressed Eritrea's economic nonviability and her dependency on Ethiopia for foodstuffs. As the Ethiopians put it, "the economies of Eritrea and Ethiopia are interdependent that the prosperity of Eritrea will depend on the prosperity of Ethiopia which in turn depends upon the obtaining of access to the sea through the return of Eritrea."[67]

In regard to security, Ethiopians contended that all invasions directed against Ethiopia had had their origins either in Eritrea or in Italian Somaliland, the return of which to Italy might entail the repetition of aggressive invasions. Obviously this well-calculated strategy was bent on creating a nonexistent eminent danger so as to convince the great powers and the United Nations, a fact later made evident by John Spencer who admitted that, "[a]fter the Fascist invasion of 1935, Italy could scarcely be expected to attack Ethiopia a second time."[68]

Finally, the emperor repeatedly emphasized, the injustice visited upon Ethiopia by Italian aggression in the 1930s which a fortiori necessitated the forfeiture of Italy's colonial title to Eritrea and thus the latter's reversion to its "legal owner." The twisted logic is that the reversion of Eritrea to Ethiopia would recognize "the existing historical, racial, and cultural, and economic and geographical ties which bind Eritrea integrally to Ethiopia and redresses in part the injustices visited upon Ethiopia by the fascist regime."[69]

The purpose of invoking the question of reparation through the acquisition of Eritrea was, of course, to arouse a guilty conscience among the great powers and the United Nations for not coming to the aid of Ethiopia during the Italian aggression. At the time Ethiopia had been forsaken by the League of Nations. But the question was whether Eritrea, the first victim of Italian aggression, should be involved in reparation for what Italy had done to Ethiopia. At any rate, sentimentalization of the issue was in Ethiopia's favor.

An important element in the Ethiopian diplomatic offensive, in the 1940s and in subsequent decades, was the acquisition of John H. Spencer, an American legal and foreign affairs advisor. Aided by the French-educated Ethiopian Vice Foreign Minister Aklilou, Spencer came to build an elaborate diplomatic machinery for Ethiopia. He was able to exploit skillfully his knowledge of the political psychology of both Westerners and Abyssinians to the advantage of the latter. His "adoption" into the imperial system was facilitated by his philosophical temperament and right-wing republicanism. Possessing all the necessary abilities to persuade, manipulate, caricaturize facts, and distort realities, Spencer soon proved to be a linchpin in the process that reached its crescendo with the Ethiopian acquisition of Eritrea and the complete incorporation of Ethiopia into the Western camp. He attended every conference on Eritrea and drafted every memorandum on Eritrea submitted to any international conference. In fact, the emperor was said to have played a minimal role in the acquisition of Eritrea. The proof of this comes from Spencer's own political autobiography: "During these four years of searching for a solution to the Eritrean problem, the Emperor, to the best of my knowledge, played a compliant role, almost never objecting to, always approving our proposals. I fail to recall a single suggestion which he had to offer with regard to the Eritrean formula as it evolved into its final text."[70]

Egypt's claim to Eritrea was the same as that of Ethiopia. Egypt hoped to maximize her interest in the region by annexing Eritrea to the Sudan since her ambition was to become master over the Anglo-Egyptian condominium of the Sudan after British withdrawal from the area. Egypt submitted a memorandum in 1946 to the Paris Peace Conference containing her claim to Eritrea based on historical and economic grounds. Egypt's historical claim was that "[t]he African coast of the Red Sea was markedly Arab in character."[71] In support of the economic importance of Eritrea to the Sudan, the memorandum stated, "Furthermore, from the economic and commercial point of view, Massawa is indispensable to the Sudan. It is a natural outlet for Kordofan and Darfur and through it foreign goods can reach the Sudan."[72]

Aside from the strategic significance of Eritrea to the Egyptian security interest, Egypt also had a vital interest in Ethiopia itself. Egypt receives more than 80 percent of its water from Ethiopia via the Nile River. The acquisition of Eritrea would enable Egypt to exert its influence on political development in the region to prevent Ethiopia from being able to use water as a political weapon against Egypt.

In light of the multiplicity of external interests in Eritrea, there were certainly historical limitations to its international capacity. The problems peculiar to Eritrea in the postwar years emanated from the fact that Eritrea did not have recognized international status before Italian colonization. It was a new entity brought about as a result of a series of Italian conquests that created conditions for its statehood. Consequently, the emergence of Eritrean nationalism aspiring for independence had to face obstacles from regional and international forces.

Many claimants to the territory arose in order to block Eritrea's full-fledged national independence and maximize their own interests. Eritrea's inherent inability to overcome external elements that posed a threat to the realization of its aspirations is attributable to a number of factors. First, the Eritrean question appeared on the international scene at a time when pressures that would create the cold war were building up. Consequently, the Eritrean issue came to be viewed in the context of East-West conflict in which both blocs had a stake in the disposition of Eritrea. Second, a solution to the Eritrean question was sought at a time when the international state system was at a crossroad in its transition after a generalized war. Third, although the principle of self-determination had been enshrined in the newly adopted charter of the United Nations, in view of the novelty of the charter and the uncertain character of the organization at a time when the direction of international relations was not yet determined, the application of the principle was ignored in the interest of power politics. Fourth, since Eritrea was one of the first three colonies to appear as a candidate for national independence, it posed the first serious challenge to the colonial order. In response, the West had to do everything to prevent the establishment of a precedent that would jeopardize its traditional colonial possessions. Fifth, the bipolar nature of international politics and the absence of a significant number of states that had passed through the same experience as Eritrea, which could have aided it in diffusing the concentration of voting power in the two contending blocs, significantly militated against independence. At that time, only three African countries, Egypt, Ethiopia, and Liberia, were independent and the first two were claimants to Eritrea. In other words, the tripolarization process and the resultant tripolar character of the United Nations occurred after the 1960 developments from which other African and Asian colonies benefited, and Eritrea was caught in the earlier bipolar process.

Finally, since all the administrative, political, and material resources of Eritrea were in the hands of the British, Eritrea lacked the necessary ingredient of public authority to achieve independence. All its opponents could use their diplomatic connections and access to the international forum to negotiate, strike compromises, exert influence, and solicit assistance. The Eritreans lacked all these elements for channeling internal and international resources, which could have facilitated the establishment of international connections and, when necessary, guaranteed the satisfaction of some strategic needs of certain powers. For example, in March 1949, when a company of four Eritrean nationalists decided to take the Eritrean case in person to the United Nations, they had to pass many British hurdles. As they did not have passports, they had to travel on a British military permit to Cairo and from there make their own arrangements. In addition, they were allowed to transfer only 500 pounds to Cairo where they had to convert the pounds into dollars. The British political advisor, Robert W. Mason, even argued that it was expedient to use delaying tactics to dissuade the Eritrean nationalists from making the journey to New York. As he observed, "All this will take time and it seems to me very unlikely that they will be able to get to America in time. While we do not want to appear to restrict them I suggest we should not make any effort to expedite their journey since I am sure they would be a nuisance to our Delegation at Lake Success."[73] Mason even trivialized the seriousness of the desire for Eritrean nationalism by suggesting that the nationalists would be content to stay in Cairo for two or three weeks since they had never before been outside Eritrea.[74]

In short, while Eritrea's doors were open to all claimants, Eritreans were deprived of all diplomatic, political, and financial resources. Given the multiplicity of external interests in Eritrea and the strength of the contenders, Eritreans suffered from objective historical limitations. For one thing, since the socioeconomic class structure in Eritrea was in a state of flux, the capitalist powers could not be certain that a full-fledged Eritrean compradorial (or native intermediary) class would be able to maintain state power in subservience to the West. In addition, since the West had full access to the Ethiopian state apparatus and its control over the Ethiopian feudo-compradorial classes was ensured, Western support of the Ethiopian claim was far more politically profitable.

Diplomacy in Motion

Pursuant to the Potsdam protocol reached by the big powers in the summer of 1945, the governments of Great Britain, the USSR, the United States, and France formed what they called the Council of Foreign Ministers (CFM) to consider the disposition of the former Italian colonies of Eritrea, Libya, and Italian Somaliland. In this matter, the council was to be guided by two principles. First, it was to consider wholesale disposition of the colonies. No other solution was acceptable. Second, the council would adhere to the principle of unanimity, meaning that each of the powers could defy any solution. It was clear from the beginning that, amid the heat of East-West conflict, the participants would never reach any solution.

The only constructive proposal submitted to the first session of the CFM in London in September 1945 was enunciated by the United States. The U.S. plan provided for United Nations collective trusteeship for each colony. Each would be governed by a neutral administrator with full executive power, assisted by an advisory committee. The administrator was to be appointed by and responsible to the United Nations Trusteeship Council. Under this plan, Eritrea was to become independent after a period of ten years.[75] In justifying the U.S. position, U.S. Secretary of State James F. Byrnes argued that his country's main interest in proposing this plan was the belief "that a trusteeship should be established solely to assist the inhabitants of the colonies to develop the capacity for self-government so that the people might be granted independence [and] give[n] assurance that the Italian Colonies will not be developed . . . for the military advantage of anyone."[76]

Predictably, the Soviet Union dismissed the U.S. plan as impractical and idealistic. Instead, it proposed individual trusteeship for each of the colonies with the USSR being assigned to administer the territory of Tripolitania. Foreign Minister Vyacheslav Mikhaylovich Molotov rationalized this Soviet plan on three counts. First, he argued that Russia was the most qualified state to administer the Libyan region of Tripolitania since it had "wide experience in establishing friendly relations between different nationalities." Second, Russia was legitimately entitled to Italian territory since ten divisions and three brigades of the Italian Black Shirts had invaded the Soviet Union during the war, causing enormous human and material damage. Third, Russia had the desire to have a sea outlet in Tripolitania because "the Soviet Union should take the place that is due it and therefore should have bases in the Mediterranean for its merchant fleet."[77]

France, too, was disturbed by the U.S. plan since it indicated some changes would take place in the colonial status quo. Collective trusteeship for the Italian colonies accompanied by independence would be a prelude to general disruptions of the colonial system, and France was bound to lose her African colonies. Thus, France proposed Italian administration for all the colonies as the most likely way of preserving the status quo. Britain also showed no enthusiasm for the American plan. Consequently, the first fall session of the CFM ended in a fiasco.

Viewed today, the U.S. plan was superior in all counts to any other proposal yet put forth since it made direct reference to the United Nations charter pursuant to the concept of trusteeship. Perhaps the proposal represented the American traditional orientation of anticolonialism or the principle of self-determination that had been part of its diplomatic vocabulary in international competition with its traditional Western rivals. After all, the coalescence process in the West had not yet reached its crescendo and would not until 1949. On the other hand, Molotov's request for a share in the territorial division of the Italian colonies brought to the surface the true pigmentation of Soviet Marxism, which provided the ideological facade for Russia to become an active participant in the new scramble for the territorial division of the world.

Another salient feature of the London conference was its total rejection of Ethiopia's application for the return of Eritrea. Frustrated by the result, the emperor of Ethiopia had even opened negotiations with Britain on the possible acquisition of the port of Zeila, in British Somaliland, to serve Ethiopia as a connecting sea corridor in return for the Ogaden, which Britain had been seeking from Ethiopia in order to realize its dream of creating "greater Somalia."

For this purpose, in January 1946, the Ethiopian Vice Foreign Minister Aklilou left for London to lay formally the Ethiopian basis for a quid pro quo arrangement.[78] However, Britain showed little enthusiasm for the Ethiopian project, not so much because she did not like the idea, but because she thought that it might jeopardize her plan of partitioning Eritrea, with half of it going to Ethiopia in return for the Ogaden. When it was learned that the British plan to transfer part of Eritrea, including an access to the sea, was still alive, the Ethiopian government retreated from the negotiations on the cession of Zeila.[79] In addition, John Spencer takes the credit for strongly opposing the Zeila project as it would have jeopardized Ethiopia's chance of acquiring Eritrea:

> But the most important consideration in my mind was the danger that such an exchange to obtain a miserable port below Djibouti would irreparably compromise Ethiopia's case for the return of Eritrea with its ports of Massawa and Assab. . . .
>
> I remained firmly opposed to the project if for no other reason than that it would give the four powers, and especially France, the excuse for arguing that Ethiopia had no need for Eritrea.[80]

At any rate, Ethiopia's move to retreat from the Zeila project was a most productive diplomatic venture for her.

The CFM made another try at wholesale disposal of the colonies during its second session, held in April 1946 in Paris. The Four Powers remained predisposed to their previously held positions. Only Britain seemed to budge, coming forward with a distinct plan calling for the immediate independence of Libya, exploring the advisability of dividing Eritrea with part of it going to Ethiopia, and the creation of greater Somalia by uniting Italian Somaliland, British Somaliland, and the Ethiopian province of Ogaden.[81]

To counter the British proposal, the Soviet Union modified its position by proposing joint trusteeship for all the colonies. Italy would be coadministrator of all the territories while Russia and France would become its copartners in the administration of Tripolitania and the Fezzan, respectively. Britain and the United States would assume trusteeship over Eritrea and the other remaining territories.[82]

Both the Soviet and British plans were rejected. France remained adamant in her insistence on the return of Italy to the colonies, and the United States now supported the French idea. More surprisingly, however, the Soviet Union abandoned its claims to Tripolitania and agreed to the idea of Italy returning to the colonies. Her intention was partly to obtain ground within Italy itself since the Communist party there seemed to have solidified its mass base, threatening a seizure of power.

In view of the turbulent state of East-West relations, the Four Powers were in no position to find any solution acceptable to all four of them. In October 1947, the CFM decided to send what came to be called the Four Powers Commission of Investigation to collect factual data regarding the economic and sociopolitical situation to each of the colonies under consideration.

Meanwhile, the news that the CFM might send a commission to Eritrea generated tremendous enthusiasm and political activism in Eritrea. The political arousal of the Eritrean people was so great that it alarmed many British politicians who doubted the commission's ability to assess objectively the political conditions in Eritrea. Frank E. Stafford, for example, warned that the new hopes of the Eritreans might be "destroyed by a political decision taken for other reasons."[83] He believed that the native political entities in Eritrea were mature enough to make the right decision affecting the destiny of the colony and even suggested that the political choices before the Eritrean people should be explicitly explained to them. Stafford observed: "Another point regarding self-determination, peculiar to this territory has assumed importance since I came here. If the people are to be afforded an opportunity of choosing between incorporation in the Ethiopian Empire and administration under a trusteeship, they must be given every opportunity to learn what trusteeship really means. The effect of such education on any thinking man could only be to make trusteeship a more attractive proposition than outright absorption into Ethiopia, whose present regime and state of development is not wholly admired. The right to transfer to Ethiopia would remain open during the period of tutelage, whereas outright cession would be irrevocable."[84]

Stafford further reasoned that proper education about the significance of trusteeship would diminish whatever influence Ethiopia might have in Eritrea. Since the inalienable rights of the ordinary Eritreans were involved, the alternatives "should be put fairly and squarely before them before the Commission arrives, irrespective of its effect upon the Ethiopian claim."[85] The process of political education could be carried out by means of speeches and public statements either by a representative of the United Nations or by a non-British member of the CFM.

Stafford's observation was both technically correct and logically potent. There is irony, however, in reading such noble words about fairness and justice from a man whose elementary sense of detachment would degenerate three years later into dispassionate hatred for Eritrean nationalism as he increasingly adopted an anti-Eritrean posture.

With the purposes of ascertaining the wishes of the inhabitants and gathering factual evidence on the economic and sociopolitical situation, the Four Powers Commission arrived in Eritrea on 8 November 1947 and stayed there until 3 January 1948. The commission received a total of 173 communications in the form of written and oral statements, lengthy documents, interviews, and answers to questionnaires from all parties and groups in Eritrea. The commission also visited fifteen centers throughout Eritrea where it heard representatives of organized villages and tribal sections. As expected, the commission members' interpretations of the factual data were divergent. For this reason they could not even produce joint reports on factual descriptions let alone produce a common recommendation.

According to the U.K.-U.S. description of the data, 55.2 percent of the population were in favor of Eritrean independence or an international tutelary administration leading to independence, whereas 44.8 percent claimed to support Ethiopian interest.[86] The U.S.-U.K. delegates, however, dismissed these figures as only "revealing trends of opinion." They contended that the presentations made by the Eritrean political parties were so exaggerated that they could "give no guidance as to the wishes of the inhabitants."[87]

The Anglo-American delegates further recorded that the people of western Eritrea were overwhelmingly in favor of independence and against the annexation of their region to the Sudan. Instead of acceding to the wishes of the people, however, the delegates tried to deprecate their wishes by suggesting that it was "doubtful whether the political implications of these terms [were] fully understood by their protagonists."[88]

Contrary to their expectations, the Anglo-American delegates also found that a significant "Christian minority" in highland Eritrea was anti-Ethiopian and proindependence. As they noted, these Christians "appear sincerely to believe that immediate alliance with Ethiopia would not be in the best interests of their people." In addition, they discovered that more than 90 percent of the population expressed strong opposition to the return of Italy to Eritrea in any form.[89]

The French and Russian delegates gave a different assessment of what they observed in Eritrea. Both disputed the method used for ascertaining the opinions of the inhabitants. They argued that the Eritrean sociopolitical structure was "ill-adopted" to popular consultations and since the people "lacked the experience," they were "politically immature."[90] The delegates thus dismissed the figures as having no scientific validity since the commission could not control them. The Franco-Russian computation revealed that 47.83 percent of the Eritrean population favored union with Ethiopia while 52.17 percent favored independence or trusteeship leading to eventual independence.[91] The political cynicism of the French and Russian delegates was manifested when the French delegate suggested that "the general impression left by interviews with a large number of persons belonging to all the parties is that they would accept the decision of the Four Powers even if it were contrary to the wishes expressed by their parties."[92]

Finally, the French and Russian delegates were disturbed by the lack of support among the Eritreans for the Italian claim to return to Eritrea, as both powers were favorably disposed toward the Italian position for immediate political reasons. Nonetheless, their pro-Italian position began to haunt British diplomats since it was regarded as having serious implications for Anglo-Italian relations if Britain were the only country to publicly oppose Italy's request for a return to Eritrea. This worry, in fact, quickly gathered momentum in diplomatic circles, necessitating a reappraisal of British policy in Eritrea in light of the new Franco-Russian determination to support Italy.

Subject to such anxieties, on 5 January 1948, David J. Scott-Fox of the Foreign Office entertained a number of options available to Britain. His fear was that the pro-Italian position of France and Russia might give the latter an opportunistic avenue to establish a foothold in Africa. In his view the most amenable strategy was to try to persuade the French to support British interest in Libya on condition that Britain would accede to the French pro-Italian position in Eritrea. The dilemma was, however, that this position necessarily involved repudiation of Ethiopia's claim to Eritrea. Scott-Fox reasoned that Britain was not "obliged to support their [Ethiopian] full claim to the extent of preventing any less favorable decision being reached in the C.F.M."[93]

As a way out of the dilemma, Scott-Fox proposed the cession of part of plateau Eritrea to Ethiopia and the rest of Eritrea to Italy with a guarantee for Ethiopia to freely use Eritrean ports. Admittedly, this proposition had a liability in that Italy might go communist, thereby upsetting the new strategic equilibrium that might be reached. But the alternative was worse, according to Scott-Fox. If Britain blocked any decision in the CFM, the matter would automatically go to the United Nations where Ethiopia might not get better treatment than what the British had proposed, and Italy might even receive the consent of the United Nations to establish an Italian tutelary administration in Eritrea.[94]

As the pro-Italian forces led by France gathered steam on the international scene, Scott-Fox's prognosis received attention in interdepartmental debates. The British Commonwealth Office communicated its position on this matter to the Colonial Office. Lawson of the Commonwealth Office treated the idea of reexamining the possibility of Italian tutelary administration in Eritrea with reservation. His misgiving was that if Italy became the trusteeship power in Eritrea, she would be added to the UN Trusteeship Council. This would necessarily require that another country be chosen as a member of the council to equalize the administering powers, which might upset the pro-British composition and equilibrium of the council. As Lawson noted, "If Italy should fall under Communist influence, and if the additional non-administering country were unfriendly to the Colonial powers, . . . the balance in the Trusteeship Council might be seriously altered to our disadvantage. If, therefore, any concession is made to Italy in the colonial sphere, there is much to be said for making a large enough concession to secure Italian political support and co-operation in colonial matters generally, and in the Trusteeship Council, if she is to be a member of it."[95]

As the interdepartmental debates raged, the British cabinet took up the matter in early February and reached provisional conclusions in favor of Italian trusteeship for Eritrea. The cabinet rationalized that it was important to accommodate French and American views on Eritrea in order to obtain their support for British trusteeship in Libya, where vital and strategic military facilities were located. Under this tentative scheme, Italy would return to the greater part of Eritrea while Dankalia and part of plateau Eritrea would go to Ethiopia. The decision of the cabinet seemed to be influenced by the belief that, if the case should go to the United Nations, Italy would be able to use her strong parliamentary position at the General Assembly to obtain Eritrea in the form of a trust territory. In such an eventuality, open British opposition to the Italian claim would only serve to strain Anglo-Italian relations.[96]

For a while, it seemed that Britain might endorse Italian tutelary administration in Eritrea. British diplomats were further encouraged because Ethiopia's emperor now seemed less than enthusiastic about his claim over Eritrea. According to British sources, the emperor was resigned to the idea of not getting Eritrea at all provided he got a sea corridor, probably through Assab. On 28 March 1948, a distinguished Swedish diplomat confided to British officials in Asmara that the Ethiopian emperor had decided not to press his claim to Eritrea for two fundamental reasons. First, he thought that Eritrea would be an added financial burden to an already bankrupt empire. Second, the emperor feared that Eritrea might give a fresh impetus to centrifugal tendencies in the empire, producing "a real danger that Eritrea might make common cause with the Tigre to split off from Ethiopia."[97]

In spite of such new shifts among diplomatic forces, however, the pro-Italian elements among the British were not solid enough to enforce the provisional decision of the cabinet. The War Office and the British Chiefs of Staff, in particular, were recalcitrant in their opposition to abandoning Eritrea to the Italians for strategic reasons. In early April Mitchell telegramed Bevin expressing the displeasure of the War Office with the idea of Italian trusteeship in Eritrea. Mitchell conceded that Eritrea would be of little economic value to Ethiopia since the latter did not have the means and capabilities of operating and maintaining the modern capitalist infrastructures in Eritrea without the support of international technicians. But he argued that, short of British occupation of Eritrea, it was in Britain's strategic interest to place Asmara and Massawa under Ethiopia. Mitchell's rationalizing arguments were, first, that this plan would enjoy the support of the United Nations. Second, once settled in this manner, there would be no power to threaten British expulsion from Eritrea. Third, it was unlikely that Ethiopia would be able to develop such naval capabilities as to menace British sea communications in the Red Sea, as might be the case were any other power to have possession of Massawa and Asmara. Fourth, in the event of war with any communist or other anti-status quo power in the Middle East, the possession of Massawa and Asmara would serve as "forward base, repair shops, and transit air fields." Mitchell concluded that "although it would of course be in essence a Colony, [the] Colonial power would be black, which in UNO circles would make it respectable."[98]

The opposition of the War Office finally aroused another round of interdepartmental debate over the issue of Italian trusteeship in Eritrea. In a memorandum of 15 April, Scott-Fox resurrected the idea of collective trusteeship for all three Italian colonies if the allocation of a greater part of Eritrea to Italy had an overriding disadvantage and if Britain were unable to obtain broad international support for British trusteeship for the whole of Libya. The idea had already been emphatically rejected in 1945 when the United States presented it on grounds that it might give the Russians a foothold to penetrate Africa. Now, in an about-face, Scott-Fox argued that, if the scheme of collective trusteeship were introduced at the United Nations by the Soviets or by any other power, there was a high probability that it could be forced through anyway. In such eventuality, Britain would have no choice but to conform.[99]

Scott-Fox's rationale was that collective trusteeship would reduce British commitment to stay on in Eritrea simply to prevent Italy from returning, which might in the long run provoke Franco-Italian hostility toward Britain. Even though such a collective arrangement in the administration of Eritrea was cumbersome and it might even be impossible to deflect Italy, France, and the Soviet Union from their present positions, Scott-Fox felt that British diplomatic movement in this direction was worth trying.[100]

As the multiple-power trusteeship ran into snags in view of the vehement opposition from British military headquarters, like all other schemes before it, this scheme was also dropped. In sum, the persistence of the War and Colonial offices in their anti-Italian position frustrated any British move toward pressing the Italian cause in Eritrea. This problem was compounded further by Franco-Russian intransigence on the matter.

Therefore, by the summer of 1948 the Four Powers had made no real progress. Having failed to reach any conclusion, the deputies of the CFM simply restated their respective positions. In matters regarding Eritrea, the Soviet Union proposed an Italian trusteeship with definite acceptable period and terms. Britain proposed Ethiopian trusteeship for ten years, subject to revision by the United Nations to then place Eritrea under Ethiopian administration indefinitely. France advocated Italian tutelary administration while allowing Ethiopia to annex Dankalia with full sovereignty. The United States, for its part, proposed the cession of southern Eritrea, including Dankalia, Akkele Guzai, and Seraye, to Ethiopia while postponing a decision on the remainder of Eritrea for one year.[101]

On September 15 the CFM considered the report of the Four Powers Commission. But like the commission members, they failed to produce any compromise solution on the disposition of the Italian colonies. If there were any new suggestions, it was the one submitted by the Soviet Union. At the eleventh hour the USSR suddenly changed its policy and proposed collective UN trusteeship for Eritrea and the other colonies. This proposal had been made by U.S. Secretary of State Byrnes in 1945, for which he was ridiculed by Molotov as naïve and idealist. Even though this sudden change in Soviet position surprised many observers, the Soviet proposal was categorically rejected. Thus after three solid years of intense negotiations marked by subterfuge, manipulation, wrangling, and incessant transmutations of policies, the Four Powers could not produce anything constructive to solve the colonial question. Therefore, the Eritrean question, along with that of her sister colonies, was referred to the United Nations for its recommendations.

4

The Struggle over Eritrea
in the United Nations

HAVING FAILED TO resolve their differences over postwar adjustment politics, the four big international powers finally agreed to be-
queath the colonial problem to the United Nations. The Eritrean
question, along with that of the other two Italian colonies, was formally submitted to the third regular session of the General Assembly,
which opened on 21 September 1948. The assembly immediately forwarded the colonial question to its political committee for deliberation and possible recommendations. But since the problem was new
to many members of the world body, it was decided that the matter
should be taken up during the second part of the session, which was
to resume in April 1949.

As a matter of fact, the problem soon proved to be too thorny
to solve in one session. It took the world body two solid years to
disentangle itself from the Eritrean problem. The negotiations that
took place behind the scenes were far more crucial in determining
the fate of Eritrea than those in the formal channels of the organization. In this chapter and the next, we shall be concerned with the
protracted processes of deliberations and negotiations on the question
within the United Nations itself, as well as with the diplomatic war
of attrition waged by the big powers, and its implications on the outcome of the formal processes.

The Context

UN consideration of the Eritrean issue began when the international political environment was in a state of turbulence. Three interrelated variables emerged as having crucial implications for the evolution of the Eritrean problem. These were the formation of the Western alliance, the Ethio-American connection, and the transformation of American diplomacy from one based on general containment to one based on containment/militarism.

By the time the General Assembly was holding its third regular session, U.S. capital and goods had already crossed the Atlantic Ocean and effectively penetrated the metropolitan centers of Europe and, by extension, the various overseas dependencies that had been under exclusively European control. In addition, the Marshall Plan for European rehabilitation and reconstruction had borne fruit, establishing U.S. ascendency in the sphere of economics. An important corollary to this economic development was the political concentration in the United Nations in favor of the United States because of her immense financial contribution to the world body and its agencies. The United States occupied a dominant economic position in such international financial institutions as the World Bank, the International Monetary Fund (IMF), and other subsidiary agencies. Moreover, the coalescence process in the West took on an added dimension as the apprehension of the Western powers about the spread of international communism grew more intense.

In light of these economic and political developments, the intra-West rivalry, which was the dominant feature in Western international relations during the initial phase of the postwar era, was relegated to a secondary position. The Western powers came to realize the importance of closing ranks and promoting at least an uneasy cooperation counterpoised against the rise of Soviet hegemonism. Needless to say, the net result of this coalescence process was the formation of a common Western front, although intermittent deviations from the standard requirements of the front by individual partners had occasionally been witnessed. The process climaxed with the creation of the North Atlantic Treaty Organization (NATO). Its formation was indicative of Western determination to cooperate internationally in economic, political, diplomatic, and military fields. It is our view that the formation of this alliance was responsible, in the final analysis, for the adoption of a common Western approach to the Eritrean question which proved to be the determinant factor in the kind of disposition envisioned.

Meanwhile, the United States and Ethiopia were developing new relations. In an effort to win U.S. support for Ethiopia's case, Vice Foreign Minister Aklilou had held talks with Secretary of State George C. Marshall and Senators Connolly and Randenberg in November 1948, as the third regular session of the General Assembly was in progress. During his talk with Marshall, Aklilou made an offer for the United States to remain at the communications center at Radio Marina outside the Eritrean capital in return for U.S. support of the Ethiopian acquisition of Eritrea.[1] The result of the meeting was that Secretary Marshall agreed to support Ethiopia in its claim to most of Eritrea on the proviso that the United States would retain Radio Marina and have unhampered access to military facilities such as airfields and ports in the Asmara/Massawa area.[2]

In an effort to dramatize the newly evolving U.S.-Ethiopian relations, Aklilou suggested the conclusion of a written agreement between the two countries. But in order to avoid international embarrassment and misunderstanding on the part of its allies, Washington preferred verbal commitment and assurance, and postponed formal arrangements.[3] In fact, this diplomatic rapprochement laid the foundations for what was to become one of the most durable bilateral relations in the postwar era. As Harold G. Marcus acidly observed, "The entire episode masked no conundrum or hypocrisy but revealed the texture of subsequent United States-Ethiopian relations."[4]

The shift in U.S. policy, from one proposing collective United Nations trusteeship to one endorsing the Ethiopian case, seems to have been motivated by three underlying considerations. First, Ethiopia had made a tactical move toward the East on several occasions to demonstrate to the West the extent to which it could go to gain the support of noncapitalist powers in the acquisition of Eritrea. To make matters worse, the Russian-built Ras Balcha Hospital in Addis Ababa had become operational and was run by Soviet doctors and nurses. The Ethiopian threat to defect away from the West had been indicated by Emperor Haile Selassie to President Truman in these terms: "[U]nless we can attain access to the sea, the possibility of developing the oil concession which we have granted to a large American corporation and which holds forth unlimited possibilities for the alleviation of the hard lot of our subjects, must also vanish."[5]

Ethiopia's tactical threat was put into action in 1948 when she signed with socialist Czechoslovakia an $8 million arms deal including the construction of an ammunition plant in Addis Ababa. In mid–1949, pursuant to the terms of the deal, the first shipment of 1,500 Czechoslovakian Mausers, 2,750,000 rounds of ammunition, 500 submachine guns, and 10 machine guns arrived in the French port of Djibouti.[6] The emperor's tactic here was well calculated to send a message to the West of the imminent danger of communism, when in fact, communism was more dangerous to his own authority than it was to the West. But he knew how significant Ethiopia's role was to the meaning of the United States's containment policy, and thus his tactical maneuver had the desired effect.

The second reason for the U.S. support of Ethiopian interest in Eritrea was that the level of American commercial interest in Ethiopia had by this time increased to such magnitude that it required the close attention of American policymakers. A shining example was the oil concessions won by the New York-based Sinclair Oil Company, which was highly concerned about political developments in the region in the event of British evacuation from the Horn. That concern was shared by the managers of the American military establishment.[7]

Such political expediency, coupled with strategic considerations, compelled the United States to tilt its policy toward supporting the Ethiopian case. Both business interests and managers of the military establishment concurred on the importance of safeguarding the Horn against possible Soviet infiltration. Felix Cole, U.S. minister to Ethiopia, for example, advised his government that the emperor could effectively frustrate Soviet infiltration while at the same time being dangerous by cunningly retaining some plans "in order to have someone to play off, later, if he deems it advantagious, against all the western powers, including the United States."[8]

Third, the political alignments of forces in Eritrea had cast serious doubt on the possibility of preparing the traditional elements in Eritrea to become a political client in tributary relationship to the United States. The pro-Ethiopian Unionist party, which made its presence known largely by resorting to political hooliganism and armed terrorism, was devoid of an internal social base. In addition, it had become

increasingly unreliable in view of the susceptibility of the feudal notables and ecclesiastics, who made up the core of the party, to corruption and sways and consequent mass defections. The concern about
the absence of the necessary social base in favor of the traditional
elements was made evident by U.S. Ambassador Merrell in a secret
telegram to the State Department in which he stated that the political
momentum was in favor of the proindependence forces: "Cheren
branch of Unionist Party has defected en bloc. British Administrator
estimates privately for British Embassy [in] Addis that independence
bloc commands 75 percent of Eritrea as of August 10."[9]

Furthermore, the fact that the Unionist party was one of opportun-
ist power seekers was made clear in the same telegram: "According
to British Embassy defections from Unionist Party in Eritrea are causing concern in Ethiopian Government. . . . Unionists are understood
by Drew [British Chief Administrator] to have threatened wholesale
defection to independence bloc unless Ethiopians accord immediate
and substantial support and guidance. Unionists asked Deressa [Ethi-
opian Minister] 'how many cabinet seats will Eritrea get?' and 'how
many seats in Chamber of Deputies will be accorded us?'"[10]

It appears that, having lost faith in the ability of the Eritrean traditional classes, the United States was increasingly alarmed by the growing strength of Eritrean nationalism, which was anathema to U.S.
strategic needs in the area. The United States was even more alarmed
when the Eritrean Independence Bloc held a national convention in
August 1949 and resolved to send messages to all nations asking them
to support Eritrean independence. According to American diplomatic analysts, some anti-imperialist sentiment had been detected in
the convention, which naturally heightened U.S. apprehension in regard to the ultimate objective of the bloc. For example, the same
telegram from Ambassador Merrell reflected this concern:

First Independence Bloc convention was staged [in] Asmara
10th [August, 1949]. [The] Meeting voted to send messages [to]
'all freedom loving countries' emphasizing Eritreans claim to
independence. Statement said local economic and technical resources should serve only Eritrean well-being and not foreigners, whatever their race. . . . Whether this was intended [to]
mean denial of radio port and air facilities to US and allies is
problematical but may mean Italian influence [over] indepen-

dence bloc is overrated, as embassy presumes any pro-Italian group will be in touch [with] Rome where such a statement would be unlikely at this time. Rather statement strikes embassy as example [of] growing nationalism in Muslin world and exaggerated appraisal by partially capable Muslin group of ability of Eritreans [to] govern [them]selves.[11]

Such internal political developments in Eritrea induced U.S. alarm in regard to its ability to retain Radio Marina and other military facilities in the event of Eritrean independence. No doubt this apprehension had led to a reorientation on American policy, from one based on United Nations trusteeship for Eritrea, to partial support for Ethiopia in getting a connecting corridor to the sea, finally to one of complete incorporation of Eritrea into Ethiopia. Objectively speaking, that move was consistent with the globalization of American interests and consequently with its global strategic perception. In summary, the basic conditions for the development of U.S.-Ethiopian relations were now ripe. The maturity of this growing relationship was made evident when Aklilou, accompanied by John Spencer, visited Secretary Dean Acheson at his own request on 30 March 1949, just five days before the opening of the third regular session of the UN General Assembly. At the end of their meeting, a memorandum was issued in which, "the Secretary expressed the pleasure of the American government for the military facilities which the emperor indicated he would grant to the United States in Eritrea after that area has been ceded to Ethiopia. Aklilou responded that the emperor was pleased to be of help in this matter."[12]

These newly evolving Ethio-American relations coincided with the formulation of a global U.S. foreign policy. The Truman Doctrine had long been in action when the General Assembly was considering the Eritrean question. In fact, the policy of containment had been transformed into what Jerry Sanders, in *Peddlers in Crisis*, called containment militarism, suggesting the ascendency of the national security managers and consequently the militarization of U.S. foreign policy.

Insofar as the final formulation of U.S. policy toward Eritrea was concerned, the military strategists indeed had the greater say. From the standpoint of military strategy, Eritrea was suitably located in the tropics, far enough from the magnetic storms or the aurora borealis, and had limited degrees of seasonal variations between sunrise and sunset, thereby reducing the need for numerous communications frequency changes. In the 1940s, in the absence of a sophisticated satellite communication system, the strategic location of Eritrea captured the imagination of the military strategists. In particular the Italian-built military communication center at Radio Marina was of too much strategic value to be relinquished. At the same time, the center had the following essential functions: (1) serving as a listening post for radio communications from eastern Europe, (2) relaying military and diplomatic messages from and to ships in the Mediterranean Sea and the Indian Ocean and then on to Arlington, Virginia, and (3) providing NATO with information about movement of forces whenever electrical and magnetic disturbances upset communications in those higher latitudes.[13] As a result of World War II, Radio Marina had already been under de facto U.S. control, forming part of the global U.S. network linked to U.S. communication centers in Morocco, the Philippines, and Arlington. Under the circumstances, it was extremely hard for the American military to consider abandoning such a strategically important stronghold already in its possession.

As we noted, American policymakers perceived Eritrean independence as antagonistic to the retention of the military facilities in Eritrea. Thus to obviate that possibility, the best alternative was to embrace the Ethiopian cause. The second choice was to support the return of Italy to Eritrea. But the stigma of Italy's Fascist history was still fresh in the minds of many members of the United Nations who were ready to exploit it in their opposition to the reinstatement of Italy as an international power. Under these circumstances, it would be extremely difficult for the United States to convince many delegates to warrant a passage of a resolution in favor of Italy. Moreover, since Italy's return would be only in the form of assuming trusteeship responsibility, retention of American military installations in Eritrea would be considered contrary to the principle of the trusteeship system and virtually impossible to justify legally.

Another corollary factor was the readiness of Ethiopia to participate in the international anticommunist crusade. While the Eritrean question was still on the United Nations' floor, the emperor sent a contingent of several thousand men to South Korea, attached to the Seventh U.S. Army, thereby making Ethiopia the only non-NATO country in Africa and the Middle East to contribute troops to the anticommunist crusade.[14] In fact, Ethiopia's readiness to accept a sub-servient position under the United States' hegemony presented an excellent opportunity for American policymakers, which they quickly seized.

Under these circumstances, then, in the autumn of 1948, the American Joint Chiefs of Staff began considering the strategic value of Eritrea. The admiral of the fleet, William Leahy, then chairman of the Joint Chiefs of Staff, outlined what American military policy would be in the Red Sea area, arguing that the general policy should take into account not only "our overall requirements in the frame-work of our global strategy, but also the security interests of our po-tential allies, particularly Great Britain" since the basic concerns of Britain and America "were so interrelated that they must be consid-ered as a whole."[15] Furthermore, Leahy contended, Eritrea was too strategic to be left out of U.S. global strategic considerations. He ad-vised the Secretary of Defense, "The Joint Chiefs of Staff would state categorically that the benefits now resulting from operation of our telecommunications center at Asmara—benefits common and of high military importance to both United States and Great Britain—can be obtained from no other location in the entire Middle East—East-ern Mediterranean area. Therefore, United States rights in Eritrea should not be compromised."[16]

The policy deliberations on Eritrea were drawn to their logical conclusion in December 1948, when James Forrestal, the Secretary of Defense, wrote to the Secretary of State reflecting the general con-sensus of the national security managers on the importance of acquir-ing Eritrea. As he stated:

From the standpoint of strategic and logistical considerations it would be of value to the United States to have refineries, capable of supplying a substantial portion of our aviation needs, located close to a crude supply and also close to areas where naval task forces would be operating and where airfields would be located, yet far enough removed to be reasonably safe from effective enemy bombing.

With respect to the Middle East, refineries located in Italian Somaliland and Eritrea would meet the foregoing conditions provided prospective development of adequate crude supply for these refineries also reasonably safe from effective enemy bombing, is realized. Therefore, as a long-range provision of potential military value, it is believed that concessions or rights should be for United States interests to construct and operate refineries in Italian Somaliland and Eritrea. These rights should include necessary transportation and port concessions, together with air and naval base rights and communication facilities.[17]

Forrestal was cautiously mindful that a search for concessions would have implications on the possible invocation of similar interests by other potential enemies of the United States. As he admonished:

It would appear that demands by our probable enemies for concessions of like nature would be invited if effort were made by the United States to include the matter of concessions to us in prospective United Nations agreements for the disposition of former Italian colonies. This would obviously be undesirable from the military viewpoint. It would, however, be satisfactory from the military viewpoint, if the matter could be handled by separate agreement with friendly nations desiring control of Italian Somaliland and Eritrea.

In view of the fact that these concessions or rights, if granted, may never be utilized, the United States government is not justified at this time in making any commitments, either factually or implied in return for these concessions.[18]

It was on consideration of these recommendations that the State Department pursued a policy of separate behind-the-scenes negotiations with Ethiopia on the possible retention of her military facilities in Eritrea on the basis of quid pro quo. It is self-evident that Secretary Marshall's apparent refusal to make a formal commitment to Ethiopia on this matter in the autumn of 1948 was consistent with Forrestal's advice. This analysis compels us to maintain definitively the position that U.S. policy toward Eritrea was essentially the product of deliberations within the military circle to which the Department of State succumbed. In cognizance of these military factors, the State Department now formulated a definite policy on Eritrea that amounted to the total negation of the colony's right to independence. Consequently, a top secret document was handed over to the U.S. delegation at the United Nations for its guidance in matters relating to the disposition of the former Italian colonies. The contents of the document revealed the true essence of American foreign policy, in particular toward the former Italian colonies.[19]

In regard to Eritrea, the document instructed the U.S. delegation to support cession to Ethiopia of southern Eritrea, including the Danakil coasts and the districts of Seraye and Akkele Guzai. It was to propose that a decision on northern Eritrea be postponed for at least one year with the interim committee being authorized by the General Assembly to study the fate of northern Eritrea. "The recommendation calling for the postponement of the decision on northern Eritrea is based primarily on the strategic requirements that the American military facilities at Asmara be left in cooperative [British] hands for the time being." In the event that the above two conditions were not met, however, the delegation was to support any proposal for the wholesale absorption of Eritrea by Ethiopia. The rationale for the advisability of this policy was that the cession of the territory to Ethiopia "might satisfy Ethiopian demands that will be able to help to counterbalance the return of the Italians to Somaliland and will be applauded as an act of justice by all nations and dependent peoples all over the world."

With respect to the status of Libya, the U.S. delegation was to support the division of the territory into its subcomponents: namely, Cyrenaica, Tripolitania, and the Fezzan. It was to give unqualified support to the British effort to obtain trusteeship over Cyrenaica because the United States recognized, "that British strategic bases and facilities in Cyrenaica were vital to the maintenance of the Anglo-American position in the eastern Mediterranean." The delegation was to propose that the question of Tripolitania and the Fezzan be postponed for one year to be studied by the interim committee of the General Assembly since they involved U.S. strategic requirements in the area and in particular the American airbase at Mellaha and the British airfield at Castel Benito, both of which are near Tripolitania. The document stated:

> It is evident that these requirements make the future of Tripolitania of more concern to the United States than to the United Kingdom since the British expect to build up and maintain their position in Cyrenaica. The British agree with us that it would not be possible for them to obtain a trusteeship over Tripolitania

at this session of the General Assembly. Since no other solution could guarantee us continued use of the airbase facilities and because of the seriousness of the East-West conflict, it is considered vital that the decision with respect to Tripolitania and Fezzan be postponed at this session of the Assembly.

In connection with Italian Somaliland, the U.S. delegation was advised to support Italian trusteeship as a gesture of recognizing Italy's need and aspiration to retain some influence in her former colonies.

Having thus defined the perimeter within which the diplomatic team would operate, the State Department admonished the team that this policy guideline was the sine qua non of U.S. diplomacy, from which no deviation was allowed. It warned thus: "The above recommendations are based on the position taken by the United States in the CFM discussions on this subject and are consonant with general recommendations of the National Security Council approved by the President. Since this position, especially that part of it pertaining to Libya and northern Eritrea, finally affects our national interest, it is very important that the delegation maintain the position taken in the CFM." As we shall see later, this policy outline essentially remained U.S. policy throughout the third, fourth, and fifth sessions of the General Assembly. In fact, the policy was crucial in determining the course of events in Eritrea.

However, we must not overstate the U.S. role in the predetermination of the decision to link Eritrea to Ethiopia. As a matter of truth, Great Britain was the single most important catalyst in bringing the United States and Ethiopia together on the Eritrean issue. Mindful of Britain's diplomatic significance at the United Nations, the emperor admonished his diplomatic czars to pay closer attention to British overall policy in the region. Taking cognizance of this fact, on 29 September 1948, Aklilou received a special audience from Ernest Bevin, British foreign secretary, in which Bevin expressed his continued support for Ethiopia's claim to Eritrea, contingent upon Ethiopia's willingness to support British trusteeship for Cyrenaica. Furthermore, Bevin warned the Ethiopian foreign minister that a British-type solution was unlikely to obtain a two-thirds majority at the United Nations. Thus, Aklilou had to start lobbying the Latin American countries immediately to support any future Anglo-Ethiopian plan.[20]

In keeping with this new Anglo-Ethiopian understanding, Great Britain soon mobilized her diplomatic resources to convince the United States in the direction of the Anglo-Ethiopian plan. In October, George Clutton of the Foreign Office's African desk was instructed to open negotiations with John Foster Dulles, then head of the U.S. delegation to the United Nations, on the imperial allocation of Eritrea. Until this point in time, the United States had been fully committed to the idea of the partition of Eritrea in which southern Eritrea would go to Ethiopia while a decision on the rest of the colony, including Asmara and Massawa where important U.S. military communications were located, would be postponed for one year. Though concurring in principle on the idea of partition, Britain wanted Asmara and Massawa to be included in that portion to be ceded to Ethiopia. In addition, Dulles was insistent that Britain abandon her Ethiopian trusteeship scheme for Eritrea. On 22 October a breakthrough was generally achieved in the negotiations, and the United States agreed to the inclusion of the entire Christian highlands area of Eritrea and Massawa in Ethiopia. Consequently, Clutton decided to seize upon this new U.S. move and he asked the Foreign Office for authorization to make an outright deal. As he noted:

> [I]t is the very best that we have been able to get out of Americans after three weeks of negotiation.
>
> I therefore hope that you will allow me to clinch the bargain with Foster Dulles while they are in this frame of mind, since it is essential that we should have them lobbying firmly on our behalf and as quickly as possible. As you know, if we are in agreement with them their influence with the South Americans, who may swing this whole business, may be a decisive factor.[21]

The Foreign Office characterized the negotiation with Dulles as satisfactory and gave to Clutton a go-ahead. By the first week of November, the two delegates thus reached a formal agreement on the partition of Eritrea as outlined. The United States was persuaded to change her position once the delegate felt "that satisfactory arrangements could be reached with the Ethiopians for the retention" of the U.S. military base in Eritrea.[22]

In keeping with this Anglo-American agreement, on 7 December 1948 the Foreign Office finalized its policy formulation on Eritrea along the lines of the U.S. plan and officially submitted it to the United Nations. According to the British plan all of Eritrea except for the western region was to be ceded to Ethiopia. "The procedures and technical conditions" for the transfer of Eritrea were to be determined bilaterally between Britain and Ethiopia. Eritrea was to be handed over to Ethiopia within four months of the decision's coming into effect.[23]

Some political elements in Britain had voiced their objection to the newly formulated Anglo-American policy on Eritrea and had even asked for a revision of British overall policy toward the colony. The most persistent opponent of this policy was Lord Jowitt, the lord chancellor. On 22 January 1949, the lord chancellor wrote to Bevin asking him to send one of the Foreign Office's experts on Eritrea to discuss the matter with him. In addition to expressing his desire to strengthen Anglo-Italian relations, Jowitt argued that it was deplorable to cede any part of Eritrea "to a more or less primitive savagery."[24]

In light of Jowitt's annoyance, Bevin instructed the Foreign Office to prepare a memorandum for the lord chancellor detailing the reasons behind the Anglo-American proposal to partition Eritrea. Furthermore, to supplement the memo, on 2 February Clutton visited the lord chancellor. Notwithstanding these supplements, however, the lord chancellor remained adamant in his opposition to the plan. He even complained that, "having made a mistake in restoring the Negus to his Empire instead of placing it under United Nations control, we were now proposing to hand over a further piece of territory to be mal-administered by barbarians."[25]

Jowitt reinforced his opposition by arguing that the cession of Eritrea to Ethiopia would only serve to shatter Italian self-respect and to make that country vulnerable to communist "subversion." As a way out of this policy dilemma, Jowitt finally proposed three alternatives. First, if it were impossible to restore Eritrea to Italy, it should be placed under the trusteeship of another European power. Second, if it were too late to change British policy, Bevin should do everything to prevent the French from straining Anglo-Italian relations by posing themselves "as the champions of Italian claims against the wicked British." Third, Britain should leave to the Americans the entire matter of proposing the cession of Eritrea to Ethiopia at the United Nations.[26]

Clutton, of course, seized upon the last point and assured the lord chancellor that the plan was precisely to leave the matter to the United States to do the dirty work at the United Nations. As we shall see, it was the United States that assumed total responsibility for marketing the British idea of partitioning Eritrea along predetermined cleavages. At any rate, in view of the preponderant influence of pro-Ethiopia forces in Britain, the lord chancellor's opposition failed to gather momentum to derail the Anglo-American plan. In sum, when the struggle over Eritrea began, in addition to the already turbulent state of international affairs, Eritrean nationalists had to reckon with the "Europeanized" and mythical components of Ethiopia's international image, the emperor's international popularity, and the Anglo-American front.

The Struggle Begins

The second part of the third regular session of the General Assembly was opened in April 1949 to deal with some unfinished business. Since the question of the former Italian colonies had been referred to the First Political Committee of the assembly for its deliberations during the first part of the session, the committee considered the matter from 5 April to 13 May 1949. The lines were now so clearly demarcated that the respective protagonists were determined to pursue their particular interests by trying to establish solid constituencies within the United Nations. In this section we shall present the various views and proposals put forth by the contending forces.

The Western Thesis

When the committee sat to consider the question of the Italian colonies, the cold war had already reached its crescendo; in consequence, the issues involved were seen in terms of East-West conflict. The four Western powers (the United States, France, Britain, and Italy) were all concerned to equal degrees about the spread of communism and the gradual crumbling and disintegration of the imperial network which was largely dependent on the colonial system. Thus the importance of closing ranks became obvious to them, despite differences in perceptions of how best to safeguard Western interests.

Britain and the United States now adopted a common approach

to the Italian colonies. On the basis of a common strategic consideration, they proposed to the First Political Committee that Eritrea
should be partitioned with its larger segment going to Ethiopia, that
Tripolitania should be granted independence as a way of conciliating
Arab and Moslem opposition, that Cyrenaica should be placed under
British trusteeship authority, and that Somaliland should be allocated
to Italy. It is important to note here that this strategic allocation was
consonant with the policy guideline reviewed in the previous section.
In fact, the policy was reproduced verbatim to the first committee
by John Foster Dulles: "The inhabitants of Libya have gone far
toward autonomy. The Assembly should insist that Tripoli should
be granted full independence. In view of the importance of the region and the strategic balance of the Mediterranean and the Near
East, he felt that Libya ought to be placed under the trusteeship system. . . . The United States representative considers that the United
Kingdom should be invited to administer Cyrenaica."[27]

Turning to Eritrea, Dulles expounded to the committee that "the
population of Eritrea was neither homogeneous nor ready for independence. To avert the possibility of the territory being used in any
future time as a basic threat to Ethiopia and to give to that state
access to the sea, the eastern part of Eritrea, including the port of
Massawa and the town of Asmara, should be incorporated in Ethiopia. As for that part of the population of western Eritrea which has
more affinities with its western [Sudanese] neighbours, it appears that
a separate solution should be sought for it."[28]

With respect to Italian Somaliland, Dulles urged that it should
be allocated to Italy. His rationale for this allocation was that Somalia
did not have "any great strategic importance in connection with the
maintenance of international peace and security."[29] Thus, he recommended that Italy should be invited to assume trusteeship administration of Somalia for a predetermined duration.

It was evident that the Anglo-American proposal was made in conjunction with their global strategy whose ultimate goal was the retention of these colonies within the imperial network by making some
adjustments among the Western powers. Needless to say, the overwhelming majority of the local populations in all three colonies were
emphatically against those arrangements. They were categorical in
their opposition to the partition of their territories and the return

of Italy to the colonies in any form. This opposition was unequivocally made clear by the representatives of the respective populations
who were accorded hearings by the first committee.

In principle, France, too, had always been in favor of retaining
the Italian colonies within the Western orbit. But as to the means
of achieving that objective, she differed significantly from her partners. She saw the Anglo-American proposal as setting dangerous
precedents for other colonies to begin demanding independence. In
particular, the independence of Libya served as a brilliant star in
French North Africa and therefore was anathema to French interest
there. Thus, for political reasons of her own, France proposed a
wholesale return of the former colonies to Italy, with the exception
of the Danakil region of Eritrea, which was to be ceded to Ethiopia
as a connecting corridor to the sea.[30]

Under these circumstances, based on objective international conditions, it had become a commonplace to the three Western powers
that the imperial system could only be preserved by either partitioning the territories or by adopting the cliché of the trusteeship system
under the Western powers. This shared power was necessary because
the return to direct colonial administration by any one power was
as impossible as any contemplation of granting complete independence because it would necessarily jeopardize the maintenance of the
colonial status quo.

In presenting the Italian case, Foreign Minister Count Sforza reminded the First Political Committee of Mazzini's contribution to
Western democracy and of the fight put up by democratic Italians
against Fascism. As if the delegations hearing his speech were igno-
rant of Italy's recent treatment of its colonial subjects, Sforza tried
to make a case out of his sentimentalizing speech. In his words, "Italy,
a country of peasants and artisans devoid of any racial prejudice,
was perfectly fitted to give those areas the needed assistance."[31]

On the question of Eritrea, Sforza brought Italian arguments into
perspective by stating that Eritrea "had never belonged to Ethiopia."
Placing Ethiopian authority upon "that state would be no solution.
It seems that the complexity of the problem had never been given
sufficient consideration." Furthermore, Sforza maintained that administration of Eritrea was beyond Ethiopia's actual or potential capabilities. More important, however, from the perspective of Italian

interest, he stressed that "no matter what legal guarantees were provided to safeguard the status of Italians in Eritrea, annexation by Ethiopia would inevitably bring about a decline in Eritrea's economy because it would certainly nullify the very real contribution made by the Italian community." Sforza also expressed Italy's opposition to any attempt at annexation or partition of Eritrea simply for reasons of military security or otherwise, since Italian trusteeship authority over Eritrea would be of a temporary nature and since Eritrea's eventual independence would in no way pose a threat to Ethiopia. Like the French delegation, however, he proposed that, for ethical and economic reasons, Ethiopia should be granted access to the sea through the port of Assab.[32]

Finally, calculated at obtaining the favor of European allies, Sforza stressed the paramount importance of Italy's participation in the European economic and politico-military processes within the context of which its request for the return of Eritrea should be viewed. In his own terms, it was extremely important to "examine the problem in question from a purely European viewpoint. In the course of the past few weeks, a treaty had been concluded between France and Italy providing for a customs union to be followed by an economic union. A body had been set up within the framework of the organization for European economic cooperation for the centralization of economic programs, preparations had been made for the signing of the pact of European economic union and the North Atlantic Treaty had been signed. Those recent international developments, exemplifying as they did the constructive spirit reigning in Europe, would help to establish the conditions necessary for European peace, stability and security."[33]

The connection made by Sforza between European politicoeconomic cooperation and the disposition of Eritrea had, of course, no relevance to the solution of the problem in question. But the message was clear enough; Western powers had now established a general framework within which individual interests had to be adjusted. According to this framework Italy was entitled to receive what was due to her in light of her partnership in NATO and other political and economic institutions. The division of the pie, however, had to be determined in accordance with the power distribution within the Western alliance. And this rule by which particular interests were adjusted would remain true as long as the common perception of the specter of world communism haunted each member of the alliance.

The Soviet Antithesis

The Soviet position at the General Assembly amounted to no more than a rehearsal of previous views. Andrey Gromyko told the First Political Committee that the disposition of the Italian colonies was being dragged out simply because of the imperialist designs of the Western powers. He lashed out in particular at Britain for having the ambition to strengthen its quasi-monopolistic position in the Mediterranean and Red Sea areas. Gromyko charged that the failure of the Council of Foreign Ministers to reach any settlement for the colonies was in the main due to the British imperial idea of greater Somalia and the partitions of Eritrea and Libya. He thus observed, "[I]t was not difficult to understand that those proposals had derived from the United Kingdom's desire to improve its position in north and northeastern Africa at the expense, not only of defeated Italy, but also of Ethiopia." Therefore, "the failure to reach an agreement was principally due to the desire of the United Kingdom for expansion in those areas."[34]

In addition, in Gromyko's terms, the problem was further compounded by American support for British de facto control over Eritrea and the other colonies without any justification. France's obstinacy in supporting the Italian case was also a factor obstructing the solutions for the colonies.[35] Furthermore, Gromyko charged that the ulterior motive of the Western powers was to maintain their firm hold in the former Italian colonies in order to utilize them as strategic bases for attacking the Soviet Union and other democracies. Like some Western powers, however, the Soviet Union supported the idea that Ethiopia should get an access to the sea through the port of Assab. But in general, it rejected the idea of partition or annexation of Eritrea. As Gromyko observed, "It was inadmissible that Eritreans be taken away from one state and subjected to the control of another state or group of states solely in the interests of the governments concerned and not on the basis of the interest of the United Nations as a whole."[36]

Soviet concern with respect to the disposition of Eritrea was primarily motivated by its own security considerations as well as by the need for obtaining some foothold in the Middle East and the African continent. In Soviet strategic perception, however, acquisition of Eritrea or any other Italian colony by assuming a trusteeship role or by becoming a copartner with Italy in such an undertaking was now completely out of sight in view of the USSR's limited audience at the United Nations. This audience was almost exclusively confined to its Eastern European allies, which numbered no more than six. Therefore, the only feasible alternative now left for the Russians was to insist on obtaining the support of non-Western states for the idea of collective trusteeship, which they had ridiculed as impractical and utopian when the Americans had proposed it in 1945. In any case, Gromyko introduced a motion in the committee for the idea of collective trusteeship for Eritrea. According to this Soviet plan, Eritrea was to be governed by an administrator appointed by and responsible to the trusteeship council. The administrator was to be assisted by an advisory council composed of seven members, including one representative each from Britain, the United States, the Soviet Union, France, and Italy, and two Eritreans. In addition, territorial concession was to be made to Ethiopia in order to obtain access to the sea.[37]

Nevertheless, since the Soviet proposal was quintessentially antithetical to the political arrangement enunciated by the West and since its hidden purpose was to obtain some means of establishing Soviet influence in Eritrea, making it subversively anti-status quo, it was apparent from the outset that the West would not accept Soviet inclusion in such a scheme for Eritrea.

Restatement of the Ethiopian Case

In presenting the Ethiopian case, Aklilou, Ethiopia's vice foreign minister, read to the First Political Committee the all-too-familiar arguments based on religion, history, language, race, and social structure shared by the peoples of Eritrea and Ethiopia. In addition, he raised the economic, social, and security needs of Ethiopia.[38]

First, Aklilou contended that Eritrea and Ethiopia were economically interdependent. Ethiopia had always been the supplier of agricultural goods to Eritrea and thus, he argued, Eritrea could not exist as an independent economic entity since she lacked agricultural potentialities. In his opposition to the return of Italy to Eritrea, Aklilou pointed out that war-ravaged Italy was in no position to develop Eritrea economically.

However, Aklilou's argument against the economic viability of Eritrea was not convincing, especially to the Latin American delegates who had a perceptible predisposition in favor of Italy. With the adoption of the UN charter which had elevated the political precept of self-determination to a legal status, economic arguments could not be invoked in considering the potential for political independence of any nation. As a matter of fact, the entire international state system has always been economically interdependent. In view of the cosmopolitan character of modern capitalism, commodities of every nature must cross every international boundary in search of markets. Thus, if there had been exchange of commodities between Eritrea and Ethiopia, nothing would and should obstruct the commercial relations that had existed before by virtue of the emergence of Eritrea as an independent entity. So long as the economic interdependence or complimentarity of the two economies was dictated by the objective conditions of international capitalism, continuation of that process was in the mutual interests of the countries concerned. Furthermore, nations like Somalia and Djibouti, economically poorer in resources and potentialities than Eritrea, had been allowed to become independent entities. According to the charter, economic factors have never been and should never be counted as part of the criteria for statehood.

In all cases, and under all international practices, only political criteria have been in vogue since the principle of self-determination has been based on juridicopolitical conditions. Thus, if the Eritrean people wished to give higher value to their political rights than to their economic conditions, and were determined to protect those political rights no matter what the economic cost, it was their political choice.

In addition, the argument that Ethiopia was economically more capable than Italy to administer Eritrea was equally unconvincing in view of the qualitative difference between the feudal economy of Ethiopia and the highly advanced capitalist system of Italy. In that respect, Ethiopia had nothing to offer Eritrea. If economic capability in the sense of stimulating economic development in Eritrea, was to be a deciding criterion, then Eritrea would have been far better off under Italy than under Ethiopia.

Second, in regard to security, Aklilou argued that Eritrea "has only served Italy as a base from which to attack Ethiopia."[39] This argument seems to have convinced some of the newly emergent states since Aklilou emphasized the recent Italian aggression on Ethiopia and consequently the need for reparations. He successfully pushed the argument to the fore and sentimentalized it so as to draw the attention and sympathy of the members.

However, two important things had to be taken into account in assessing the validity of the Ethiopian argument in favor of her security need. One was the fact that the return of Italy to Eritrea as a trust power was not the only condition, and indeed was not a condition at all, for resolving the Eritrean question. The demand for Eritrean independence was the prime condition militating against any Italian presence in Eritrea, more important than the likelihood of any future aggression on Ethiopia. But if immediate independence for Eritrea failed to carry a conviction, it could have potently been argued that a neutral country other than Italy should have assumed trusteeship responsibility over Eritrea until her capacity for self-government and independence was adequately demonstrated. However, since Ethiopia's main preoccupation was with the acquisition of Eritrea in her entirety to aggrandize the Ethiopian empire, those two alternatives were unacceptable to the emperor.

Third, Aklilou contended before the committee that, since the peoples of Eritrea and Ethiopia were historically linked, those factors of common religion, history, and race would make the union of the two territories the most natural solution to the problem. In justifying his case, he argued that more than 100,000 Eritreans were living in Ethiopia at that time and that Ethiopia had already granted Eritreans the widest representation in the Ethiopian administration. Therefore, "the fact that a large number of Eritreans were currently employed in Ethiopian government services would facilitate a smooth and speedy return of Eritrea to Ethiopia guaranteeing the representation of Eritreans in the country's administration."[40]

This last point, like the previous two, suffers from several incongruities, especially when one considers the fact that Ethiopia had never known any meaningful census. Not only did Ethiopia not know the exact number of Eritreans living there, until very recently Ethiopia did not even know the number of her own population. The glaring contradiction in Aklilou's presentation was revealed in another speech to the General Assembly in which he stated that there were 200,000 Eritreans living in Ethiopia.[41] Even if the number was correct, it had no relevance to the consideration of the fate of Eritrea. Eritreans living in Ethiopia, who had adopted Ethiopian citizenship, could not determine the political processes in their parent country.

The percentage of Eritreans in the Ethiopian administration was also a dubious claim. It was true that the emperor had elevated a number of Eritreans in his imperial bureaucracy, but he did so for the purpose of using them as a pawn in the chess game against his provincial rivals, in particular the Shewan nobility in whom he had no faith. Since Eritreans had no stake in the depoliticization process in the provinces of Gojjam, Gondar, and Tigrai, where the emperor's chief rival groups were entrenched, it was extremely essential for the emperor to speed up the induction of Eritrean emigrés into his imperial bureaucracy to offset the numerical superiority of his possible antagonists. Corollary to that fact was that, since Ethiopia did not have the necessary trained administrative cadre and since by choice or necessity Ethiopia had already become part of the global capitalist structure, requiring the creation and maintenance of a modern bureaucracy, the induction of Eritreans into the Ethiopian system was of paramount importance in the modernizing process. But more importantly, the emperor had to create the impression that Eritreans were highly represented in his administration as a way of convincing as many members of the United Nations as possible.

The Position of the Latin Group

The Latin countries, which constituted one-third of the entire United Nations membership at the time, were the most cohesive group in terms of political solidarity and voting behavior. But they were caught between the political clienteleship they owed the United States and their loyalty to their shared heritage and affinities with Italy. Consequently, their general approach to the question of Eritrea reflected this dilemma. In essence, however, their position was not antithetical to the general orientation and strategy of the West. They were insistent that the particular interest of Italy had to be given a preponderant weight in matters affecting her former colonies. Paradoxically enough, the arguments of the Latin representatives were often couched in concepts of justice and law.

In presenting the Latin position, the Uruguayan delegation stressed the cultural ties that existed between his country and Italy and the latter's contribution to world cultural development for which reason alone she should be allowed to exercise trusteeship authority over Eritrea with the exception of a strip of territory to be ceded to Ethiopia on grounds of morality and justice. He urged the committee to take action on the basis of justice and law; for that reason, the United States' proposal was good enough.[42]

Arce of Argentina charged the big powers with misusing their international status in regard to the Italian colonies. He suggested that "victory did not confer rights, especially when it had been won in the name of justice, for it would be contradictory to annex a territory, a procedure incompatible with both justice and law and undemocratic in nature."[43]

Echoing the Anglo-American proposal, Arce argued that "Ethiopia, a country which had been invaded, had a moral right to reparations." Consequently, he proposed that southern Eritrea should be annexed to Ethiopia while the remainder of Eritrea should be assigned to Italy under the trusteeship system. "Thus justice will be done to Ethiopia and a new outlet will be opened for the surplus Italian population."[44]

Likewise, Belaunde of Peru began his speech by cherishing the interest and rights of the local inhabitants within the framework of which the United Nations had to resolve the colonial problem. In Belaunde's terms, the points of justice to be considered were the achievement of harmony among nations and the interests of the local population. However, the achievement of harmony among nations should take precedence over the interest of the population. As he observed, "Nothing could be done for the latter unless favourable conditions of international cooperation were created. The task was, therefore, to reconcile the interests of the powers which had done so much for the development of the Mediterranean region: Spain, the United Kingdom, France, and Italy."[45]

On the basis of this twisted logic, Belaunde proposed that Italy be returned to Eritrea as a trustee power while Ethiopia be given a strip of territory with an access to the sea. With all impunity Belaunde assured the committee that "Peru, which was proud to acknowledge the high virtues of its Italian population, was in a better position than any other country to recognize the colonizing talents of the Italian people." On the other hand, fearful of offending Britain, Belaunde added in a conciliatory tone, "The close ties and the debt of gratitude which linked Latin America to the United Kingdom as well as practical common sense demand, however, that a solution should be found in respect of Cyrenaica which would help to maintain and strengthen the harmony which should exist between the United Kingdom and Italy."[46]

All remaining delegations from Latin America reproduced these views verbatim, and in justifying their positions all of them made reference to the principles of justice and law. They even distorted history in an effort to embellish the image of Italy. For example, the Chilean delegate Santa Cruz, said that "the Italian people had not exercised a policy of racial discrimination."[47] Moreover, some Latin delegates falsely argued that the overwhelming population of Eritrea desired the return of Italy.

In summary, from the point of view of the Latin group, Italy was the only country capable of bringing about progress in Eritrea. To diffuse any strong opposition from Ethiopia to the realization of Italy's return to Eritrea, they all agreed to concede portions of the colony to Ethiopia. For the Latin group, Ethiopia's sentimentalization of the issue by making constant reference to Fascist aggression was a serious political handicap militating against their own position. Consequently, the Latin delegates expressed their readiness to concede to Ethiopia's claim on moral grounds while sometimes alluding to ethnographic and historical factors as a means of justifying that position.

The contrast drawn by the Latin delegations between Italian civilization and Ethiopian backwardness was an attempt to obviate any possibility of annexing the whole of Eritrea to Ethiopia at the expense of Italy. To them, justice meant entitling Italy to full restoration of her colonial possessions. The absurdity of their arguments is demonstrated by the frequent references they made to moral questions on which basis Ethiopia was to receive parts of Eritrea as compensation for the injustices committed by Italy by denying Ethiopia's right to national self-determination and independence, although, in fact, Eritrea was the primary object of Italian aggression and injustices.

Eritreans Appear on the Floor

Pursuant to proposals made by some delegations, representatives of Eritrean political organizations were given hearings by the first committee in an effort to ascertain the wishes of the population. Thus, for the first time in four years since the Eritrean question had been on the international forum, Eritreans appeared on the United Nations's floor, not in their capacity as active participants in the international decision-making process affecting their destiny, but as a mere source of information that might aid the committee in its deliberations on the question. But the more sensible explanation is that the purpose was merely to give credence to those who proposed that Eritreans should be heard, thereby giving the necessary legal pretense to the proceedings of the first committee.

In any case, the first to be heard by the committee was the representative of the Moslem League of Eritrea, Ibrahim Sultan Ali. In countering the thrust of the Ethiopian argument that stressed the religious affinities of the two peoples based on Christianity, Ibrahim placed the emphasis of his argument on the Islamic character of Eritrea. He contended that 75 percent of Eritreans were Moslems by faith and were totally against any form of connection with Ethiopia. In addition, he argued, in terms of ethnic, socioreligious, and linguistic characteristics, the non-Moslem population of Eritrea was not homogeneous and shared no affinities to the Ethiopian people. In Ibrahim's parlance, Eritrea had been under different powers for centuries and had never formed part of Ethiopia. "If the proposed annexation were carried out," he warned, "it would undoubtedly be contrary to the principles of the Charter which guaranteed peoples the right to choose their own government. Eritrea had no common important economic interest with Ethiopia."[48]

Ibrahim also reminded the committee of the historical antagonism, both religious and ethnic, between the peoples of Eritrea and Ethiopia. Thus, the annexation of Eritrea to Ethiopia would be extremely dangerous to the welfare of the Eritrean people, and in particular to its Moslem segment. As he observed:

> Having thus no ethnic, religious, historical or economic bonds with Ethiopia, the Eritrean Moslems were strongly opposed to the annexation of Eritrea to Ethiopia. Owing to the different political structure of Eritrea and the contribution it might make to the equilibrium of that sector of Africa and the Middle East, the Eritrean Moslems request the United Nations to grant independence to their country. Annexation of the territory to Ethiopia would lead to tragic conflicts. Ethiopia would follow a policy of oppression there and commit acts of violence against the

members of the Moslem League as had been proved by the attack as a result of which Sheik Abdel Keber [President of the Moslem League] had recently succumbed as he was preparing himself to come to the General Assembly as a member of the Moslem League.[49]

Finally, Ibrahim pointed out that 80 percent of Eritreans, including Copts, were in favor of an independent, united Eritrea. In a reply to the question by the Belgian representative as to what the preference of the Eritrean people would be if the General Assembly were to place Eritrea under the trusteeship system instead of granting it immediate independence, Ibrahim maintained that his party would be in favor of direct United Nations trusteeship.

Muhammed Abdullah of the Nuova Eritrea Pro-Italia party was heard next. As its name suggests, the Pro-Italia party was largely financed and controlled covertly by Italians and thus had on its agenda the independence of Eritrea after a reasonable period of Italian trusteeship. According to Muhammed, the general conditions in Eritrea were not favorable for the country to assume immediate independence and thus Eritrea had to be placed under Italian trusteeship since Italy was the "best qualified" to assume such responsibility in light of its social and political maturity.

Reasons adduced by Muhammed in favor of Italian trusteeship included: (1) Italian was the only foreign language spoken in Eritrea and would facilitate intellectual and technical development; (2) knowledge of the Italian language would enable Eritreans under Italian trusteeship to take a greater part in the administration of their country; (3) Italian residents in Eritrea had greatly facilitated the development of Eritrea and their exodus from Eritrea would thus hinder the country's economic progress.[50]

Finally, Muhammed expressed his vehement opposition to the annexation of Eritrea to Ethiopia, stating that historical racial antagonisms would make it impossible for Eritreans to live in peace. He also maintained that the idea of partition was equally dangerous as it was contrary to the wishes of the people. In Muhammed's terms, in view of the profound evolution throughout the sixty years of Italian administration, Eritrea had constituted a political, social, economic entity and was entitled to take the road to independence. Though he maintained that Italian trusteeship would serve the cause of justice and civilization by putting an end to the unbearable situation in Eritrea under the British, Muhammed warned that, "rather than taking a hasty decision such as the annexation of Eritrea to Ethiopia or an Ethiopian trusteeship, it would be better for the United Nations to make a thorough inquiry into the wishes of the Eritrean population."[51]

The third organization to appear before the First Political Committee was the pro-Ethiopian Unionist party. In fact its leader, Tedla Bairu, had nothing new to offer but a repetition of the parental views expressed by the Ethiopian delegation. Tedla argued that the other parties did not represent the true desires of the Eritrean people and emphatically rejected the idea of Italian trusteeship.

According to Tedla, aside from ethnic, linguistic, and religious ties that bound Eritrea to Ethiopia, Eritrea had always constituted the most important part of Ethiopia for thousands of years: "Above all, Eritrea shared a profound sense of nationality with Ethiopia and that sense of nationality had been reinforced by the common struggle against Italy and by the fact that Ethiopia alone had protected and cherished Eritrean interest."[52] Like the other parties, however, Tedla completely rejected the idea of partition.

Ironically enough, Tedla Bairu, who did everything to convince the committee of the historical, ethnolinguistic, and socioreligious affiliation of Eritrea to Ethiopia, was to recant completely what he had said at the United Nations when he joined the Eritrean Liberation Front in the 1960s. Like all born-again nationalists, he subjected Ethiopia to a blanket condemnation for her false claim to Eritrea; nevertheless his testimony and later defection were reflective of the nature of the pro-Ethiopian party in Eritrea.

The most telling testimony yet to be given was by Casciani, representative of the Italo-Eritrean Association. On behalf of his organization, Casciani requested the immediate independence of Eritrea within the geographical boundaries that existed on 1 January 1935. According to Casciani, Eritrea was a composite of different ethnolinguistic and socioreligious groups bound together by intermarriage and common economic interests. For almost a century these groups had lived side by side in cooperation and mutual respect, the contribution of each community being essential to the welfare of the others. He thus categorically objected to either partition on the basis of race, religion, or geography, or annexation of Eritrea to Ethiopia.[53]

In his opposition to the idea of ceding Eritrean ports to Ethiopia, Casciani noted that "the ports of Massawa and Assab were essential to the economic life of Eritrea as, far apart from the contribution of the fishing and allied industry, those ports provided the only outlet for the trade and traffic of the hinterland. To detach them from Eritrea would be like denying Genoa to Italy or Marseilles to France."[54] In addition, he pointed out that Ethiopia's need for an access to the sea would be fully satisfied by granting her special facilities, including the establishment of free zones to enable her to use those ports. He also reminded the first committee that all the political parties in Eritrea were unanimous in their demand that the geographical integrity of Eritrea be maintained and that that unanimity in itself was an eloquent evidence of the interdependence of the Eritrean regions and their inhabitants.

Finally, Casciani advised that, if Ethiopia was prepared to recognize Eritrea's independence, it would be possible to conclude perpetual treaties of nonaggression, trade, and cooperation between the two countries which might contribute to progress and welfare of the peoples in the Horn.

In retrospect, the testimonies of the Eritreans before the committee seemed to have made little or no impact on the perceptible predispositions maintained by the committee's delegations. If any purpose was served by the appearance of Eritreans on the floor, it was only that the deliberations of the General Assembly came to bear some legal semblance provided by the appearance of Eritrean representation in the form of consultation. It had become obvious that Eritrean independence failed to correspond with the particular interests of the major actors. What is of paramount interest to the historian is, however, that all the political organizations heard by the committee were categorically in favor of maintaining the territorial integrity of Eritrea, and three out of four favored complete independence or trusteeship leading to independence.

The "Third Road" Position
Inspired by the idea of justice rather than by considerations of strategic needs or political expediency, a few countries appealed to the spirit and letter of the United Nations charter in considering the Eritrean problem. The Saudi delegation poignantly drew attention to the fact that disagreements among the big powers should not gov-

ern the proceedings of the committee and that the condition of Italy's overpopulation or her heritage of civilization and culture was irrelevant to the problem in question. The Saudi delegation argued that the only road to solving the Eritrean problem was to grant it independence and, if that were not feasible, to arrange trusteeship. According to the Saudi position, the guiding principles in considering the Eritrean case were (1) preservation of Eritrean unity under all circumstances, (2) establishing the primacy of the interest of the Eritrean people, (3) establishment of trusteeship only to aid the Eritreans in their progress toward independence, and (4) selection of an administering authority in accordance with the desires of the people.[55]

In subscription to the Saudi position, Iraq charged that the strategic interests of the big powers were the only problems on the way to finding an acceptable solution to the Eritrean question. The delegate added that the approaches of the big powers were in flagrant contradiction of the principle of self-determination and the trusteeship system. In regard to the claims of Ethiopia, he argued that Ethiopia could get an access to the sea "provided that such a solution did not contravene the wishes of the Eritrean people and their right to self-determination."[56]

The most outraged spokesman for the "third road" position was the Philippine delegate, who condemned in the strongest possible terms the attempt at allocating the Italian colonies to different powers. He thus questioned, "[W]ere those territories really to be shared out like goods [between Egypt, Ethiopia, Italy]? With the exception of Antarctica, such a division of territories . . . must be considered as belonging to the past. It was a mistake to speak of the disposal of the former Italian colonies. The real question was the future of those peoples, the destiny of human beings. The primary and fundamental principle was whether those territories belonged to those peoples who inhabited them. They have to be consulted to the extent to which their wishes could be expressed. What had to be borne in mind was their welfare and their future as independent nations."[57]

Finally, the Philippine delegate urged that any solution to the Eritrean problem, as well as to disposition of the other colonies, "had to be based on the Charter to the fullest possible extent and particularly on article 73 which states that the interests of the inhabitants of those territories were paramount. The United Nations could not, therefore, impose on those populations a decision contrary to their wishes."[58] He also referred to the fact that the representatives from Eritrea had expressed themselves in favor of direct United Nations trusteeship to be followed by independence in which the world body was duty-bound to assist the Eritrean people to develop their own free political institutions.

The Yugoslav delegate expressed similar views. He singled out the strategic basis of the Anglo-American proposals as being the conception of their African military strategy. As he observed, "It was a matter of a new partition of Africa much resembling the scramble for Africa which had taken place during the second part of the 19th century, but legalized by the General Assembly of the United Nations."[59]

The Yugoslav representative also rejected the idea of Italy returning to her former colonies on grounds that Italy had concurred with the Anglo-American strategy of military and economic expansion. The evidence cited in this regard was that, before the North Atlantic Treaty was signed, the Italian Foreign Minister Count Sforza had pledged that his country would offer military bases and facilities to NATO within Italy, and by extension in Eritrea and the other colonies over which Italy would assume trusteeship authority. This arrangement would immediately violate the principles and provisions of the trusteeship system.[60] The point that military bases might not be allowed in the former Italian colonies was, indeed, what United States policymakers feared most, and that was why they drifted toward supporting the Ethiopian case since it offered the least resistance to the acquisition of military installations in Eritrea.

For his part, the Turkish representative emphasized that the right of nations to self-determination should be the only guiding principle in considering the Eritrean question. Although immediate independence for Eritrea was the best solution, provisional trusteeship for reasons of gaining political experience and economic progress was also acceptable. Turkey laid out the following conditions for a decision on the Eritrean problem: (1) placing Eritrea under a state with technical and economic means and democratic ideals needed to guarantee political development toward Eritrean independence while at the same time ceding a strip of land to Ethiopia with an access to the sea; and (2) the trusteeship regime to be provisional and not to exceed ten years.[61]

This approach, which we have called the third-road position, indeed represented the assertion of a third force in the process of international politics, namely that between the oppressed nations that occupy the intermediate zone and the major powers. The strength of that third force has always been subject to historical vicissitudes in view of internal political developments in each country often marked by instabilities as well as the susceptibility of internal classes to concerted manipulations by the major powers. Therefore, during the initial phase of the emergence of this force (the 1940s), the consistency of support by those countries belonging to this group was shaky and unreliable. As we shall see, many of the delegates who initially supported the right of the Eritrean people to independence would defect to the Western position.

Proposals Voted On
From the various aspects of the debate, two types of general proposals emerged. The first set of arguments resembled those of the Berlin Conference of 1885. An excellent example was the argument advanced by the Dutch representative, who held that the interest of Italy constituted the most vital element in the maintenance of European stability and prosperity. "Furthermore, Italy had a dense population on the soil which was partly not very fertile and was partly poor in raw material. Italy badly needed an opportunity to utilize constructively its considerable surpluses in energies and people."[62] According to this line of reasoning, rather than the wishes and interests of Eritrea's inhabitants, the interests of external powers were to assume overriding consideration, and international peace and security were to be defined in terms of the General Assembly's ability to "harmonize" relations among the major powers in their competition to realize their policy objectives on the basis of the requirements of the imperial network.

The second category of arguments included the ones represented by the third-road position and genuinely inspired by the spirit of the charter of the United Nations. Other countries manifested behavior based on their polycentric position, such as Burma and Denmark. But since sooner or later they were to support the Latin or Anglo-American position, they could be put in the category supporting European stability.

The underlying factor in all these variations of the arguments was the contradiction in the general process of international relations, in the light of which the various proposals on Eritrea should be analyzed. This contradiction or conflict had three principal aspects. First, the diplomatic contradiction between the so-called Latinos (i.e., Italy, France, and Latin American countries) and Anglos (i.e., Great Britain and the United States) was a concentrated reflection of the absence of any monolithic configuration within the capitalist imperial network. In other words, the traditional modalities of competition among the capitalist powers had continued into the postwar era. Furthermore, Italy's capitulation to the Anglo-Saxon-dominated coalescence process was not yet fully realized. It is within this context that the differentiations in policy orientations and corresponding proposals by the Western capitalist countries must be understood.

However, since there was another overshadowing element of contradiction in the international process represented by the Soviet Union, which was perceived as the general threat to capitalism, the aspect of the Latino-Anglo contradiction had by necessity to recede into the background. Had it not been for the presence of socialism as a dominant feature in international relations, the nature of the contradiction between Italy and the Anglo-American clique would have in all probability been different in texture and magnitude. Consequently, the proposals presented in connection with the disposition of Eritrea would have resulted in different outcomes.

As already mentioned, the Bolshevik revolution had introduced a new element of contradiction, that of socialism, into contemporary international relations. Both by definition and by objective, socialism presupposes the elimination of capitalism and its eventual supercession by a higher form of socioeconomic formation. Socialism thus requires the full mobilization of ideological, political, diplomatic, economic, and military forces against capitalism. Conversely, in recognition of this definition and objective of socialism, the capitalist powers inevitably had to mobilize their forces against the specter of world communism. The net result of this antagonism was that every international issue was viewed in the context of the contradiction between capitalism and socialism. Eritrea was caught between these two antagonistic relationships, and therefore it was obvious that the Eritrean question would be viewed in terms of that contradiction.

The third element of the contradiction in the international process stood in obvious contradistinction to the first two elements. This aspect might be referred to as the contradiction between the oppressed and oppressor nations. It was made evident by the delegations that adopted the third-road position emphasizing the right of nations to self-determination and the charter of the United Nations as the sole guiding instrument in determining the fate of oppressed or colonial nations. In my view, this position represented the incipient process of tripolarization of international relations that was to become the dominant feature, at least within the United Nations, in the 1960s, when the process of decolonization reached its high watermark. It was unfortunate that the Eritrean question appeared at a transitional historical juncture when bipolarity in international politics was the dominant feature and when countries like Yugoslavia and India, which in part reflected the interest of the future, were numerically inferior.

In sum, it was in cognizance of these aspects of the contradiction that the various proposals for the disposal of Eritrea and her sister colonies were formulated at the United Nations. It is to the consideration of these plans that we now turn.

The British draft resolution provided for the incorporation of Eritrea into Ethiopia with the exception of the western province, which was to be annexed to the Sudan. The draft was immediately endorsed by Ethiopia and the United States for obvious reasons.[63]

The British draft resolution provided the largest possible portion of Eritrea, including the two Eritrean ports, to be annexed to Ethiopia. Therefore, under the circumstances, partition of Eritrea along the lines of this draft was the optimum Ethiopia could hope to get. To win acceptance of this draft resolution, the Ethiopian delegate had to once again invoke the feeling of collective guilt among the members of the United Nations. Accordingly, he "urged the committee to take a decision favourable to his country which had suffered so great an injustice at the hands of fascist aggressors."[64]

In justifying the United States position in favor of this draft resolution, John Foster Dulles also maintained that the British proposal was the only workable solution since it recognized the ties of Eritrea's population with the peoples in Ethiopia and the Sudan. Although this argument provided the rationale for justifying the position taken, the actual intent of the United States was purely strategic.

As anticipated, however, the British proposal provoked great diplomatic uproar among Italian, French, and Latin American delegations and Eritreans as well. Tarchiani of Italy maintained that the partition of Eritrea as envisaged in the British plan would completely destory the economic life of Eritrea, ending all hopes of progress in east Africa. In addition, he called the attention of the committee to the fact that all of the Eritrean political organizations, with the exception of the Unionist party, had urged that Eritrea be given independence within its traditional boundaries. "Acceptance of the United Kingdom's proposal with regard to Eritrea would set a dangerous precedent as many nations had, in fact, been created as a result of historical accidents. What mattered was the feelings and desires of the local population which, according to their representatives, were overwhelmingly in favour of their national unity in order to attain independence at the earliest possible date."[65]

The most angry political overtures were heard from Latin American delegations. Arce of Argentina described the British package as self-serving. "With regard to Eritrea, the proposal was even more reactionary since it provided for the arbitrary partitioning of the territory between Ethiopia and the Sudan." Arce added that while he "was quite ready to recognize and to respect the right of Ethiopia, that did not mean that his delegation favoured annexation by the latter territories. The populations were opposed to Ethiopian rule. Furthermore, Argentina could not ignore the fact that the transfer of the greater part of Eritrea to the Anglo-Egyptian Sudan meant nothing less than its incorporation into a British colony."[66]

For her part, France rejected the British plan on grounds that it made no allowance for certain factors such as the wishes of the local peoples, the interest of international security, and Italy's special position on the matter. France added that the views of the various representatives of the Eritrean population had been extremely contradictory and therefore further information was needed before any determination could be reached with certainty as to their exact wishes.[67]

Objectively speaking, these rationalizations by Italy and her Latin allies were presented merely in defense of their particular interests rather than on behalf of the welfare of the Eritrean people. More importantly, it revealed the prevalence of a contradiction between the Latinos and the Anglos within the imperial network, the diffusion of which was crucial for the coalescence process. The temporary acuteness of that contradiction was revealed by the Italian delegate himself when he lavishly praised his allies in these terms: "The words of the representatives of the great nations of Latin America, the well considered and effective support of France, and the expressions of appreciation of other delegations had been received with deep feeling and gratitude by the whole Italian people."[68] At any rate, this analysis suggests that passage of the British plan was impossible without first diffusing the combined Latin opposition.

On behalf of eighteen Latin American countries, the Mexican delegation introduced a draft simply stating the general principles, desires, and interests of the local population in Eritrea. The Latin American plan was built on the assumption that Eritrea was not ready for independence, and that thus the only solution was to prepare the Eritrean people toward that end under international trusteeship composed of Britain, Italy, France, the United States, and Ethiopia. In this way, the Latin group hoped that Italy would be able to regain her international status.[69]

The Soviet Union also introduced a draft resolution calling for a collective international trusteeship for Eritrea with the participation of the USSR, the United States, Britain, France, and Italy. The difference between the Latin and Soviet plans was, in essence, one of exclusion or inclusion of the Soviet Union in the trusteeship scheme. In any case, the Soviet plan received an audience only in Eastern Europe and Pakistan.[70]

India and Iraq each introduced a draft resolution that reflected the wishes of the countries that had adopted the third-road position pursuant to the principles of the charter of the United Nations and the concept of self-determination. According to the Indian plan, direct UN trusteeship was the only proper way of keeping Eritrea and the other colonies out of the sphere of big-power rivalry and protecting the inhabitants from alien domination. The significance of this plan lay in its direct reference to the concept of referendum to ascertain the wishes of the Eritrean people. The plan recommended "that steps be taken immediately to ascertain the wishes of the people of Eritrea as to whether they desire incorporation with Ethiopia and that, for this purpose, a special commission appointed by the United Nations be dispatched to Eritrea to ascertain the wishes of the people either through plebiscite or, if this be unsuitable, by other means appropriate to the circumstances of the territory and to report to the

General Assembly in the light of its inquiries in different parts of Eritrea whether the whole or any part of Eritrea should be amalgamated with Ethiopia."[71] Similarly, the Iraqi draft recommended that the General Assembly dispatch a five-member commission to Eritrea to ascertain the real wishes of the people as to their future political status and to report to the fourth regular General Assembly session.[72]

After all the plans had been introduced, it momentarily seemed that the Eritrean case had captured many supporters. Many delegates began to express views in support of the Indian-Iraqi drafts. One of them, the Haitian representative, stated that, if justice, equity, and the charter of the United Nations were to be respected, the United Nations should adhere to the desires of the Eritrean people as expressed by their representative organizations and that, for this purpose, the United Nations should send an inquiry commission to Eritrea whose findings should be accepted. The representative added that he had previously "fully supported the Ethiopian demands. But in view of the opposition which had been expressed by certain of the Eritrean spokesmen, it was clear that no decision could be taken until the population had been consulted. . . . [I]t might perhaps, therefore, be appropriate to undertake a plebiscite."[73]

In view of the multiplicity of such divergent plans, the First Political Committee eventually resolved to set up a minicommittee, which came to be known as Subcommittee Fifteen, to consider the plans hitherto submitted or that might be submitted to the first committee.

Ironically, however, just the day before Subcommittee Fifteen began its session to carry out its new assignment, the General Assembly learned from a dispatch of the Associated Press that secret Anglo-Italian negotiations had resulted in the settlement of the Italian colonies. It was reported that, after having consultations with United States officials, Count Sforza had stopped in London on his way home and had met with British Foreign Secretary Ernest Bevin. At the end of their meeting, the two diplomats produced what was to be known as the Bevin-Sforza plan in which Italy was to receive Tripolitania and Somaliland while Britain and France were to retain Cyrenaica and the Fezzan, respectively. Eritrea was to be partitioned between Ethiopia and Anglo-Egyptian Sudan.[74]

Having received his instructions from London, the British representative in Subcommittee Fifteen then introduced the contents of the Bevin-Sforza plan as if it were a new British initiative. Now the contradiction between the Latinos and the Anglos seemed to have been resolved, and thus the Anglo-Italian plan was assured of safe passage. And indeed, it received the stamp of Subcommittee Fifteen. All other proposals were rejected.

Many countries, however, defied the action of Subcommittee Fifteen on legal grounds. Iraq, for example, opposed the Bevin-Sforza plan on two counts. First, Subcommittee Fifteen had exceeded its terms of instruction since it was supposed to consider only those plans already submitted or that might be submitted to the First Political Committee of the General Assembly. Since the Anglo-Italian proposal had been directly forwarded to Subcommittee Fifteen, bypassing the first committee, the normal procedure agreed upon had been violated. Second, certain provisions of Subcommittee Fifteen were at variance with the spirit and letter of the charter of the United Nations as all the local inhabitants of all the colonies had objected to the return of Italy in any form.[75]

Likewise, the Haitian delegate attacked the Bevin-Sforza plan as a flagrant violation of the legal jurisdiction of the United Nations, because the matter had been legally referred to the United Nations by virtue of the fact that the Four Powers had failed to reach any settlement of the question. Therefore, since the United Nations was considering the matter, the Anglo-Italian deal contravened the provisions and principles of the world organization.[76]

In view of the heated controversy over the Bevin-Sforza plan and its subsequent adoption by Subcommittee Fifteen, Poland proposed that the representative organizations from the colonies should be accorded new hearings by the first committee. For obvious political reasons, Britain, however, adamantly stated that it was "useless and dangerous"[77] to hear again the various views of the representative parties and groups. From the British point of view, it was perfectly clear that the local populations were categorically against any form of partition or the return of Italy. Therefore, to avoid any inevitable political embarrassment, it was of paramount importance to block the proposal for a new hearing. But the Polish plan was adopted by a majority vote and the parties were heard again.

Meanwhile, the three Eritrean political organizations previously heard formed the Eritrean Popular Front and asked to be heard collectively. As the British feared, the Eritrean spokesman, Ibrahim, unequivocally denounced the Bevin-Sforza plan. Ibrahim raised two important questions, one relating to the wishes of the Eritrean people and the other to the principle of international law.

In regard to the first question, Ibrahim maintained that the Anglo-Italian agreement "was contrary to the aspirations of the Eritrean people for immediate independence. The Eritrean people are opposed to any idea of partition or annexation of any part of its history to any country whatever." In connection with the second question, he charged that, from the legal point of view, the plan was contrary to the principle of the Atlantic Charter that affirmed the sanctity of the right of nations to self-determination. He then requested that a United Nations committee be invited to decide that point of law.[78]

Finally, Ibrahim asked that the First Political Committee send a commission composed of neutral countries, not directly having particular interests in the matter, to make a field survey of the ethnic and economic division of the Eritrean people. In his view, only such an investigation could demonstrate the desire of the Eritrean people for independence within the existing boundaries. If immediate independence was impossible, however, he invited the United Nations as a whole to assume trusteeship over Eritrea.

Nevertheless, the new hearing accorded to the Eritreans had no impact at all as the Latin delegations were now effectively manipulated and swayed, thanks to the capitulation of Italy to the Anglo-Saxon circle. Thus it became evident that the Latin group was ready to vote in favor of the Bevin-Sforza plan. On 13 May 1949 votes were cast on all the hitherto discussed plans. As expected, the Bevin-Sforza plan was passed, receiving a majority vote, and was transmitted to the full session of the General Assembly for its approval.

However, as the General Assembly began consideration of the recommendations of the First Political Committee, there arose serious difficulties owing to the combined resistance of Arab, Moslem, and Asian nations supported by the Soviet bloc. The Arab countries were particularly incensed by that part of the Bevin-Sforza plan that dealt with the partition of Libya. After long heated debate, marked by innuendos and constant bickering, the whole question took on a new twist. The third-road position seemed to have prevailed. Because many countries consistently showed preference for this position in favor of self-determination, the General Assembly was beset with insurmountable legal questions.

In any case, after a plethora of amendments and repetitions of old ideas, votes were cast on the Bevin-Sforza plan: first on each separate section of the plan dealing with territory and then on the whole package. The proposal on the partition of Eritrea was approved by thirty-seven votes with eleven against and ten abstentions. The proposal for a wholesale disposition of all three colonies was, however, rejected by thirty-seven votes with fourteen in favor and seven abstentions. But since the rules of procedure demanded that a solution be sought simultaneously for all three of the Italian colonies, the Eritrean question had to continue as part of the general issue until approval for the other two was obtained. Thus the struggle over Eritrea continued.

5

The Struggle in the United Nations Continues

THE QUESTION OF the Italian colonies was again taken up for consideration during the fourth session of the United Nations General Assembly in the fall of 1949. But during the interim period between the third and fourth sessions some strategic realignment of forces inside Eritrea occurred. The Eritrean nationalists counted the defeat of the Bevin-Sforza plan as a victory for Eritrean nationalism and quickly began to capitalize on it. The Italians also now seemed convinced that neither the annexation of Eritrea to Ethiopia nor Italian trusteeship over Eritrea was a feasible alternative. Consequently, Italy began to agitate its supporters inside Eritrea to join the nationalists in the cause of full-blown independence. The idea of independence thus became a meeting ground for both nationalists and pro-Italian forces in Eritrea. The new enthusiasm and anti-Ethiopian feelings were so high that even Mason could write that the native Eritreans were "intoxicated" by the idea of independence just as people "who have tried alcohol for the first time in their lives."[1]

Out of this well-coordinated movement emerged what was to be called the Independence Bloc of Eritrea, an umbrella organization of eight political groups joined on the platform of fighting for the ultimate independence of Eritrea. The coalescence process that occurred in the summer of 1949 clearly demonstrated that the majority of Eritreans were in favor of complete independence. Mason acknowledged this fact when he reported to London that the nationalist parties "have all joined up on the Independence platform, I think that there can be no doubt that they represent a clear majority of the country. Two thirds seems to me a reasonable guess, but sixty percent would perhaps be safer. . . . On the whole, therefore, it is the view of most people here with long experience of the country that the idea of Independence has aroused more enthusiasm than the idea of Union did. I agree with this view."[2]

The Independence Bloc found leadership in the political genius of Ibrahim Sultan Ali, secretary general of the Moslem League. Ibrahim distinguished himself as a formidable leader in the early 1940s when he threw himself behind the emancipation of the serfs movement in western Eritrea. Since then, he had been regarded as a threat to the aristocratic order in Eritrea and, by extension, to the feudal order in Ethiopia. This in the main explains why most of the Moslem aristocrats in Eritrea challenged his leadership in the Moslem section of the Eritrean population. But with his political astuteness and superior articulation of the interests of the masses, Ibrahim was able to maintain the relative cohesion of Eritrean Moslems.

In practice, Ibrahim showed his followers his unwaivering loyalty to the party and dedication to the country. For example, one time when the Moslem League had completely run out of money to discharge its proper functions, he appealed to the faithful Moslems to send goatskins as a tribute to God when they killed goats on a given holiday. Then Ibrahim sold the skins at profit and earned about 2,000 pounds, enough to put the league back on its feet. This earned him tremendous respect from his followers.[3] Ibrahim's political innovation earned him the respect of Christian Eritreans as well, and he became the unanimous choice of both Moslems and Christians to be leader of the Independence Bloc. In sum, he was admired by friends and foes alike. For example, Paddock, an American diplomat, warned his government that "Ibrahim should not (repeat not) be underestimated."[4]

The political coalescence in Eritrea under the leadership of the Independence Bloc was further supplemented by Italy's diplomatic activism on the international scene. Failing to obtain trusteeship over Eritrea, Italy now seemed fully committed to supporting Eritrean independence as the best alternative to Ethiopian annexation. The new Italo-Eritrean alliance, however, had both its blessings and its drawbacks for Eritrean nationalism. Ibrahim knew well the diplomatic utility of Italy, particularly with respect to her ability to influence the Latin American countries. A temporary rapprochement with Italy on the idea of independence thus opened an international forum for Eritrean nationalists. Internally, however, it had negative consequences for the cohesion of the Independence Bloc. The bloc was an amorphous collection of parties, many of which had strongly objected to Italian participation in Eritrean affairs. To ordinary Eritreans, Italy represented a symbol of past colonial exploitation and oppression, and it was extremely difficult for Ibrahim to convince all constituent parts of the bloc of the diplomatic significance of a temporary alliance with Italy. Britain and Ethiopia quickly seized upon these misgivings to blackmail Ibrahim as an agent of Italian interest in Eritrea, which made the bloc vulnerable to internal dissensions. With the benefit of hindsight, one could argue that any move toward an alliance with Italy was wrong, given the political psychology of the ordinary masses in Eritrea, but it is equally reasonable to argue that, given Italy's international connection with the Latin group, the move to accept Italian international hegemony and work with pro-Italian forces in Eritrea could not have been a political error.

These developments, both internal and international, generated political trauma for Britain, the United States, and Ethiopia. The latter was, in particular, perturbed by events in Eritrea as the influence of the Unionist party began to dwindle rapidly. In an apparent effort to prevent the complete collapse of the Unionist party, Ethiopian officials led by five senior ministers flooded the Eritrean capital, ostensibly for health reasons. Expectedly, the Independence Bloc had repeatedly asked the British administration to stop the arrival of Ethiopians. Initially, the administration had downplayed the whole matter, but as tensions between Eritreans and Ethiopians in Asmara increased, Brigadier F. G. Drew, chief administrator of Eritrea, was finally forced to report to London: "The continued intensive and open intervention by the emissaries from Addis Ababa in the internal political field has now reached a stage where it is a matter for some considerable embarrassment to the Administration. . . . It could not now possibly be denied that this intervention is the object of their visit and I do not think that the individuals in question will even be disposed to deny it. We have every reason to believe that their activities are carefully organised and that each has been assigned a different political party to work upon."[5]

Furthermore, Drew noted that the presence of Ethiopians in Eritrea was a political liability both internally for security reasons and internationally as it might tarnish British "neutrality" in Eritrea. Consequently, he proposed to the Foreign Office that some form of mild representation be made to the emperor, stating "that the presence of these visitors is proving a matter of embarrassment to the Administration."[6]

Nonetheless, Drew's proposal touched off a controversy over the propriety of making representation to Ethiopia. In particular, Sir Victor Mallet, British ambassador to Rome, and Dan W. Lascelles, British ambassador to Addis Ababa, seemed locked in a war over turf as they put emphasis on different aspects of the British strategic equation. Mallet warned that British confrontation with Italy over Eritrea would have serious repercussions on future Anglo-Italian relations.[7] In his view, to preempt a crisis in Anglo-Italian relations over Eritrea, the granting of autonomy for the whole of Eritrea was the ideal solution. He dismissed the all-too-familiar argument that any semblance of Eritrean autonomy might lead to bloodshed or Ethiopian invasion of Eritrea as nonsense. As he noted, "I can see no real reason why autonomy for the whole of Eritrea under Ethiopian sovereignty should lead to bloodshed. . . . Local autonomy would at least have the advantage of giving Eritrea a better chance of maintaining its higher level of civilisation instead of being dragged down to the Ethiopian level."[8]

Lascelles, however, strongly disagreed with Drew and Mallet on the question of Ethiopian intervention in Eritrean politics as well as on the idea of autonomy. From Lascelles's perspective, in light of the significance of Eritrea to Ethiopia, the latter had every right to influence Eritrean politics in such a manner as to advance her cause and to prevent the slippage of Eritrea from Ethiopian hands. "Since no other power now asserts any claim on the territory, it would not appear that these Ethiopian visits could give rise to any justified demands from other quarters for similar facilities." He further defended this by saying that the Ethiopians were only making private contacts with political parties.[9] From Lascelles's standpoint, Ethiopia could not afford to lose by default whatever influence she had in Eritrea. "[M]oreover it is quite natural that the Ethiopian Government

should make these special proselytising efforts at a moment when
. . . the local political situation is rapidly evolving to their detriment.
If they can, by such efforts, put a stop to defections from the Unionist
to the Independence camp, it will be politically well worth their while
to do so."[10]

In regard to the uneven sociocultural development that existed
between Eritrea and Ethiopia, Lascelles had earlier disputed Mallet's
position on the question. From his perspective, Ethiopia's acquisition
of Eritrea was crucial for the economic development and political modernization of Ethiopia, as the union of the two countries would serve
to "accelerate this process by leavening the mass. The need of the
Ethiopian Government for competently trained officials is acute. . . .
In these circumstances, can we be at all sure that it would be
'morally wrong and politically an error' to leaven the mass by giving
this African territory to an adjacent African State, even if it does
mean 'economic and social regression' for the territory in question?"[11]

Since Lascelles's views were in conformity with the general position
of the Foreign Office, he was declared the winner in the controversy
and Drew's suggestion of protesting Ethiopian meddling in Eritrea
and Mallet's arguments were rejected. Sir William Strang had already
told Mallet that Bevin was by no means prepared to depart from
his original idea of partition. Strang further contended that there
were no prerequisites for the suggested autonomy for Eritrea.[12] By
rejecting Mallet's proposal and the suggestion to protest Ethiopia's
intervention in Eritrea, Britain once again made the Eritrean political
arena open to external meddling and agitation.

Like her partners, the United States also was apprehensive about
the political developments taking place in Eritrea. Accordingly, it sent
Paddock to make an assessment of the internal correlation of forces
and report to the State Department. On 28 August 1949, Paddock
sent a fifteen hundred-word telegram outlining his impression of the
relative strength of the Independence Bloc. In his first report, Paddock blamed the waning influence of Ethiopia in Eritrea on the Ethiopian liaison officer Negga in particular, and on Ethiopia's policy in
general. He noted, "My estimate is that Ethiopia lost golden opportunity by not following forceful policy locally and by leaving Unionists
to local leaders in lieu [of] guidance supplied from palace Addis has
shown weakness by sending ministers [to] Asmara and that Nega's
claim of Unionist strength is completely incorrect. . . . I would place

the fig[ure for strength of Independence Bloc] at 60 or 65% not 75%."[13]

In view of the strength of the Independence Bloc, Paddock advised the State Department to refrain from reasserting the U.S. plan of partition so as not to contribute to the political strength of the Independence Bloc by providing an anti-imperialist platform. An open U.S. position on partition, he cautioned, would only serve to unite the partners of the Independence Bloc. In his view the Bloc was likely to split up if its members were "not cohered by what might seem to them [an] Anglo-Amer[ican] intervention."[14]

In his second message of 29 August, however, Paddock modified his earlier assessment about the bloc's strength. Now he advised the State Department that the bloc would remain united throughout the fourth session of the General Assembly, and thus warned that the department should expect Ibrahim to make a strong attack on U.S. policy. He assured the department that the Independence Bloc was prepared to invoke the principle of self-determination enshrined in both the Atlantic and UN charters. Paddock felt that Ibrahim was capable of convincing as many delegates as possible and to obtain majority votes in favor of Eritrea's right to independence.[15]

Realignments at the United Nations

On the eve of the General Assembly's fourth session, Britain, Ethiopia, and the United States were as determined as ever to force their plan of partition through the General Assembly. The Italo-Eritrean forces were, however, equally well positioned to put up a herculean fight against the three anti-Eritrean partners.

On 21 September, the General Assembly took up the Eritrean question afresh. The session merely heard ritual reproductions of the arguments of the contenders involved. But some important reorganization of the political dispositions of the contenders took place, and within that framework some results were achieved.

In the first place, for the first time in four years Eritrea became detached from her sister colonies. Libya and Italian Somaliland were to become independent in due course. Thus the procedure of wholesale disposition was formally abandoned. Second, the Soviet Union for the fifth time changed its position and now advocated independence for Eritrea. In countering all other proposals, the Soviet delegate introduced a draft resolution calling for Eritrean independence after five years of direct United Nations trusteeship.[16]

Third, the Soviet move to support Eritrean independence had only a boomerang effect in the sense that the West increasingly became resistant to the idea of independence. Under these circumstances, Ethiopia's chances of obtaining Eritrea with the full support of the West was assured. Aklilou himself lavishly praised the West to the extent of exonerating the capitalist powers from accusations of pursuing colonial policies. He told the assembly, "The great powers which had been accused of imperialism, namely the United Kingdom, France, and the United States, were the first countries which made the first move in the Assembly in a campaign to bring an end to the unhappy period of imperialism in Africa."[17] Oddly enough, France and Britain were still holding more than forty African nations in colonial bondage, and they were actively pursuing imperialist policies.

Another tactical move by the Ethiopian delegate was to paint a dim picture of the Eritrean capacity to maintain a stable system of government if allowed independence. "Since the territory had neither the economic resources, necessary trained personnel, nor the the essential foundation for political unity, the immediate and inescapable result of such a step would be revolution, disorder, bloodshed and inevitable foreign intervention and interference."[18] As we shall see, the significance of this move was to draw the attention of the General Assembly to the terrorist upsurge in Eritrea, which was being encouraged and financed by Ethiopia with the purpose of creating an anarchic image of Eritrea. In so doing, Ethiopia provided the raw material for the argument that Eritrean independence would pose a threat to peace and security in east Africa.

Another Ethiopian tactic was to create a sense of collective guilt among the members of the United Nations by reminding them that the League of Nations had failed to come to the aid of Ethiopia in the 1930s. Aklilou lamented "that the United Nations, which is following the example of the League of Nations, had been unable to impose its moral prestige to bring about the adoption of a just solution that would satisfy the requirements of peace and security in East Africa."[19]

It thus seemed that the complaints and appeals of Ethiopia in conjunction with the tendency of the West to endorse wholly the Ethiopian claims had diffused the political momentum that had been gathering in the General Assembly in favor of Eritrean independence. Ethiopia and the West joined hands to forestall the materialization of the proposals for Eritrean independence presented by the Soviet Union, Poland, Czechoslovakia, Pakistan, and many others. The hope of the proponents of Eritrean independence was dashed when the Chilean delegation proposed that the information presented was not adequate enough to make a resolution and thus a commission of investigation should be dispatched to Eritrea to gather factual information. Consequently, Subcommittee Seventeen of the First Political Committee of the General Assembly introduced a draft resolution to send a commission to Eritrea. This resolution was adopted by a majority vote.

The commission was directed by reference to ascertain the wishes of the inhabitants and to make recommendations accordingly:

In particular the commission shall take into account:
A. the wishes and welfare of the inhabitants of Eritrea including the views of the various racial, religious and political groups of the provinces of the territory and the capacity of the people for self-government;
B. the interest of peace and security in east Africa;
C. the rights and claims of Ethiopia based on geographical, historical, ethnic or economic reasons including in particular Ethiopia's legitimate need for adequate access to the sea.[20]

Five countries, namely Burma, Guatemala, Norway, Pakistan, and the Union of South Africa, were selected to compose the United Nations Commission for Eritrea. Ironically, the selection of these countries was based on the available power distribution in the General Assembly. Norway was the consistent advocate of unconditional union of Eritrea with Ethiopia and thus was thought to represent Ethiopia's interest. Throughout the sessions of the General Assembly, Burma had exhibited a polycentric position, and as such she was winnable to the most powerful position. Pakistan was the representative of the third road, consistently making references to the charter of the United Nations and the principle of self-determination, which she advocated for Eritrean independence. On the other hand, Guatemala, being a member of the Latin group, advocated either Italian trusteeship or independence for Eritrea, and thus was regarded as representing Italian interest. The most shocking, however, was the selection of South Africa. At that time, the Union of South Africa had just questioned the competence of the United Nations to preside over the question of Namibia—a nation that had been seeking political disentanglement from South Africa. It was a public secret that South Africa's position was antithetical to the conception of self-determination. Moreover, it had been only two years since the government of South Africa had legally instituted the abominable system of apartheid. At any rate, the selection of that government for membership in the commission was in the interest of the West.

It was thus clear from the beginning that each member of the commission had been predisposed to certain perceptible notions, and it was not hard to predict what kinds of proposals would be produced by the commission. The commission arrived in Eritrea in February 1950 and stayed there only six weeks.

When the commission arrived in Eritrea, the political situation in the territory was extremely tense. The net result of the coalescence of the Independence Bloc was that members of the pro-Ethiopian Unionist party began deserting en masse. For a moment it seemed that the Ethiopian case in Eritrea was hopelessly dead. Stunned by this development, the Ethiopian authorities and their supporters in Eritrea transmogrified their frustration and anxiety into armed violence. In light of the presence of the United Nations Commission for Eritrea, it was of paramount importance for Ethiopia to foment anarchy with a view to increasing the visibility of its supporters and creating an anarchic image of Eritrea.

In late September 1949 shifta (terrorist) activity in Eritrea took on a new dimension as the terrorists began attacking nationalists and police posts in large numbers. For example, on 28 September a band of shifta numbering between fifty and seventy-five engaged British security forces, killing one, wounding another two, and capturing five policemen.[21] On 6–7 October another band of shifta killed an Arab and two Italians in Asmara. Three of the shifta were reported to have been wearing police caps, suggesting that they were professionally trained members of some Ethiopian units. Drew noted that although shifta activity had been common in Eritrea throughout the

1940s, the concentration and frequency of shifta attacks had become an immense security problem. His conclusion was that the majority of the shifta were Ethiopians plentifully supplied with arms from across the frontier.[22]

In light of this security breakdown in Eritrea, the British Foreign Office made a formal protest to Ethiopia through her ambassador in London. The Ethiopian ambassador, Abebe Retta, was told that the unleashing of the Unionist cohorts on a terrorist rampage was damaging the Ethiopian cause in Eritrea. While promising to convey the message to his government, Retta complained that "the Italians, who were much better organized and had much more experience of political propaganda than the Ethiopians, would take no notice of our representations and that the Unionist Party and the Ethiopian Government would only suffer if they observed the rules of the game."[23] On 7 December senior British military officers gathered in the Foreign Office to consider the security implications of the shifta in Eritrea. They agreed on the need to send additional funds to curtail the shifta activity, to send a ship to Massawa as a show of British resolve, to reinforce the military in Eritrea, to further strengthen the police force by another two hundred men, to undertake a combined mopping up operation by the police and the military, and to ban temporarily all political activities in Eritrea.[24]

The arrival of the UN Commission in Eritrea certainly did not help settle the problem. As its presence boosted the morale and political enthusiasm of the nationalists, it also undermined the morale of the pro-Ethiopian forces. The result was an escalation of violence against the nationalists and Italians. In sum, between October 1949 and the arrival of the commission in February 1950, nine Italians, one Greek, one Indian, three Christians, and four Moslem supporters of the Independence Bloc were murdered. Hand grenades were thrown at Eritrean and Italian supporters of the bloc in Asmara, Massawa, Decamare, and other towns. Agrocommercial concessions were raided and ransacked and thousands of livestock belonging to Moslem tribesmen were looted.[25]

The political terrorism reached its climax in February 1950 when a bloody riot killing fifty persons broke out between Moslems and Christians in Asmara after a bomb was thrown at the funeral procession of a Moslem who had been murdered by a band of shifta.[26] The fact that Ethiopia was behind these terrorist activities was amply demonstrated by the commission's own findings:

> Information received from the British administration from time to time was that the shifta bands mainly attacked those persons who were opposed to union with Ethiopia. It was common knowledge in Eritrea that these gangs withdrew from Eritrea into Ethiopia whenever they were pursued by forces of law and order and that the Tigrai province was used by them for rest and perhaps sanctuary. . . . These [BMA] reports . . . showed clearly that many of the gangs came from Ethiopia into Eritrea and that, if some of their members were wounded, they were treated in the hospitals of Ethiopia.[27]

On 16 March, as shifta outrages continued unabated, Drew requested London to increase the Eritrean police force by three hundred men and the British officers by another twenty-seven men as well as to arm the Moslem tribesmen in Eritrea to defend themselves.[28] In being vocal about Ethiopian intervention in Eritrea, Drew apparently had three overriding concerns. First, he did not want to lose a single British life in Eritrea. Second, he did not want to incur any cost in order to maintain security in a territory that Britain was about to abandon. Third, he felt that the lack of internal security was a matter of international embarrassment to the adminstration. In regard to the last point in particular, members of the UN commission had expressed serious reservations about Britain's ability to maintain law and order in Eritrea. General Theron of South Africa, for example, had expressed the view that "an extremely bad impression had been created in the minds of the Commission by the continued terrorist outrages committed in the Unionist cause."[29]

With this in mind, Drew had confronted the Unionist party with three challenges: first, to completely "dissociate" itself from terrorist acts committed in the past; second, to exhort its cohorts "not to injure their cause" by participating in future terrorist acts; and third, "to cooperate with the administration in giving information or in effecting the arrests of persons—who committed terrorist acts." Under sustained pressures, the Unionist party had belatedly issued a statement accepting the first two challenges while rejecting the last one.[30]

The hostile political agitation and armed violence of the Unionists were sanctioned by the Eritrean Coptic Church which publicly announced in the official organ of the Unionist party, *Ethiopia*, that those who were in favor of independence would be barred from church facilities for baptism, marriage, and burial places, and would receive no communion or absolution.[31] In connection with the role played by the church, the Guatemalan and Pakistani members of the commission observed:

> With regard to the influence of the church in favour of annexation, it is important to point out that the Coptic Church in Eritrea depends hierarchically upon Ethiopia. The Commission was informed about interference by religious authorities of that church in favour of annexation and the ideas of the Unionist Party. It also heard complaints about threats and reprisals by the leaders of the Coptic Church of Eritrea against those who opposed annexation. The commission heard allegations to the effect that several Copts had been excommunicated because they did not hold the same political views as those of the Unionist Party. At nearly all the gatherings of the Unionist Party, a large number of priests were seen with church emblems and it was obvious that the church was using its influence over the laity. And some priests and monks complained that they had been threatened or actually excommunicated by the Abuna of the Coptic church for refusing to support the Unionist Party.[32]

Terrorism and ecclesiastical meddling in Eritrean politics were reinforced by open British hostility toward the nationalists. Of course, the BMA did not approve of armed violence for the reasons narrated above. But in general the British government was wholly committed to the destruction of Eritrean nationalism since it posed a serious challenge to the British plan of partitioning Eritrea. In fact, when the UN commission arrived in Eritrea, the Foreign Office designated Frank E. Stafford as the British liaison officer in Eritrea. Stafford's mission was threefold: to coordinate the Anglo-Ethiopian political offensive against Eritrean nationalists, to break up the anti-Ethiopian political parties in Eritrea, and to persuade the individual members of the UN commission to support the British plan of partition.

As we saw in Chapter 3, Stafford earlier had convincingly argued that a proper political education had to be given to the Eritrean people so that they could make an informed political choice over matters affecting their destiny. He had even cautioned that annexing Eritrea to Ethiopia without the explicit wishes of the Eritrean people would be a tragic mistake. In his view, even if independence seemed premature, the Eritreans were entitled to the benefits of the trusteeship system and he had advised that they should be discouraged from electing to join Ethiopia since doing so would foreclose their future options. Three years later, however, Stafford's sense of political detachment degenerated into political careerism as British policy in Eritrea became openly hostile.

Stafford started his mission on 27 January 1950, when he met the Ethiopian emperor in Addis Ababa for consultation on strategy and tactics. The emperor gave lavish praise to Britain for sending Stafford "as this was a concrete measure to help Ethiopia to achieve our mutual object in the disposal of Eritrea."[33] The emperor assured Stafford that the Ethiopian liaison officer in Eritrea, Negga, would work in close consultation with Stafford and would strictly follow his "advice in matters connected with the activities of the UN Commission." Furthermore, the emperor expressed his pleasure that Stafford was prepared to work with all political parties in Eritrea to influence and manipulate the course of events there.[34]

Before he left the palace, Stafford counseled the emperor that attaining the support of the majority of Christian Eritreans alone was not sufficient to convince the UN commission to be in favor of Ethiopia. He thus suggested that a concentrated effort should be made to obtain the support of Moslem Eritreans, too.[35]

In February Stafford began in earnest his work of breaking up the nationalist parties in Eritrea. The first target was the Liberal Progressive Party (LPP). Its existence as a distinct Christian bloc opposed to the annexation or partition of Eritrea concretely vitiated the Anglo-Ethiopian argument that all Christian Eritreans were unionist. In fact, Stafford succeeded in breaking up the party by discretely fomenting rivalry and suspicion among its leaders. As he bragged, "The important thing is that we have now substantially reduced the number of Christian non-unionists on the Plateau."[36]

The disaffected elements from the LPP formed what they called the Liberal Unionist Party on the platform of conditional union, or federation, with Ethiopia.

Encouraged by this split, Stafford next turned his attention to the

Moslem leaders in the Eritrean plateau. Though he felt unable to persuade them to come out in favor of some form of union with Ethiopia, Stafford thought he could stir up some political bickering in the nationalist camp that might encourage the Moslems "at least to break away from the Independence Bloc." He confided to Clutton that "I hope within the next few days to be able to inform you of the formation of yet another political party favourable to our cause."[37]

As part of his strategy, Stafford began to woo the Moslem aristocrats in western Eritrea. He suggested that Ibrahim was an Italian agent, and this certainly was effective since Ibrahim had already demonstrated an antifeudal orientation that had alienated him from the Moslem aristocrats. The internal class polarization within the Moslem League thus provided ample opportunity for Stafford to exploit. As a matter of fact, he succeeded, as the Moslem chiefs came out in favor of forming a separate party, which they soon named the Moslem League of Western Eritrea, with a platform for British trusteeship or inclusion in the Sudan. This squarely fit the British plan of partition.[38]

Stafford's mission was not yet complete. He next turned to another constituent member of the Independence Bloc, namely the Independent Moslem League of Massawa. He wrote to Clutton that this party was "almost our only hope in the Red Sea Province."[39] To sum up, Stafford was relatively successful in breaking up the Independence Bloc. However, he cautioned that the Anglo-Ethiopian cause could only be safeguarded if the new forces were "properly primed in the right answers to give to the Commission when it gets down to the job of ascertaining the wishes of the population."[40]

A cautionary note must be attached to this analysis: the Independence Bloc was not completely destroyed. The waivering elements in the Eritrean movement were removed from it, and thus the strongest of the nationalists remained within the bloc, now even more determined and more tenacious to continue their struggle against the Anglo-Ethiopian front.

In addition, Stafford had encountered some stiff opposition from his own Ethiopian counterpart, Negga. Although Britain and Ethiopia had agreed in general terms on the expendability of Eritrea, their imperial demands were different, and their strategies were at odds. This inevitably led to a serious clash between Stafford and the Ethiopian liaison officer. The source of this clash was the contradictory desires of the two officers as to who should have exclusive control over the agenda of the Unionist party. Negga was wholly committed to the acquisition of Eritrea in her entirety. He thus indoctrinated the cohorts of the Unionist party to support this plan when expressing their views to the UN commission. Conversely, Stafford was in favor of having the Unionists express their support for partition. Stafford tried to convince the Unionists on the basis of the maxim that, since the wholesale absorption of Eritrea by Ethiopia was unlikely, "half a loaf is better than no bread at all." Since he was not successful in this, however, he accused Negga of disseminating anti-British propaganda among Unionists that the partition plan was a British intrigue. The conflict between the two became so sharp that Stafford requested the Foreign Office to convey his complaints to Aklilou. He stated that the initial agreement between the two countries "was to destroy the argument that the only point on which all political parties are agreed is that partition is unacceptable" and to this end the Unionists were supposed to express their views to the commission in favor of partition.[41] Stafford was particularly disturbed by the fact that almost all of the Unionists expressed their views against the idea of partition. Even the loyal pro-British member of the commission, General Theron of South Africa, confided to Stafford that in view of the strong objection of the Unionists to partition, he could only support trusteeship for Eritrea. In appealing to the Ethiopian authorities Stafford said he hoped the damage done by Negga could be repaired if the Unionist leaders were persuaded to provide a document to the UN commission retracting their previous opposition to partition and expounding the change in their attitude.[42] Much to Stafford's chagrin, Negga, however, "consistently obstructed this line of action, preferring to rely upon his own outmoded futile ideas. If partition solution is not recommended by the Commission and I am now very pessimistic about it, the blame will lie squarely upon him [in] his refusal to be guided by my advice."[43]

Stafford's final ammunition was to appeal directly to John Spencer, the American advisor to the Ethiopians, who he thought could be of help by restraining Negga from hostile activity. But that did not help, and on 16 March Stafford sent another message to London: "The other severe handicap under which my work is suffering is the obstinancy, to put it generously, of Col. Negga in obstructing my efforts to obtain from the Unionist Party a statement that they are willing to agree to the severance of the Western Province from Eritrea provided that the rest is ceded to Ethiopia. . . . He is of the type of Ethiopian who is still fascinated by the result of the battle of Adowa and considers that if only the Ethiopians were allowed to fight it out now they would soon have Eritrea within the Empire."[44]

Another important part of Stafford's mission was to work upon the members of the UN commission to obtain their support for the British plan of partition. Although he claimed to have converted three out of five, the Pakistani and Guatemalan delegates rejected all his propaganda efforts. Dr. Garcia Bauer, the Guatemalan delegate, strongly detested the British political manipulations. Stafford described Bauer's principled position on the Eritrean question as a reflection of a "national inferiority complex."[45]

To this anti-British camp was added the principal secretary of the UN commission, Schmidt, who represented the Secretariat of the United Nations and was accountable only to it. His constitutional obligation was to make sure that the commission followed the correct procedures and principles in ascertaining the wishes of the Eritrean people, as laid down in the UN charter. But his adherence to and advocacy for strict observance of these procedures brought him into sharp conflict with British officials in Eritrea. To begin with, Schmidt questioned the legality of the UN commission as then constituted and the procedures it adopted. Furthermore, he was naïvely optimistic that regardless of the commission's recommendation, the General Assembly would assist the Eritreans in exercising their right to national self-determination. As Drew warned the Foreign Office, "The Principal Secretary, Schmidt, seems obsessed with the idea that independence or Trusteeship leading to independence is the right answer and the only right answer which the U.N. will be disposed to accept."[46]

Schmidt sincerely believed that nothing could stop Eritrean nationalism from being consummated in full-blown independence. The only obstacle he saw to this end was the British occupation of the country and the negative British propaganda campaign. For Schmidt the strategic importance of Eritrea was the main reason why the British did not want to leave the question to be decided on the basis of the UN charter, and his very emphasis on the charter brought him into open antagonism with the British. In addition, he dismissed the British argument stressing the economic nonviability of Eritrea as pure "imperial acquisitiveness." In the eyes of the British, his potent legal arguments, coupled with his UN and European connections, made Schmidt a danger to the British plan. As Drew noted, "It is self evident that his [Schmidt's] views and his position as the Principal Secretary of the U.N. Commission for Eritrea make him a most dangerous man from the point of view of H.M.G. He had on a previous occasion made it clear to me that in his view economic considerations did not count in determining the future of the territory."[47]

In light of the contradictory interests in Eritrea, the British were not so sure whether they would be able to influence the decision of the UN Commission for Eritrea. Drew, who was in touch with the political reality in the colony, reached a gloomy conclusion about the prospect for the British plan of partition. He thus suggested that Britain should request the United Nations to take the Eritrean question off the agenda for a minimum of ten years with the continuation of the British administration.[48]

Drew was not alone in this assessment. Some officials in the Foreign Office had gone even farther, probing the morality and the legal expediency of partitioning Eritrea. On 17 March R. S. Scrivener produced a memorandum outlining the fundamentals of this new British thinking. He argued that the majority of Eritreans were against any association with Ethiopia. "Quite apart, however, from what the inhabitants do or do not want," the memo argued, "the merits of a solution which would give four out of the five Eritrean provinces to Ethiopia is open to question. The maladministration, corruption, and oppression in Ethiopia is notorious and . . . is getting worse as the days of British wartime administration recede. It must be assumed that, no matter what safeguards may be drawn up on paper for the non-Ethiopian communities of Eritrea, such conditions will emerge in any territory placed under Ethiopian administration."[49]

In addition, the memorandum questioned Ethiopia's capacity to protect the 360-mile-long Eritrean coast against gunrunners, drug traffickers, and slave traders without jeopardizing British interests in the region. Moreover, Italy's future hostility toward the British plan was another dimension to be considered in regard to the British policy in Eritrea.[50]

These dissenters in the Foreign Office described the British argument that stressed the political and economic nonviability of Eritrea as a fallacious scare tactic. They substantiated their line of reasoning by referring to Togoland and the Cameroons, which were considered unsuitable for statehood and yet they were trust territories. They also stated that the question of economic viability concerned not only Eritrea, but also many other countries that were either independent or trust territories. The absence of sociopolitical unity, after all, "in no way debars a solution on the lines of trusteeship."[51]

The all-too-often sentimentalized argument that stressed Ethiopia's unfortunate experience with Italy was equally dismissed as unwarranted by these analysts. Although Ethiopia's experience under Italian occupation deserved sympathy, the dissenters argued that "this on its own can scarcely justify our present policy; and in the past territorial awards made by third parties on these grounds have rarely been of lasting benefit to the recipients."[52]

Based on their recast analysis, the dissenters in the British Foreign Office proposed a collective trusteeship regime for Eritrea to be administered by Western powers for an indefinite duration until the direction of the wishes of the Eritrean people were fully ascertained.[53] But, although the arguments encapsulated in the memorandum were cogent, this new line of thinking failed to obtain currency, and thus Stafford was given a green light to continue with what he had been doing in Eritrea.

These were the circumstances under which the UN Commission for Eritrea labored to ascertain the real wishes of the Eritreans. Its task was made doubly difficult by Unionist terrorism, ecclesiastical meddling, and active Anglo-Ethiopian manipulations.

The commission began hearings in highland Eritrea. No doubt the Unionist party had its strength in this heartland. Its strength was mainly due to the combined influence of the clergy and the Christian nobility on the peasantry, not to mention the terrorist rampage. In addition, the strength of the party was further magnified by the fact that the same Unionist cohorts were expressing views to the commission at different meeting places. Stafford himself acknowledged this fact in this way: "Another foolish trick of the Unionist Party from which I have in vain tried to dissuade them, is the movement by devious routes of numbers of their storm troopers and party officials from one meeting place to another where their faces are promptly recognized by the Commission."[54]

In the western and eastern regions of Eritrea, the Unionist party was virtually nonexistent. In fact, the dismal showing of the party became a matter of political embarrassment to Stafford as he accompanied the commission to those regions. In western Eritrea the Unionist party's showing was so poor that Stafford ridiculed the Unionists by saying that the party "could only muster some twenty harlots and a few tramps and the commission was in two minds as to whether to accept this as a representative gathering of respectable inhabitants."[55]

The position of the Unionist party was even worse in the Red Sea region. In fact, Stafford described the situation as a "dead loss" to the Anglo-Ethiopian cause since not even a "single voice was raised in favor of union with Ethiopia."[56] In general, the Independence Bloc showed a preponderant following in both the western and eastern regions of Eritrea. In fact, as a result, many nationalists were overly optimistic that they had made an indelible impression on the commission in favor of Eritrean independence.

The UN commission completed its mission in Eritrea by 8 April and left for Ethiopia the next day, presumably to make some survey of the economic, sociopolitical, and administrative conditions there. According to the original itineraries, the commission was supposed to start its survey in Ethiopia on 1 April, but the British used a delaying tactic to prolong the stay of the commission in Eritrea and thus to shorten its stay in Ethiopia. To begin with, the Ethiopian authorities were reluctant to receive the UN commission and only agreed to do so under British pressure. When the commission suggested in mid-March that it would travel by road from Asmara to Addis Ababa, British and Ethiopian officials were perturbed lest the members of the commission see for themselves the primitiveness of the Ethiopian economy, the malnutrition of the people on the roadsides, and the archaic state of the political system, all of which might significantly reflect on Ethiopia's ability to administer Eritrea. The pronouncements made by the Pakistani and Guatemalan delegates that they intended to visit "several centers" did not help to assuage the fears of the British and Ethiopians. The emperor's advisor, John Spencer, was particularly nervous that the commission's travel by road might enable the members to observe for themselves "the visible imperfections of the Ethiopian administration."[57]

Of immediate concern to both British and Ethiopian authorities was the fact that the emperor's subjects in Wallo and Tigrai were languishing under the ravages of what seemed to be the perennial famine to which the Ethiopian government paid little or no attention. Exposure of this situation was considered damaging to the Anglo-Ethiopian case. In fact, the matter posed a moral and political dilemma to senior British diplomats in Addis Ababa. Lascelles, for example, frankly admitted that "[i]n all this business I myself have been rather torn between the feeling that the Commission *ought* to see how bad things are in Ethiopia before deciding whether she should acquire any further territory, and the knowledge that if it did so this would tend to diminish the chances for the solution advocated by His Majesty's Government."[58] Finally, however, the British were able to manipulate the situation by encouraging the South African member of the commission, General Theron, to raise the question of travel by road as superfluous and time-consuming. The other members were genuinely convinced of Theron's argument, and the idea of traveling by road was never revived. In light of this well-calculated maneuver, the commission spent only three, rather than the originally planned twelve, days in Ethiopia, in Addis Ababa. No time was left for the commission to see provincial centers and rural areas in Ethiopia.

The worry of the British and the Ethiopians was not over yet, however. The issue of what the commission might see in the Ethiopian capital itself and of what it might hear from foreign residents in Ethiopia continued to haunt the Anglo-Ethiopian strategists. Lascelles became increasingly nervous about the hypothetical questions that could be raised by members of the commission. He was not even sure what answers to give if he were asked certain questions pertaining to the competence of Ethiopia to administer Eritrea. In his view, if the members of the UN commission had taken their job "honestly and seriously," their international obligation would be to "estimate for themselves how far the Ethiopian state can be regarded as worthy of acquiring Eritrea or any part of it." Particular questions pertaining to the character of the Ethiopian state, the treatment of socioreligious and racial minorities, the financial insolvency of the state, and the corruption of the judicial system were disturbing to Lascelles.[59]

Predictably, honest answers to these questions were not forthcoming from Ethiopian authorities. Nor would foreign nationals volunteer such information since they were "more or less dependent on the goodwill of the Ethiopian authorities and therefore unable to afford to speak their minds." The only people unaffected by the political whims of the Ethiopian government were members of the diplomatic corps within Addis Ababa. Lascelles even acknowledged the potentially informative utility of the diplomats to the members of the commission if they seriously wanted to find out about the nature of the Ethiopian administration. As Lascelles observed, "If I were a member of the Commission, I should make a bee-line for them and do my best to pump them."[60]

Under these bewildering circumstances, Lascelles finally asked the British Foreign Office for explicit advice as to how he should handle the hypothetical questions troubling him. He specifically wanted to know whether it was appropriate to lie or to tell the truth. He was caught between choosing political opportunism to retain his senior position and submission to the dictates of his moral conscience. As he noted, "The true replies to almost all the relevant questions . . . would be damaging to the Ethiopian case—which it is the policy of H[is] M[ajesty's] G[overnment] to further. For the fact of the matter is that Ethiopia is not in the least worthy to acquire Eritrea or any part of it."[61]

What bothered Lascelles was not so much the act of lying itself as the political embarrassment that might result from exposure after telling a lie about what was common knowledge in Ethiopia. He proposed his own way out: "As it would obviously be bad policy—quite apart from being unacceptable to myself—to give untrue answers about matters which are common knowledge here, the choice seems to lie between hedging and a plain, general refusal to say anything. I am inclined to favour the latter alternative."[62]

The Foreign Office concurred with Lascelles that hedging was a risky business. It thus simply advised him to evade questions pertaining to the nature of the Ethiopian state by focusing on the British plan to partition Eritrea. This meant that Lascelles had to find ways to make the entire discussion revolve around the British plan rather than around the issue of Ethiopian competence to administer Eritrea. The Foreign Office further noted that it did not have any ready-made tactic to deal "with the question of Ethiopia's fitness to govern all or part of Eritrea." Lascelles was thus advised to "take the line that there is no ideal solution to the problem of Eritrea's future, and that a more competent administration than the Ethiopian one could no doubt be found." But, according to its rationale, such adversarial arguments could be assumed away by pointing out to the commission that "the desire for government by persons of one's own race, rather than by a more qualified foreign administration, is a widespread political phenomenon which has to be accepted."[63]

Thus, by the time the UN commission arrived in Addis Ababa, the British and Ethiopians had a strategy in place to withhold or distort any substantive information from members of the commission. The situation could not be more ideal for the British. Not only were the members of the commission exhausted from their turbulent stay in Eritrea, but the opportunity they had to see the situation in Ethiopia for themselves was extremely constrained by time. They were never able to "pound" foreign diplomats to find out about Ethiopia's fitness to acquire Eritrea, nor were they able to see any part of Ethiopia outside the capital. The delegates were distracted from their mission by ceremonious itineraries and skillfully organized receptions. Breathing a sigh of relief, Lascelles admitted that "[a] special effort was made to convert Pakistani delegate by mustering 'domesticated' moslem notables at all receptions." Although, as he also noted, "[e]vidence of stage management was rather painfully obvious," it made no apparent impact on the commission.[64] On 12 April 1950 the UN Commission for Eritrea left Addis Ababa for Geneva to start drafting its final report to the Interim Committee (I.C.) of the General Assembly.

The Anglo-American Offensive

In the aftermath of their failure to force through their scheme of partition at the General Assembly, Britain and the United States agreed on the need to develop a common approach to the Eritrean question. For this purpose, they formed an Anglo-American coordinating committee. The committee was charged with the task of developing a common strategy in the event that the UN Commission for Eritrea recommended Eritrean independence. The strategy was to search for a formula that might be acceptable to the advocates of Eritrean independence while at the same time enabling Ethiopia to obtain all or substantial portions of Eritrea. The initial steps were geared toward obtaining Italian and Ethiopian support for the would-be Anglo-American compromise formula regardless of the findings of the UN commission.

The United States believed that the federation of Eritrea and Ethiopia was the alternative to Eritrean independence. The British, however, were less than enthusiastic about the idea of federation, although they accepted it as a temporary tactical maneuver. The joint diplomatic offensive thus crystalized around this American initiative. Accordingly, approaches along these lines were made in January 1950 to both Italy and Ethiopia, with talks held in Washington, Geneva, and London. The talks held in the first two cities were conducted under American sponsorship with a view to bringing Italians and Ethiopians together around the issue of federation. Certainly, both Italy and Ethiopia were anxious to avail themselves of U.S. meddling, albeit for different reasons. The Italians realized that Eritrea was the cornerstone to long-term Italo-Ethiopian relations, and thus they thought that it was in their interest to resolve all their differences with Ethiopia.

There were three circles in Italian politics, however, that made the formulation of any coherent Italian diplomacy impossible. One group, led by Count Zoppi, the czar of Italian propaganda, was determined to restore Italy's international power status, which did not preclude the restoration of Eritrea to Italy. The minimum he would accept was an unconditional Eritrean independence, as a way of preserving Italian influence in Eritrea. The second group was led by the Anglophile Italian ambassador to London, Duke Gallarati-Scotti. Gallarati was insistent about the need for engineering a new avenue for Italy's incorporation into the Western union, which could be achieved only by meeting British demands in Eritrea. To him, Italy's international status could be restored only by forging a new partnership with Britain and the United States. Count Sforza's group was in between the other two groups. In light of these contradictory political dispositions, Italian diplomacy showed marked volatility and inconsistency.

On 11 January 1950, Gallarati and Strang of the British Foreign Office held talks on procedural matters to start dealing with the Eritrean question. Calling Eritrea the thorniest issue in Italo-Ethiopian relations, Strang argued that Ethiopia had every right to object to being flanked by Italian trusteeship in Somalia and Eritrean independence. Gallarati concurred with Strang's assessment and expressed his readiness to consider Ethiopian sovereignty in Eritrea in terms of the American suggestion of federation.[65]

With this understanding, Clutton and D'Ajeta from the Italian emassy started talks on the future of Eritrea relative to Italo-Ethiopian relations. Both agreed that long-term Italo-Ethiopian relations were contingent upon a compromise solution on Eritrea. D'Ajeta proposed that Ethiopia should abandon her position on Eritrean annexation in return for Italian renunciation of Eritrean independence. The likely outcome would then become federation, the American plan. Clutton, however, was less than optimistic about federation since that formula was bound to weaken the British plan to partition Eritrea. Clutton evoked some legal arguments pointing to the impracticality of federation since the concept presupposed the equality of Eritrea and Ethiopia. More important, even if the question of practicality were resolved, Italian and Ethiopian views on the concept of federalism were irreconcilable. From the Ethiopian point of view, federation meant complete economic union and complete Ethiopian sovereignty over Eritrea in matters of defense and foreign relations.[66]

Although Clutton used this legal argument merely to preempt the materialization of the American plan, his reasoning was nonetheless potent. From the Italian standpoint, federation should empower Eritrea with the necessary ingredients of public authority to ensure its autonomy and distinct identity. According to D'Ajeta, these ingredients should include the creation of "personal union" between Eritrea and Ethiopia under the Ethiopian crown, entrusting the administration of Eritrea to an international body appointed by the United Nations, internationally guaranteeing the constitution of Eritrea, and establishing a customs union between the two countries as the basis for future integration.[67] Clutton and D'Ajeta finally agreed that the subject matter was becoming too delicate to be handled at a junior level and thus proposed that the Eritrean question should be discussed at a higher level. But before they departed, Clutton made it clear that the Italian proposition was totally unacceptable to the Ethiopians.

In the meantime, on 27 January 1950, the U.S.-sponsored Italo-Ethiopian talks in Geneva produced a tentative agreement on the Eritrean question. The terms of the agreement included: recognition of the fact that the future of Eritrea should be determined by the General Assembly in response to the findings of the UN commission; Italo-Ethiopian noninterference in Eritrea's internal affairs during the commission's investigation, preparation, and submission of its recommendations; nonexpression of any particular solution by either party prior to the completion of the commission's inquiry in Eritrea; and, upon the completion of the Commission's report, undertaking discussions under the auspices of the United States and Britain with a view to evolving a mutually acceptable solution before the General Assembly's Interim Committee (I.C.) considered the Eritrean question.[68]

The last condition in the agreement is of interest. The tentative agreement to undertake mutual consultations before the I.C. considered the report of the commission was designed to develop a common strategy to circumvent the adoption of any solution not amenable to Italy and Ethiopia. As such, it was consistent with the Anglo-American strategy to develop an alternative to Eritrean independence irrespective of the commission's findings and recommendations. More important, however, the whole package was designed to neutralize Italy from providing an international forum for the Eritrean question, not to mention the moral and political support Italy was rendering to the Eritrean Independence Bloc. But the agreement had unintended consequences for Ethiopia, too. The tentative agreement not to meddle in Eritrean politics while the commission was undertaking its inquiry would have deprived the Unionist party of active Ethiopian financial, political, and military support. It was obvious to both the Unionists and the Ethiopians that, without these conditions, the Eritrean Independence Bloc was in a superior position to convince the UN commission of its relative strength in Eritrea. Precisely for this reason, Ethiopia was the first to reject the principles of the Geneva accord. Thus, the American-sponsored Italo-Ethiopian talks ended in failure.

Beginning in April, both Britain and the United States began canvassing members of the UN Commission for Eritrea in an apparent effort to influence their report. The American representative in Geneva held several talks with members of the commission to explain U.S. views. General Theron, in particular, showed enthusiastic interest in what the United States had to say and even suggested that the State Department present its views in writing to the commission. The U.S. representative's prognosis was that three of the five commission members were leaning toward supporting the Anglo-American position.[69]

The American embassy in Rome, however, presented an entirely different assessment about the commission's division. In his telegram of 18 May, Dunn, the American ambassador to Italy, argued that three of the five commission members were likely to come out in favor of UN trusteeship leading eventually to Eritrean independence. He observed, "It would seem, therefore, that despite our best effort to convince the Commission of the excellence of our position, literally the only enthusiastic support on horizon for US-UK position continues to be US and UK." In the ambassador's view, if even one member of the commission recommended independence, it was certain that the General Assembly would obtain a two-thirds majority "and the pro-independence delegates could almost surely muster the one-third plus one vote to block any other solution."[70]

Based on this analysis, the ambassador recommended that the State Department develop a watered-down version of trusteeship as the alternative to UN trusteeship for Eritrea. In his view, such a strategy would meet the minimum requirements of the United States without necessarily alienating the proindependence forces. The elements of the scenario he depicted include the following. First, the commission could not ascertain the true wishes of the Eritreans due to the lack of "their political maturity and organization" and hence its report would likely be inconclusive. In an effort to establish preconditions necessary for ascertaining the wishes of the people, the UN would ask the British administration to create local institutions that might eventuate in the formation of Eritrean self-government. The BMA would then continue negotiations with Ethiopia with a view to forming a customs union between Ethiopia and Eritrea. Finally, the General Assembly would consider the disposition of Eritrea, taking into account the wishes of the people as expressed through their local self-government without prejudice to the attainment of full Eritrean independence or complete union with Ethiopia.[71]

The State Department, however, soon realized that the ambassador's prognosis was not favorably received in London and declined any further exploration of his recommended suggestions. Instead, the department decided to intensify its diplomatic efforts to convince Britain of the need for bringing Italy and Ethiopia together once again while continuing to lobby the UN Commission for Eritrea. The State Department gave particular attention to Pakistan with a view to dissuading her from endorsing a UN trusteeship for Eritrea. On 24 May, Assistant Secretary of State George McGhee told the secretary general of Pakistan's foreign ministry "that Eritrea could never be a viable state and that it was therefore unrealistic and dangerous to press for its independence." Furthermore, the alternative of UN trusteeship to independence "would mean letting Russia into Africa for the first time."[72]

U.S. Secretary of State Dean Acheson also had personally appealed to Sforza during their talks in London. In fact, Sforza was reported to have said that the "declaration of independence of Eritrea was a dead letter." In light of Italian prevarications in the past, however, the State Department could not be so sure about Sforza's ability "to face the logical consequences" of his remarks at home since Italian public opinion strongly favored Eritrean independence.[73] At any rate, Sforza's remarks gave some glimmer of hope, prompting the British and Americans to double their diplomatic efforts to bring Italy and Ethiopia together. This effort was successful as both parties resumed talks on Eritrea in early July. In fact, American officials exuded optimism that the Italo-Ethiopian talks in London would produce a preemptive strategy before the I.C. took up the Eritrean question, as both countries seemed to have accepted Anglo-American hegemony in the matter.

Before long, however, the American ambassador in London began complaining about the inability of Ethiopians to comprehend Italy's strong parliamentary position at the United Nations and about their excessive "reliance on the righteousness of their cause," not to mention their naïve optimism about their ability to influence the proceedings of the General Assembly. On the other hand, he appreciated Italy's "realism" despite her strong influence with the Latin American nations.[74]

Despite their willingness to proceed with the Anglo-American instructions, Italy and Ethiopia still maintained wide differences as to the exact definition of federation. The Italians had been in favor all along of a "personal union" approximating the one between Denmark and Iceland before 1944, whereas for Ethiopians federation meant annexation in all but name.

An additional problem was that the Italians were deeply committed to developing specific details for the federal arrangement, which should include the formation of an Eritrean self-government, division of powers between the federal and the local governments, the undesirability of the presence of Ethiopian troops in Eritrea, inclusion of the United Nations during the transition period, and prior agreement as to who should draft the federal constitution. For Ethiopia, such specifics were beside the point and had to be dealt with after the adoption of the federation formula.[75]

These Italian arguments evoked serious concern in the Anglo-American circle since they presaged the emergence of similar expressions at the I.C., even if Italy could be persuaded to abandon these arguments for now. Some countries might bring up the point that the United Nations should set up in Eritrea a trusteeship as a transition to prepare the colony for self-government relative to article 76 of the charter. It was also possible that the General Assembly might become immersed in details about the federal constitution; the probable inclusion of democratic features in it was perceived as ominous.[76]

Parallel to the Italo-Ethiopian talks, representatives from Britain, the United States, and Italy held a tripartite conference on Eritrea between 30 June and 3 July. The overarching purpose of the conference was to apply a Machiavellian stroke to Italy to change her posture on the question of Eritrean independence. The Anglo-American position offered the following basic conditions requisite for Italy to change her posture: (1) settlement of the Eritrean question was the key to resolving all outstanding differences between Ethiopia and Italy and would allow Italy to find additional outlets for her economic interests in Africa; (2) failure to resolve the Italo-Ethiopian differences over Eritrea would have unfortunate consequences not only for Italian interests in Africa but also for the general interest of the West, since there was an imminent "danger of Communist penetration in any circumstances of tension or disturbance"; (3) should Italy change her posture on the substance of Eritrean independence, Ethiopia would be prepared to normalize relations with Italy and even give additional outlets to Italian economic interests in Ethiopia; (4) should Italy pledge to accept a compromise formula along the lines of federation, Ethiopia would do the same, and any compromise acceptable to both countries had the best chance of acceptance at the United Nations; (5) Britain and America would ensure the provision of a special charter for the Italian communities in Eritrea; (6) should Italy accept the above conditions, the United States would extend generous economic assistance to the Italian government.[77]

The Italian representative, Count Vitetti, noted his agreement to most of the conditions. He even assured his Anglo-American counterparts that his mission was to discuss the terms of a compromise for-

mula and the tactics that should be acceptable to both Ethiopia and
the United Kingdom. He further declared that Italy was against all
forms of trusteeship or independence as such moves might pave the
way for Soviet penetration not only into Eritrea, but also into Ethiopia.[78] Vitetti added that, should the Anglo-American delegation propose cession of Eritrea to Ethiopia, the Italian delegation at the
United Nations would not object to it. Instead, the delegation would
merely state the Italian position while the Italian government worked
with the Latin American countries on a compromise plan.[79]

At last, the representatives from the three Western countries
agreed on three key questions: that Ethiopia and Italy should give
moderate speeches at the United Nations leaving room for a compromise formula while on the surface adhering to their original
positions; that all substantive questions pertaining to a federal constitution should be excluded from the proceedings of the General
Assembly; and that any discussion pertaining to the framing of the
constitution for the Eritrean state should also be excluded from the
proceedings.[80]

Despite concurrence on the above questions, other differences had
yet to be resolved. From the Italian point of view, Eritrea's autonomy
should be wide enough so as to ensure the protection of the Italian
community there. Vitetti rejected the Anglo-American proposal to
provide a special charter for the Italian community in Eritrea since
such a plan would form the Italians into a permanent political opposition to Ethiopian authorities and hence a constant source of strain
in Italo-Ethiopian relations. The plan also would make the Italians
an object of political resentment by Eritreans. Furthermore, the presence of Ethiopian troops in Eritrea was considered to be dangerous
to the preservation of Eritrea's autonomy.[81]

The differences over the definition of the federal formula became
even more apparent when Brusasca, the undersecretary in the Italian
foreign ministry, joined the conference on 3 July. Brusasca asserted
that Italy was not prepared to accept a solution on Eritrea that was
not commensurate with Italy's international obligations. Any decision
on Eritrea had to be taken in consultation and cooperation with the
Latin American nations. From his standpoint, a compromise plan
submitted to the United Nations should also take full account of the
territorial integrity of Eritrea and the effective formation of a self-

government enabling all Eritreans to participate in the economic development and civil affairs of their country.[82]

Brusasca's proposals were seen by the Anglo-American representatives as infringing upon Ethiopia's sovereignty. From the Anglo-American point of view, a large measure of Eritrean self-government was incompatible with the requirements of Ethiopian sovereignty, and the representatives were not prepared to support any plan that would diminish the emperor's sovereignty over Eritrea.[83]

At the end, the Anglo-American representatives were able to obtain an Italian pledge not to agitate actively for Eritrean independence at the United Nations. For all intents and purposes, the Italian delegation to the Interim Committee would not exchange ideas on the question of Eritrean independence with other delegations. In fact, in a second tripartite conference held on 17 July, Vitetti reassured the Anglo-American representatives that Italy would never support any solution other than federation, even though the fundamental principles had yet to be worked out.[84]

The diplomatic offensive that started in January did not produce the desired results from the Anglo-American perspective but, despite seeming Italian intransigence, the groundwork for a deal between the participants had been laid down. When the I.C. began its deliberations on the report of the UN Commission for Eritrea in mid-July, the Anglo-American delegations did not have a ready-made formula as they had hoped to produce before the I.C. began consideration of the report. Nonetheless, they had a tentative, Januslike strategy that would enable them to pursue the old lines of argument while leaving room for subsequent modifications pursuant to the shifts in the parliamentary correlation of forces. The British Foreign Office instructed its delegate to continue defending the British plan of partition. At the same time, he was advised to frame his speech in such a manner as to allow him to make modifications should the need for a compromise arise. The Ethiopian foreign minister was also advised to be restrained from engaging in provocative and bellicose exchanges.[85] The Norwegian and South African members of the UN commission were encouraged to start immediate canvassing for support of their recommendation. The Foreign Office also advised that the effort to bring Italy and Ethiopia together should continue even during the proceedings of the I.C.[86]

On 11 July Acheson, too, instructed his diplomats to work closely with the British delegation to preclude any possible exploitation of Anglo-American differences on the Eritrean question. According to Acheson's prescription, the American delegate would first propose the partition of Eritrea "and then tone down" to leave room for a compromise along the lines of federation. Furthermore, for the first time Acheson made an inference about the connection of the Eritrean question to U.S. anxiety over the Korean crisis, and he advised the American delegate to bring the relationship of the two to the attention of the I.C. so that it might take prompt action on the Eritrean issue.[87]

The UN Commission's Report Considered

Having completed its investigation, the UN Commission for Eritrea sat in Geneva between 3 and 17 May 1950 to write its draft report to be submitted to the I.C. Two distinctively different descriptions of the facts emerged, relative to the preconceived dispositions of the members.

The delegates of Burma, the Union of South Africa, and Norway subscribed to the same factual review, which led them to conclude that close political association between Eritrea and Ethiopia was of imperative necessity. They said the Eritrean people lacked the capacity for self-government and that the bulk of the people were illiterate. "Moreover, the leaders of the community have no knowledge of the responsibilities of government and possess no administrative or judicial experience other than in the regulation of tribal affairs and the application of customary law."[88] Another component element in their argument was the question of peace and security. The ad hoc logic justifying this argument was that:

Eritrea is a very rugged and broken country, and this fact has throughout made adequate policing difficult and costly. Strategically, the external defence of Eritrea is rendered complicated by her long coastline and flat coastal plain and by the absence of natural frontier barriers in the interior. Whether or not peace and security could be maintained in such conditions would, however, be influenced less by pure strategic considerations than by the ability of the territory to meet the cost of policing and defence, by the degree of internal unity or dissension and by the political relationships with neighbouring countries. . . .

[T]he creation of a separate Eritrean State entirely on its own would contain all the elements necessary seriously to prejudice the interests of peace and security in East Africa, now and in the future.[89]

In reality, these arguments pointing to the incapacity of the Eritreans to govern themselves, the disunity of the population, and the conjured-up threat of Eritrean independence to peace and security were the same arguments used by Ethiopia and its supporters. It is hard to imagine how the absence of natural barriers to external aggression or the presence of a long coastline could justify the sellout of a nation in an international system supposedly based on principles of sovereignty, equal rights, and self-determination. After all, Eritrea was not the only country exposed to external aggression. Probably more than 90 percent of the world's nations are in no position to withstand aggression by big powers in the absence of internationally recognized principles and constraints. In any case, the argument is belied by the fact that the Eritrean resistance movement has been able to put up a fight for nearly thirty years against Ethiopian annexation in which the United States and the Soviet Union have taken turns sanctioning and, in most part, financing Ethiopia's military occupation of the territory.

Another justifying element adduced by these three commission members was that the majority of the Eritrean people were in favor of political association with Ethiopia. But that statement was sharply contradicted by their own confession: "In the circumstances obtaining in Eritrea, however, accurate figures cannot be compiled."[90] Furthermore, when confronted with questions during the General Assembly debate on the issue, Donges, the South African delegate to the U.N., admitted that "for Eritrea as a whole, it could not thus be said with certainty how many people were in favour of union with Ethiopia and how many were in favour of independence. Opinion seems to be fairly evenly divided. It appeared, however, that the majority of the inhabitants were opposed to partition."[91]

Despite their unanimity on the factual review, however, the three delegates differed in the type of political association they envisaged for Eritrea. Initially, during the general discussions at Geneva, the South African representative had proposed Ethiopian trusteeship for Eritrea with the view to its eventually forming part of Ethiopia, while the western part of Eritrea was to be temporarily under British administration until the people there were in a position to make up their minds between joining Ethiopia or the Sudan.[92] (We recall that this proposal had been originally submitted by the British to the last session of the Council of Foreign Ministers in London in 1948.) Nonetheless, having learned that the political tendency in the Anglo-American circle was toward a middle road in the disposition of Eritrea so as to avoid open political embarrassment and, above all, to ensure the association of Eritrea with Ethiopia one way or another, the South African delegate withdrew his proposal for Ethiopian trusteeship over Eritrea and joined with the Burmese representative in recommending federation as the approporiate solution to the problem.[93]

In proposing federation, the delegates from Burma and South Africa maintained that two irreconcilable political tendencies existed in Eritrea, one toward union with Ethiopia and the other toward independence.

> These respective claims have the stamp of validity and they have been steadfastly put forward by these two political groups. As these claims are irreconcilable, it is impossible fully to satisfy the demands of either group without causing a grave miscarriage of justice to the other. A fair but effective compromise is, therefore, necessary. . . .
>
> The total integration or incorporation of Eritrea into Ethiopia would arouse popular Moslem antagonism and might lead to internal strife with possible external intervention. The immediate or future independence of Eritrea, without close association with Ethiopia must result in the economic disruption of Eritrea and in political upheaval on the part of the Coptic population.[94]

Based on this analysis, the Burmese and South African delegates strongly argued that federation was the most feasible solution that would ensure "the maintenance of peace and security in East Africa. For such a plan recognizes the inalienable right of the people of Eritrea to fashion their own destiny, in conjunction with their federal partner on certain common problems, without the wishes and aspirations of either of the two main sections of the people of Eritrea being subordinated to those of the other."[95]

Obviously, the Burmese and South African delegates were reading their own preconceived notions into the final report. The fact that two political strains existed in Eritrea was unquestionable. But the issue was to find out whether one of the two groups had superior strength, which could have been ascertained by the adoption of a democratic procedure during the commission's time in Eritrea. As we have seen earlier, even British and American officials had admitted that between 65 and 75 percent of the Eritrean people were in favor of independence. That fact alone belied the tendency of the commission members to divide the Eritrean people along religious lines.

Procedurally, too, the conduct of the investigation was out of the ordinary. From the point of view of practical international law and the charter of the United Nations, the only appropriate method to ascertain the wishes of the Eritrean people was by means of an organized plebiscite. Since that was not done, the so-called federal plan did not recognize "the inalienable right of the people of Eritrea to fashion their own destiny." In fact, it was an outright usurpation of that "inalienable right" since federation is a political system created by two or more independent states on the basis of free and voluntary participation and consent of the people concerned or their appropriate organs of government.

Although he agreed with the delegates of Burma and South Africa on the necessity of the close association of Eritrea with Ethiopia, the Norwegian representative, Judge Qvale, differed from them in the form of association he recommended. As a matter of fact, of all the documents and speeches presented to the United Nations, those of Norway were the most distinctly marked by offensive and elitist remarks. An explanation of this political behavior is hard to come by, for only forty-five years before Norway had seceded from Sweden with whom she shared a Nordic culture and civilization. In any case, in recommending the unconditional reunion of Eritrea with Ethiopia, Norway claimed to have been "fully satisfied that the overwhelming majority of the people of Eritrea are in favour of such a reunion."[96]

It is hard to understand how the Norwegian delegate could establish this "fact" since by his own admission the problem of computation was marked by "the absolute impossibility of checking the figures given by the various groups as to the number of their adherents."[97] The delegate apparently simply searched for rationalizing justifications for the position he had taken before he left New York. As he argued in a separate memorandum, all other political forces in Eritrea, with the exception of the Unionists, were merely political sycophants: "[T]he opposition parties did not appear until 1946 and 1947; they were obviously born out of the political possibilities presented by the discord between the Powers about the future of Eritrea, and were created by a handful of ambitious Eritreans, partly former officials in Italian service, who by uniting their groups . . . [gave] to the newborn political activity an aspect of religious differences."[98]

The Norwegian approach to the history of the region was so one-sided that, in fact, the Norwegian delegate did a better job than Aklilou of Ethiopia in the articulation, perfection, and presentation of the Ethiopian case. The political situation in Eritrea was, according to him, purely artificial, resulting from "a confusion in the mind of the primitive masses who are supposed to support the independent movement as to the true meaning of the word 'independence' in opposition to the word 'union.'"[99]

It is obvious that the delegate from Norway was determined to see the complete integration of Eritrea into Ethiopia regardless of the desires of the people. The only obstacles he saw to the realization of this plan were political developments in western Eritrea where the nationalists had their stronghold. At one point western Eritrea had threatened to secede from the rest of the country to form a separate independent state if the Christian highlanders had opted for union with Ethiopia. Norway, however, admonished against acceding to the wishes of the people in western Eritrea, arguing that any question about western Eritrea could be considered only if it posed an obstacle to the smooth transfer of Eritrea to Ethiopia. The memorandum stated, "In case it should be found, however, that the opposition of the Western Province presents an obstacle to the union of Eritrea with Ethiopia, we would not be opposed to its provisional exemption from such a union, nor to its continued administration by the British Government for a period to give the people of the Western Province the opportunity of deciding in fuller knowledge which of their two neighbouring countries they wish to join."[100] The memorandum claimed that allowing western Eritrea to secede would contribute to the fragmentation of the nationalists and thus weaken their resistance. "[I]f, in determining the future status of Eritrea, the Western Province were excluded, the adherents to the Independence Bloc in the rest of the country would find themselves reduced to a trifling minority compared to the numerical strength of the Unionists, since the parties opposing union with Ethiopia have most of their adherents in the Western Province."[101]

Norway's memorandum demonstrates that, in the main, the members of the commission were not prepared either to analyze objectively and report the facts as they appeared or to ascertain the wishes of the Eritrean people. Of the three separate memoranda submitted to the Interim Committee, the one presented by Pakistan and Guatemala was by far the most objective and least contradictory. It was, at least, the only one based on legal arguments and the principles of justice and self-determination as embodied in the charter of the United Nations.

In their memorandum, the commission members from Guatemala and Pakistan acknowledged that the Unionist party had larger followings in the highlands. But they added that its strength was mainly based on political coercion and terrorism, and that thus it was difficult to determine the precise size of its adherents. For example, "prominent leaders of political parties favouring independence have been attacked, such as the President of the Independent Eritrea Party, Mr. Woldemariam [a Christian] on whose life four attempts have been made. Such criminal practices make it difficult to ascertain even approximately the true desire of those who now declare themselves in favour of annexation as it cannot be said that, in every case, the spontaneity of their political affiliation is guaranteed."[102] Nonetheless, these two delegates affirmatively concluded that the majority of the inhabitants were in favor of independence, and they proposed independence for Eritrea, to be preceded by ten years of direct United Nations trusteeship. In justifying their proposal they argued that

the Eritreans have the right to independence, since a majority of the population claims it and there are no juridical reasons justifying any other procedure. Under present conditions, there is nothing to justify a different solution for this territory. Independence does not exclude subsequent decisions taken in a democratic way by the people of Eritrea to link their country in

the form of confederation or federation or even of unconditional union with Ethiopia, when it happened to be the unmis-
taken wish of the people, should the occasion arise. But that
is not the case at present and it is not possible to tie the fate
of one country to that of another in advance and irrevocably,
when a large part of the population rejects that solution and
demands independence.[103]

The report of the United Nations Commission for Eritrea containing the three separate proposals was submitted to the Interim Committee of the General Assembly on 13 July 1950 for its deliberation.
For the time being Britain and the United States seemed to have
a strong position on the I.C. as they were able to rally behind them
all western European countries with the exception of Sweden and
the Netherlands. Sweden was uninterested in the Eritrean issue and
expressed no views one way or the other. The Netherlands was originally in line with the Anglo-American circle, but later deserted in
favor of UN trusteeship for Eritrea. As Luns, the Dutch representative, suggested to Stafford, the Dutch government was influenced
by some elements in the UN Secretariat who were said to be strongly
in favor of UN trusteeship. In fact, Stafford and Luns both concurred
that Schmidt, the principal secretary of the UN commission, was the
culprit behind the Dutch desertion.[104]

While agreeing in principle to federation, Italy was still insistent
about granting a wide measure of autonomy to the Eritrean state.
Thus, since Italy was reluctant to give the green light in favor of
the Anglo-American plan, the Latin American states remained as adamant as ever in their position against any solution unacceptable to
Italy. The Soviet bloc and other non-European countries also rallied
behind the Latin bloc. Consequently, the I.C. was beset with insurmountable paralysis. Now Britain and the United States became more
determined than ever to break up the Latin bloc as a way of diffusing
the political concentration at the I.C. in favor of Eritrean independence.

The stalemate in the I.C. proceedings was further complicated by
the Burmese proposal to make the federal plan a genuine federation.
Some of the items proposed by Burma included (1) the government
should be based on a tripartite federal structure, namely a separate
central federal government and separate governments of Eritrea and

Ethiopia; (2) the federal government should be composed of the executive, the legislative, and the judicial branches; (3) the federal legislative structure should be composed of two chambers of deputies, with election to the first chamber based on proportional representation of the population as a whole while election to the second chamber based on equal representation of the Eritrean and Ethiopian peoples; (4) the federal executive branch should be responsible to the legislative assembly; (5) the federal court should be the final court of appeal with regard to constitutional matters and all of its decisions should be final; and (6) both states should enjoy full powers of local self-government except in matters of defense, external affairs, finance, and interstate commerce and communications.[105]

These Burmese suggestions were particularly offensive to the Ethiopian delegate. The proposal denoted equality between the two states and thus was sharply contraposed to the Ethiopian self-perception of superiority, especially when considering the mythical component in the international image of Ethiopia. The democratic nature of the proposal, albeit limited, in which the executive branch would be responsible to the federal legislature and the federal court would be the final court of appeal, would undoubtedly strip the emperor of his absolute powers.

In light of Italian intransigence and the new Burmese suggestions, the debate over Eritrea at the I.C. could not move any further. After five weeks of heated deliberations on the federation formula, the Anglo-American alliance failed to obtain complete Italian capitulation or the acquiescence of the Latin American states. The result was a complete impasse. The United States then took the Eritrean question into behind-the-scenes talks. Muniz of Brazil, the president of the Interim Committee, acknowledged that, when an impasse was reached in the Interim Committee, "confidential discussions had been initiated by the United Kingdom and the United States delegations."[106]

The Struggle Deferred

Britain and the United States were encouraged by the fact that federation had become an inescapable buzzword. But now their task became how to water down the concept in order to make it amenable to Ethiopia which, for all practical purposes, was against the substance of federation. On the other side, Italy was still intransigent about obtaining a genuine federal structure within which a modicum of political security for her nationals in Eritrea could be ensured. To resolve these contradictory positions, on 23 and 24 August, Charles Noyes, U.S. representative, and Frank Stafford organized an underground conference in which Italian and Ethiopian representatives participated. The Brazilian president of the I.C., Muniz, and his Mexican assistant, P. Nervo, were also present throughout these talks. Britain and the United States obtained Italian capitulation to the Anglo-American plan and Ethiopia, too, accepted the deal.[107]

Since Aklilou insisted on the abandonment of the three-government model envisaged in the Burmese proposal, Muniz and Nervo acceded to the Ethiopian version of the formula in which Eritrea was to be federated with Ethiopia under the sovereignty of the Ethiopian crown. Spencer bragged: "In attaining that formula, we were greatly aided by Stafford and Noyes. Charles Noyes, an excellent constitutional lawyer, was flexible enough in his mental processes to abandon the U.S. constitutional model in favor of federation wherein the Ethiopian government was, at the same time, the federal government. The same was the case with Ambassador Nervo. . . . Muniz, in particular, ultimately obtained acceptance of that special formula."[108]

The next step was to change radically the Burmese suggestion about the federal legislature, which stipulated an equal representation of Eritrea and Ethiopia and the accountability of the executive to the legislature. Here, too, the coconspirators agreed that the Ethiopian parliament should serve as a federal parliament with some Eritrean representatives participating in it. As Spencer recorded:

After many hours of discussion, it was agreed by Muniz, Nervo, Stafford, Noyes, Aklilou and me that the existing Ethiopian parliament enlarged to accommodate delegates from Eritrea on the proportional basis would become the federal parliament.

In order to obtain this concession on the legislature, the concept of an imperial federal council in which Ethiopia and Eritrea would be equally represented was agreed to on condition that its functions would be purely advisory. In that way, the principle of proportional representation was respected for the legislative branch while still offering the Eritreans equal representation on an advisory basis.[109]

In essence, Eritreans were to participate only in the political dress rehearsal, and not in the actual decision-making process. And as long as they did not participate in that process, it did not really matter what ceremonious positions they occupied.

With respect to the federal judicial system, the conspirators agreed that the Ethiopian judicial branches in Eritrea should also serve as the federal courts. Thus a separate system of federal judiciary was ipso facto ruled out. Having assumed the title of federal courts, these Ethiopian courts would have jurisdiction over defense, foreign affairs, currency and finance, and external and interstate commerce and communications. In taking credit for winning this concession, John Spencer bragged, "I had insisted upon this language because those terms would enable Ethiopia in any discussion to rely upon the meaning assigned to those words in U.S. constitutional practice. Charles Noyes acceded to my wishes on this point. I also insisted upon insertion of the word 'including ports' to ensure that Massawa and Assab could provide access to the sea for Ethiopia and would fall exclusively under federal (Ethiopian) jurisdiction."[110] In making reference to the American constitution, Spencer forgot that the American constitutional system was based on the three-branch model of government and was fundamentally based on the democratic principle of checks and balances.

With these changes, the Burmese proposal was completely undone. The provisions relating to the legislative and judicial branches were reshaped to the liking of Ethiopia and in such a manner as to ensure the adoption of the formula by the waverers in the General Assembly. Direct reference to the establishment of a separate federal government was deliberately excluded so as not to provoke any hostility to the plan. As Spencer again boasted, "Eventually, we agreed on a formula reflecting these solutions for the legislative and judicial branches of the federal government at the same time avoiding all reference to the basic reality that no separate federal government would be established."[111]

It was this formula that was to be called a "compromise" solution. In one respect, it was indeed a compromise, but only among the conspirators. No Eritrean representative or pro-Eritrean independence country participated in these discussions. Italy was the only force that could have prevented the materialization of the formula.

Thus, by the end of August, it seemed that the Anglo-American plan was assured of safe passage in the I.C. To test the water, Muniz informally submitted it to a special conference of selected members of the United Nations who were considered potential cosponsors. Initially, the would-be cosponsors inquired about the U.S. position on the draft since they did not have prior information about the underground talks. Without going into specifics as to who had participated in the talks, the American delegate stated that the draft was a product of "exhaustive" negotiations, and that it was "the best possible compromise."[112]

The plan, however, ran into snags once again as Italy reversed her position on the matter. On 5 September Ambassador Tarchiani informed Assistant Secretary McGhee that the federation formula was not acceptable to Italy. Tarchiani argued that, as diluted as the plan was, the Italian government could not sell it to the Italian people. Moreover, such a complete sellout of Italian rights would be considered very damaging to the international image of Italy, in particular among her Latin allies. The ambassador pointed out many deficiencies in the formula. First, he argued that Muniz and Nervo were unable to obtain the acquiescence of the Latin American delegates without making substantive changes in the plan. In addition, the formula was not acceptable to most non-European states. Second, even if the I.C. could pass the plan, once the Eritrean case was submitted to the Ad Hoc Political Committee, the Soviet Union would no doubt introduce a draft resolution in favor of Eritrean independence, with which it would be extremely difficult for Italy not to associate herself. Third, in view of the fact that the question of Eritrean independence enjoyed the widespread support of the Italian people, the Italian government in supporting the federation plan would inevitably be a victim of an embarrassing political fallout. Fourth, in view of their pro-Ethiopian position, the British could not be relied upon to ensure the smooth implementation of any federal solution.[113]

McGhee's response was prompt and blunt. He rejected Tarchiani's complaints outright. McGhee contended that the United States was not prepared to go any further than the compromise plan.[114]

In the meantime, Anglo-American differences over the federation formula were also surfacing. Unlike the United States, Britain was delighted to see a change in the Italian position against the plan. To begin with, Britain never considered federation a viable alternative to partition. She had merely accepted the idea as a tactical means to hush the proindependence forces at the United Nations and to kill the whole idea of Eritrean independence so that she could resurrect her original scheme to partition Eritrea. As early as 25 July, Drew had described the federal package as useless since it would quickly "develop into annexation" of Eritrea by Ethiopia. Drew argued that "the implementation and the continued existence of a federal solution will ultimately depend on the command of whatever troops are located in Eritrea. If these are subject to the orders of the Emperor, any autonomy or self-government in Eritrea will last for just so long as the emperor sees fit."[115]

Drew had an ulterior motive, namely reversion to the old British plan of partition. He urged the Foreign Office the consider a divide-and-conquer strategy by focusing on the ethnic heterogeneity of Eritrea which would supposedly make the coexistence of Moslems and Christians unlikely.[116] Under his scenario Eritreans would never be able to produce any formal agreement on the form and substance of a federal structure for the whole of Eritrea, but he insisted that federation as a tactic would serve British diplomacy well. His prescription was that Britain should press for federation at the I.C., laying on the table all detailed elements of the federal structure to be followed by publication of the plan. The next step would be to propose to the I.C. the participation of all Eritrean political parties in the debate. Drew's cynical hope was that the Eritrean leaders would voice all their fundamental differences in debate on the federation plan, thereby making it impossible for the I.C. to formulate a plan acceptable to all Eritreans. This would ensure the inevitable revival of the British plan of partition and its subsequent adoption by the United Nations.[117]

Stafford, too, liked Drew's Machiavellian strategy and exuded optimism that the Eritrean Independence Bloc would never accept anything less than independence whereas the Unionist party would do anything to block the formation of an autonomous Eritrean state. He thus suggested that Britain should develop a scheme that could be adopted "by the General Assembly which is almost certain to be rejected by both the two almost equal divisions of the people of Eritrea, whose aims are directly opposite to one another and who will oppose this solution for quite different reasons."[118]

Unlike Drew, Stafford did not like the idea of allowing Eritreans an access to the international forum as their presence "would reopen channels for intrigue, misrepresentation and confusion which have befogged the issues on previous occasions."[119] Like Drew, Stafford was confident that the convocation of an Eritrean assembly to consider framing a constitution would certainly lead nowhere since the Eritreans would "remain in their separate boxes and will never agree upon a constitution for a separate state of Eritrea under Ethiopian sovereignty which gives neither side what they want." Under these circumstances Stafford hoped that partition would reemerge as the only alternative acceptable to both contending parties in Eritrea.[120]

Given this British mood, Italian backtracking became a welcomed move to British diplomats. Thus, by the beginning of September, the United States alone was wholly committed to the idea of federation. From now on, Ethiopia's hopes for the acquisition of Eritrea were in the hands of the United States.

In the Korean crisis, Ethiopia found a new trump card to play as a way of obtaining sustained American support for the acquisition of Eritrea. Ever since Acheson made an inference about a connection between the protraction of the Eritrean question and U.S. anxiety over the looming Korean crisis, the Ethiopian emperor had been harping on this new opportunity. In mid-July Ethiopia contributed $100,000 Ethiopian to be used for medical supplies in Korea.[121] Furthermore, on 12 August the Ethiopian emperor expressed his desire to help "the United States in its struggle in Korea." In making an offer of troops, the emperor pledged that his country would always be on the side of Britain and the United States.[122]

Acheson welcomed the Ethiopian offer of troops and characterized it as "an outstanding example to other nations of the importance placed on carrying out its international and United Nations obligations by a small country which was formerly a victim of aggression."[123] However, he instructed Ambassador Merrell to advise the emperor to make the offer directly to the secretary general of the United Nations. Once the offer was accepted by the United Nations, Ethiopian officials would then meet with representatives from the U.S. departments of defense and state to work out details of logistics to transport the Ethiopian troops to Korea.[124] Thus, Eritrea was once again used as a meeting ground for U.S. and Ethiopian relations.

Ethiopia used the Korean crisis as a means of obtaining unconditional U.S. support for its claim to Eritrea while the United States began to use Eritrea as a means of broadening U.S. international legitimacy of its position in Korea by the inclusion of a black state in the crusade against international communism. This was of enormous propaganda value for U.S. war efforts. One State Department memorandum explained the desirability of using Ethiopian troops in Korea because "of the great propaganda value of including among the UN armed forces a contingent of troops from an independent, colored nation in Africa, which would help to offset the Soviet claim that the Korean war is white imperialist aggression against the colored races of the world."[125]Thus, notwithstanding British wavering and Italian intransigence on the Eritrean question, Ethiopia increasingly became dependent on the United States to push her claims through the United Nations. On 15 September Assistant Secretary McGhee reassured Aklilou and Spencer that the United States would do everything to ensure the acquisition of Eritrea for Ethiopia.

In the meantime, Britain was inching toward complete repudiation of the federal plan. On 18 September, Roger Allen, head of the Africa department in the Foreign Office, argued in a memorandum that the federation formula was dead, as Muniz and Nervo had failed to produce an agreement from the Latin American bloc. He contended that Britain had always considered the idea of federation completely impractical and suggested that the Foreign Office should contrive new tactics to deal with the shifting forces at the United Nations by stirring up a movement for the adoption of the partition plan.[126]

This sudden backtracking in British diplomacy prompted Assistant Secretary McGhee to leave for London on 19 September, heading a U.S. delegation for talks with a British Foreign Office team that was headed by Michael Wright, assistant undersecretary of state for foreign affairs. The exchanges between the Americans and the British were heated. McGhee charged that the Italians were playing an obstructionist role simply to obtain a favorable position in Eritrea. He added that the Latin American states were not prepared to accept the federation formula until they received an indication from the Italian government in this direction.[127]

In reponse, Wright argued that Britain had no legal obligation to continue administering Eritrea. He even threatened that if the United Nations reached a solution unacceptable to Britain, his country would be justified in taking a unilateral action to implement what-

ever plan she deemed necessary. He further contended that British
subscription to the federation formula was simply contingent upon
Italo-Ethiopian agreement.[128]

Infuriated, the Americans argued that their commitment was to
Ethiopia and not to Italy. They even challenged the argument that
the British could unilaterally withdraw from Eritrea or implement
a decision contrary to their international responsibility. As long as
any formula was acceptable to Ethiopia, the United States was prepared to push for the acceptance of that formula even in the face
of Italian opposition at the United Nations.[129]

After long, heated exchanges, Wright and McGhee finally agreed
on a tentative plan based on two scenarios. The first was that the
United Nations might endorse Eritrean independence preceded by
some form of international tutelary administration. In this case, Britain would immediately withdraw from Eritrea, leaving the decision
to be implemented by somebody else. The second was that the United
Nations might fail to produce any solution at all at this session. In
such an eventuality, Britain would have three choices: unilateral implementation of the original U.S.-U.K. plan of partition irrespective
of UN sanction, immediate withdrawal from Eritrea, and/or continuance of British administration in Eritrea for another year.[130]

Nonetheless, since unilateral British withdrawal might have negative repercussions that might encourage the proindependence forces
to coalesce, the Anglo-American team finally agreed to patch up their
differences over Eritrea and to continue working on the federation
solution. They even agreed not to require Ethiopia to make any further concessions on Eritrea, and to force the plan through the General
Assembly even in the wake of Italian objections "by breaking up the
Latin American bloc."[131]

During the last week of September, Acheson, too, became heavily
engrossed in the Eritrean question and took personal charge over
the diplomatic offensive. He appealed directly to Bevin and Sforza
to support the federation plan unconditionally. Bevin promised unequivocal support and, without complete surrender, Sforza expressed
his readiness to cooperate with the Anglo-American circle if he were
not required to commit Italy to championing the federation formula.[132]

Ethiopia, nonetheless, asked for increased effort to obtain Italian
submission. The Ethiopians feared that, without prior Italian capitu-

lation, it would be extremely difficult, if not impossible, to break up the Latin American bloc. Failure to do so might enable the Eritrean Independence Bloc to count on a coalition of the Latin, Arab, and Soviet blocs to push the independence platform through the General Assembly. In fact, on 22 September, John Spencer forcefully argued that any plan that excluded Italian participation or acquiescence involved certain risks for Ethiopia. He thus urged that some avenues should be explored to include Italy in the federation formula. Consequently, Spencer and Noyes developed what they called a package broadening the framework of the negotiations on Eritrea to include other issues of importance to Italy. The package suggested the formation of a mediation group that would propose to both Italy and Ethiopia points of agreement on the text of the Anglo-American draft plan, the removal of Ethiopian objection to the implementation of Italian trusteeship in Somalia, the settlement of reparation questions, the retention of some fifty foreign experts in Ethiopia, and the resumption of full diplomatic relations between Italy and Ethiopia. Once an agreement was reached on these points, the document could officially be published for use by the Italian government to justify its position on the question before the Italian parliament and the Italian people.[133]

The State Department spared no time in giving its full approval to this confidential package. But before any advance on the substance of the plan could be made, the I.C. ran out of time as it transferred the Eritrean question to the Ad Hoc Political Committee of the General Assembly. The latter took up the discussion where the I.C. had left off and debated the Eritrean question and all the proposals submitted to it for nearly three weeks between 8 and 26 November.

It was during this debate that Italy finally capitulated to the Anglo-American circle and gave written endorsement of the federation formula. Fourteen of the eighteen Latin American countries then defected en masse, abandoning their longstanding anti-Ethiopian position. The Arabs, too, led by Egypt which was a claimant to Eritrea, supported the American formula. One of the ironies of the time was that Syria and Iraq, which were consistently anti-imperialist at least in rhetoric, endorsed the federal formula. Yet these two countries were to be the staunchest supporters of Eritrean nationalism from the 1960s on. On the other hand, Israel, still enjoying her honeymoon as a new state, opposed the formula and supported Eritrean independence. Yet Israel was later to be one of the foremost suppliers of arms to Ethiopia, and was charged with the task of training the most notorious counterinsurgence elite troops to be used against the Eritrean nationalists.

Thus on 20 November the United States led a constellation of thirteen other countries to introduce the draft resolution on the federation formula, which was adopted by thirty-eight votes in favor, fourteen against, with eight abstentions. On 26 November, the Ad Hoc Political Committee transmitted its resolution to the full session of the General Assembly for its approval.[134]

On 2 December 1950, the General Assembly considered the federation formula. Before the votes were cast, the pro-Eritrean independence countries were allowed to give their eulogies. One of the most moving speeches, marked by its profound legal depth, was given by Ambassador Ichaso of Cuba who maintained that the plan was unacceptable because of its "peremptory" character.

> We understand by an agreement of federation an instrument in which each party is fully conscious of its feelings, its ideas and its convictions. . . . We consider that the United Nations should assist all colonial territories to obtain their independence sooner or later as circumstances may require. The draft resolution approved by the Ad Hoc Political Committee, which provides for federation, closes all roads to Eritrean independence, whereas the proposal for independence presented by the delegation of Pakistan, which we supported, does not close the road to federation, but simply leaves that a matter to the free determination of the Eritrean people. . . . I feel that to give independence to Libya, Somaliland, and not to give the same treatment to Eritrea constitutes an act of discrimination in the solution of the problem of the former Italian colonies.[135]

Castro of El Salvador also categorically rejected the idea of federation, stating that his country's traditional policy based on the

> respect for the right of self-determination of peoples makes it impossible to vote in favour of that draft which predetermines the future political structure of Eritrea and provides for a feder-

ation between Eritrea and Ethiopia. It is clear that it has been impossible to consult the people of Eritrea in order to find out their wishes. It is true that a Commission visited the country, but this is not the way to solve the problem affecting the entire population. To determine whether the people of Eritrea wanted federation, there would have had to be a plebiscite and a plebiscite was not held. The delegation of El Salvador felt that the opinion of the whole population of Eritrea had not really been sought. Therefore, when a particular political structure is decided for Eritrea, be it federation or confederation, monarchy or republic, we consider that the United Nations is attempting to solve a problem which only the people of Eritrea can properly themselves solve.[136]

Likewise, Garcia Bauer of Guatemala reminisced about his visit to Eritrea as a member of the commission and chose to leave the verdict to history. As he solemnly observed, "During our travels in Eritrea we were able to see how important were the parties which formed the Independence Bloc and that experience convinced us that the greater majority of the population opposed the idea of federation which the Ad Hoc Political Committee approved. Nor can my delegation agree that this plan for so-called federation recommended by the Ad Hoc Political Committee can be considered a compromise solution or a well balanced solution as it has been called. But it is not up to us to reply to that argument. Time will answer those who make that assertion."[137]

Members of the Soviet bloc also gave similar speeches condemning the draft as a product of the political huckstering of the West and cursing in particular American imperialism as the chief beneficiary. In the view of the Eastern European delegations, the Eritrean question was part of a larger reality connected with the general crisis of the colonial system, which the West was endeavoring to maintain. Thus, the federation formula was a pre-emptive venture on the part of the West to delay the inevitable liquidation of the colonial network. Aside from being a false and unjust solution depriving the Eritrean people of the fundamental and inalienable rights to decide freely their own destiny, the formula was a smoke screen for the annexation of Eritrea. Vavricka of Czechoslovakia probed the validity of the formula: "The federal form of government which will possibly be imposed on Eritrea is not based on the free, spontaneous and democratic expression of the will of two sovereign states. It is merely a mask for the annexation of little Eritrea by a larger and more populous state. . . . What influence can the representatives of the people of Eritrea, a country of only one million inhabitants, have in legislative bodies where the representatives of Ethiopia will speak for sixteen million inhabitants? How will the Eritrean people's right to free development be safeguarded in such a federation and under such conditions?"[138]

The proponents of the draft resolution gave no speeches on the day of voting. Assured of its adoption, they were content to listen to the political eulogies of their opponents. The result was that the federal formula was approved by forty-six votes with ten against and four abstentions.[139]

In approving the federation formula, known as the Federal Act, rather than searching for a lasting solution to the complex problem on the basis of its charter, the United Nations opted to remove the Eritrean question from its floor. In effect, the United Nations was pushed into contortions to preside over what became the legalization of the sellout of the former Italian colony. This is the most overlooked aspect of the Ethio-Eritrean conflict. The roots of the present Eritrean problem lie in the very decision of the United Nations to link Eritrea to Ethiopia under the guise of federation. In sum, the United Nations' decision to federate Eritrea with Ethiopia represented, not the resolution of the struggle that had been going on for five years, but its deferment.

6

The Federal Act Implemented

ON 14 DECEMBER 1950, the General Assembly of the United Nations elected Dr. Eduardo Hanze Matienzo of Bolivia to become UN commissioner in Eritrea. He was empowered to implement the Federal Act,[1] to draft a constitution based on that act in consultation with the inhabitants, and to approve it on behalf of the United Nations. Matienzo arrived in Eritrea in February 1951 and immediately began touring the country to explain the aims and terms of the Federal Act. The commissioner commenced his onerous task by declaring that "the solution which has now been adopted is a middle of the road plan which should give satisfaction not only to those who want Eritrea to be united with Ethiopia, but to those who want Eritrea to be independent."[2]

In fact, it was the "middle of the road" character of the resolution that was to create conditions for what became excessive self-confidence and self-assurance among Unionists and Ethiopian authorities, because they knew that they could sooner or later do away with the "middle of the road" plan. Conversely, the nationalists were perfectly aware that the plan would not work in view of the anachronistic nature of the Ethiopian system in face of the political pluralism in Eritrea. It took no time for Matienzo to discover the prevailing mood of political dejection among the population. For example, the commissioner's report summarized the general mood in these terms: "In spite of the acceptance of the idea of federation, however, the

177

commissioner had an impression of pessimism among the population which he ascribed to the lack of security in the territory. He also had the feeling that a number of people did not fully believe in the federal solution or in the possibility of it being carried through. On all possible occasions, therefore, he attempted to instill a spirit of optimism and self-confidence into the population."³

It was under these conditions that Matienzo initiated his formal consultations on the draft of a constitution for Eritrea. In view of the extremely hostile political atmosphere, it was clear from the beginning that the commissioner's task would not be easy. In this chapter we shall analyze the elements of conflict during the preliminary stage of drafting the Eritrean constitution and the gradual erosion of the rights and privileges of the Eritrean government that would lead to its formal liquidation.

The Beginning of the End

The Aklilou-Matienzo Confrontation

Before starting his formal consultations with the government of Ethiopia and the Eritrean people in regard to the constitution to be installed in Eritrea, Matienzo issued a working memorandum specifying the items for possible inclusion in the Eritrean constitution. Some of the basic elements included the question of human rights and political liberty, designation of official languages, determination of spheres of jurisdiction between the government of Eritrea and the federal government, the electoral principle to be followed in the organization of the government, designation of an Eritrean flag, and determination of the structure of the legislature, executive, and other branches of government.⁴

On the basis of this memorandum, Ethiopian Foreign Minister Aklilou, his advisor John Spencer, and Matienzo held four meetings in May and July 1951. The meetings revealed that Aklilou was still predisposed to the earlier position held by his government which was in substance antithetical to the smooth implementation of the Federal Act. Regressing to his old theme, Aklilou even questioned the legal validity of the UN document and suggested that remedial solutions should be sought in order to make the federal plan workable. That position led him to open confrontation with Matienzo on the actual interpretation of the technicalities and purposes of the federal instrument.[5]

Aklilou contended that by virtue of the absence of a separate federal government, the UN Federal Act created an association between Eritrea and Ethiopia closer than any classical form of federation would give. Therefore, the concession given to Ethiopia appeared great, but the Federal Act contradicted this concession by allowing for Eritrea a "very broad measurement of self-government." To show the incongruous nature of the UN document, Aklilou drew comparisons between the Federal Act and the federal constitutions of the United States, Australia, Germany, and many other nations. The crux of his argument was that Eritrea had been accorded a greater measure of autonomy than that provided for by any other federal constitution in which the local governments would assume certain limited powers and the general powers were naturally reserved for the central authority. Furthermore, Aklilou argued, it had been presumed in all federal constitutions that maintenance of peace and order was contingent upon the full authorization of the central government to enact legislation affecting internal security and order. Thus, since the Federal Act under consideration contained no clause bestowing upon the Ethiopian government, which was recognized as the federal government, adequate jurisdiction over security matters, "the powers reserved to Eritrea had been left intact, a unique feature in a federal constitution."

Aklilou also contended that the federal governments of certain Latin American countries were given broad powers in such matters as public health, education, and labor, while the UN Federal Act did not confer such rights upon Ethiopia. Hence the Federal Act was out of the ordinary.

In an effort to further substantiate his position, Aklilou referred to the Australian system in which the federal parliament had the prerogative to legislate for the entire federation regarding civil and criminal procedures, whereas Ethiopia had no such prerogatives under the Federal Act. In the case of the United States, Australia, Mexico, and others, the laws enacted by the central government were valid throughout the confederate states. Particularly in Brazil, "[t]he federal government had wide powers of intervention." Having enumerated all these stipulations, Aklilou charged that Ethiopia was deprived by the Federal Act of all the necessary elements of public authority. Aklilou emphasized in particular Eritrea's "incapacity" to govern over Eritrea herself in view of the rampant security problem in the territory. Aklilou thus complained "that in the absence of the usual provisions for the legal recognition of decrees and laws of confederate states, it had no guarantee whatsoever that any of the federal laws, decrees and privileges would be respected in Eritrea."

Finally, by way of recommendation, Aklilou proposed that the closest possible link between the Eritrean executive and the imperial government of Ethiopia be established. Moreover, he wanted the Eritrean chief executive, who was to have veto power over Eritrean legislation, to be appointed by the emperor. He also proposed that there should be a close relationship between the education, health, and labor of the two countries since Ethiopia was to represent Eritrea in all international matters. He recommended that Amharic, the official Ethiopian language, be the official language for Eritrea and that the Ethiopian flag should be the only flag for both countries.

It appears that, despite a compilation of comparative data, Aklilou missed the main point. In drawing a comparison between the UN Federal Act and the federal constitutions of other countries, he systematically brushed aside one important point, namely the fact that the UN Federal Act was an attempt at grafting democracy to a feudo-Byzantine-type imperial structure, whereas the federal constitutions in the United States, Australia, Germany, and others were products of historical, political contracts that the federal partners democratically concluded on the basis of their mutual interests. Moreover, the federal governments in those countries are founded upon the three-government model, to which, as we recall, Aklilou had vehemently objected when Burma had proposed the traditional form of federalism. Under the tripartite federal structure, the central government becomes a "neutral arbiter" in the service of all confederate states governed by the equilibration process of checks and balances. But in the case of the Ethio-Eritrean federation, the imperial government of Ethiopia was designated both as the government of Ethiopia and as the government of Ethiopia and Eritrea, a unity completely alien to the concept of federalism. In any case, in an effort to avert early abortion of the Federal Act, Matienzo took one step forward to confront Aklilou on legal grounds. Matienzo's profound legal interpretation of the Federal Act is summarized thus.[6]

Matienzo reminded the foreign minister of the fact that Ethiopia had expressed strong opposition to any "undue measure of autonomy" for Eritrea and of her concern about the disadvantages that could emanate from such a move. But, despite such expressions of concern, Ethiopia had voluntarily yielded to the outcome of the negotiations, and therefore she was not now entitled to make any changes in the Federal Act. Matienzo observed thus:

> However, the fact was that the resolution, which had been accepted after the careful examinations referred to by Mr. Aklilou in the most recent statement, was binding upon everyone. *Roma loquita est, causa finita est.* If that was true of the parties concerned, a fortiori the commissioner as the representative of the United Nations had to conform strictly with the resolution from which he could delete nothing and to which he could add nothing. At most he could only interpret, in case of need, the text which was on the whole quite clear. . . . The commissioner, whose means of action were limited and who was directly answerable to the General Assembly, was absolutely debarred from tampering with properly defined settlements produced after closely reasoned negotiations which affected important interests and involved great powers on either side.

In regard to Aklilou's complaint that the Federal Act gave Eritrea an "undue measure of autonomy," more than enjoyed by many states that were members of a federal union, Matienzo observed, "Although that was absolutely true, it was hardly right to infer, as the minister of foreign affairs had done, that it was therefore expedient to strengthen the control of the federal government in order to safeguard the federation. Surely, the United Nations will not take back with one hand what it has given with the other, and by enabling the federal government to exercise control over the government of Eritrea, leave the latter with illusory power only."

In reference to Aklilou's doubts as to the future capability of autonomous Eritrea to govern herself, Matienzo accepted the possibility of security problems in Eritrea, but stated that such problems would not be a sufficient reason for tampering with the international instrument of the Federal Act. As he observed, "The responsibility was not Ethiopia's but the Assembly's, for by deciding upon autonomy, it had ipso facto accepted all the inherent risks." Matienzo further counseled that "he could not undertake to give an opinion about the ability of Eritrea to govern itself since the matter had been settled by the General Assembly and by the trust placed in the Eritrean people." In this respect, Matienzo was more categorical in rejecting the minister's view: "The argument that Eritrea could not make use of its autonomy should be dismissed out of hand, for if that was so, an entirely different solution ought to be contemplated and the case would immediately come within the scope of chapters 12 and 13 of the trusteeship system of the Charter."

In reference to Aklilou's argument that there should be the closest possible link between the Eritrean executive and the emperor, Matienzo maintained that such a link would of necessity exist. But, he added, he did not mean that the Ethiopian emperor could take part in the appointment of the Eritrean chief executive "or a fortiori control" him.

In the matter of a flag, Matienzo argued that member states of a federation always had their own flags, and therefore there was nothing wrong with designating a flag for Eritrea. With respect to the language question, he maintained that the wishes of the people of Eritrea should be given primary consideration.

Finally, in reference to Aklilou's contention that the Federal Act stood in sharp contradistinction to the internationally accepted concept and practice of federation as applied in the United States, Australia, Germany, and other countries, Matienzo maintained that the analogy was inappropriate since the Ethio-Eritrean situation markedly differed from those situations under which federal arrangements were made. "It is possible that the text of the resolution contains a mixture of the just and unjust. But it must not be forgotten that the situation under consideration differs appreciably from the case of two previously constituted states which had decided to federate. In the case in question, a state with stable institutions and traditions was to be associated with a unit as yet unformed. The only material to which to refer was, therefore, the document which had received the approval of the United Nations."

In this confrontation between the Ethiopian foreign minister and the UN commissioner in Eritrea, Matienzo was superior in all counts, particularly in the legal sense. The Ethiopian position was extremely dangerous to the proper implementation of the Federal Act. As

Matienzo admonished: "It is possible to proceed by successive stages from a slight limitation of Eritrean autonomy to its complete destruction." Astounded by the strong position and strong language taken by Matienzo, Aklilou finally apologized for the impression created by his arguments that he was against the autonomy of Eritrea. At face value, his apology was an acknowledgement of defeat, but in reality it was a temporary retreat in order to gun down the aims and purposes of the Federal Act at a later, more opportune time. Although the unflinching stand of Matienzo seemed to have averted an outright incorporation of Eritrea and to be a victory for Eritrean autonomy, Aklilou's explicit opposition to the widest possible Eritrean autonomy was an ominous indicator of what would come later.

The Security Problem
While Aklilou and Matienzo were engaged in a fierce legal battle, Eritrea was being subjected to the terror of a highly organized brigandage sponsored and armed by the imperial government of Ethiopia. The continuation of this political terrorist campaign had two objectives. The first was to intimidate the nationalists during the preliminary stage of drafting the constitution in hope that they would not pursue too far their goal of obtaining "the widest possible measure of autonomy," whereby the Ethiopians hoped to persuade Matienzo to abandon some of the legal arguments he had been advancing. The second objective was to create an anarchic image of Eritrea, lending credibility to Aklilou's argument that Eritrea was wholly incapable of governing herself. Eritrea's anarchic image would then enable Ethiopia to obtain a concession to assume responsibility for Eritrea's internal security because the federal charter had specifically provided that Eritrea would maintain its own independent police force. From the point of view of Ethiopian strategy, control over Eritrean internal security would immensely facilitate the immediate erosion of the autonomous rights and privileges of the territory.

At the time that Matienzo was touring Eritrea, the Unionist bandits or shifta, as they were officially called, intensified a wave of terrorism against Eritrean nationalists including party leaders. As we saw in Chapter 5, the Ethiopian campaign of terrorism was greatly complemented by the recruitment of unemployed ex-Italian soldiers. In the context of economic uncertainty some of the ex-soldiers engaged in

banditry as a means of earning their living, and some of these economically displaced soldiers were recruited by Ethiopia to advance
her cause in Eritrea. Prominent among these shifta were the Mesazgi
brothers, who had served in the Italian colonial army. When one Italian carabiniere killed one of the Mesazgi brothers in December 1948,
the other brothers went on a rampage, terrorizing Italians in highland
Eritrea and killing at least eleven.[7]

In 1951, the incidents of banditry throughout Eritrea increased
to an average of 130 per month, as opposed to 85 incidents per month
in 1950.[8] The activities of the shifta generally took the form of political terrorism directed against both Europeans and Eritreans who supported the implementation of the Federal Act and the democratic
process. Armed holdups of trains, buses, and individuals, destruction
of property and cattle, raids on agro-commercial concessions, and
attacks on villages and police posts were the chief means employed
by the armed gangs.[9]

In view of the progressive increase in lawlessness and terrorism,
in both scope and magnitude, and the consequent difficulties he encountered in carrying out his task of consulting the people, on 31
March 1951 Matienzo communicated his concern about the situation
to the British chief administrator. He described the deteriorating security situation as a grave emergency. In this communication, Matienzo stated that the activities of the shifta were undermining public
opinion, destroying the feeling of security and self-confidence of
Eritreans, and obstructing the proper execution of the UN resolution.
He proposed that the institution of amnesty programs, accompanied
with severe punitive measures against those shifta who would refuse
to take advantage of them, might alleviate the security problem.[10]

Nevertheless, during April, the security situation deteriorated further, endangering more lives and property. Consequently, on 1 May
1951, on the eve of the day he was to commence formally consulting
the Eritrean people on the draft constitution, Matienzo announced
the postponement of his plan. He expressed his views in these terms:

I do not believe that it is advisable, from the psychological point
of view, to begin these consultations at a time when the population, which desires peace and security above all else, is in danger.
Furthermore, I do not think that it is proper that I should travel
about the country flying the flag of the United Nations over

roads stained with the blood of people attacked by the terrorists. While I know that there are cases where the UN flag has had to be flown over roads stained with blood, it has been as a symbol of the UN stand against aggression and in the protection of human rights. Finally, my conscience will not allow me to travel at present throughout the territory with an armed escort while the inhabitants whom I desire to meet will run the risk of ambushes and attacks from shifta when coming to meet me.[11]

Under this increasing pressure from the UN commissioner, on 19 June 1951, the British chief administrator proclaimed a general amnesty to all shifta who surrendered themselves to the government within one month.[12] Furthermore, in an effort to bring an end to this daunting security problem, Britain sought the cooperation of Ethiopia, which was in the driver's seat in matters of arming and harboring the shiftas. Some portions of Eritrea were also placed under martial law. The result was that, during the one-month period of general amnesty, 1,330 shiftas gave themselves up to British authorities, and another 93 were arrested and a number of them were hanged. In addition, many shiftas crossed the border into Ethiopia and surrendered to Ethiopian authorities, where they probably felt most at home.[13]

In this way, the security problem in Eritrea was resolved. In my opinion, much of the credit should go to Ethiopia because, as the initiator of the problem, she was finally cooperative in dealing with it. Since the shiftas received their moral stimulation, their political direction, and their arms from Ethiopia, it would have become very difficult, if not impossible, to bring an end to the security problem without Ethiopia's participation in dissuading her Unionist allies and curtailing their activities. It seems that Ethiopia was finally convinced that, in light of the refusal of the nationalists to cave in to political banditry and intimidation, continuation of political terrorism would only delay the implementation of the Federal Act. From the point of view of Ethiopia, it was advisable to halt political intimidation and armed assaults until the UN commissioner left Eritrea, as it had become obvious that Matienzo would in no way carry out his task under those circumstances. Moreover, since the security problem was perceived by the outside world as largely the creation of Ethiopia, continuation of the brigandage was tarnishing Ethiopia's international image. After all, Ethiopia was still insistent upon her claim to Somalia; therefore, it was in Ethiopia's future interest to resolve the shifta problem in Eritrea.

UN Decision Implemented

On 11 July 1951, soon after the security issue was resolved, Matienzo formally announced that consultation of the Eritrean people on the draft constitution was under way. Meanwhile, the Eritrean Independence Bloc, in a letter to the UN commissioner, had declared that it had decided "to change its name to the 'Eritrean Democratic Front' in order to adapt to the new situation." The bloc also indicated its readiness to respect and give effect to the UN decision in accordance with the principles, intentions, and recommendations of the General Assembly.[14] Accordingly, all the parties that comprised the Eritrean Democratic Front were consulted jointly.

The views expressed by the Eritrean Democratic Front on the draft Eritrean constitution included the following proposals.

1. A bicameral legislature consisting of a house of representatives and a senate should be set up with a structure that would create a system of checks and balances by maintaining equal representation in the senate so as to offset domination of the lower house by pro-Ethiopian Unionists.

2. The chief executive should be elected by the two houses of the parliament in a joint session.

3. The chief executive should appoint his ministers from among Eritreans, maintaining an even balance between Christians and Moslems.

4. The chief executive should be liable to dismissal by the Eritrean legislature on the basis of a no-confidence vote.

5. Since no mention was made in the Federal Act of the Ethiopian emperor's representation in Eritrea and since the presence of his representative would certainly pose a threat to Eritrean autonomy, allowing the emperor to have his own representative in Eritrea with or without power was objectionable.

6. Tigrinya and Arabic should be the only official languages of Eritrea.

7. The flag of the federation should be separate from that of Ethiopia, and Eritrea should have a distinctive flag of its own.

8. The Ethiopian government could not be the federal govern-

ment, and thus the federal government ought to be distinct from both the Eritrean and Ethiopian governments.

9. Some guarantee, in the form of intervention in the event that the UN resolution and the Eritrean constitution were altered or violated against the will of the Eritrean people, should be obtained from the United Nations.[15]

The Unionist party merely rehearsed the views expressed by Aklilou. During his consultations, throughout the provinces of Eritrea, Matienzo discovered that the views expressed by the people were the same as those already expressed by the political parties. The most controversial issues involved the designation of a flag, the number of assemblies, official languages, and the representation of the emperor. The people also explicitly expressed their desire that the United Nations should guarantee the Eritrean constitution and that a permanent UN observer should be placed in Eritrea to oversee its autonomy.[16]

The formal consultations with Eritrean political parties and people were closed on 8 October 1951, and Matienzo left for Geneva to begin drafting the constitution. In this endeavor, he was assisted by a British constitutionalist, a Dutch jurist, and a Swiss professor of public international law. Although the final legal document produced by Matienzo was not pleasing to the nationalists as a whole, it did, nonetheless, represent a partial victory for them in the sense that the tradition of Eritrean political pluralism, the principles of a democratic electoral system, the due process of law, and the freedoms of speech, association, and religion were all guaranteed. Much to the chagrin of the Ethiopian authorities, Tigrinya and Arabic were enshrined in the constitution as the official languages of the land. Still another victory for the nationalists was that a new flag, distinct from that of Ethiopia, was designated for Eritrea.

Matienzo also rejected the Ethiopian suggestion that the Eritrean chief executive should be nominated by the emperor. According to the drafted constitution, the head of the executive was to be elected by the Eritrean parliament and was responsible to it. The chief executive was to appoint his own secretaries to the various departments of the government and, on recommendations of the president of the parliament, he would appoint judges; all other civil servants were to be selected by the Eritrean Civil Services Commission on the basis of merit.

In regard to the legislature, the Unionist idea prevailed, as a unicameral parliament was set up with sixty-eight seats equally apportioned between Christians and Moslems. In the 1952 election, the Unionist party captured thirty-two seats while the various nationalists parties won the remaining thirty-six seats. Despite the continuous political intimidation and the projected Ethiopian ascendency, the political forces opposing or having reservations against Ethiopia still commanded nearly 52 percent of the popular vote.

Under the circumstances, the concession obtained for the nationalists on the judicial system was substantial. The Eritrean constitution provided for an Eritrean Supreme Court, a high court of justice, and district courts, all independent of the executive and the legislature. Thus Eritreans were to litigate their cases before Eritrean judges in Eritrean courts applying Eritrean laws.

However, on two crucial points, the nationalists lost the battle. The Eritrean constitution provided that the Ethiopian emperor would have his own representative in Eritrea with official functions to promulgate laws passed by the Eritrean parliament, annually to read a speech from the throne, and to send back legislation to the Eritrean parliament for its reconsideration if they encroached on non-Eritrean jurisdictional matters.

The greatest anomaly in the Eritrean constitution was, however, that it provided for the Ethiopian government to become the federal government. This was not Matienzo's fault, however, for it had been the intent of the framers of the Federal Act, about which Matienzo could do nothing. Nevertheless, the constitution did not provide for a neutral arbiter to monitor the implementation or violation of the UN resolution. It was hardly possible to understand how an Ethiopian government could ipso facto become "above" Ethiopia and Eritrea and reconcile their contradictory interests, when that government was the reification of Ethiopian absolutism. Since the core of any federal government has always been the presence of a neutral arbiter or third government in the federal structure, the absence of that element alone signified an ipso facto negation of Eritrean autonomy. It revealed the sham character of the so-called Ethio-Eritrean federation. In fact, it merely represented the beginning of the end, and would facilitate the eventual incorporation of Eritrea into Ethiopia.

In any case, the Eritrean government was set in motion on 15 September 1952, having authority over domestic matters that included maintenance of internal security, internal taxation, education, health, labor, development of internal commerce and industry, and an Eritrean budget, while the federal Ethiopian government was authorized to have control over currency and finance, defense, and external and interstate commerce and communications. In retrospect, the adoption of the Eritrean constitution and the institution of the Eritrean government, and consequently the departure of Hanze Matienzo, heralded, not the execution of the UN Federal Act, but the continuation of the endless struggle begun in the 1940s.

The Federation Terminates

No sooner had the Eritrean government been set in motion, than Ethiopia adopted a two-pronged policy geared toward the devitalization of the Eritrean economy and the depoliticization of Eritrean society. As part of its economic policy, the imperial government dissuaded foreign investors and entrepreneurs, under threat of expulsion, from engaging in business activity in Eritrea. The federal government, which was for all practical purposes the government of Ethiopia, unilaterally abrogated the agreement between the Eritrean government and an Italian company, Fiat, to set up an automotive factory in the Eritrean town of Decamare. Likewise, it abrogated another agreement between the Eritrean government and an electric company, Sadaw, to build a hydroelectric scheme involving cotton plantations in western Eritrea and the setting up of a textile factory in 1954–1955. In addition, many factories such as textile, tanning, and earthenware, were either shut down or relocated in Ethiopia.[17] For example, in 1958 there were 165 industrial establishments in Eritrea and only 55 in Ethiopia. Three years later, however, the number of industrial establishments decreased to 83 in Eritrea while those in Ethiopia increased to 95.[18] Eritrea's regressive underdevelopment was, in effect, making an ironic contribution to Ethiopia's modernization. Objections to such steps devitalizing the Eritrean economy were vehemently expressed by Eritrean nationalists, but to no avail. Even the pro-Ethiopian John Spencer admitted that "the Ethiopian government turned a deaf ear to complaints of withholding customs revenues from duties on imports for use in Eritrea."[19]

According to Bereket Habte-Selassie, the emperor of Ethiopia had three objectives in mind in devitalizing Eritrea's economy: to weaken

Eritrea's economy and thus prove its nonviability as an independent economic unit; to undo the syndicalization of Eritrean labor since it was regarded as the bastion of Eritrean nationalism and above all as a model for emulation by its Ethiopian counterpart, which the emperor feared most; to attain access to Eritrea's skilled labor, which Ethiopia had long coveted.[20] The net result of this policy was that the Eritrean working class was effectively disbanded, leading to the massive exodus of its members in two directions. One segment left for the Sudan and the Middle East in search of employment, while another section flocked to Ethiopia following the relocated factories there. As Spencer acidly observed, "The Eritreans soon proved themselves to be the Irish of Ethiopia."[21]

This policy of economic devitalization was accompanied by a concerted effort to depoliticize Eritrean society. Since the beginning, relations between the two partners of the federation had never proceeded as envisioned in the Federal Act. These strained relations were soon "provoked by the appointment of Shoans rather than Eritreans to local federal offices and favoritism in awarding federal contracts and concessions."[22]

The next step taken by Ethiopia was the declaration of war on Eritrean trade unions, political parties, and the press. The political activities of the parties, with the exception of the pro-Ethiopian Unionist party, were curtailed, and eventually the parties were banned. Important party personages were thrown in jail. Similarly, the General Union of Eritrean Labour Syndicates was banned, and its leader, Wolde-ab Woldemariam, was politically so harassed that he was compelled to flee the country. Some other nationalist leaders followed suit. Having obtained political sanctuary in Nasserite Egypt, Wolde-ab and his colleagues began broadcasting to the Eritrean people from Cairo, urging them to resist the withering away of Eritrean democracy and autonomy.[23]

Seeing the steady erosion of Eritrean democracy, the Eritrean parliament issued a memorandum in 1954, stating that it would submit the Eritrean case to the United Nations unless the intrusions by Ethiopian authorities into the political life of Eritrea were stopped. This warning was conveyed to Ethiopia through the chief executive. The reaction of the emperor's representative was, however, a blunt refusal. In March 1954, in his speech before the Eritrean parliament, he declared that "[t]here are no internal nor external affairs as far as the office of His Imperial Majesty's Representative is concerned, and there will be none in the future."[24]

This recalcitrant behavior finally precipitated a crisis in the relations between the two partners. The chief executive of the Eritrean government resigned four months after the Ethiopian representative gave his blunt speech. He was replaced by a quiescent cohort of the emperor, Asfaha Wolde-Michael, who had been second in command in the Ethiopian representative's office. The president of the Eritrean parliament, Idris Muhammed Adem, was also dismissed a year later and was replaced by another Unionist, Dimetros, a clergyman in the Coptic Church.

Having reduced to impotence both the executive and legislative branches of the Eritrean government, Ethiopia seemed to have secured a freer hand in Eritrea. In 1955, it exerted intensive pressure on the Eritrean parliament to end the federation in favor of unconditional union of the country with Ethiopia. Although the Eritrean parliament was not competent to terminate the federal structure by its sheer vote, it was the most tempting instrument for Ethiopia to use to provide the necessary legal pretext for abolishing the federation. The attempt, however, did not materialize. Although it was not clear why the termination of the federation was delayed, John Spencer claims credit for saving the federation. He noted, "I immediately opposed the project, pointing out that were Ethiopia to accept the proposal, she would seriously aggravate the already delicate situation at the United Nations where Italy was opposing Ethiopia in a boundary dispute over the Ogaden."[25]

In 1956, Tigrinya and Arabic were officially banned as languages of the land and were replaced by Amharic as the only official language of the empire. Ethiopian courts also preempted litigations between Eritreans that otherwise might have fallen under Eritrean court jurisdiction. This arbitrary legal procedure was later legalized by a decree designed to include Eritrea within the legal jurisdiction of Ethiopian courts. In that way the Eritrean judicial system was reduced to complete impotence. Furthermore, on the eve of the 1956 parliamentary elections, Proclamation 121 was issued, enabling elections to be held without the supervision of the independent electoral commission that had been authorized by the constitution to supervise all elections. Although the Eritrean attorney general, a British national, had fought the illegality of Proclamation 121 in the Supreme

Court, where it was declared unconstitutional, the emperor's representative defied the court and conducted the elections, in which only the Unionist party officially participated, in a draconian fashion under strict Ethiopian control.

In 1957, once again, the Eritrean parliament was asked to vote in favor of terminating the federation altogether. Here again, Spencer claims credit for saving the nominal federation: "Once more I entered my opposition. The level of support by Egypt and Syria for the dissident movement in Eritrea had now given rise to serious concern."[26] If Spencer is correct, then only exogenous reasons, namely Arab support for Eritrean nationalism, dissuaded the emperor from aborting the federal structure at that time.

In any case, Ethiopia continued destroying the remaining insignia of Eritrean identity and official seals of the Eritrean government. In December 1958, the Eritrean flag was lowered, and in September 1959, Eritrean laws were replaced by the Ethiopian penal code. In May 1960, the Eritrean parliament, packed by Unionists, voted to change the names "Eritrean government" to "Eritrean administration" and "chief executive" to "chief administrator." Even the seal of the Eritrean government was changed to read "Eritrean Administration under Haile Selassie I, Emperor of Ethiopia."[27]

Such measures, however, never failed to provoke stiff resistance by Eritrean nationalists, albeit limited to peaceful means in the form of appeals. For example, in late 1957, Muhammed Omar Kade, former member of the Eritrean Supreme Council, and Wolde-ab Woldemariam traveled to New York to submit a memorandum in person to the secretary general of the United Nations. In this memorandum, they declared that "the frustration of the Eritrean people is pushing them to the verge of a revolution. Their patience has reached its breaking point. Mindful of the fact that the prolongation of the present state of affairs . . . may jeopardise world peace, they decided to appeal to the United Nations. The United Nations, having disposed of the destiny of a nation by the said resolution and having reserved the right to verify its implementation, should at least, inquire into the facts of this complaint, and find out whether its Resolution has been actually carried out or utterly abrogated. A Commission of inquiry should be assigned to Eritrea to examine, on the spot, the grievances."[28]

Even though the United Nations was insensitive to their case, the nationalists persisted in their diplomatic endeavor to draw the attention of the world community to their cause. In 1958, the exiled politicians, Ibrahim Sultan Ali, Wolde-ab Woldemariam, and Idris Muhammed Adem, revived the Eritrean Democratic Front and renamed it the Eritrean Liberation Movement, with the view to intensifying their diplomatic offensive. As Robert Hess observed, "At first they bombarded the United Nations and the governments of Britain, the United States, France, Italy, and the Soviet Union with letters and petitions protesting Ethiopian violations of the federal charter and of the Eritrean constitution. Their fears of progressive Ethiopianization of the territory through Amhara dominance were not baseless; Eritrean political parties, under constant pressure from the Ethiopian government, diminished in strength, while the Eritrean parliament, apparently packed by order of Addis Ababa to insure a pro-Ethiopian majority, provided no effective opposition to Ethiopian policy."[29]

In 1959, leaders of the Eritrean Democratic Front once again urged the United Nations to review the Eritrean case and to put pressure on Ethiopia to refrain from further violations of the autonomous rights of Eritrea. In a letter to Secretary General Dag Hammarskjöld, copies of which were distributed to foreign embassies in Cairo, they appealed to save Eritrea from being completely annexed to what they called "the rotten empire of Ethiopia." Moreover, they charged the United Nations with exposing the Eritrean people to wanton genocide by Ethiopia under the mask of federation.[30]

Aside from the onerous task of substantiating their case, the old guards of Eritrean nationalism had to break through the mythical component of Ethiopia's international image and particularly the emperor's popularity. For example, Haile Selassie was described by Hammarskjöld, to whom the nationalists were appealing, as "a symbolic landmark, a prophetic figure in the path of man's struggle to achieve international peace through international action."[31] Under such circumstances, the repeated appeals by the nationalists to the world body in part reflected their political naïveté as to the organization's nature and the purpose of the federation, and in part their faith in justice and law and even in the integrity of the United Nations.

Emboldened by the insensitivity of the United Nations to the appeals of the nationalists, Ethiopia began a drastic move to do away completely with the federal structure. On 15 November 1962, without any previous notice but at the behest of the Ethiopian emperor, the chief administrator of Eritrea drove to the Eritrean parliament, which was then surrounded by Ethiopian armed forces. There he read the following statement: "The statement that I am going to read to you is the final issue of the Eritrean case, and there is nothing you can do other than accepting it as it is. We render the federation null and void, and henceforth we are completely united with our motherland."[32] Henceforth Eritrea constituted the fourteenth province of the Ethiopian empire.

From the point of view of law, the unilateral termination of the federation by Ethoipia was a direct contravention of the Federal Act and a flagrant violation of the right of the Eritrean people to national self-determination. But, since from the very beginning the decision to federate Eritrea with Ethiopia had been illegal and contrary to the principles and purposes of the charter of the United Nations, the subsequent developments in Ethio-Eritrean relations simply took their natural course. As indicated, Eritrean nationalism, with its inherent capitalist orientation, obviously represented a threat to Ethiopian absolutism. Therefore, the emperor's action in terminating the federal structure was a strategic preemption against the menace posed by Eritrean pluralism in favor of maintaining the status quo. But at the same time, the flourishing of Eritrean nationalism, with its inherent drive toward the creation of an independent Eritrean state, was in no way to be denied. As the spokesman of the Eritrean Independence Bloc had told the General Assembly in 1950, "The right of that people to independence could not be disregarded without the risk of creating in East Africa a situation dangerous to peace and security, for the people of Eritrea would never accept Ethiopian domination. . . . [They] would not tolerate the name of Eritrea being struck off the map of the world."[33]

The Eritrean Armed Struggle

Upon the installation of the federation, Trevaskis had offered the following words of wisdom for Ethiopia:

It is for Ethiopia to make her choice. The temptation to subject Eritrea firmly under her own control will always be great. Should she try to do so, she will risk Eritrean discontent and eventual revolt, which . . . might well disrupt both Eritrea and Ethiopia herself. Though an autonomous Eritrea has admittedly unwelcome implications for Ethiopia, her need for a loyal and stable Eritrea far transcends any inconvenience a federal relationship may imposed upon her. It is to her own interest as well as to Eritrea's that she should ensure that the Federation survives in the form its authors intended. The future of the Federation, and indeed of the whole group of young countries in North East Africa, is likely to be affected by the course that Ethiopia takes. She has acquired a great responsibility.[34]

Ethiopia did not heed Trevaskis's prophetic warning. As a result, Eritrean exiles in Cairo formed the Eritrean Liberation Movement in 1958, with a view to initiating political agitation inside Eritrea against the erosion of Eritrean autonomy. The response to the formation of this front was dramatized by the simultaneous emergence of two movements in Eritrea, one in the lowlands and the other in the highlands. While the one operating in the lowlands was known as the Eritrean Liberation Movement, the other operating in the highland region came to be called Mahber Showate, or Cells of Seven, since each unit of the organization was composed of seven members in order to maintain the needed secrecy.[35]

These movements were successful in galvanizing a mass mobilization against Ethiopia's advances. For example, in 1958, Eritrean workers were agitated to stage a general strike and demonstrations in reaction to the lowering of the Eritrean flag and the introduction of the Ethiopian labor law into Eritrea. During these massive demonstrations, Ethiopian forces killed over eighty persons and wounded another five hundred.[36]

After several such incidents, the Eritrean exiles in Cairo became convinced that the road to peaceful opposition to Ethiopia's intrusive steps was blocked. They formed the Eritrean Liberation Front on 1 July 1960 to initiate armed struggle. The nationalists collected some £6,500 and smuggled into Eritrea a consignment of outdated Italian rifles.[37] Consequently, on 1 September 1961, the Eritrean nationalists fired the first bullet against Ethiopian troops. Henceforth, Eritrea's quest for national self-determination took on a military dimension.

The increased measures of repression taken by Ethiopia only enhanced the visibility of the nationalist forces. As early as 1963, there were already three thousand Eritreans in Ethiopian prisons under suspicion of sympathy for the nationalist movement.[38] By 1965 the actual fighting guerrilla forces had reached more than 3,000. In the same year, the Eritrean nationalists obtained international visibility when the Sudan announced that it had seized eighteen thousand tons of Czech arms destined for the Eritrean nationalists.[39]

Although Ethiopia never acknowledged the existence of an armed insurrection in Eritrea, the military confrontation escalated in the second half of the 1960s, causing a serious security problem. As a result Ethiopia's second army division had to be put on a war footing. The army was increased from 6,000 to 8,000 troops.[40] In 1967, as part of its counterinsurgence measure, the second division began a massive mopping up operation in western Eritrea, which resulted in the destruction of three hundred villages. Thirty thousand refugees also crossed into the Sudan.[41] The military strategy of the second division increasingly alienated the army from the people and thus encouraged popular support for the nationalists. As the head of the Israeli military delegation, attached to the Ethiopian armed forces, said, "The 2d Division is very efficient in killing innocent people. They are alienating the Eritreans and deepening the hatred that already exists. Their commander took his senior aides to a spot near the Sudanese border and ordered him: 'From here to the north—clean the area.' Many innocent people were massacred and nothing of substance was achieved. There is simply no way that the Ethiopian army will ever win the struggle over Eritrea by pursuing this line."[42]

The year 1970 saw a dramatic increase in guerrilla activities in both rural and urban areas. In May a unit of Eritrean nationalists engaged 3,000 Ethiopian troops in a fierce battle in the vicinity of Massawa, inflicting heavy casualties on the Ethiopians. In retaliation, Ethiopia destroyed a number of villages in Akkele Guzai, where thirty-two persons were killed under sympathy for the nationalists. Another eighty-eight persons were killed after resisting resettlement in the Massawa area. In November, Eritrean nationalists broke three important bridges and derailed a cargo train. On 21 November the second army division general was killed by Eritrean guerrillas. In reprisal, Ethiopia killed one thousand civilians.[43]

Under these circumstances, most of Eritrea was placed under martial law. Under this emergency law, the ministry of defense was empowered to relocate inhabitants in certain areas, which amounted to a strategic hamletization designed to enable the government to keep the movements of the inhabitants under surveillance. In addition, the ministry was empowered to set up military courts to try anyone suspected of sympathy or cooperation with the nationalist forces.[44]

When the Ethiopian revolution exploded in 1974, many hoped that the Eritrean problem would be resolved peacefully. But that hope was dashed early when the Ethiopian military council, the Dergue, excluded Eritrean political prisoners from the list it submitted to the emperor for release. To make matters worse, two hundred Eritreans were massacred at Om Hager and another four thousand fled to the Sudan.[45] In response to the Om Hager massacre and the discrimination against Eritrean political prisoners, the twenty-three Eritrean members of the Ethiopian parliament resigned. In December 1974, fifty Eritrean students were strangled to death by piano wire. Furthermore, many thousands of Eritreans were detained without formal charges being filed against them.[46]

Violation of human rights worsened further under the military government. Mary Dines recounted:

On the morning of 13th March 1975, a group of 300 Ethiopian soldiers on their way from Asmara to Keren, passed through the village of *Woki* (population about 2,500) at 7.00 a.m. They rounded up the villagers on a piece of waste ground and shot 37 dead. After this, most of the people fled into the hills, but the rest, believing there was nowhere safe to go, or that nothing else would happen remained. On their return on 14th March, the Ethiopians stopped again. They then proceeded to slaughter nearly 500 people in the most gruesome way. Many women, children and old men were bayonetted and pregnant women were slit open. The Ethiopians then killed all the livestock and set fire to the houses. The slaughter was arbitrary and had no political connection with opposition forces. There are three mass graves outside the village.[47]

The demolition of Woki and the massacre there were representative of the norm. In 1975 alone, Ethiopian troops destroyed 110 villages and tens of thousands of civilians were killed in the process.[48] The most disgusting atrocity was committed when, in March 1975, one hundred patients were taken from the Asmara hospital and killed as part of a "scorch the earth" policy.[49] In December 1977, Amnesty International reported, "In Eritrea, the State of Emergency imposed under the former Government has continued in force, with the same kind of atrocities against civilians, use of torture, and arbitrary killings of alleged supporters of the secessionist movements, as under Emperor Haile Selassie's rule."[50] These massacres and arrests continued unabated into the 1980s.

On the political balance sheet, the Ethiopian policy of repression merely served to further alienate the Eritrean people and became an important element in the galvanization of popular support for the nationalist forces. The net result was that between 1974 and 1977 the nationalists were able to liberate 95 percent of Eritrea. But the Ethiopian revolution failed to resolve the Eritrean question on the basis of a democratic procedure that would respect Eritrea's right to national self-determination.

Perspectives on the Federal Act

The Eritrean issue was a simple colonial question that the UN transformed into a political enigma and a human tragedy by linking Eritrea to Ethiopia under the guise of federation. The UN move was certainly unprecedented. From the point of view of law and political principles, federation signifies a political system arrived at by two or more sovereign states who freely determine a form of government appropriate to them. The decision to install a federal structure must emanate from the true desires, not of a third party like the United Nations, but of the parties concerned, to form a larger political unit that will reflect the mutuality of their interests, needs, and aspirations.

Aside from the legal and political arguments against the UN-created federation, the fact that there was, between the Ethiopian and Eritrean systems, an organic incompatibility that later defined their relationship gave an apocalyptic character to the UN decision. In retrospect there were two possibilities when the UN installed the federation: immediate dissolution of the federation and absorption of Eritrea into Ethiopia as part of the general absolutization and centralization process, or a further democratization of the federation by a process that might have destroyed the feudal order in Ethiopia. As Ethiopian absolutism and Eritrea's political pluralism could not coexist, a struggle between the two systems became inevitable, a struggle for either absolute centralism or political diversification.

In fact, when the opponents of the federation formula expressed strong reservations about the UN decision, they were pointing to this reality. Their arguments and concerns are placed in their proper historical context below in order that students of the Horn might appreciate the proponents' detached prognosis about the future of the federal structure.

Historic Abyssinia was an aggregate of loosely connected Amhara and Tigrayan political formations mediated by the universalism of the Coptic Church. Abyssinian rulers vying for control of the central state had first to obtain the submission of their provincial rivals, either through the mediation of the church or by the use of force. Periodic payments of tribute were essential elements of submission. To meet their tributary obligations, the vassal kings carried out predatory incursions into neighboring states. Such internal struggles for power and the collection of tribute gave the Abyssinian state a character of self-expansive inherency. Menelik's southward expansion is a case in point. After submitting to Yohannes, Menelik paid, in December 1880 alone, 50,000 talers in cash, six hundred mules and horses trimmed in gold and silver and loaded with grain, and 150,000 talers worth of other items.[51]

To meet his increasingly onerous tribute payments, Menelik began a series of campaigns into adjacent states. In the early 1880s, for example, he invaded Arussi and returned with 100,000 cattle.[52] Once in motion, the process of expansion became self-feeding. The availability of fabulous material resources, such as gold, ivory, livestock, coffee, and slaves, in the non-Abyssinian formations, coupled with the pressure of tribute payment to Yohannes and the need to finance the import of arms, compelled Menelik to embark upon these southward campaigns. In November 1894, for example, tempted by the fabulous riches and dense population of Welamo, Menelik conducted a bloody campaign against this prosperous kingdom during which about 119,000 Welamo were either killed, wounded, or captured. Thirty-six thousand cattle were also taken.[53]

In sum, between 1875 and 1900, Menelik incorporated more than fifty ethnic formations into his kingdom, thereby doubling his dominion in resources and population. By incorporating such multiple formations, Menelik laid the basis for Ethiopia's future problems. As

Clay and Holcomb commented, the ease with which Menelik acquired such vast colonial possessions was attributable to four major factors. First, the Abyssinian conquest occurred over a period of two decades so that the various ethnic formations were incorporated into Abyssinia by piecemeal. This preempted the possibility of collective resistance to Amhara advances. Second, the co-optation of some local elites into the Abyssinian state assisted in the easy consolidation of Amhara hegemony. Third, the Abyssinians were able to transfer their stockpiles of arms obtained from Europe to the conquered areas and to establish military garrisons to maintain order in those areas. In addition, their control of the trade routes deprived the subject peoples of their effective commercial and communication channels. Fourth, in an effort to obtain favors from Menelik, many European powers indirectly assisted him to maintain and consolidate his possessions. They provided him with a massive injection of arms and technical and military advisers.[54]

This last point was particularly crucial since it distorted the balance of power in the region. For example, when Menelik invaded the coffee-rich kingdom of Kaffa, his forces were equipped with 20,000 relatively sophisticated European arms as against the 300 superannuated guns at the disposal of the Kaffa monarch. If needed, Menelik had the capacity to collect 196,000 soldiers at any given moment.[55] Between 1880 and 1900, Menelik imported 1 million rifles and 47 million cartridges from Europe.[56] This massive arms buildup was financed by resources obtained from the Abyssinian colonies. Although it was dropped in the face of German government opposition, the fact that Menelik was able to place an order, in 1893, for 100,000 rifles and 5 million cartridges from a Hamburg firm, dramatized the significance of these colonies in arms transactions.[57] Thus, as McClellan commented, the Abyssinian armed presence coupled with the Amhara self-perception of invincibility and innate superiority promoted a sense of hopelessness and futility among the subject peoples in their collective resistance to Abyssinian occupation.[58] After all, the absence of capitalist elements in the Abyssinian modes of production in itself was a sufficient preemption to the emergence of any collective psychological makeup among the subject peoples, a precondition for joint anticolonial resistance.

The far-reaching legacy of Abyssinian conquest was, however, the universalization of slavery and the feudal mode of production. Slavery was an integral element of Abyssinian society. Adjacent regions inhabited by peoples with darker complexion were frequently raided for slaves. These captured slaves were used for servile labor in agrarian production and domestic work. But with the conquest of these vast areas by Menelik, enslavement assumed a cardinal economic significance as it came to be used as an important source of commercial revenues. Slaves were obtained either during the campaigns that led to the conquest of the colonies, or by means of armed raids into the colonies later. Menelik actively participated in this commercialization of the enslavement process. As Timothy Fernyhough has nicely documented, between 1870 and 1895 an average of 4,000 slaves were annually exported via the Somali and Eritrean coasts. In addition, the regions south of Kaffa yielded about 8,000 slaves annually, and the annual export of slaves via Kumbi and Garo reached 5,000 slaves. The 1894 Welamo campaign yielded 15,000 slaves in which the imperial share was 1,800 slaves in addition to 18,000 heads of cattle.[59]

During the first three decades of the twentieth century, slavery continued as an integral part of the Ethiopian economy. In 1912 Lij Iyasu, Menelik's successor, led 10,000 armed men into the southwestern colonies of the empire and returned with some 40,000 slaves to Addis Ababa. In Gimira alone, his soldiers captured up to 8,000 slaves.[60] In the aftermath of the 1919–1920 influenza epidemic, which decimated the slave population in Ethiopia proper with a resultant reduction in servile labor, slave raiding and trade were on the increase. In 1922, for example, the Amharic governor of Maji pledged his colony for slaves. His successor also later looted Maji and took a number of slaves along with 18,000 head of cattle and 50,000 sheep. The governor's wife also conducted armed raids in the area, capturing 92 slaves. According to one estimate, the population of Maji fell from 40,000 in 1910 to 4,000 in 1922.[61]

It is believed that in a matter of three decades between 1898 and 1929 some 360,000 slaves were exported from the Abyssinian colonies. The demographic consequences of the slave trade were drastic. For example, an Abyssinian official informed a European observer that, by the mid–1920s, the population of Kaffa decreased from 250,000 to 10,000. By 1912, the population of Gimira had already declined from 100,000 to 20,000.[62]

Although important antislavery elements were germinating in the Ethiopian agrarian structure, the final impetus for the abolition of slavery in Ethiopia came from outside. The British Anti-Slavery Society was particularly vocal about these matters on behalf of the Ethiopian slaves. In fact, the matter became an international issue when Ethiopia applied in 1919 for admittance to the League of Nations. Ethiopia became a member of the league only after four years of diplomatic struggle, but her membership was conditional upon her commitment to abolishing slavery. In an effort to comply with the conditions imposed upon her, Ethiopia proclaimed two antislavery imperial edicts, one in 1924 and another in 1931. Notwithstanding these proclamations, de facto slavery continued. In 1932, for example, the Anti-Slavery Society reported that at least one-fifth of Ethiopia's population were still slaves.[63]

Only the Italian occupation of Ethiopia in 1935–1941 brought the slave mode of production to an end. In 1936 the Italians are said to have emancipated 600,000 slaves.[64] Although this figure may have been inflated for propaganda purposes, there is no doubt that the Italian conquest of Ethiopia provided the practical means of abolishing slavery altogether. After restoration, a revival of slavery was unnecessary for both domestic and international reasons. The slave owners themselves were displaced because of the war, and the increasing demand for agrarian labor made slavery obsolete. In addition, the emperor availed himself of the British presence in Ethiopia to solidify the state machinery to cope with the problem. In 1942 he abolished the legal status of slavery by decree. The law established twenty years' imprisonment, forty lashes, a fine of 10,000 Ethiopian dollars, a combination of these, or death for those persons engaged in slave trading or transporting. During the first year of the law, the high court in Addis Ababa tried 130 slave-related cases and convicted 120 persons, of whom many were executed.[65]

Thus, slavery as a distinct mode of production was ended by the beginning of the 1940s, but the social stigma and the pejorative historical connotations persisted in Ethiopian society. After all, the freed slaves were displaced both structurally and socially and their genuine rehabilitation required undiminished restoration of their means of livelihood from which they were detached by force. The imperial government was unwilling to rehabilitate them in the structural sense. When the opponents of the UN-created federation spoke of Ethiopia's backwardness and Eritrea's relative advance, they were pointing precisely to this objective reality.

The other legacy of Menelik's conquest was the universalizing of the feudal mode of production throughout the region. Menelik established garrison towns throughout the colonies. These garrison towns assumed reponsibility for the administration, collection, and transmission of revenues to the center. The colonial administrators received land and the labor of indigenous cultivators in lieu of monetary remunerations for their administrative services. This system came to define the relationship between the Amhara and the subject peoples. The indigenous population became Gabbars, an Amharic term equivalent to serfs. Upon conquest, Menelik confiscated two-thirds of the land and distributed it among his generals, soldiers, the nobility, and the church. Indigenous laborers were assigned to work on the land for these classes. The allocation of land and serfs was dependent on the length of service and rank of the settler-colonists. For example, a common soldier received between 40 and 120 hectares of land and ten or more serfs. A garrison commander received up to 800 hectares of land and over seventy serfs whereas a provincial governor received extensive tracts of land and up to three hundred serfs. The obligations of the serfs to the Amhara settlers included the surrender of part of their produce as tribute, tithe, provision of honey, meat, and firewood, grinding the landholder's share of grain, helping in building his houses and fences, caring after his livestock, and providing military services.[66]

While abolishing slavery, Haile Selassie simply modified serfdom by replacing it with feudal tenancy. Instead of abolishing the feudal order, he directed his efforts toward creating a correspondence between the modernization of the Ethiopian state and the control of production apparatuses by harnessing the latter to the former. Soon after restoration in 1941, the emperor embarked in all earnest upon a process of centralization, an imperative precipitated by the fact that he had to cope with the various separatist tendencies to form feudal principalities. For the emperor, the creation of a centralized state apparatus capable of eliminating feudal particularism at the superstructural level was of the first order of importance. To this end he began depoliticizing the nobility, building a modern army, and neutralizing the Coptic Church.

To undercut the power of the nobility, the emperor issued a series of decrees prohibiting the aristocracy from having its own standing army and police force. In this way, the nobility was rendered impotent as a military aristocracy. In addition, the collection of agrarian taxes was centralized by the Ministry of Finance, thereby removing the nobility from public production apparatuses. The old aristocrats were either shipped out of the country as ambassadors or were assigned to distant regions as governors. Some of them occupied nominal positions in the Ethiopian parliament or in the Imperial Council of Advisors, where they were kept under the constant surveillance of the emperor.[67]

The manipulative strategy to depoliticize the aristocracy was carefully worked out. First, though deprived of their political power, the aristocrats were not affected economically. In fact, their economic position was further consolidated as they were rewarded with more land in return for acquiescence in their political subservience and loyalty. Assignments to peripheral regions of the empire also enabled them to snatch more land from the non-Abyssinian peasantry. For example, during his governorship in Illubabor and Kaffa between 1942 and 1955, Ras Mesfin acquired over 2 million hectares of land, excluding the estates he built in Shoa and Hararage. Another warload snatched 900,000 hectares in Hararage alone. Other lesser nobility grabbed up to 200,000 hectares in Sidamo.[68] Thus, loss of political power was overcompensated by the inclusion of the aristocracy in the control of production apparatuses.

Second, the centralized institutions of the state were cast in such manner as to ensure the continuance and solidification of Amhara dominance. In shuffling the Amhara nobility from one place to another, the emperor made every effort to assure that each move was consistent with the interest and destiny of the Amhara as a nation. The pattern of recruitment, retention, and elevation of his officials clearly reflected this phenomenon. For example, one study revealed that, between 1942 and 1966, the proportion of Shoan Amhara appointed to positions of vice minister and higher was 62 percent. For the same period, the numerical superiority of subprovincial Amhara governors in the non-Abyssinian regions was: Wellega—74 percent, Illubabor—80 percent, Kaffa—71 percent, Sidamo—81 percent, Arussi—90 percent, and Hararage—74 percent. In addition, some 70 percent of all district governors in these regions were of Amhara origin. Seventy percent of military officers were also Amhara.[69]

The third essential element in the depoliticization of the nobility was the role of the Coptic Church. The church provided the necessary elements of legitimation by mystifying the place of the emperor in Ethiopian society and spreading the idea of the divine right of emperorship. With the church behind him, the emperor transmogrified himself into a supernatural figure. In return for their legitimizing functions, the 20,000 Coptic churches and the 170,000 members of the clergy were generously rewarded with land grants. By harnessing religion to the modernizing imperatives of the state, the church increased its economic role in the agrarian structure. A somewhat deflated figure given by the central church treasury revealed that the total of church holdings in 1962 was 3.4 million hectares. But since various studies put the estimate of church land holdings at between 28 and 40 percent of the country's total arable land, the figure given by the church was certainly incomplete. In addition, when new agrarian tax laws were passed in 1967, the Coptic Church, which had received 11.5 percent of the total agrarian revenues, was exempted from taxation.[70] Thus, the clergy was as much interested in the preservation of the status quo as the emperor was.

Finally, the modernizing process had an external component. By capitalizing on foreign military assistance, the emperor built a modern 45,000 strong armed force supplemented by another 20,000-man territorial army and another 18,000 man police force.[71] The emperor was able to utilize this modern force to crush centrifugal forces, sometimes augmenting it by foreign assistance. For example, in the 1943 Weyane revolt in Tigrai, the emperor asked for British intervention in crushing the insurrectionists. British jets bombarded rebel concentrations and villages and even dropped bombs at a marketplace in the Tigraian capital, killing seventy persons and wounding many more innocent civilians.[72]

While the British fought alongside Ethiopia internationally to acquire Eritrea, they were also heavily involved in aiding the emperor to create a modern state machinery capable of coping with internal oppositions. This explains why British authorities, as we saw in Chapter 5, were overly concerned when the UN Commission for Eritrea proposed to visit many provinical centers in Ethiopia. They were nervous that members of the commission might see for themselves what Ethiopia was, thereby jeopardizing the chances of her acquiring Eritrea.

At any rate, this basic tendency in the Ethiopian state to weld into one entity the various traditional centers of power was facilitated by the introduction of dependent capitalism, which itself had an inherency toward centralization. To put it differently, the modernizing tendency toward uniformity in economic, political, legislative, and military development simulated the European pattern of state formation. Two fundamental factors, however, distinguished Ethiopian absolutism from other kinds. First, imperial centralization in Europe was accompanied by full-fledged capitalist development and by the consequent politicization of society with bourgeois ideas and values. In contrast, the process in Ethiopia, although able to contain the traditional forces of decentralization, took on the opposite direction, i.e., restriction of capitalist development and effective depoliticization of the Ethiopian society. The disarticulation between tradition and modernity was not so great as to warrant a bourgeois revolution resulting in the democratization and growth of modern institutions compatible with the bourgeois conception of government and society.

Second, unlike European absolutism, which was led to its eventual disintegration by the development of capitalism, Ethiopia's absolute monarchism benefited from two mutually reinforcing processes, namely the feudalization of the modern bureaucrats and the commercialization of the old aristocrats. These processes profoundly militated against the organic transformation of the Ethio-Eritrean federation into a genuine one.

By necessity, the emperor staffed his bureaucracy with members of the educated elite. To obtain their co-optation, he conferred land titles upon them. The net result of this allocation was that the Western-educated elitists found themselves in possession of abundant land for which they had to secure the labor of tenants, whereby they became absentee landlords. In becoming so, they were reduced to virtual impotence, unable to bring about any change in the status quo along the lines of bourgeois democracy, which obviated the possibility of any democratic development in Ethiopia. Thus, since restoration, the land allocation process moved in two directions. While more land was allocated to the nobility and clergy, another portion was granted to the strategic modern elite. Between 1941 and 1970, the government allotted 4.9 million hectares of land to these forces. Of this figure, no more than 20 percent went to the peasantry.[73]

Grants were intimately tied to political imperatives. For instance, after the restoration land grants averaged between 60,000 and 70,000 hectares per annum, but after the 1960 aborted coup, the grants averaged between 150,000 and 175,000 hectares per year, reflecting the emperor's concern with internal opposition to his rule both in Eritrea and in Ethiopia.[74] On the eve of the Ethiopian revolution, about 2 percent of the Ethiopian population thus owned 80 percent of the land, and between 65 and 80 percent of the peasants were tenants who surrendered between 50 and 75 percent of their produce to the landlords.[75] In a nutshell, the maintenance and strengthening of the feudal order became beneficial, not only to the old aristocracy, but also to the newly co-opted modern elite which were effectively feudalized. With this regressive metamorphosis of the modern elite, the possibility of any antifeudal democratic revolution also disappeared.

The regression of the strategic elite was reinforced by the commercialization of the nobility that controlled the capitalist networks. The emperor and members of his royal family actively participated in this process, often using foreign intermediaries to cover up their involvement. In the 1940s, aided by the appearance of Western commercial interests in the Horn, which stimulated the production and export of coffee, gold, and other raw materials, the royal family and the nobility quickly established monopolies over the important lifelines of the Ethiopian economy, thereby precluding the formation of an indigenous entrepreneurial class.[76]

The commercialization of the aristocracy was later extended to the agrarian sector. With the estimated potential of between 6 and 8 million hectares suitable for cultivation, coffee was a particular attraction. In the early 1950s only 90,000 hectares were under coffee cultivation. The commercial significance of this monocrop was dramatized when the export of coffee jumped from 15,000 tons in 1949 to an average of 65,000 tons in the early 1960s.[77] Coffee plantations were gradually supplemented by the introduction of agro-technology into such areas as sugar and cotton production. As a result of what came to be known as Ethiopia's green revolution, by 1974 there were five thousand agrocommercial plantations with 750,000 hectares under cultivation.[78]

Mechanization of agrocommercial plantations was stimulated by the exemption of import duties on fertilizers, farm machinery, tractors, and fuels. Agrarian investments above $200,000 U.S. were exempted from income tax for three to five years. Cheap farm credits were also made available through the Agricultural Development

Bank.[79] Mechanization, however, did not involve any trickle-down to the peasant masses. The agrarian structure and the credit arrangements simply favored the rich and excluded the poor. The Agricultural Development Bank, for example, did not grant loans below $5,000 Ethiopian, and a farmer had to prove entitlements to a minimum of 40 hectares of land in order to qualify for such loans.[80]

Mechanization had unintended consequences for the feudal order, however. Mechanization and agrocommercialization increased the value of the land and hence the rental demand for it. In consequence, thousands of tenants were evicted.[81]

The evicted tenants began drifting to the urban centers for menial employment. Thus, unemployment became one of the major problems facing the overextended imperialist state. Furthermore, the imperial bureaucracy reached the limits of its absorptive capacity. Every co-optation now entailed a major cost. The consequence was that as the modern segment of the Ethiopian population increased, the number of the educated elite excluded from the imperial bureaucracy also increased. Dependent capitalism, which was intended to help preserve and strengthen the feudal order, was instead undermining it. Herein lies the historic coincidence of Eritrean nationalism and the new capitalist forces in Ethiopia. Capitalism was grafted to the feudal order to give it stability, and Eritrea was acquired to aggrandize the Ethiopian empire. Both purposes became self-defeating in the end, as Eritrean nationalism and Ethiopia's new elements converged to destroy the feudal order. Eritrea's significance was that it gave depth and context to these new forces. In short, at the time when Eritrea was linked to Ethiopia, the emergence of a full-fledged feudo-commercial oligarchy resulting from the processes of feudalization of the strategic modern elite and the commercialization of the traditional forces was complete.

It was to this empire, run by this oligarchy, that Eritrea was linked under the guise of federation. Given the distribution of strength between the two countries, Eritrea was in no position to upturn the status quo in favor of a democratic process in which both partners of the federal arrangement could benefit. In substance, what was asked of the Eritrean nationalists was to agree to the reduction of their competence to the narrow interests of the Ethiopian oligarchy by accepting a pseudofederal arrangement. Having been denied its right to external self-determination, Eritrea was, in effect, also denied its right to arrange its internal life since the envisaged autonomy represented an inherent contradiction of the interests of the Ethiopian oligarchy.

By envisaging autonomy for Eritrea, the federal plan seems to have drawn a distinction between external self-determination, which was denied to Eritrea in view of its association with Ethiopia, and internal self-determination, in which the Eritreans were left to arrange their lives internally in accordance with their wishes. But in the absence of parallel development in Ethiopia, namely the institutionalization of democracy, any separation of the external from the internal was certainly a construction of subterfuges.

7

Evolution of the
Ethio-American Connection

THE FORMATION OF United States interests in Eritrea was essentially a by-product of the globalization of what has been euphemistically called American security interest. The development of a coherent U.S. policy toward Eritrea was conditioned by two factors. First, Eritrea provided a strategic contiguity of the Middle East. Though peripheral, Eritrea was considered a strategic buffer for the maintenance of U.S. interests in the area. The military rationale that the center should be protected did not preclude the need to protect the periphery.

Second, Eritrea attracted American strategists in view of the existence of an elaborate military infrastructure built by the Italians. As part of the war effort, the U.S. Army had already occupied these military installations. In keeping with global imperatives, the U.S. military establishment resolved to transform the temporary occupation of these installations in Eritrea into a permanent one.

Initially, U.S. economic interests in Eritrea were marginal. The only noticeable commercial interest was represented by the Arabian-American Oil Company which maintained an office in Asmara to recruit Eritrean workers for the Arabian oil fields. Shell also operated a sizable oil storage at Massawa for the U.S. Navy.[1]

Articulation of U.S. Interests in Eritrea

The United States was thus preoccupied mainly with the acquisition and maintenance of Radio Marina, the communications center in Asmara built by the Italians. After the U.S. Army took it in 1942, the United States expanded it. The center occupied three important sites in Asmara and had three station transmitters capable of receiving signals from all parts of the world. The geographical location of Asmara insulated these sites from atmospheric disturbances and seasonal variations, thus avoiding the necessity for numerous frequency changes. In addition to monitoring enemy radio communications, the center was used to relay military and diplomatic messages to and from U.S. ships in the Indian Ocean and the Mediterranean Sea.[2]

In the eyes of American strategists, these imperatives necessitated the disposition of Eritrea in such manner as to ensure U.S. dominance in Eritrea. Initial U.S. perception about Eritrea's susceptibility to communist infiltration precluded Eritrean independence. The perceived volatility of Ethiopian politics and her inherent internal instability also made the allocation of Eritrea to Ethiopia an undesirable option. Thus at the beginning, when the Eritrean question was being considered, the primary American option was to have Eritrea under either British or American control. The U.S. commanding officer of Radio Marina had confided to Robert Mason that "if U.N.O. decided to place this country under Ethiopia the station would have to be moved, possibly . . . to Cyprus or Kenya, subject to our consent. He said it would be a pity to move from Asmara, which was very suitable for their purpose, but it would be impossible to maintain it if the British were to leave."[3]

Nonetheless, the seeming intractability of the Eritrean problem and the turbulent state of international affairs eventually influenced the United States to settle for the allocation of Eritrea to Ethiopia under conditions that would ensure U.S. military dominance in Eritrea. Having obtained this desideratum, the United States turned to implementing its military plans in Eritrea. On 11 December 1950, just nine days after the adoption of the federation formula, Assistant Secretary of State McGhee suggested to Aklilou and Spencer that "some time before the implementation of the Eritrean federation resolution is completed representatives of the United States and Ethiopia should get together to discuss United States interests in a telecommunications base facility at Asmara and in an air and naval base facility at Massawa for use in times of emergency."[4] The Ethiopian response was of course positive. In light of these developments, in a progress report on policy document NSC/19-E, Undersecretary of State James Webb informed the National Security Council about the mutual satisfaction of Ethiopia and the United States over the acquisition of Eritrea and about the preliminary steps taken to formalize the U.S. presence there. In conveying this message, Webb said that "the principal strategic interest of the United States in Eritrea is in having the right to use certain military facilities in that territory. . . . United States strategic requirements call for the operational availability" of the "essential" bases and communications center in Asmara and Massawa.[5]

Although American policymakers exuded confidence that they would have no difficulty in consolidating their military hold on Eritrea, negotiations with Ethiopia became tougher than anticipated. The emperor was astutely prepared to squeeze more out of the United States by harnessing the negotiations on the defense installations in Eritrea to Ethiopian requests for U.S. arms and economic assistance. In fact, the emperor had three overriding goals. The first was to translate into reality the national myth that the traditional Ethiopian boundaries extended to the Indian Ocean. The Ethiopian file on Somalia was not yet closed, even though the latter was destined to be independent in 1960. The second was to build a strong national army capable not only of defending the gains, but also of expanding the frontiers of the empire. Third, Haile Selassie wanted to graft modern production apparatuses to the feudal order, not only to give it stability, but also to obtain the needed revenues to support the first two objectives. In these three areas, total U.S. commitment and assistance were critical. As early as March 1950 the emperor himself articulated these objectives to McGhee as requiring full U.S. support. In trying to justify his pleas for more U.S. aid, which would have included thirty fully equipped fighter planes, the emperor argued that "[w]ith the increase in national and international responsibilities resulting from the eventual return of Eritrea, it is necessary that these purchase orders . . . be completed with the least possible delay."[6]

Later, in a memorandum to the State Department, the emperor drew a connection between Ethiopia's military and economic modernization and her obligations to participate in the anticommunist crusade. He reasoned that it was "the duty of Ethiopia to suppress Communism" but the "suppression of Communism depends upon successful carrying out of his program of economic development however, Ethiopia's needs for economic assistance have been relatively ignored by US."[7]

These insistent pleas placed the American policymakers in an awkward position. They had to analyze Ethiopia's nagging demands for arms in light of U.S. legal requirements and Ethiopia's overall strategic utility to U.S. global security. Under the law, Ethiopia was not yet eligible for reimbursable assistance. Thus, without changes in existing legislation, the State Department could not grant her requests for more arms. And even with such changes, determination on Ethiopia's eligibility had to be made on the basis of a clear demonstration of her ability to defend herself or to "participate in defense of area of which she is a part is important to security of US." In addition to such legal and political requirements, the department cautioned that prior U.S. commitments to other areas might preclude Ethiopia from receiving any substantial quantity of arms in the foreseeable future.[8]

In an effort to narrow the widening rifts in U.S.-Ethiopian relations over the question of U.S. assistance, Ambassador Merrell recommended that a reputable American general be sent to the emperor with some shipment of arms in order to explain to him how the United States perceived Ethiopia's role in the defense of the free world.[9] The Office of International Security Affairs concurred with the ambassador's recommendation and sent a memorandum to the Department of Defense underlining the principal aspects of U.S.-Ethiopian relations. This involved the magnitude of U.S. military aid to Ethiopia and formalization of the U.S. military establishment in Eritrea. But the memorandum cautioned that the cost of military equipment sent to Ethiopia should not exceed the military importance of that country to the United States. It thus urged that the emperor should be placated by sending a high-ranking official to help him understand the objectives of American policy and the limits of his subservient role. "In addition to displaying American interest in Ethiopia it is felt he could explain to the Emperor our conception of Ethiopia's role in the defense of the non-Communist world and particularly to dissuade him from military expenditures beyond the capacity of his country."[10]

Despite the American explanation, Haile Selassie became even more determined to hold Eritrea hostage until the United States made generous concessions regarding the supply of arms and economic aid. Under these circumstances, the policymaking institutions in Washington began to scramble to find ways to at least partially satisfy Ethiopia's requests for assistance. In March 1951 the Department of State enunciated the overriding political imperatives as the prevention of communist influence over Ethiopia and maintenance of Ethiopia's pro-Western orientation, establishment of a stable administration "in the areas under Ethiopian sovereignty," and ensuring continuing Ethiopian participation in U.S.-sponsored international security arrangements. The department concluded that these imperatives would require the satisfaction of Ethiopia's demands.[11]

What made outright rejection of Ethiopia's requests for help extremely difficult was Ethiopia's participation in the Korean War, where she had sent 5,000 troops attached to the Seventh U.S. Army.[12] In supporting a move to satisfy Ethiopia, the department urged that the newly evolved U.S.-Ethiopian relations "would strengthen another weak area exposed to Communist penetration and subversion and thus contribute to the stability of the Near East and the Red Sea area."[13]

Since Ethiopia was important to U.S. security in the Red Sea basin because of the military installations in Eritrea, arming Ethiopia was also in American interest. But the American leaders deferred as to the amount of arms to be given to Ethiopia. The primary interest of the United States was to use Ethiopia effectively at the lowest possible cost without being required to meet all her requests for arms. Ethiopia's imperial ambition to emerge as a regional power by acquiring Somalia and by building a strong army was too expensive a venture for the United States to endorse. Hence, the most essential question was how to convince the emperor to accept his dependence on the West without straining the delicate relations. If Ethiopia were disgruntled, initiation of talks on the defense installations in Eritrea would be extremely difficult. American strategists finally concurred with the idea of sending a high-ranking general to Ethiopia to appease the emperor and possibly to ward off a repetition of his pleas for U.S. arms. For this purpose, Gen. Charles L. Bolte, Deputy Chief of Staff for Planning, U.S. Army, was selected to visit the emperor. An enlarged conference of the heads of various agencies was held in May 1951 to discuss the content of Bolte's mission. They agreed that Ethiopia had a minimal need for security against external aggression, but that a general security breakdown could occur in Eritrea after the federation was implemented. General Bolte foresaw the possibility that the Ethiopians might need U.S. arms to maintain internal security in Eritrea where the U.S. defense installations were located.[14]

In concurring with Bolte, McGhee added that "the emperor required armed forces to maintain law and order within Ethiopia itself since some of the tribal chiefs in some of the remote areas were inclined to be rebellious." McGhee then counseled that "General Bolte should give to the Ethiopians assurances in regard to whatever he thought could be provided within the framework of present legislation and regulations."[15]

Before his departure, Bolte was advised to emphasize to the emperor that the United States was not prepared to make any additional commitment unless it was absolutely vital to the defense of the free world. A further rationale was that no aggression against Ethiopia by her immediate neighbors was likely. The possibility of communist insurrection in Ethiopia was ruled out and its geographical location made direct Russian aggression a remote possibility.[16]

General Bolte successfully completed his mission to Ethiopia on 5 July 1951. In his report Bolte declared that he was assured by Spencer "informally that the Government of Ethiopia would welcome a continuance of the US Army Radio Station at Asmara, Eritrea." In return for this pledge, Bolte recommended that the United States should set up a training program in Ethiopia for the replacement of the Ethiopian contingent in Korea, should guarantee to protect Radio Marina, and should extend reimbursable military and economic assistance.[17]

Notwithstanding such mutual pledges, the two countries still delayed defining the exact role of Ethiopia in the global U.S. security network and the amount of arms Ethiopia should receive. The problem was complicated when Aklilou complained in a memorandum of 30 January 1952, that Ethiopia did not receive military assistance from the United States commensurate with her participation in the Korean War.[18] This Ethiopian complaint dragged out the talks over the defense installations. In October 1952, U.S. Secretary of State Acheson and Aklilou met in an apparent effort to break the stalemate in these talks. Aklilou argued that, if the Ethio-American agreement on base rights were confined to Eritrea alone, Ethiopia would be accused of disposing of Eritrea's rights shortly after her placement under Ethiopian sovereignty. His post hoc logic was that such accusations could be deflected only by broadening the base-rights agreement so as to include Ethiopia herself, that is, the United States should develop and use additional military facilities inside Ethiopia. He further contended that Ethio-American relations were one-sided in favor of the United States. As he noted, it was "customary for a bilateral agreement to be so framed that all the granting and giving is not reserved to one of the parties." His argument was that if Ethiopia concluded a military agreement in Eritrea without a suitable quid pro quo, "many European bees will want an equal right to sip the Ethiopian honey."[19]

Acheson was not persuaded by Aklilou's arguments and he resisted being outmaneuvered on the question of additional military facilities in Ethiopia. On 30 March 1953, another round of talks was held between high-ranking U.S. and Ethiopian delegations. Aklilou reiterated that Ethiopia was seeking a strategic partnership with the United States that would elevate Ethiopia to the status enjoyed by Greece and Turkey. In heated exchanges, Aklilou's cynical opportunism began to show when he disingenuously suggested that Ethiopia was more important to the United States than the Arab states with which the United States had a stronger relationship. Aklilou then tried to qualify his remarks by saying that Ethiopia "is neither for nor against the Arabs; she is neither for nor against 'Colonial Powers'." The message was clear. Ethiopia was a loyal ally to the United States insofar as the latter would not encounter any difficulty from Ethiopia in furthering her policy in the region.[20]

The Americans were not impressed with the Ethiopians' offer of additional military facilities as a means of squeezing more aid from the United States. Though the United States expressed gratification at the unique generosity of the Ethiopians to mortgage their country for military dollars, the American delegates graciously declined the offer. There was no compelling reason to incur additional costs for military redundancy when the United States already had unhampered access to Eritrea. As General John E. Hull, vice-chief of staff, U.S. Army, noted, "All the U.S. wants is a continuation of what we have in Eritrea." The general contended that what Ethiopia needed was not a heavily armed offensive army, but a lightly equipped mobile force to cope with the country's internal security needs. But he also warned that there should be no ambiguity as to questions involving the size of the Ethiopian army, its equipment, and the costs of equipping and operating it since these questions had to be grappled with by the Ethiopians themselves.[21]

The mutual intransigence of the two delegations finally resulted in a stalemate. In fact, the intractability of their relative positions had to do with the contradictory perceptions of the two countries about their relationship. The Americans approached the question from their postwar global ascendancy and gave Ethiopia a mere satellite status. On the contrary, the frame of reference for the Ethiopians was the nineteenth century, when they were able to establish regional hegemony by colluding with European powers and sometimes by playing one power against the other. Now the Ethiopians sought similar treatment and equality from the United States, and they never hesitated to remind the Americans that they could change their loyalty if their wishes were not met. The alternative they had in mind was of course the Soviet Union. This they had demonstrated in the late 1940s when the United States refused to supply Ethiopia with arms. The emperor had signed an $8 million arms deal with Czechoslovakia, including the construction of an ammunition plant in the Ethiopian capital. In 1949 the first shipment of 15,510 rifles and machine guns and about 2.8 million rounds of ammunition arrived in Ethiopia, and in 1950 Ethiopia received 20 tanks from Czechoslovakia.[22]

The Americans did not take lightly the possibility of an Ethiopian shift to the East. The United States was therefore first to give in. On 6 April 1953, Undersecretary of State Walter Smith, in a letter to the secretary of defense, proposed that the status of Ethiopia be elevated and that she receive preferential treatment in regard to U.S. military assistance. Smith remarked that the Ethio-American talks had hitherto made it "evident that the Ethiopians are not prepared to conclude the kind of base agreement we have been seeking without assurances for adequate military assistance from us." This assurance would involve furnishing essential arms and a military mission, which the Ethiopians considered "virtually as a gift."[23]

Smith recommended that Ethiopia be counted among Middle Eastern states so as to enable her to receive portions of the extraordinary funds of $26 million reserved for such expenditures. From Smith's point of view, both the elevation of Ethiopia's status and the granting of limited funds could be justified along the following lines: Ethiopia's contribution to the war effort in Korea had both propaganda and military value; arming Ethiopia would contribute to the defense and security of U.S. military installations in Eritrea; Ethiopia could turn to other powers for arms, in which case American influence, prestige, and interest would enormously suffer; and Ethiopia was willing to join any U.S.-sponsored military formation in the region.[24]

In a letter of 8 May, the secretary of defense concurred that Ethiopia's strategic location made it of direct importance to the defense of the Middle East and thus to the security of the United States. On the same day, Smith communicated to the director of mutual defense security requesting that the president of the United States should find Ethiopia eligible for U.S. grant military assistance. The letter noted that "for maximum effect on the negotiation of our base rights agreement with Ethiopia, it is important to obtain approval in principle of grant military aid before the Ethiopian Foreign Minister leaves Washington next week." Consequently, on 12 May President Eisenhower signed the finding that Ethiopia was eligible for full U.S. military assistance.[25]

On 22 May 1953 Walter Smith signed the Mutual Defense Assistance Pact, in the presence of Aklilou, providing for grant military aid. On the same day Ethiopia and the United States signed the Defense Installations Agreement covering U.S. base rights in Eritrea.[26] With the signing of these two military treaties, the process of transforming Eritrea from a European colony into a U.S. military fortress and an Ethiopian manor was complete.

U.S. Policy in Action

Upon the signing of the Defense Installations Agreement, Radio Marina was renamed Kagnew Station in honor of the Ethiopian contingent that had fought in Korea. The treaty gave the United States unbounded "rights, powers and authority . . . for the establishment, control, use and operation of the Installations for military purposes." Moreover, Article XVIII of the treaty provided for the exemption of the U.S. government and its contractors "from the customs laws and regulations of Ethiopia, including those relating to inspection and seizure, and from customs duties, taxes or any other charges imposed on materials, equipment, goods and supplies brought into, procured in, or taken out of Ethiopia and used in the construction, maintenance, support or operation of the Installations." U.S. military and civilian personnel in Eritrea were also exempted from similar economic obligations.[27]

Soon Kagnew Station became a $60 million military complex connecting Europe with the Far East in the U.S. global communications network. Initially it was staffed with 1,800 personnel, whose number progressively increased to 3,500. The United States paid Ethiopia about $12 million annually in the form of military aid.[28] In essence, then, Eritrea provided Ethiopia the military resources it needed for the containment and suppression of Eritrean nationalism. Furthermore, Ethiopia received huge quantities of U.S. arms plus a military mission to train the Ethiopian armed forces, much of which was used against the Eritrean insurrection.

Having stabilized her military relations with the United States, Ethiopia now shifted gears to seek economic aid. In June 1954, Aklilou led a high-level Ethiopian delegation to Washington for this purpose. A major part of his mission was to obtain U.S. partnership in the exploitation of Eritrea's resources, particularly in the areas of fishing and expanding the ports. Aklilou said that the development and expansion of the Eritrean ports of Massawa and Assab were critical to Ethiopia's political, military, and economic security. According to his projection, the development of the ports would involve 80 percent of Ethiopia's foreign exchange earnings, which the Ethiopian economy could not absorb without adverse economic consequences.[29]

With respect to the fishing industry, the Ethiopians claimed that the trawlers operating on the Eritrean coast were able to export 900,000 pounds of fish annually, and thus the potential for foreign exchange earnings was even greater if the fisheries were modernized. While appreciating the potential contribution of fishing to the Ethiopian and Eritrean economy, the Americans, however, contended that it was premature for the United States to extend the $2.5 million long-term loan requested for the development of fisheries in Eritrea without first making feasibility studies there.[30]

When the Ethiopians spoke of the development of the Eritrean ports, they meant expansion of Assab and not of Massawa. The Americans were curious to know why the Ethiopians placed the emphasis on the development of Assab while Massawa was the better port and Ethiopia was still making use of Djibouti to import goods destined for eastern and central Ethiopia. They also asked why Ethiopia had not taken the matter up with the World Bank where such financial assistance was usually handled. The Ethiopian reply was that the number of ships visiting Assab had increased by some 30 percent in tonnage. They contended that Massawa was farther from the regular sea-lanes than Assab, and would involve additional time losses for ships wishing to visit the Eritrean coast. They further argued that the use of Djibouti to import or export goods was not in Ethiopia's interest since the French were charging excessive dues. As to the option of obtaining the needed financial assistance from the World Bank, the Ethiopians argued that the French and the British would block their request applications.[31]

While the Ethiopian answers had some elements of truth, they certainly concealed important facts. The debate over the relative importance of Massawa versus Assab was purely political, and as such brought one fundamental element of difference between the United States and Ethiopia to the surface. From the American point of view, Massawa was of enormous strategic value, hence its development was warranted. In addition to having important oil storage facilities for the U.S. Navy, Massawa was an important air and naval base for the United States in times of emergency. There was also a political consideration. The development of Assab would attract more ships away from Djibouti, carrying goods destined for Ethiopia. This would have certainly intensified competition between Assab and Djibouti, much to the chagrin of the French. The United States became reluctant to subsidize Ethiopia's competitive edge at the expense of U.S. relations with France. These factors explain why the United States was hesitant to endorse Ethiopia's plans.

The Ethiopians had two fundamental reasons for ignoring the development of Massawa. For one thing, the commercial lifeline of the Eritrean hinterland was entirely dependent on the economic prosperity of Massawa, and choking it off would speed up the desired process of destroying the Eritrean economy. Second, the Ethiopians were well aware of what would be the logical consequences of their unilateral action to abrogate the federal structure some time in the future. In the event of Eritrean insurrection, it was certain that, as seen from experience, the transporting of goods to and from Massawa would be entirely disrupted. Their insistence on the development of Assab was intended to bypass the problems of such an eventuality. In addition, Ethiopians always thought that Assab could easily be detached from the rest of Eritrea and be placed under effective Ethiopian control without adverse economic or military disruptions.

As the discussions over the development of Assab became acrimonious, the Americans inquired whether the United States could finance other projects while Ethiopia used its own resources to finance the Assab project, in order to avoid political friction with the French. But Aklilou responded that he saw no reason for political embarrassment since the United States openly sponsored the Ethio-Eritrean federation, including the return of the ports to Ethiopia. He even asked to see higher officials in the U.S. government if this question was not resolved, at least in principle, immediately. Taken aback by Aklilou's remarks, John E. Utter, director of the State Department's Office of African Affairs, retorted that "principles" involved money. He added, "In our democratic government it takes time; perhaps in other forms of government decisions can be made sooner." Utter reminded Aklilou that the United States would never commit itself to long-term loans without meeting the requirements of the law and without studying Ethiopia's ability to repay and without the facts supporting the Ethiopian case.[32]

The message was clear and bitter; the Ethiopians had failed to convince their American counterparts. But Aklilou, accompanied by Spencer, was allowed to see Assistant Secretary of State Henry Byroade on 7 July 1954. In an apparent effort to placate the Ethiopians, Byroade emphasized that the potential for U.S. economic aid to Ethiopia was great, but had to be provided within the framework of U.S. legislation. Out of courtesy, he expressed regret for the misunderstanding over the Assab project, saying simply that there were no funds available for this project and suggesting that Ethiopia should make feasibility studies of the port. Once the economic analysis was completed, then the United States would consider Ethiopia's application for a loan. Byroade announced that the United States had allocated $500,000 in military aid as a demonstration of American good intentions while at the same time intimating that it had no connection to the economic discussions under way.[33] The message was clear: the Americans were trying to placate the Ethiopians by offering some aid so as not to risk their complete alienation.

The Ethiopians recognized the message, but Aklilou became even

more determined to pursue the Ethiopian case, which drew him into
more heated exchanges with Byroade. The latter now became crisp
in his responses and reiterated that the Assab project must be economically and financially justified, and should be financed through
ordinary loans by taking into account its profitability and ability to
amortize the debt. Byroade added that if, however, "the ports are
based on political and national necessity, some other approach might
be necessary."[34] Here Byroade touched the essence of the problem.
The project involved not a question of economics, but one of politics.
Though couched in diplomatic language, the reasons for Ethiopia's
insistence on the development of Assab were purely political, and
a political case could not be economically justified. Ethiopia feared
that an economic analysis might reveal this fact and might point to
developing Massawa as a rational economic undertaking. Aklilou
tried to evade the crux of the matter by suggesting that financial
receipts alone were not crucial to justify the importance of these ports
to the Ethiopian economy as a whole. Byroade replied that he understood "the political reasons for the ports," but that he still wanted
to know the economic aspect of the project.[35]

The net result of these heated exchanges was a stalemate, and the
Americans have never since offered to finance the project of Assab.
Nonetheless, for fear of disturbing the geostrategic context of its military presence in Eritrea, on 27 October 1954, the U.S. government
offered $3 million in military aid to Ethiopia.[36] It was hoped that
this would placate the Ethiopians, who had left Washington disap-
pointed four months earlier.

The immediate effect of this minor controversy over the Assab
project was that the United States refrained from saying anything
when Ethiopia began to criticize the substance of Eritrea's autonomy,
lest it antagonize her further. In fact, over time, the United States
came to appreciate Ethiopia's obsession with the potential danger of
Eritrean nationalism as much as Ethiopia shared U.S. apprehension
about the growing radicalism of Nasserite Egypt. Against this background of a deepening military relationship, on 26 December 1957,
the two countries signed yet another agreement under which the U.S.
provided military equipment, materials, technical advice, and services. A major segment of this agreement reads: "The purpose of
this program is to increase the capacity of Ethiopia to produce, maintain, repair or overhaul military equipment and materials used for

the purposes of common defense, such increased capacity being needed for the mutual defense of the free nations of the world."[37]

After the 1960 coup, the United States and Ethiopia signed another secret agreement under the terms of which the United States offered to train, equip, and modernize the some 40,000 Ethiopian armed forces. The United States once again "reaffirmed its continuing interest in the security of Ethiopia and in its opposition to any activities threatening the territorial integrity of Ethiopia."[38] This assistance was aimed at the containment and suppression of Eritrean nationalism, the prevention of a general security breakdown in Ethiopia, facing the Somali challenge over the Ogaden, and enabling Ethiopia to participate in regional security arrangements if and when called upon by the United States. The proximity of the U.S. defense installations in Eritrea to the operational base of the nationalists was particularly of concern to the United States. Thus, direct U.S. involvement in the suppression of Eritrean nationalism was significant in the 1960s. A U.S. advisory group was attached to the Ethiopian Second Army Division in Eritrea, and the United States gave aerial support to the Ethiopian ground forces. The United States even gave 2,000 tons of wheat to Ethiopia to recruit peasant workers to build a military airstrip at Keren, close to the base areas of the nationalists.[39] When the Eritrean nationalists began to obtain international visibility, in 1964, the United States sent a team of counterinsurgency experts, and in 1966 she sent more than 100 counterinsurgency advisors to Eritrea for a period of three years, under the scheme known as Plan Delta, to help the Ethiopian army deal with the military situation there.[40]

The Ethio-American connection had an Israeli component. Ethio-Israeli relations dated back to 1958 when Israel proposed the formation of an alliance of non-Arab states, including Ethiopia, to counter pan-Arabism and the spread of communism in the region. But since Ethiopia did not want to widen the anti-Ethiopian front in the region, the idea never materialized. Nonetheless, a cordial relationship between the two countries continued to deepen over the years. For example, Israel was credited with playing a critical role in aborting the 1960 coup against the emperor. Together with the American forces in Eritrea, Israeli officers coordinated the campaign of the loyalists to quell the insurrectionists.[41] Thereafter, the Israeli military commitment in Eritrea steadily increased. Israel maintained a group of counterinsurgency experts in Eritrea attached to the Ethiopian army. After 1964, Israeli officers were charged with the task of recruiting, training, and equipping the notorious counterinsurgency commandos. Members of this military elite were even sent to Israel for advanced training. In addition, Israeli officers gave special assistance to the Ethiopians at the company and battalion levels. It was even reported that Israeli officers took part in the Ethiopian offensive of 1976 to relieve the besieged town of Naqfa from the Eritrean guerrillas.[42]

According to Israeli and American defense analysts, the Israeli anti-Eritrean posture was primarily motivated by security concerns. Israel viewed the Eritrean revolution essentially as an extension of pan-Arabism. Eritrean independence was thus perceived as facilitating a potential Arab blockade of the Red Sea whereby Israeli commercial vessels would be subject to constant harassment. In this sense, Israeli involvement in Eritrea was considered a preemptive military exercise against Eritrean nationalism. In addition, Israel wanted to forge important links with influential African states to weaken Afro-Arab solidarity, which was considered prejudicial to the Arab-Israeli conflict. As the seat of the Organization of African Unity (OAU), Ethiopia was considered a key link in this Israeli effort. The Israeli presence in Eritrea and Ethiopia was considered essential, enabling Israel to exert pressure on the Arab states from the western shores and southern tip of the Red Sea. Needless to say, Israel could supply arms to the Southern Sudanese Liberation Front only through Eritrea and Ethiopia.[43]

A closer look at these reasons, however, makes the analysis superficial. As Tom Farer cogently argued, there are higher factors that would militate against such a threat to Israel's security. First, the potential blockade of the Red Sea or harassment of Israeli ships in the area by any Arab state would necessarily entail Israeli countermeasures. Such undertakings would also drain the economic and military resources of the most important Arab states, like Egypt, that have the capacity to undertake a blockade. To put it differently, the Arab states are as vulnerable, if not more, as Israel is to any blockade of the Red Sea since that action would have wider international ramifications. Second, access to additional military facilities in Eritrea would not in any way enhance the capacity of the Arab states to attack or harass Israeli ships in the Red Sea. The Arab states already possess important air and naval facilities in the Yemens, Saudi Arabia, the Sudan, Egypt, and Somalia. Eritrea's contribution to such a military configuration would then amount to redundancy. A third factor is that Israeli air superiority and the capacity for long-range flight and midair fueling, plus the availability of a strong Israeli navy equipped with long-range missiles, make the idea of a blockade an improbable project. Fourth, historical experience shows that Eritrean nationalists would be guided more by prudent raison d'être than by any revolutionary fervor that might link them to pan-Arabism.[44]

If the above analysis is correct, Israeli motivation for involvement in Eritrea was purely political. Israel has been fighting against diplomatic isolation by the concerted efforts of Arab states. Thus, the argument in favor of forging an alliance with Ethiopia as a countermeasure to Arab diplomacy is plausible. Moveover, the Ethio-Israeli alliance against the Arabs was readily facilitated by their shared traditional anti-Arab orientation. Another motivation is economic. Several Israeli companies owned meat- and fish-processing plants and agro-commercial plantations in Eritrea and Ethiopia, and they were active in the construction sector. In any event, the addition of Israel to the Ethio-American equation was a most welcomed development for Ethiopia since she was the chief beneficiary of this triangular relationship. Israeli officials and pro-Israeli forces in the United States actively lobbied on behalf of Ethiopia for the aid she received from the United States. This, in part, explains why Ethiopia was able to receive more than one-half of the total U.S. military aid to Africa and about one-fifth of its economic aid to the continent.

Between 1953 and 1976, Ethiopia received $279 million in military aid and $350 million in economic assistance. In the same period, 3,555 Ethiopian officers received their military training in the United States. In 1973, half of the 3,055 Ethiopian students abroad were enrolled in American universities. Furthermore, on the eve of the Ethiopian revolution in 1974, of the $593 million (Ethiopian dollars) external debt of the country, $532 million was owed to the United States or to U.S.-dominated international financial institutions.[45] The United States was also Ethiopia's major economic partner, absorbing 38 percent of Ethiopia's total export, including 70 percent of its coffee. For example, in 1973, the United States absorbed $72 million of Ethiopia's $187 million export.[46]

In the wake of the Ethiopian revolution, the Ford administration,

on Secretary of State Henry Kissinger's insistence, even accelerated
its military aid to Ethiopia in an apparent effort to forestall Eritrean
independence. For example, U.S. military aid to Ethiopia increased
from $23.9 million in 1974 to $37.6 million in 1975 and to $41.9
million in 1976. The cash sale of arms also increased from $5 million
to $20 million in 1975 and $200 million in 1976.[47] The administration
tried to justify its involvement in the newly erupted Ethio-Eritrean
war for the control of Asmara through distortions of historical facts.
During a congressional hearing on the Ethio-Eritrean conflict, Acting
Secretary of State for African Affairs Edward Mulcahy, for example,
falsely reported that "the UN conducted a plebiscite" in Eritrea and
that the federal compromise was a product "of conflicting objectives
on the part of the population for the future of the territory." Moreover, in a reply to a question as to what sparked the Eritrean insurgency, Mulcahy incorrectly claimed that "there was a sentiment
within Ethiopia, a sentiment shared by a large part of the population of Eritrea, for complete integration into Ethiopia as the 14th
province. . . . [B]ut it is my understanding that the Eritrean Parliament voted to divest itself in effect of the autonomous status that
had been guaranteed and to accept a provincial status in Ethiopia.
This was done as a result of a democratically elected parliament."[48]

Certainly, this statement is an obvious distortion. Using the same
logic, he might have said that the U.S. Congress could compromise
U.S. independence in the name of integration if it wished to do so
because it was elected democratically. The real question is, if there
really was a shared sentiment for integration on the part of the
Eritreans and if the federation was abolished democratically, what
else could spark an Eritrean insurgency and how could it be sustained
without popular support? This deception by the administration reveals that the United States was still reluctant to acknowledge the
abnormality of the federal arrangement and the U.S. role in it, much
less the illegality of the unilateral abrogation of the federal act.

Many expected that the U.S. government would intervene in the
Ethiopian revolution on behalf of the emperor to the extent of using
the Eritrean movement as a counterforce to the military regime. Instead, the United States opted to forge a new alliance with the
Dergue. A constellation of reasons explains this continuity. The first
had to do with the strategic depreciation of both Eritrea and Ethiopia
in the wake of technological breakthroughs in satellite communica-

tions. Eritrea had been chosen for its ideal geographic location that insulated the communications center from the vicissitudes of atmospheric change, but the use of sophisticated satellites diminished Eritrea's strategic utility and hence the military facilities there reached their diminishing return. In 1974 the United States had already begun to phase down its radio facilities in Eritrea. In March 1975 there were only 44 military personnel in Eritrea running the defense installations, which had once been staffed by 3,500. In addition, an alternative to Eritrea was found in Diego Garcia, thereby reducing the potential vulnerability of U.S. bases in Eritrea to hostile attacks, possibly by Eritrean nationalists. In light of these significant changes in technology, the United States saw the political developments in Ethiopia as not menacing enough to warrant active involvement to rescue the emperor.

Second, the United States had urged the emperor to pursue a policy of "stability with progress," by taking such important measures as land reform, modernization of the judicial system, devolution of power, and partial restoration of Eritrea's rights. These suggestions were not accepted favorably. Moreover, it is suggested that the United States was taken aback by the emperor's attitude to the tragic famine of 1973, in which 4 million people were affected and about 200,000 died. Consequently, Washington saw continued association with the emperor as an international liability.[49]

The third rationale for the U.S. decision not to support Eritrean nationalism was that sudden cessation of arms to Ethiopia would result in Eritrean independence whereby the capacity of the Arab states to control the Red Sea would be greatly enhanced, posing a security and economic danger to Israel. The logic here was that, inasmuch as Eritrea was widely perceived as the extension of pan-Arabism, Ethiopia was regarded as the extension of Israel's security zone.[50]

Fourth, the consummation of Eritrean nationalism was seen as setting a precedent that might trigger balkanization trends in Ethiopia and throughout Africa, with implications that might upset regional strategic balances. It was further argued that if the United States permitted this to happen, her international credibility would be considerably damaged. As Mulcahy stated, "Moreover, the black African states do not want to see the disintegration of Ethiopia. . . . They would be very critical of us if we were to withdraw our support from the Ethiopian Government at this crucial time. Some African states have, in fact, already expressed to us in confidence their deep concern for the present situation."[51]

Finally, American decision makers had developed a strong sense of natural alliance with the Ethiopians. Having internalized this sense into a conventional dogma, they developed categorical imperatives based on the following clichés: (1) being the second most populous state in Africa, Ethiopia has great market potential; (2) Ethiopia's traditional anti-Arab orientation and pro-Western posture have been critical to the security of Israel and the West; (3) by virtue of her being the seat of the OAU, and because of the diplomatic preeminence she enjoys in Africa, Ethiopia has been the key link in U.S.-Africa policy; (4) for reasons of geopolitics, whoever controls Ethiopia also dominates the Horn of Africa with enhanced capacity to monitor and control developments in the Red Sea basin and in the northwestern quadrant of the Indian Ocean; (5) all other elements in the Horn of Africa, including Eritrea and Somalia, have been seen as satellites that revolve around this centripetal force called Ethiopia; thus failing to control Ethiopia would necessarily result in the satellite elements falling apart to the detriment of vital American interest in the area. Encapsulated in this form, this strategic myth gave birth to the continuity thesis in U.S. foreign policy.

The End of Pax Americana

The year 1977 saw a dramatic souring in Ethio-American relations. This was triggered by a series of events that neither the United States nor the Dergue could control. The Dergue resisted paying compensation for American firms that were nationalized in 1975. The most dramatic political event, however, was the palace coup by Colonel Mengistu Haile Mariam on 3 February, in which seven of his most powerful contenders were murdered. Within twenty-four hours, Mengistu received a succession of congratulatory messages from Moscow, Havana, and other Eastern European capitals. This development set the tone for what was to follow. Thereafter, Ethiopia officially condemned U.S. imperialism by name and the CIA was used as a scapegoat for Ethiopia's political and economic malaise. Moreover, it was during this time that the Dergue's campaign known as the Red Terror, launched against the left oppositionist forces, reached its climax.

The Carter administration responded by numbering Ethiopia among dictatorships charged with gross human-rights violations. Subsequently, Congress was informed of a substantial reduction in U.S. military aid to Ethiopia, with only $10 million projected for 1978. The number of U.S. military advisors in Ethiopia was reduced to less than half. In justifying these actions, the deputy assistant secretary of state for African affairs told a Congressional committee: "Let me first say that we are very much concerned by the use of American military equipment in suppressing indigenous movements inside Ethiopia. Obviously people are getting killed. . . . We are also concerned by the gross violations of human rights in Ethiopia."[52]

The assistant secretary stressed that the administration was merely scaling down the grant assistance to Ethiopia, not eliminating it. He rationalized the continuance of limited U.S. military aid to Ethiopia on the basis of three factors: retention of a long-standing relationship with Ethiopia should not be disturbed by regime changes; forestalling any precipitation of the Dergue's shift to the Soviet Union for arms supply was essential; and continued arms assistance to Ethiopia would serve as a "balancing factor on the Horn." By the same token, the official indicated the painful dilemma facing the administration. "I will tell you very frankly that it is a very difficult decision to make because we would be reluctant to abandon Ethiopia to total Soviet domination. On the other hand, we do not want to see our weapons used in this fashion."[53]

The Carter administration was, however, outpaced by developments in Ethiopia. In counterreaction to the American administration's action, on 23 April the Dergue announced the closure of all U.S. military facilities in Eritrea and Ethiopia and all military personnel were ordered to leave immediately. On 27 April the United States reacted by announcing the suspension of all military aid to Ethiopia, including the delivery of $65 million worth of arms already paid for.[54] Unlike the protracted evolution of Ethio-American relations in the 1940s, the termination of these relations in the 1970s was abrupt and cataclysmic. The immediate international ramification was that every step in the weakening of the Ethio-American connection contributed considerably to the deepening of Ethio-Soviet relations.

As many commentators have rightly suggested, there were mutual barriers to any meaningful U.S.-Dergue alliance. First, the frequent reports of mass executions in Ethiopia and military repressions in

Eritrea had become a source of constant international embarrassment for the United States. For the Dergue, too, maintaining relations with the United States, which had already become a target of the Ethiopian revolution, was perceived as detrimental to the socialist credentials of the regime. It was inconsistent with the Dergue's ideology to be dependent on the United States, the leading supporter of the previous regime. Second, the Dergue's pro-Soviet orientation was more in keeping with its policy of nationalization and reign of terror. Alliance with the Soviet Union was also intended to undercut seriously much of the support given to Eritrea by pro-Soviet countries. Third, the conservative pro-American Arab states in the Red Sea basin had increasingly adopted a hostile attitude toward the Dergue and thus gave an added incentive to the United States to minimize relations with the Dergue.[55]

In any event, the estrangement in Ethio-American relations touched off a new controversy over whether to continue or modify U.S. policy toward Ethiopia. The controversy was played out between Zbigniew Brzezinski, the national security advisor, and Cyrus Vance, the secretary of state. The debate was essentially an effort to solve complex problems of the Horn by traditional methods. The elements of the debate were subsumed under the familiar intellectual perspectives of globalism versus regionalism; that is, one side was concerned with the interrelationship of the Horn to global geopolitical concerns while the other sought to evaluate U.S. policy options in the Horn within a regional context.[56]

Paradoxically, the rebel against the continuity thesis was Brzezinski, Kissinger's co-ideologue in matters pertaining to Soviet international behavior. In his view there was a direct correlation between Soviet involvement in Ethiopia and its international behavior or its larger global strategy. He further argued that the turbulent situation in the Horn "offered an opportunity to damage the Soviets by tying them down in a costly and endless struggle and even forcing them to back down in a confrontation."[57]

Brzezinski urged Carter to deploy a naval force to the region, to provide air cover to Somali ground forces, and to funnel military aid to Eritrean nationalists in order "to tie down the Soviets and Cubans in a bloody and inconclusive struggle."[58] Brzezinski pursued this line to the extent of invoking the principle of linkage between Soviet involvement in the Horn and detente. In his words, "The Soviets must be made to realize that detente, to be enduring, has to be both comprehensive and reciprocal. If the Soviets are allowed to feel that they can use military force in one part of the world—and yet maintain cooperative relations in other areas—then they have no incentive to exercise any restraint."[59]

Vance's rebuttal was premised on an entirely different view of Soviet international behavior. He contended that Brzezinski's "grand design interpretation" of Soviet behavior was essentially flawed and that the situation in the Horn was a paradigm case of Soviet exploitation of targets of opportunity created independent of Soviet international activism. He said that Ethiopian nationalism would in the long run be strong enough to preclude any permanent establishment of Soviet presence in the Horn as relations between the two countries would inevitably sour, resulting in Ethiopia's pro-Western reorientation. In keeping with this analysis, Vance argued in favor of retaining a political pipeline with Mengistu while simultaneously strengthening relations with other forces in the region. Vance regarded position of open hostility toward Ethiopia as counterproductive inasmuch as it would deepen Ethio-Soviet relations.[60]

In this inconclusive debate, the Eritrean question was overshadowed by the Ethio-Somali conflict. In suggesting the funneling of arms to the Eritrean nationalists, what Brzezinksi had in mind was making tactical use of the Eritreans as a counterforce against the Ethiopian regime so as to weaken the Soviet presence in the region. For Vance, the Eritrean question was tangential to the strategic debate, since in his mind Eritrea constituted simply an internal Ethiopian problem.

The Eritrean question began to loom as a policy problem for the Carter administration only in March 1978 after the decisive defeat of the Somalis in the Ogaden. The attention to Eritrea was prompted by two overriding considerations. First, the administration saw the Eritrean question as the key element of destabilization in the Horn, ensuring the ungovernability of the region under Soviet dominance, and thus precluding the consolidation of pax Sovietica. Second, just as South African intervention in Angola provided the pretext for active Soviet-Cuban militarism, the presence of Somali troops in the Ogaden provided an ostensible justification for Cuban military intervention on Ethiopia's side. In such a situation, the administration feared that active American countermeasures could be interpreted by African states as support for Somali aggression against Ethiopia's "territorial integrity." However, there was at least tacit international understanding that the Eritrean insurgency was provoked by Ethiopia's systematic denunciation of Eritrean autonomy and that the parameters of the nationalists' objectives were indigenously determined.

Moreover, there was no physical presence in Eritrea of outside forces on the side of the nationalists to justify any Cuban military action. Thus, if the Cubans intervened, their action would set an entirely new precedent on the African continent, upsetting regional equilibria. If legitimized in Eritrea, the next targets of opportunity for the deployment of Cuban troops could be Zaire or Namibia. Given this perception, containment strategy thus became the American approach.

In early April, as Soviet and Cuban involvement in Eritrea became imminent, the U.S. administration embarked upon a new offensive to contain and limit the damage of Cuban military presence in the Horn. On 3 April in a speech before the Nigerian Institute of International Relations in Lagos, President Carter officially denounced the feverish preparations by the Soviets and Cubans for military action in Eritrea. He observed that "military intervention of outside powers or their proxies in such disputes too often makes local conflicts even more complicated and dangerous and opens the door to a new form of domination. We oppose such domination, such intervention."[61]

These concerns were echoed in European, particularly in British, public opinion. On 5 April an Eritrean support committee in the British House of Lords was formed. Its stated aims were to publicize the Eritrean quest for national self-determination and independence, to give out information about the horrendous situation in Eritrea, to dissuade external powers from intervening in Eritrea, and to bring the plight of Ethiopian prisoners of war in Eritrea, whose existence the Dergue repudiated, to the attention of the world.[62] This certainly contributed to a chilling in Anglo-Ethiopian relations and for a while it seemed that the Eritrean case was gathering steam in the West. On 8 April Dr. David Owen, the Labourite foreign secretary, publicly urged the United Nations to speak out against the feverish Soviet and Cuban preparations for military offensive in Eritrea.[63]

Earlier, on 7 April the U.S. State Department, in a written statement to the press, reiterated the growing concerns of the West about

Cuban engagement in Eritrea. The statement noted that "the imposition of a military solution (in Eritrea) through the use of foreign forces would only increase the bloodshed and suffering, would not be durable and would not contribute to a reduction in regional tensions. Unfortunately we have information that the number of Cuban military personnel in Eritrea is increasing and there is evidence that they have engaged in combat."[64]

The Carter administration, however, did not extend its concerns over Eritrea beyond verbal condemnation to concrete diplomatic actions. Even when the Eritrean nationalists were driven back from the areas they had gained during the 1975–77 period, the administration watched the military imbalance in Eritrea with indifference. The Eritrean problem was soon overshadowed by developments in Iran and Afghanistan, to which the administration diverted attention. Now, the U.S. fear of a serious disruption of oil flow from the Persian Gulf as a result of Soviet presence in the region almost became a reality. Econometric projections did not help to assuage the fears of the administration about this possibility. According to a 1979 report, the gulf states owned 364.8 billion barrels of the total proven reserves of 445 billion barrels owned by OPEC as a whole, and produced an average of 20.7 million barrels a day of the total 30.6 million barrels a day produced by OPEC.[65] According to 1980 estimates of the Congressional Budget Office, the interruption of Saudi oil alone for a period of one year would cost the United States some $272 billion, would increase unemployment by 2 percent, and raise inflation by 20 percent. In addition, it would slash the U.S. gross national product (GNP) by 5 percent and that of Europe and Japan by 7 percent and 8 percent, respectively. A complete cutoff of total gulf oil for one year, on the other hand, would slash the U.S. GNP by 13 percent, Europe's by 22 percent, and Japan's by 25 percent.[66]

In light of these economic scenarios, the imbalance in the military configuration, both in the Horn and in the gulf region, heightened the strategic importance of the Horn. The Eritrean question was pushed to the back burner, if not entirely forgotten.

Contrary to ideological rhetoric, the installation of the Reagan administration in 1981 brought no change in U.S. policy toward Eritrea. It simply reiterated the continuity thesis with two overriding objectives in place. The first involved the ouster of the Soviet Union from the Horn as a precondition to bringing Ethiopia back to the Western orbit, thereby eliminating the Soviet threat to the gulf region and to southwest Asia. The second objective was to obtain military facilities in the Horn of Africa. As Acting Assistant Secretary of State Walker stated, "We do not believe that our search for these facilities will exacerbate tensions in the area or draw us into local conflicts."[67] This was in effect a reaffirmation of the traditional U.S. policy not to support Eritrean nationalism or the Somali claim to the Ogaden, in order to avoid any conflict with Ethiopia. As Walker contended, Ethiopia was in control of Eritrea and the Ogaden; as a result, the administration would have time to review U.S. policy options in the area. In Walker's terms, "In effect, this current equilibrium on the ground does not drive the United States to make urgent policy decisions."[68]

Another imperative for the Reagan administration was to build on what Carter had started before leaving office, i.e., economic and military consolidation of the front-line states in the Horn of Africa. For example, in August 1980, the Carter administration and Somalia had already signed an agreement under which the U.S. provided $40 million in military credit assistance, $5 million in budgetary support, and $11 million for Somali port development in return for military access to Somali facilities.[69]

In keeping with this, in 1981 the Reagan administration announced that 39 percent of the total U.S. military and economic assistance to Africa would be devoted to the coastal states in the Indian Ocean and the Red Sea. For fiscal year 1982, the administration proposed $401.3 million in military and economic assistance to the Sudan, Somalia, and Kenya.[70] Further assistance to Ethiopia was subsumed under humanitarian aid. Moreover, for all intents and purposes, all commercial relations with Ethiopia were left intact.

Despite such efforts to placate Ethiopia by not supporting the Eritrean movement, the Reagan administration expressed disappointment in Ethiopia. Walker acknowledged that the United States was "not sure what signals the Ethiopians are trying to send us and their own neighbors. Thus far the effect of their attacks has far outweighed the tentative conciliatory steps they have taken."[71]

Notwithstanding such complaints and setbacks, the administration still refused to accept the legitimacy of the Eritrean question. The United States simply continued to harp on the continuity thesis and on the geostrategic importance of the Horn to U.S. regional security in which Ethiopia was the key element. On 27 April 1983, Chester Crocker, assistant secretary of state for African affairs, tried to justify this policy: "Our strategic interests in the Horn of Africa are strictly corollary to our broader interests in southwest Asia and the Indian Ocean, and our military activity in the Horn, including our acquisition of access rights in Kenya and Somalia, is directed at protecting these larger interests. We harbor no hostility toward Ethiopia, a nation with which we have a history of long and close ties even if we have had differences in recent years; we recognize and fully support the sovereignty and territorial integrity of all the states of this region, including Ethiopia."[72]

Crocker's remarks set the tone for the rest of the Reagan era. In pledging allegiance to Ethiopia's territorial integrity, Crocker was sending a signal that U.S. posture toward the Horn was premised on the repudiation of Eritrean nationalism and Somali claims to the Ogaden. Thus, the Reagan administration left no mark on the Ethio-Eritrean conflict.

In summation, successive American administrations, from Truman to Reagan, faithfully adhered to the unbroken continuity thesis in regard to U.S. foreign policy toward the Horn of Africa, where they created a fundamental regional imbalance by sponsoring the Ethio-Eritrean federation. The initial U.S. perception about Eritrea was that it was susceptible to communist penetration and thus was a danger to U.S. military interest in the area. The historical paradox is, however, that Soviet penetration occurred, not in Eritrea, but in Ethiopia, a country the United States had regarded as the bulwark against the spread of communism. American policymakers have not yet acknowledged their political error in regard to the regional configuration or the possible injustice toward the cause of the Eritrean people.

8

The Ethiopian Revolution and the Ethio-Soviet Connection

EVERY REVOLUTION INVOLVES historically complex and politically loaded questions that seek immediate resolution. The 1974 Ethiopian revolution was one of those cataclysmic social revolutions that took both the forces of reaction and the agents of change by surprise. The revolutionary convulsions stirred more violent conflicts than could be resolved and unleashed forces too large to control. Agrarian reforms, state power, the institutionalization of political democracy, and the outright repudiation of age-old national oppression were all monumental tasks that required the formulation and implementation of revolutionary strategies.

But precisely because state power was not conquered by the agents of change, the Ethiopian revolution was deflected from its historic course and hence failed to resolve the Eritrean problem within a democratic framework. Two major factors led to the early abortion of the Ethiopian revolution: the emergence of the military as a dominant element in Ethiopian politics and the intervention of the Soviet Union.

In retrospect, the fragmentation of both Ethiopian revolutionaries and Eritrean nationalists contributed considerably to the political solidification of the Dergue by allowing it to steal their revolutionary slogans. In search of a social base, the Dergue tried to substantiate its revolutionary credentials by taking drastic steps that included the nationalization of land and industrial enterprises. The purpose was to harness the urban and rural production apparatuses to the central state and thereby to ensure the consolidation of political power and the continued collection of economic surpluses. These steps were eventually translated into total alienation of the revolutionary forces from their potential social bases as the Dergue was able to develop its own universal version of socialism by moving from one end of the political spectrum to the other.

These desperate moves by the Dergue were externally reinforced as the Soviets began to intervene on its side. Here, too, Eritrean nationalists and Ethiopian revolutionaries watched the growing Soviet-Dergue relations with indifference. They grossly underestimated the Dergue's ability to speak the language of socialism and the extent of Soviet opportunism. Instead of exposing the initial Soviet moves, the anti-Dergue forces continued to appeal for Soviet ideological and political support. They even released congratulatory fliers when the Soviets began to engross themselves in the Angolan crisis, supporting the Popular Liberation Movement of Angola (the MPLA). They forgot that what they were watching on the historic mirror was the image of their own future. Once the Soviets were entrenched in Ethiopia, it became too late for Eritrean nationalists and Ethiopian revolutionaries to undo what had been done by political ineptitude and cowardice and by their own timid evasions of ideological debate.

This chapter will bring into focus the implications and results of the Soviet-Cuban intervention for the Eritrean movement.

Soviet Search for Dominance

Opinions diverge on the underlying motivation of Soviet interventionism in Horn affairs. Almost all analysts use the same data in formulating the thrust of their respective arguments, but reach different conclusions. This suggests that the contradictory propositions about Soviet behavior stem from the struggle between intellectual perspectives, rather than from the objective identification of causality. A brief review of these contending approaches to Soviet international behavior is in order to shed some light on why the Soviets exchanged the Eritreans and the Somalis for the Ethiopian military regime.

The Western conservative intellectual orientation points to the inherent inability of African states to resist the ideological blandishments offered by the Soviet Union. Hence Soviet advances in the

Horn and other parts of Africa are essentially viewed as part of a larger historical process destined to undermine Western interests and influences by capitalizing on Africa's vulnerability. Recent Soviet moves in Ethiopia and Afghanistan are cited as evidence of Soviet global strategy to outflank Western interests in the Red Sea and the gulf region. The emphasis of this perspective is that Soviet support for the development of a military infrastructure, training, arms transfer, and establishment of military networks will in the long run be sufficient to bring about both the quantitative and the qualitative transformation of the African state into one capable of a pro-Soviet status quo.[1]

A more liberal interpretation of Soviet behavior in Africa holds that recent Afro-Soviet relations are essentially aberrant phenomena. The premise is that since the Soviets offer only instruments of liberation from colonial domination and repression rather than instruments of development, African nationalism and nonaligned postures will in the long run preclude any permanent Soviet presence in Africa. The argument runs further that the inherently unstable African political and ideological formations have nothing to do with either capitalism or communism. If anything, they reflect the transitional character of African polities, such as in Ethiopia, during which time the USSR might obtain temporary influence. From this benign analysis flows an optimistic conclusion that, once stability is achieved, the African regimes will reorient themselves toward the general direction of the West.[2]

It is worth noting that U.S. foreign policy toward the Horn has hitherto been premised on this optimistic orientation. The political prescription has been that persistence and perseverant waiting are essential until significant cracks in Ethio-Soviet relations develop and stability is achieved. If Afghanistan is a premier model, this perspective may be right. Passionate believers in the dialects of international power politics may agree on this assessment. But the conditions and forms under which the Soviets will eventually leave the Horn remain to be seen.

In any event, other analysts assume away the previous two perspectives as oversimplifications of Africa's order and disorder. Instead, such international commentators as Dimitri Sims and David Albright have been peddling the notion of Soviet opportunism as an explanation for recent Soviet interventionism in the Horn and elsewhere.

The gist of their argument is that the contemporary militarization of Africa has its own logic, which has manifested itself in such forms as Southern African and Eritrean insurgencies, the collapse of the ramshackle empire of Ethiopia and of other weak states, and cross-border conflicts like the one between Ethiopia and Somalia. These objective conditions have thus offered a wide range of openings for Soviet penetration.[3]

Albright contends that, since these continental conditions invite external involvement, recent Soviet activism in Africa is reactive and opportunistic: reactive because the Soviet Union was responding to African developments and Western involvements in African affairs. For example, the argument goes, if the Dergue had not charted a socialist path, "it is debatable whether Moscow would have had the chance to enhance its position in Africa." Moreover, the Soviet move was opportunistic insofar as the Soviet Union took advantage of openings that presented themselves irrespective of existing Soviet policy or commitment. An illustration often cited to make this point is the transposition of Soviet support for Eritrea and Somalia against Ethiopia to Soviet support for Ethiopia against Eritrea and Somalia.[4]

Petras and Morley have offered a lucid variant of the opportunism thesis to explain Soviet involvement in the Ethio-Eritrean conflict. They have argued that the newly evolved Ethio-Soviet relations reflect neither the radicalism of the Dergue nor the growth of Soviet "social imperialism," but rather an opportunistic move on both sides. From the Soviet point of view, the move was made to compensate for its declining influence in the Middle East and north Africa in the wake of its expulsion from Egypt and the Sudan. After all, the Soviets embraced the Dergue only after 1977 when they saw the Dergue's capacity to solidify its power base. As the argument goes, had it not been for the waning influence of the Soviet Union in the region and for the Dergue's anti-American behavior, the Soviet Union would not have moved in to bolster the Ethiopian regime against Eritrea and Somalia.

In this sense, then, the Soviet move has essentially been reflexive and opportunistic, seeking to establish a political foothold and mili-tary facilities on the Eritrean coast to offset the loss of its air and naval facilities in Somalia. Explicit in this analysis is the optimistic prediction of a Soviet ouster from Ethiopia resulting from the Soviets' inability to develop structural relationships since the Soviets by nature could not penetrate structural formations. By the same token the Dergue's main objective in developing state-to-state relations with the USSR has been to prevent the political and military disintegration of Ethiopia and to retain its colonial possessions in Eritrea. According to this thesis, under these conditions Soviet eviction from the Horn becomes inevitable.[5]

The opportunism thesis is obviously subjective, as it confuses appearance for essence and tactics for strategy. In doing so, it blurs the substantive driving forces of Soviet behavior. Based on conditionality and ad hoc logic, the premise of the arguments is essentially flawed. To argue that the Soviets would not have embraced the Dergue if the latter had not charted a socialist path is, for example, like saying that the Soviets would not have embraced the Ethiopian regime if the Bolshevik revolution had not occurred in Russia in 1917 in the first place.

Another flaw is that proponents of the opportunism thesis take tactics for strategy, and in doing so they obscure the underlying motivation of Soviet behavior which is concealed beneath the seemingly contradictory and opportunistic moves. To unravel the substance, one has to ask what end purpose the Soviet Union serves by its opportunistic and reactive moves. Petras and Morley contend that Soviet involvement in the Ethio-Eritrean war has been a result of reflexive Soviet behavior and a drive to compensate for its declining influence in Egypt and the Sudan. But the real question is why the Soviet Union would want to obtain and maintain political influence and military facilities in these countries in the first place. Without objectively answering this question, we cannot explain with certainty the motive for Soviet intervention in the Horn.

The most important lesson that the Soviets learned from the Marxist textbook has been that the basis of any foreign policy should be the objective analysis of factual international conditions. They have scrupulously studied the dialectics of international power politics. The resultant behavior of this learning process has been that the Soviets have been able effectively to concentrate on the weakest links of the international capitalist order at any given moment as a strategy of transforming the status quo by piecemeal in the absence of objective conditions for well-coordinated global action. Therefore the Soviet moves that appear opportunistic and reactive to some analysts are essentially tactical moves designed to serve the long-range strategic determination. If the USSR abandoned the Eritreans and Somalis in favor of Ethiopia, the abandonment would still be consistent with its cost-benefit ratio and analysis, which must be explained within the context of its strategic determination. Recent Soviet behavior in the Horn does not in any way contradict the traditional notion that all imperial powers actively engage in the creation of opportunities for dominance and exploitation and then make effective use of any openings that occur. If the Soviets seem to have emphasized the latter, it is only because of their relative international weakness. Hence their foreign policy is determined in relation to the political and military disposition of international forces. To be sure, my analysis points to the contention that Soviet intervention in the Horn could be characterized as opportunistic only in the sense that the Soviets have effectively harnessed ideology to their geopolitical considerations to the extent of duping many intellectuals and politicians.

The Soviet Union is, like any other traditional imperial power, driven by geostrategic, economic, and military considerations. To concretize the analysis, as Legum noted, the Soviet Union has always harnessed African developments to its continental objectives. It has provided arms mainly to be used as instruments of repression against the masses to such African dictators as Bokassa, Idi Amin, Macias Nguma, and many others. There is also ample evidence that the Soviet Union coerced many left-wing organizations, like the Algerian and the Sudanese Communist parties, to support nationalist, yet anticommunist governments. The USSR even forged a close alliance with Nasserite Egypt in the face of a horrendous persecution of Egyptian communists by the Nasserites. Many African liberation movements, like the African National Congress, have capitulated to Soviet coercion to reject Chinese aid outright and to publicly denounce the Chinese ideological line as a precondition for receiving Soviet aid. Those who challenged this coercion, like Mugabe's Zimbabwe African National Union (ZANU), were denied any Soviet aid.[6]

Many analysts have suggested the following objectives as the basis for Soviet activism in Africa: (1) establishing an irreversible ideological and economic presence in Africa commensurate with the USSR's global status; (2) weakening and eventually eliminating Western dominance and influence in Africa; (3) promoting her political security interests and enhancing her power-projection capability by acquiring air and naval networks similar to those of the West; (4) maintaining her ideological hegemony by countering Chinese challenges in Africa; (5) moving the nonaligned bloc closer to Moscow by allying herself with black national-liberation fronts; (6) denying strategic resources to Western economies by encouraging African states to take nationalization action.[7]

Crucial economic considerations clearly substantiate this analysis. Despite a seventy years' drive toward industrialization, the process of capital accumulation in the Soviet Union has not been realized to the satisfaction of the state bureaucracy. Soviet politicians and economists have not effectively grappled with the problems associated with technological lag, uneven economic development between regions, climatic factors, and demographic conditions to achieve modernization and efficiency of the Soviet economy. For example, 80 percent of Soviet hydrocarbon energy is located in Siberia where consumption is relatively low and the logistics of transport and communication are extremely cumbersome. The net result has been that the Soviet economy stagnated and hence could not compete internationally to realize the conditions for internal capital accumulation. The political realization of this structural problem thus triggered a drive toward intensive modernization of the Soviet economy, which in turn initiated an extroverted orientation of Soviet leaders to integrate the Soviet economy into the global economic order to compete for technology, market, raw material, and capital. The need for intensive modernization has brought an added strain on the Soviet hydrocarbon energy, which must be supplemented by imports.[8]

Petroleum production occupies a crucial place in these economic determinations. Intensive economic modernization means in the long run greater consumption of hydrocarbon energy, a critically finite resource. Soviet oil production has already begun to dwindle. According to Western analysts, in 1977 Soviet petroleum production reached 11.44 million barrels a day, of which 1.5 million barrels were being exported to its satellites in Eastern Europe and another 1.5 million barrels to hard-currency countries for about $8 billion. This analysis suggests that since petroleum export accounts for 50 percent of Soviet foreign-exchange earnings, the question of hydrocarbon energy is a crucial component of Soviet foreign policy. A decrease in oil production to 8 million or even 10 million barrels a day would have far-reaching domestic and international repercussions for the Soviet Union, accentuating her economic and political vulnerability.[9]

Moreover, according to 1977 CIA estimates, the USSR and its European allies were expected to import between 3.5 million and 4.5 million barrels of oil daily by the second half of the 1980s. Despite discrepancies in projections, any amount of oil import would end the much-talked-of self-sufficiency of the Soviet economy and would certainly deprive it of the much-needed hard currency to pay for imported technology, foodstuffs, and raw materials. As Marshall Goldman observed, if the Soviet Union had not had oil in 1979, for example, its hard-currency earnings would have dropped from $11 billion to $6.5 billion. By the same token, if it were to import as much as 3 million barrels of oil a day, the Soviet import bill would grow to $58 billion annually, resulting in an annual trade deficit of about $52 billion.[10]

Fluctuations in prices for oil on the world market in recent years have further aggravated the stagnation of the Soviet economy, which, for example, saw zero growth between 1980 and 1985. Finance Minister Boris Gostev acknowledged in 1988 that the Soviet Union had lost $64 billion in revenue since 1985 alone as a result of a slump in prices for petroleum. Consequently, the USSR has been incurring budgetary deficits for years, the 1988 deficit being $58 billion.[11]

Soviet demand for imported raw material is not as insignificant as some analysts suggest. In the late 1970s, the Soviet Union was importing 11 percent of all the raw materials it needed to sustain domestic production, including almost half of its bauxite. Moreover, it was importing 10 million tons of feed grains for livestock in addition to substantial import of wheat to supplement poor harvests.[12]

Climatic factors are important contributors to the growing Soviet global dependency for foodstuffs. The 1988 harvest, for example, fell to a record low of 195 million tons. This meant that the Soviet Union would have to import 30 million tons of grain to make up the difference for the 1989 domestic consumption.[13]

These economic determinations point to the Soviet need to compete for both resources and markets in the Third World. The global thinking of Soviet leaders and the resulting international behavior of the Soviet Union directly emanate from these economic determinations. Due to the temporal and structural lags in the Soviet economy, its economic competition in the Third World necessitates the attainment of political and military footholds for a number of reasons. First, to the extent that Soviet goods are inferior in quality, they are noncompetitive in the advanced countries and hence must be exported to the Third World. Even there, they have to compete with commodities from the advanced countries. To avoid failure, the Soviet Union has been trying to create favorable political conditions by cultivating state-to-state relationships by supporting anti-Western regimes. The net result of this political clienteleship has been that the anti-Western regimes have become increasingly dependent on the Soviet Union. Under these conditions, as Goldman rightly noted, Third World markets have ideally become receptive to Soviet goods, making the USSR the largest exporter of machine tools to these countries.[14]

Moreover, Soviet economic assistance to Third World countries has hitherto been directed toward the development of extroverted economies in those countries so as to enable the Soviet Union to import their outputs. This unequal economic relationship has been characterized by the fact that these countries have been forced to buy inferior Soviet goods at prices 20 percent higher than world market and to sell their own products to the Soviet Union at prices 20 percent or more lower than world market. Their dependency has been further accentuated by the fact that Soviet industrial goods have been bartered for Third World raw materials and crops.[15]

Second, Soviet economic competition and militarism have been coextensive. To begin with, the Soviet economy has been militarized for national security reasons. The snowball effect is that the maintenance of the largest military apparatus in the world has necessitated the development, production, and continual sophistication of war machines, siphoning off the most productive components of the Soviet economy. In fact, over the decades, the Soviet Union became the most efficient producer of arms, which became a crucial component of its economic competition with the West in the Third World. The transitional and unstable political forces in the Third World have been readily receptive to such military exchanges and developments. Thus the export of arms has been used in two ways: to cultivate and support anti-Western regimes and to obtain hard currency. In other words, while the export of arms served to support Soviet economic penetration and political dominance, it has at the same time been used as a means for the generation of cash to strengthen the process of internal capital accumulation. Between 1974 and 1979, for example, the Soviet Union sold $20 billion worth of arms, capturing 43 percent of the total world market.[16]

Third, internal political stability and the ultimate survival of the Soviet system has been contingent upon keeping the economy running. As recent events have clearly shown, the ever-deepening economic crisis in the Soviet Union has continually undermined its basis of political concentration. The immediacy of this impact has been felt in the satellite states.

In light of these structural dynamics and the potential for apocalyptic scenarios should the Soviet system fail, Kremlin leaders have been seeking external outlets to support the internal process of capital accumulation, a precondition for intensive modernization of the economy. Seen in the context of this analysis, the argument that economic components underlie the motivation for Soviet activism in the Horn of Africa is even more cogent. For preponderant economic reasons and geopolitical considerations, Africa and the Middle East hold the key to Soviet Third World policy. Increasing Soviet economic and military aid to countries in these two regions supports my analysis. For example, between 1975 and 1979, the Soviet Union extended $6.6 billion in military aid to states in these regions, Ethiopia being one of the chief beneficiaries. By 1979, the Soviet Union had some 27,000 economic technicians in these regions and the value of Soviet arms agreements there had reached $24.9 billion, making the Soviet Union the chief arms supplier to twenty-one countries. By the end of the 1970s, the number of Soviet and Eastern European military advisers had reached 12,000 in these two regions alone. And the number of African and Middle Eastern students in the Soviet Union had reached some 22,000.[17]

The role of the Soviet Union in the Ethio-Eritrean conflict should be placed within this theoretical framework. I could find no other reasons than economic and geopolitical ones that have propelled the Soviet Union to engross itself in the messy political affairs of the Horn. These reasons are not different from the ones that have motivated the United States since 1945. In fact, there is a striking symmetry between the U.S. and Soviet perceptions of the strategic utility of the Horn. Like the United States, the Soviet Union views the region as a strategic adjunct to the Indian Ocean and the Middle East. Given this premise, two fundamental reasons explain the motives for Soviet involvement in Horn affairs. First, the Horn is too strategically important for the Soviets to leave to the quasi-monopoly of the U.S. Lying on the periphery of the Middle East and the Indian Ocean, the Horn commands the western shores of the Red Sea, the north-western quadrant of the Indian Ocean and the oil lifeline from the Persian Gulf to Europe and America. The importance of the region was underscored in February 1978, when the Soviets began to become engrossed in Eritrea, by the Soviet Ministry of Foreign Affairs in these terms: "The Horn of Africa is primarily of military, political and economic importance. The importance of the region is mainly because of its situation where the two continents of Africa and Asia meet. There are many good harbours in the Persian Gulf and in the Indian Ocean. Moreover, there are maritime routes which link the oilproducing countries with America and Europe."[18]

This Soviet assertion is not without substance. Any power that controls the Red Sea will be able to control the shortcut between Europe and the Far East. Cruising via the Red Sea rather than around the Cape of Good Hope reduces the distance from the Black Sea to the Asiatic ports of Soviet Russia by almost 70 percent. More important, the Horn is in an ideal geostrategic situation close to the oil lifeline should the Soviets decide to deny the West access to this oil. Additionally, control of the Horn will enable the Soviets to obtain access to the Indian Ocean in their strategic competition with the United States.

The Indian Ocean has been the focal point of superpower rivalry, not only for its military value, but also for its importance as a source of economic resources. The Russians depend on the sea as a source of protein far more heavily than any Western power does. The Indian Ocean has over the decades become an important operating area for Soviet trawlers, providing more than one-fifth of their catches.[19]

Furthermore, dominance of the Red Sea and the Indian Ocean is crucial for controlling and protecting the pro-Soviet littoral states in the area. Today between 45 and 50 percent of Soviet military and economic aid goes to such Red Sea and Indian Ocean coastal states as India, Viet Nam, South Yemen, and Ethiopia.[20] In short, in so far as the shipment of military equipment and oil to states within its sphere of influence and to its Asiatic territory is concerned, the sea route is too important for the Soviet Union to leave to the quasi-monopoly of the United States. Herein lies the crux of U.S.-Soviet rivalry over the Horn, which has become an inescapable part of the general political texture of the region.

The second motive for Soviet involvement in the Horn region is that the Soviets share with Americans the dominant conventional thinking that whoever controls Ethiopia also controls the Horn of Africa. After all, Ethiopia is geographically twice the size of Somalia. Additionally, with 42 million people to Somalia's 4 million, Ethiopia is the second most populous state in black Africa, offering market and economic potential far greater than any of its immediate neighbors. By virtue of being the seat of the OAU and the oldest independent state in sub-Saharan Africa, Ethiopia is seen as politically superior to other states in the area for penetration of Africa. Moreover, the Soviets believe in Eritrea's inseparability from Ethiopia. So with the permanent addition of Eritrea, Ethiopia could also effectively be used for political and military dominance of the Middle East and north Africa.

In light of these advantages associated with Ethiopia, the Soviets have pinned their hopes on Ethiopia for the control of the region since the 1950s. In this endeavor, the Soviet Union applied a carrot and stick approach to courting Ethiopia. In the late 1940s, Czechoslovakia was used to supply arms to Ethiopia as a means of penetration. Throughout the 1950s and 1960s, the Soviet Union made several offers to provide any amount of military equipment to Ethiopia, though the emperor declined the offers in order not to jeopardize his special relations with the West. Nonetheless, the emperor judiciously cultivated diplomatic relations with the Soviet Union, partly to justify his ostensible neutrality in the wake of the newly evolving nonaligned movement and partly to improve his bargaining position with the United States by referring to the Soviet Union as an alternative source of military and economic aid.

In 1959, Haile Selassie became the first African head of state to visit Moscow, upon which he received $102 million in long-term loans. Thereafter, Ethiopia and the Soviet Union signed a number of technical, educational, and commercial agreements. Consequently, the Assab oil refinery, the botanical laboratory at Ambo, and the Bahr-Dar Polytechnic Institute were built with Soviet aid.

Soviet strategists, however, never harbored any illusion that this carrot approach alone would be sufficient to penetrate Ethiopia. They were simultaneously searching for regional allies, which they found in Somalia and to some extent in Eritrean nationalism, to counter U.S. presence in Eritrea and Ethiopia. The Soviets began to pour military and economic assistance into Somalia for this purpose, the emphasis being on creation of a military infrastructure and modernization of the Somali army. According to Western sources, between 1962 and 1976, the Soviet Union provided $1 billion worth of arms to Somalia, giving her both quantitative and qualitative superiority over her neighbors. By 1975, Somalia had more than 100 fighter planes, 250 tanks, 300 armored personnel carriers, and 23,000 soldiers. Anywhere from 1,000 to 4,000 Soviet military advisers were attached to the Somali army and some 2,400 Somali officers are believed to have received their training in the Soviet Union. In the economic realm, the Soviets had committed a total of $154 million, of which only 60 percent was actually used. Some 1,500 Soviet security and economic technicians were also attached to various Somali ministries. In exchange, the Soviet Union obtained access to important military facilities on the Somali ports, comparable to the U.S. defense installations in Eritrea. These Soviet installations included petroleum storage depots, a naval missile-handling facility, a communications center, and a dry dock for the Soviet navy. In addition, Somali airfields were used for long-range reconnaissance flights.[21]

The Soviets also attempted to use Eritreans as a means of penetrating the Horn. But since the Eritreans lacked formal international recognition and were less popular than the Somalis with black Africa, the Soviets refrained from openly embracing them. Instead, they encouraged their surrogate states, like Czechoslovakia, Bulgaria, Cuba, Somalia, and South Yemen, to assist the Eritreans. Thus the nationalists received arms from those countries until 1976.

The second half of the 1970s, however, saw a dramatic change in Soviet policy in the Horn when the Ethiopian revolution provided an ample opportunity for Soviet penetration. At first, the Soviets had hoped that they could manipulate the Eritreans and Somalis by controlling the Ethiopians, so they encouraged diplomatic negotiations. But when the Soviet Union and Ethiopia secretly signed a $385 million arms deal in December 1976, the texture of Soviet diplomacy changed.[22] At this time, they fully endorsed the territorial sanctity of Ethiopia and so proposed a federal union of Eritrea, Ethiopia, and the Ogaden within the framework of Ethiopian unity. The Eritreans were either to form a branch of an Ethiopian Communist party or to create their own party. Somalia and South Yemen were also to join this federation later in the process.[23]

Pursuant to the Soviet proposal, Fidel Castro visited Ethiopia, Somalia, and South Yemen in March 1977. But as anticipated, the

Eritreans and Somalis flatly rejected the Russo-Cuban mediation and reiterated their demands for their right to national self-determination. With that, the Soviet strategy to create a pax Sovietica under the rubric of federalism vanished. Consequently, the Soviets made their disaffection with the Eritreans very obvious. In May 1977, Mengistu of Ethiopia visited Moscow where he signed a secret agreement involving $500 million in arms.[24] During a banquet for Mengistu, President Podgorny claimed to have seen a connection between Eritrean "secessionism" and Western international imperialism: "Insofar as the Red Sea is concerned, recent events prove that the imperialists seek to establish their control over this region with the assistance of certain Arab countries, primarily Saudi Arabia, in violation of the legitimate rights of other states and peoples in this region and to the detriment of free international navigation."[25]

With these newly evolved Ethio-Soviet relations, the way for full-fledged Soviet involvement in Horn affairs was cleared. But when the Somalis occupied the whole of the Ogaden and most of Hararage province, and the Eritreans liberated all of Eritrea with the exception of Asmara and the two ports on the Red Sea, the Soviets, concerned over their possible inability to contain the revolutionary process in the region, began to surface. Thus they rushed the delivery of arms to Ethiopia in an unprecedented fashion.

Between 26 November 1977 and 6 January 1978, Soviet transport planes made more than fifty flights into Ethiopia carrying arms and personnel. More than 225 Soviet air force cargo planes, some 15 percent of her transport fleet, was involved in this massive operation. The planes included the long-range Antonov 22 and Tupelev-76, the heaviest planes in the Soviet inventory. The maximum payload of an Antonov 22 is 80 tons.[26] In addition, a flotilla of Soviet ships cruised from the Black Sea into the Eritrean ports on the Red Sea where they unloaded heavy guns, artillery, rocket launchers, and armed vehicles and tanks.[27]

This complex arms delivery operation, the first of its kind since World War II, was coordinated by means of a spy satellite that the USSR had deployed recently. American surveillance ships of the Sixth and Seventh fleets and satellites closely monitored this increased Soviet naval and air traffic. Pakistani, Iranian, Turkish, Israeli, and Greek radar stations also picked up this heavy volume of traffic. By the beginning of February 1978, in addition to the heavy guns, artillery, and ground-to-ground missiles, the Dergue had received four hundred Soviet tanks and over fifty MIGs. Soviet and East German military advisers, logisticians, and pilots were also flown into Ethiopia. More than 10,000 Cuban troops arrived in Ethiopia to reinforce the 100,000 in the Ethiopian army and the 150,000 in the militia.[28] Soon the Cubans organized themselves into one mechanized and two infantry brigades. A Soviet army general, V. I. Petrov, was put in command of the Ethiopian ground forces.[29] In addition, a new High Military Committee, comprised of eight Russians, four Ethiopians, and three Cubans, was charged with the task of planning and coordination of the forthcoming military operations.

Having completed the feverish preparations, the High Military Committee opted to meet the Eritreans and the Somalis separately. Thus, in February 1978, the first air and ground offensive was launched against the Somali-backed Western Somalia Liberation Front (WSLF), and 88,000 Ethiopian regular and irregular troops were deployed in addition to the 10,000 Cubans in the Ogaden.[30] By the end of the month the war on the eastern front was over with the defeat of the Ogaden Somalis.

Emboldened by this swift victory in the east, the Russians and Ethiopians now turned to the north against the Eritreans. As early as December 1977, the Soviets had been actively involved in military campaigns against the Eritreans. When the guerrillas captured three-fourths of Massawa, two Soviet warships joined four Ethiopian ships bombarding guerrilla positions to preempt the total capture of the port. At least forty Soviet technicians were stationed at Massawa to operate the heavy artillery, the BM-21 multiple rocket launchers, and other sophisticated weapons. South Yemeni elements also participated in the operation, flying Soviet MIGs and driving Soviet tanks.[31]

In January 1978, as a prelude to the general offensive against Eritrea, the Ethiopian air force, now largely piloted by Russians and Cubans, began bombarding guerrilla positions, towns, and villages, using napalm and cluster bombs. Raymond Wilkinson, a UPI correspondent who was inside Eritrea, reported:

Ethiopian warplanes are bombing Eritrean towns with napalm and cluster bombs in an apparent systematic campaign to terrorize the civilian population and disrupt the guerrillas' fight for independence. The campaign began at the start of the new

year. . . . I was in Tessenei when Ethiopian warplanes, painted
in desert camouflage, bombed the town and the neighboring
village of Ali Gidir twice within four hours. Swooping out in
the mid-day sun as Tessenei slumbered during its daily siesta,
two Soviet-built MIG–21s, recently shipped to Ethiopia as part
of a massive arms buildup, skimmed over the town dropping
bombs. . . . Four hours later, the Ethiopian planes were back,
wheeling for several minutes in the clear sky and dropping napalm and deadly cluster bombs. . . . One napalm bomb devastated several thatch huts. A cluster bomb fell nearby, battering
the area with shrapnel. . . . The cluster bomb's canister was re-
covered later. In stencilled English were the words "bomb cluster." Several other bombs fell on a nearby farm.[32]

By the end of January, the once flourishing town of Tessenei, with
over 25,000 population, was reduced to shambles with less than 5,000
people remaining. As a prelude to further military action, in mid-
March the Soviets began a campaign of vilification and distortions
against the Eritrean movement. On 16 March, *Pravda* carried an article accusing the Eritreans of collaboration with Western imperialism
and Arab reactionary forces in an attempt to weaken the Ethiopian
revolution and deny Ethiopia her access to the sea. In *Pravda*'s words,
"In these conditions the Eritrean separatists are involved in a game
played by others [and are] objectively helping the realization of imperialist designs." The newspaper self-righteously added that "[t]he
genuine interests of the population of the province coincide with the
interests of the entire Ethiopian people which is striving to build life
on new principles."[33]

As part of their frantic war preparation, on 23 April the Soviet
Union sent to Ethiopia an additional twenty MIG-23s.[34] The actual
troop movement against Eritrea began in May 1978, when the Dergue
assembled 150,000 regulars and irregulars along the Tigrai-Eritrean
border. By August, the Ethiopian troops recaptured most of the
towns held by the nationalists. But they could not completely dislodge
them from the strategically important towns like Keren. Therefore,
they launched a second offensive of encirclement and suppression
in mid-November. Two Soviet generals, eleven colonels, and about
two hundred lower-echelon officers organized this new offensive, em-
ploying 150,000 Ethiopian troops. In addition, Soviet spy satellites

and Soviet-piloted helicopters and jets provided the planners with photographs and intelligence data about the positions and movement of the guerrillas. General Petrov, who had conducted the successful offensive against the Ogaden Somalis earlier, now became commander of the Ethiopian ground forces while another Soviet general took charge of the air force. When the offensive began in five directions against the nationalists, the eleven Soviet colonels commanded the front-line units. Lieutenant Colonel Alexei Alexandrov was in charge of the Ethiopian forces on the western front, while Lieutenant Colonel Vassily commanded the eastern front. Lieutenant Colonel Eduard was in charge of the northern front. Eduard was wounded at the battle for Elaboret, not far from Keren, and later died in Addis Ababa.[35]

After the strategic retreat of the nationalists from Keren, 100,000 civilian Eritreans fled their sanctuaries in the mountains in northern Eritrea. Some 5,000 Eritreans were either killed or injured in air strikes and artillery bombardments. In addition, 8,000 received temporary treatment for exhaustion. About 40 villages were razed to the ground, and another 120 villages were severely damaged.[36]

The second offensive drove the guerrillas from all towns except Naqfa into the rugged mountains of Eritrea. From the point of view of military strategy, the Soviet intervention introduced a new element into the Ethio-Eritrean armed conflict, namely a high degree of sophistication in military technology. Moreover, Ethiopia became totally dependent on Soviet military technology and thus provided a new location for the Russians to test their new weapons and military strategies.

Unlike the February 1978 offensive against the Ogaden Somalis, the repeated blitzkrieg-style offensives against the Eritreans could not destroy the Eritrean national resistance. Therefore, the Soviets and Ethiopians had to launch many offensives. In fact, since 1978 and until the time of this writing, the Eritreans have seized the military initiative and the Soviet-backed Ethiopian forces are on the run. Like the United States, the Soviet Union has again proved itself to be wrong in its assessment of the strength of ethnocentrifugal forces in the Horn. But, given the Soviets' past extroverted orientation, there seemed to be no other alternative from their point of view to using the Horn of Africa as a means of expanding their security zone in the region. However, the new introverted orientation of

Gorbachev seems to amount to official repudiation of past Soviet foreign policy. As we shall see in the next chapter, the new orientation suggests that the fundamental changes taking place in Eastern Europe may have positive implications for the Eritrean problem.

The Role of Proxies

Following the Soviet lead, many of the traditional supporters of Eritrea defected to the Ethiopian side and shared the division of labor of intervention as it suited them. In this regard, the activities of Libya, South Yemen, East Germany, and Cuba were particularly noticeable.

Between 1969 and 1975, Libya was an outspoken supporter of Eritrean nationalism, providing considerable material and diplomatic assistance. In 1976, Muammar Qaddafi reversed his policy and threw himself behind the Ethiopian regime. During the initial phases of Ethio-Libyan relations, Qaddafi extended to Mengistu $150 million in outright grants to be used for the suppression of Eritrean nationalism.[37]

Ever since its independence, South Yemen, too, had been an important ally of Eritrea. Eritrean nationalists used Aden as a transit entrepôt for arms and provisions. They enjoyed the unconditional support of Yemeni leaders until South Yemen changed sides under Soviet pressure in 1976. By January 1978, there were 2,000 Yemeni troops in Ethiopia, positioned to bolster the Ethiopian army. As the war clouds over Eritrea and the Ogaden darkened, Premier Ali Nasser Muhammad flew to Moscow in early February for special talks with Soviet leaders. Ali Nasser took a public position concurring with the Soviets that the Eritreans and the Somalis "played into the hands of imperialism." He pledged his country's respect for Ethiopia's territorial integrity and agreed to make every contribution to its struggle against Eritrea and Somalia. He also reaffirmed that Aden would continue to be used as a staging post for massive Soviet arms to Ethiopia. By then, South Yemeni troops were reported to have played an active combat role against Eritrea.[38]

Pursuant to the international cooperation in support of Ethiopia, the East Germans were assigned to developing communication and intelligence apparatuses with particular emphasis on building an elaborate security network to cope with internal opposition to the regime.

Of the proxies, the most visible and most active has been Cuba.

Cuban military intervention in the region has been of critical importance to the Ethiopian regime as it effectively deflected the Ethiopian
revolution and has enabled Ethiopia to achieve a transient victory
over the Somalis and to contain the Eritreans. Because of the considerable magnitude of the Cuban intervention and because of her opportunistic moves, the remainder of this chapter is devoted to an
examination of the origin and evolution of Cuban-Eritrean relations
and to Cuba's later betrayal of Eritrea.

Cuba's policy toward the Horn began to evolve in the mid-1960s
when she cultivated cordial relations with Eritrean nationalists. Starting in 1966, Cuba had warmly enbraced Eritrean nationalism as an
indigenously authentic and internationally credible movement. Consequently, some Eritrean guerrillas received their drilling in Cuba.
Castro's open advocacy of Eritrea's inclusion in the nonaligned movement helped Eritreans obtain their anti-imperialist credentials in the
otherwise hostile international political environment.

In addition, Cuban propaganda organs gave ample coverage and
analysis to the Eritrean movement. In 1969, for example, the Cubans
unequivocally characterized the Eritrean question as a popular struggle against Ethiopian colonialism. In their words: "The Eritrean revolution is a struggle for national independence and for their liberation
from Ethiopian colonialism."[39]

In the early 1970s, the Cubans broadened their interest in the
Horn by embracing the Somali cause. In August 1972, in a joint communiqué, Cuba's minister of external affairs "expressed the support
of his government to the Somali peoples in their desire for reunifica-
tion."[40]

Cuba's public affirmation of the justness of the Eritrean and Somali
struggles represented an open repudiation of Ethiopia's imperial acquisition. This affirmation was justified on the basis of the principle
of national self-determination, and Cuba's support for the Eritreans
and Somalis was placed within the context of "proletarian internationalism." But Castro's opportunism was unmasked when he endorsed
Soviet involvement in the Horn in support of the Ethiopian regime.
In an about-face, Castro blamed the Eritreans and Somalis for making demands on Ethiopia and ascribed this as the reason for Cuban
intervention on Ethiopia's side. Castro charged that, while the Somalis
launched an aggression on Ethiopia, the Eritrean "secessionists in the
north of the country, clearly in coordination with the Somali attack,

were intensifying their military operations all along the existing front lines. It was at this juncture that a situation arose where only resolute and determined internationalist help to support the heroic struggle of the Ethiopian people would have saved the independence, territorial integrity, and the Revolution in their country."[41]

According to this opportunistic description of events, the Eritrean and Somali problems were reactions to the Ethiopian revolution while, in fact, they were integral parts of the major factors that contributed to the Ethiopian revolution, and as such, they were awaiting answers from it. Despite this fact, Castro pushed his bizarre analysis further by likening the Eritrean movement, which he had characterized in 1969 as a struggle against Ethiopian colonialism, to the southern secessionism in the United States during that Civil War. Echoing the Soviets, Cuban propaganda media denounced Eritrean nationalists for collaboration with imperialism and Arab reaction.[42]

The purpose of this propaganda was to set the ideological tone for Cuban intervention in Horn affairs. In February 1977, a Cuban division general, Arnaldo Ochoa Sanchez, visited Ethiopia with no reasons given. This was followed by Castro's visit to the region in March when he organized a conference of Ethiopian, Somali, and South Yemeni leaders to discuss the federation option. Castro suggested that the Eritrean and Ogaden questions could be solved within the framework of a federal structure without violating Ethiopia's territorial integrity. But, insistent on their right to national self-determination, the Eritreans and the Somalis rejected Castro's mediation. This then gave Castro a spurious reason to mask his capitulation to Soviet pressures and to commit Cuba militarily to the defense of Ethiopia's imperial status quo.

In December 1977, Cuba's role in the Horn was clearly defined as Cuban troops were airlifted from Havana, Angola, and the Congo to Ethiopia. By April 1978, the number of Cuban troops deployed in the Horn reached 17,000. The Cuban forces led by General Ochoa Sanchez were immediately placed under the command of General Petrov.[43]

In mid-March, the Cubans intensified their propaganda warfare against Eritrea, and informed diplomatic sources interpreted this activism as indicating a decision to dispatch Cuban troops to Eritrea along with Soviet forces. In fact, about 3,000 Cuban soldiers had already been airlifted to Asmara where they immediately began probing the operational strength of the Eritrean guerrillas in the vicinity.[44]

However, unlike the Ogaden, the Eritrean war posed a painful dilemma for the Cubans. A number of things compounded the unwarranted nature of Cuba's meddling in Eritrean affairs. First, there was no external involvement on the side of Eritrean nationalists equivalent to South African intervention in Angola or to the Somali presence in the Ogaden to provide any ostensible pretext for Cuba's involvement. Second, Eritrean nationalists share similar anti-imperialist credentials with the Cubans in the Third World, and the Eritrean movement was supported by all anti-imperialist forces. Moreover, Algeria, Mozambique, Iraq, Guinea, Yugoslavia, and other liberation organizations and parties had publicly expressed their displeasure with Cuba's moves in Eritrea. Under these conditions, it became increasingly difficult for Cuba to justify her involvement in Eritrea without jeopardizing her reputation as independent of the USSR. Third, there was no detectable change in the basic orientation of the Eritreans, as their attitude toward the Soviets and Cubans remained the same. The EPLF, in particular, consistently pleaded with the Soviets and Cubans to reconsider their role in the Horn of Africa. It even castigated Eritreans who expressed publicly their displeasure with the Soviets and Cubans.

Under these circumstances, Castro moved discreetly in Eritrea, confining the Cuban forces to strategic matters such as building Ethiopia's military infrastructure, training, handling heavy weapon systems, flying MIGs, and providing logistical support activities and services to the Ethiopian army. The Cubans were removed from tactical battles to avoid possible capture by Eritrean forces and thus to provide a prism of deniability to the Cubans about their engagement in Eritrea. In addition, the core of the Cuban forces was deployed to the Ogaden to police the region to prevent the resurgence of the Somalis, whereby the Ethiopian army was released from the area to fight in Eritrea. In this way, the military visibility of Cuban forces in Eritrea was reduced.

Nonetheless, the Cubans continued to be an essential component of all military operations of encirclement and suppression launched against the Eritreans beginning in 1978. In 1980, there were at least 3,500 Cubans in Eritrea fighting alongside the Ethiopians.[45] During the 1982 so-called red star mopping-up operations against the nationalists, a strong Cuban infantry battalion shored up the 120,000 strong Ethiopian army in yet another attempt to destroy the Eritrean movement.[46]

Given the indigenous character of the Eritrean movement, the continued Cuban involvement in the Ethio-Eritrean conflict is certainly dubious and even unconscionable. If the point of departure of any analysis is the tradition of warm Cuban-Eritrean relations, the sudden change in Cuba's policy represented a diplomatic betrayal of Eritrea. Defenders of Cuba's African policy have created concoctions of all sorts in an apparent effort to exonerate Cuba from her intervention in the Horn. These rationalizations use faulty methodological assumptions such as the invocation of "proletarian internationalism" or "natural alliance" with the Ethiopian revolution. However, the truth of the matter is that the Cubans had supported the Eritrean movement precisely on the basis of those principles. If the Eritrean movement was a just and principled struggle against "Ethiopian colonialism," as the Cubans themselves had characterized it earlier, what makes it today "unjust" and "unprincipled"?

Any objective analysis should squarely probe the sudden shift in Cuba's policy and intervention in the Horn. It is my contention that Cuba's ill-conceived characterization of the Eritrean movement as "antisocialist" and "secessionist," and its subsequent involvement in the war is a function of the pressures brought to bear on Cuba by the Soviets, which resulted in her being compelled to support Ethiopia's imperial aims. To this extent, Cuba acted as a proxy of the Soviet Union in the Horn, contrary to her convictions and interests, in order to reciprocate the Soviet Union for its generous economic and military assistance. The following account should illustrate this point.

Historically, the genesis of the Soviet-Cuban partnership stemmed from their shared geopolitical and ideological considerations. Both countries share a siege mentality stimulated by the West's determination to counter the emergence and international spread of communism. Both countries have been subjected to varying degrees of economic restrictions, political isolation, and ideological warfare of the West. The deterministic attitude of the West gave birth to the Soviet-Cuban obsession with the danger of capitalist encirclement, which triggered the need for opening multifarious fronts against international capitalism at its weakest links, which happened to be situated in the Third World. These fronts were expected to ease the concentrated Western assailing of the Soviet Union and Cuba by diverting attention to politically hot spots in the intermediate zone. Additionally, the actual and potential economic value of the Third World has been enormous to the socialist camp in the face of the unmitigated hostility of the West. Thus, Soviet-Cuban views on the Third World have been identical, and the interests they sought have been compatible.

Situated in the geopolitically sensitive United States sphere of influence, Cuba's survival would have been particularly precarious without unqualified Soviet international guardianship and economic largesse. From Cuba's point of view, it has been an imperative necessity to help create, support, and broaden national liberation fronts in the Third World. Over time this became an essential component of Cuba's foreign policy. This, in fact, was the underlying motivation for the initiation and evolution of Cuban-Eritrean relations in the 1960s and 1970s.

The similarity of their interests and the compatibility of their views have made possible the Soviets' and Cubans' joint formulation of tactical and strategic determinations and the coordination of their military operations. But their shared global orientation has been further facilitated by the coincidence between Soviet-Cuban interests and the interests of the anti-status quo forces in the Third World. By historical accident, almost all countries in the intermediate zone happen to be former colonies of Western powers, and the regimes they left behind have been closely associated politically, militarily, and economically with former imperial powers. Hence these governments were the immediate targets of any imminent revolution. After all, these conditions have been the basis for the emergence, evolution, and growth of many of the anti-status quo forces in the Third World. The Eritrean case is a classic illustration.

The Ethio-Eritrean federation was installed by the Western powers under the leadership of the United States purely for geopolitical considerations. This UN-sanctioned federation in essence became a denial of Eritrea's right to national self-determination. Hence, any movement against this status quo (until it was later upset by Ethiopia's unilateral termination of the federal structure) became essentially a movement against Ethiopian and U.S. imperialism. For this reason the Eritreans early were able to elicit the solidarity and support of all anti-status quo forces, including the Soviets and Cubans. The illusory semblance of such a "natural alliance" served to mask the

long-range intentions of the Soviets and Cubans as they opportunisti-
cally fell to sloganeering on the principle of "proletarian internationalism."

The drawback of these international linkages has been that, failing
to draw a distinction between means and ends, many commentators
have fallen to the temptation to reiterate the Soviet-Cuban interpretations of international affairs. The stark reality is that different groups
use the same means to achieve different ends. When the anticolonial
and national liberation movements are just and legitimate, the assistance they receive also bears the stamp of a just character. Since Western assistance for these forces has not been forthcoming, the socialist
countries have increasingly identified themselves with the demands
of the liberation movements, and thus the assistance they have given
has borne the semblance of justness.

My analysis does not purport to suggest that Cuba has been a docile
proxy of the Soviet Union in the Horn, but rather that until recently
Cuba has had a vested interest in being a convenient Soviet tool there
in exchange for economic and military gains from the Soviet Union.
Within the structural framework sketched above, their reciprocal
benefits can be summarized.

From the Soviet perspective, as many writers have rightly suggested, Cuba is a strategic asset. The placement of Cuba within the
Soviet orbit enhances Soviet national security by the use of Cuban
harbors and ports to service Soviet commercial and naval vessels and
by the placement of electronic intelligence-gathering networks and
communications facilities close to the shores of the United States.
In addition, Cuba serves as an exemplary model for Soviet alliance
with nations of the Third World. By showing solidarity with the
Cuban revolution and offering generous economic largesse, the Soviet Union hopes to prove to nations of the Third World that it is
a country worth allying with. Moreover, by cultivating the image of
a natural Soviet ally, Cuba has been acting internationally to bring
the nonaligned movement closer to the Soviet Union.[47]

In return for playing these roles globally, Cuba has received all
the assistance she needs. Cuba's economic dependency on the Soviet
Union began in the 1960s when the USSR injected more than $1
billion into the Cuban economy to subsidize the production and international distribution of Cuba's sugar with a view to neutralizing the
effects of the U.S. economic blockade against Cuba.[48] The Soviet

Union has also been the chief supplier of oil to Cuba, at almost half the price of OPEC oil. Between 1967 and 1975, for example, the Soviet Union supplied 98 percent of Cuba's petroleum needs.[49]

But this economic dependency has had political consequences. In the event of Soviet-Cuban conflict on any matter, Soviet views must take precedence over Cuban ones, even to the extent of outright capitulation. An illustration of this fact is Castro's ideological squabble with the Micro Faction in the 1967–68 period. When Castro incarcerated or excommunicated members of the Micro Faction, who were reported to have shared Soviet ideological and political views, the Soviet Union reacted by slowing down the supply of oil to Cuba, with the consequence of mass discontent. At the same time the Soviet Union increased the export of oil to other Latin American countries. The growing economic dependency of Cuba and her trade deficit of $1.7 billion at the time gave the Soviets a crucial leverage to use oil as a political weapon to discipline the Cuban leader. The incident was ended only after Castro rehabilitated his pro-Soviet opponents and when he officially endorsed the Soviet invasion of Czechoslovakia on 23 August 1968.[50]

The significance of this episode lies in the fact that thereafter political capitulation became the medium of exchange for Soviet economic assistance. If placed in this context, Cuba's involvement in Eritrea seems consistent with the nature of the Soviet-Cuban relationship.

As the magnitude of Cuba's economic dependency on the Soviet Union increased, Castro gave further concessions. For example, in the aftermath of the 1970 campaign to produce 10 million tons of sugar, Castro abandoned his introverted socialist economic development in favor of the Soviet model. In return, the Soviet Union further deepened its economic assistance to Cuba. In the 1972 trade agreement, following Castro's adoption of the Soviet model, the USSR deferred Cuba's debt until 1986, to be followed by repayments over twenty-five years. New credits covering Cuba's trade deficit for 1973 to 1975 were also given free of interest charges.[51]

By 1976, 22 percent of Cuba's GNP was directly tied to the Soviet economy. Between 1961 and 1976, Cuba's exports to the Soviet Union constituted 43 percent of her total exports, while her importation of Soviet goods accounted for 52 percent of her total imports.[52]

If Soviet-Cuban relations are seen within the parameters of these economic factors, it is reasonable to argue that the magnitude of Soviet largesse determined the ideological and political direction of those relations and one could certainly establish a direct correlation between the magnitude of Soviet economic aid to Cuba and the latter's politico-military activism in Africa. For example, Soviet subsidies of the Cuban economy and military apparatus, by 1978, rose to three and a half times the 1975 levels. Since the Angolan operation, the Soviet Union has been underwriting the Cuban economy with $2.5 billion annually as compared with only $550 million in the early 1970s. In 1976 alone, sugar and petroleum subsidies amounted to $897 million and $375 million respectively. Additionally, the Cuban army was supplied with the most modern weapon systems, in appreciation of its military role in the Horn and in Angola.[53]

Parallel to Cuba's increased military role in Angola, the Ogaden, and Eritrea, Soviet-Cuban trade increased from 2.9 billion Cuban pesos in 1975 to 4 billion pesos in 1978. Between 1977 and 1980, the annual average of Cuba's commercial exchanges with the Soviet Union reached 66 percent of Cuba's total international trade, and the annual average of its sugar exports to the Soviet Union was 55 percent, with the latter buying between 3 million and 4 million tons of sugar at substantially higher prices than world market. In sum, the cumulative Soviet economic and military aid to Cuba between 1961 and 1979 stood at $16.9 billion. Even the 1980s saw no decrease in the magnitude of Soviet aid to Cuba and the level is likely to remain as high as long as Cuba retains its politico-military utility in Africa. In 1988 alone, Cuba received more than $5 billion from Moscow in economic and military aid.[54]

These were the conditions that underlay Cuba's reluctant intervention in Eritrea. The Cubans realized that their action in Eritrea was unwarranted and of enormous potential cost to their international credibility. In fact, their involvement became internationally so embarrassing that they smuggled Fr. Gobeze, a former Meison (All-Ethiopian Socialist Movement) leader, into Ethiopia from Paris in early summer 1978, with a view to overthrowing Mengistu. By placing Gobeze in power, the Cubans hoped that they would obtain the needed civilian cloak to justify their presence in Ethiopia and Eritrea.

On the balance sheet, the actual and potential cost of Cuba's military adventurism in Africa is greater than the benefits derived from it. First, Eritrea has become a watershed in exposing the real intentions of Cuba's military operations in Africa. In the case of Angola and the Ogaden, the presence of external elements provided the pretext for Soviet-Cuban involvement. But when they moved to Eritrea, many international actors and intellectuals began to question the sincerity of Cuba's international revolutionism.

Second, Cuba's military operations in Africa have considerably speeded up the process of class differentiation in Cuban society. Civilian participants in the so-called internationalist mission have been given, upon returning home, 20 percent salary differentials over internal national rates. Additionally, these returnees have been given priorities in housing and durable consumer goods. In reaction to these differences in privileges, social alignments and antagonisms are being crystallized as the capitalization process deepens.[55] The mass exodus of 125,000 Cubans in 1980 partly substantiates this thesis.

Third, Cuba's African engagement has accentuated the division between the civilian and military establishments as the civilian segment resents the growing privileged status of the military. Limited evidence suggests that this has fostered institutional jealousy to the potential detriment of the state. For example, the appointment of two division generals as vice presidents to the Council of State has not been pleasing to the technocrats.[56]

Fourth, although the toll of Cuban casualities in Eritrea and the Ogaden is shrouded in secrecy, some facts are emerging about the number of Cuban deaths in Angola. According to recent reports, 10,000 Cubans and 90,000 Angolans were killed between 1975 and 1988 in this stalemated civil war.[57] Even after suffering such casualities, the Angolan military situation remains inconclusive. In addition, after twelve years of Cuban involvement on the Ethiopian side, Eritrean nationalists are on the offensive again. In light of these developments, the cost of Cuban adventurism has been greater than the benefits derived.

Fifth, following Cuban intervention in Eritrea and the Ogaden, Sweden cut off all forms of aid to Cuba, starting in 1979. In June 1978, Canada also terminated its $10 million in trade credits and $4.4 million in technical aid to Cuba. In February 1976, West Germany had announced that Cuba would no longer be eligible for German development aid.[58]

Finally, Gorbachev's introverted orientation for the USSR seems to militate against continued Cuban presence in the Horn. In order for perestroika to take root, a temporary outbreak of "peace" is a necessary condition, meaning that important resources must be generated and allocated for the civilian economy to promote and sustain the new forces of capitalist production. This suggests that, without the deployment of massive Soviet economic and military resources, Cuba will not be able to continue playing its military functions in Africa at the same level as before. If my analysis is correct, then, this chapter should end with a note of optimism on the possibility of Cuban disengagement from the region sooner than the Ethiopian regime anticipates.

9

Eritrea: An Unanswered Question

ERITREANISM, AS A field of study, is perhaps the most complex province of nationalism, one seemingly defiant of any rational analysis. The excruciating problem lies in the fact that this longest and certainly one of the most tenacious liberation movements in this century has failed to make a dent in international politics and, by extension, in the academic world. In this sense Eritrean nationalism seems immune to the dialectics of international power politics. The concomitant ramification of this painful reality for Eritreans is that the articulation of external elements in the Horn has been moving unidirectionally in Ethiopia's favor, thereby retarding the realization of Eritrea's nationalist aspirations. Therefore, the recurrent pattern of external entanglement in the Ethio-Eritrean conflict has made the prediction of the outcome of the conflict very difficult.

Despite this fundamental difficulty in prediction, however, recent developments, if they continue to unfold at the current pace, seem to provide some guidance to the future solution of the Eritrean problem. Short of a massive external military deployment on Ethiopia's behalf, Eritrean victory seems likely. Because of their miscalculations of the dynamics and strength of Eritrean nationalism, Soviet leaders in the 1980s made the decision to intervene on Ethiopia's side. In doing so, they deepened the crisis of the Ethiopian state as they failed to resolve the Eritrean question militarily. The unintended consequences of the increase of belligerency between Eritrea and Ethiopia have been a growth in ethnic cleavages in Ethiopia and popular disaffection of the Ethiopian masses in general, resulting from the harsh economic policies of the regime. These conditions make the Soviet presence in the area precarious. In other words, economic determinations, the ungovernability of the Eritrean people, and the competition from the West all combine to make long-term Soviet dominance in the Horn highly precarious. Given the rapidity with which these factors are moving currently, this chapter could, in a very short time, probably be written in the past tense while using the same data contained herein to explain the reasons for Soviet eviction from the area.

Economic Determinations

In view of the ongoing war and the cyclical pattern of drought aggravated by the misguided economic policies of the regime, the Ethiopian economy is in shambles. The primary reason stems from the diversion of critical resources to the military sector in order to contain the Eritrean insurrection. Another equally important reason involves the regime's overall agrarian policy.

Without adequate material conditions and without a concrete plan of action, the regime nationalized the land in early 1975. Since then, the regime has been tampering with the agrarian process with a multitude of proclamations that have failed to make any appreciable difference in the lives of the working peasants. In June 1979, the government issued a drastic decree requiring the total communization of Ethiopia's agriculture within ten years. Forced resettlement of peasants into villages has been the chief means of speeding up this process. The regime boasted that 33 million peasants would be moved into newly created communal villages by 1990. By the end of 1987, 8 million peasants were herded into some 8,500 villages under intolerable conditions that have no resemblance to the ideal communes described in the decree.[1]

Since these policies lacked the needed spontaneity and free volition of the peasantry, the regime found itself constantly in open antagonism with the working peasants as they resisted forced collectivization. In early September 1979, for example, just three months after the issuance of the collectivization decree, 150 peasants were killed while resisting the forced changes.[2] In the face of the unmitigated hostility of the peasantry, the regime even began the practice of slave labor on state farms. According to one report presented to a UN working group on slavery in 1981, the government herded 15,000 laborers into trucks and transported them to Humera, in the northern region of the country, to work on a sesame harvest. The laborers were reportedly forced to work for 12 hours per day without sufficient food and water and without even makeshift living accommodations. Although the regime was compelled to repeal the practice under considerable international pressure, more than 1,600 laborers died during the harvest.[3] Additionally, in the summer of 1988, 2,000 peasants, who were forcibly resettled on a "pilot zone" in Gondar province, escaped from the project, choosing to become refugees in the Sudan.[4]

These are just a few instances that typify Ethiopia's agrarian problem, which is worsening the already harsh plight of the peasantry while at the same time eroding the power base of the regime. On balance, as the staggering statistics below will show, the regime's agrarian policy is a disaster. Agricultural production, which grew by 2.2 percent per annum in the 1960s, grew by only 0.5 percent in the late 1970s. Consequently, per capita food production for the 1976–80 period plummeted to 16 percent below its levels at the beginning of the decade.[5] The situation is worsened by the increasing and yet inefficient role of state farms in the agrarian sector. Over 90 percent of all agrarian investment goes into state farms, which have continued to produce a meager 4 percent of the country's food needs.[6] In addition to the heavy-handed intervention of the state in the economy, the agrarian classes have to deal with the extortionate collection of surpluses by the government in the form of taxes.[7]

A component element of the tax system is the price-control mechanism exercised by the Agricultural Marketing Corporation (AMC), a state agency whose task is to assess prices on agricultural commodities. The corporation's chief priority has so far been to provide food at cheap prices to the urban dwellers who are the political power base of the regime. With a 40 percent unemployment rate, the Ethiopian regime is sitting on a political volcano whose eruption must be prevented, if the regime is to survive the current crisis, by the provision of sufficient food to create quiescent urban dwellers at the expense of the rural classes.

The AMC predetermines how much food the country needs in a given year and then conveys the orders through its channels to the peasants, specifying the amounts and prices. The quotas required are so high that the peasants are left with no surplus to sell in the open market. In some instances, the official prices are lower than the cost of production, the result being that what the peasants produce is wholly absorbed by the state, partly for distribution to loyal segments of the population and partly for financing its war efforts in Eritrea.[8]

The seemingly endless recurrence of famine is another crucial threat to the regime, both as a source of human tragedy and as a potential danger to the Ethio-Soviet alliance which has failed to deal with it in a humane way. In the 1979-80 period, some 4.5 million people were affected by the famine in Eritrea and Ethiopia. Even though the regime has used the famine as a political weapon in Eritrea, the famine also significantly reduced the regime's capacity to collect agrarian surpluses since most parts of Ethiopia have also been hit by the drought. The cumulative results of mismanaging the economy and the drought have been that food production has continued to dwindle considerably. In 1980 the output of grain production fell to 300,000 tons from 600,000 tons in 1975–76. This necessitated the importation of 240,000 tons of grain to cover the difference.[9]

The same agrarian crisis and politics were replayed during the 1984–85 period, with Eritrea and Tigrai the hardest hit areas. In addition to the 2 million people displaced by the war, some 2.5 million people were affected by the famine. As the saga of famine continued to unfold in 1987, the Ethiopian regime again appealed for over 1 million tons of grain to cover its 1988 food deficit.[10] In this latest recurrence of famine, over 2 million people were expected to be affected if the international community did not donate its usual food handouts, since the Ethiopian regime has not changed its policies.

Even more apocalyptic scenarios lie ahead unless immediate political solutions are found to the regional conflicts, including the one between Eritrea and Ethiopia. According to U.S. sources, if Ethiopia's present agrarian policy is not changed, the country's food deficit will reach 2 million tons by 1992.[11] The projections of the World Bank are even more alarming. According to its recent study, Ethiopia's current food deficit of half a million tons will climb to 7 million tons by 1995. Ethiopia's present population of 45 million, which is growing by 2.9 percent annually, will increase by 90 percent to more than 5 million in the next thirty years. The study also revealed that the country's infant mortality rate today is 225 per 1,000, one of the highest in the world. The per capita income stands at $120, the fifth lowest in the world and the lowest in Africa.[12]

The regime's performance in the industrial sector is equally dismal. In the 1977–78 period, for example, industry grew by only 0.4 percent compared with 7.4 percent growth in the 1960s.[13] The main explanation is the government's misallocation of resources and mismanagement of the nationalized industrial firms. The government's response to the sagging industrial economy has been to promulgate meaningless plans and expect them to be financed externally. When the government launched a ten-year plan in 1980, it appealed to the international community for funds to finance its projects, and it expected to double the gross domestic product (GDP) by the end of the decade, to increase agrarian production and industrial output by 60 percent and 250 percent respectively, and to build 450,000 houses.[14] The paradox is that the regime still hoped to build "socialism" by relying on foreign aid. The $30 billion ten-year plan unveiled to the party congress in September 1984, for example, stipulated that 70 percent of the new projects were to be financed externally.[15]

To its chagrin, the regime found that the needed foreign funds were not forthcoming, and whatever funds were funneled into the country merely served to deepen the country's external dependency. By the end of 1982, Ethiopia had accumulated an external, nonmilitary debt of $898 million.[16] Of this figure, only $195 million was owed to the Soviet bloc, while the rest was owed to Western creditors, demonstrating Ethiopia's continued economic dependency on the West.

Although Ethiopia's external debt seems minuscule by Western standards, it is beyond the country's economic capacity to keep up with servicing its debt. Consequently, Ethiopia's international trade position is adversely affected. Monoculturally dependent on the export of coffee, which accounts for 80 percent of its foreign-exchange earnings, the country also suffered from the volatile world market price for coffee as the price for Ethiopian coffee fell by 40 percent at the beginning of the 1980s. In 1980, for example, of the total of 300,000 tons of coffee output, only 80,000 tons were exported and at a much reduced price.[17]

Furthermore, since the mid-1970s, Ethiopia's economy and foreign trade have been considerably affected by the energy crisis. In 1979 for example, her oil import bill devoured 36 percent of the country's export earnings. A year later the government announced that it was devoting 50 percent of its $500 million anticipated foreign earnings to oil imports. In light of this recurrent energy crisis, important development projects had to be either scrapped altogether or to be postponed indefinitely.[18]

The most salient factor militating against the Ethio-Soviet alliance is the militarization of Ethiopia's sagging economy. The Soviets had viewed Ethiopia as a crucial arms market so long as Ethiopia could pay the bill on time. But the prolongation of the Ethio-Eritrean war left the country with a $4 billion military hard-currency debt, wholly owed to the Soviets.[19] Every year since the present regime's accession to power, the military consumption has exceeded the total nonmilitary expenditure of the country. On the eve of the revolution, Ethiopia had only 45,000 soldiers, mostly deployed in Eritrea, with an annual budget of $40 million, whereas today the regime commands a 300,000 strong army with an annual budget of $400 million, and half of Ethiopia's army is currently deployed in Eritrea. According to international observers, 46 percent of Ethiopia's GNP is being spent on maintaining the armed forces, whose primary task has become fighting the Eritreans and other dissident nationalists.[20]

All things considered, Ethiopia has become an economic liability for the Soviet Union. The magnitude of Ethiopia's economic and military problems is probably beyond any power's capacity to solve. After all, the Soviet Union itself is economically too weak to provide Ethiopia with economic assistance enough to sustain the regime's legitimacy and to retain Eritrea within the imperial network. The meager economic contributions it has made to Ethiopia testify to this point. During the 1980 famine, the Soviet Union gave only $5 million, including 12,000 tons of grain, in outright grants to Ethiopia, a minuscule amount compared with what the West gave in food aid. Even during the disastrous famine of 1984–85, the Soviets contributed to the relief efforts a mere 2,500 tons of grain.[21]

This economic analysis illustrates that Ethiopia's growing dependency on the Soviet Union and the USSR's subsequent inability to continue sustaining Ethiopia both economically and militarily were bound to create a rupture in Ethio-Soviet relations, much to the expectation of the West. Cracks have already begun to show. In March 1985, during a brief meeting with Mengistu in Moscow, Gorbachev reportedly expressed his displeasure with Ethiopia's dismal economic performance and political deterioration. Ethiopia's inability to achieve food self-sufficiency and to repay her hard-currency debt were two issues of particular concern to the Soviet leader. Since then, commercial transactions between the two countries have steadily declined, and there has been a sharp reduction in subsidized Soviet oil supply to Ethiopia, leaving the country in its worst shape ever. Whereas Ethio-Soviet trade increased tenfold between 1977 and 1985, it has progressively declined every year since then.[22]

Faced with these harsh economic realities, the Soviets are said to have exerted pressure on Mengistu to decollectivize the peasant households and to accept the World Bank's recent recommendations for full privatization of the agrarian sector, lifting the ban on interregional exchanges of agrarian commodities, and increasing prices for agricultural products. The regime responded to these cumulative pressures by increasing prices for agrarian products between 8 and 9 percent, starting in January 1988. In return, the Soviets gave Ethiopia 250,000 tons of grain to encourage further liberalization measures. Seemingly designed to improve the Soviet image, a grain shipment of such magnitude is the first of its kind to any country in the Third World.[23]

Nonetheless, the country's economic difficulties require a far more drastic transformation of the empire, including its political institutions. The thirty-year-old war in Eritrea holds the key to this change. The regime can redirect its attention and resources to solving the country's economic problems only when and if it is willing to respect the popular will of the Eritreans and other recalcitrant nationalities and to settle accounts with them by democratic methods. Additionally, the land ought to be decollectivized, allowing for the free and spontaneous organization by the agrarian classes, and the entire economy ought to be demilitarized. Short of these conditions, Ethio-Soviet relations are bound to turn for the worse.

In addition to these endogenous factors, i.e., the military deterioration in Eritrea and the collapse of the Ethiopian economy, the dynamics of perestroika have further unintended ramifications for Ethio-Soviet relations. A restructuring of Soviet diplomacy is necessary in order to give breathing space to the new productive forces in the Soviet Union. Since Gorbachev's introverted economic orientation and hopes are pinned on achieving rapid modernization and efficiency of these newly unleashed forces of capitalist production, he needs every bit of available resources deployed in the Soviet Union, meaning that the economic redynamization and political crystallization of these forces will, of necessity, take precedence over Soviet Third World policy. There will be less resources available for international distribution. Consequently, Ethiopia's share of Soviet aid will be drastically reduced. The dynamics of perestroika and the demands of the introverted means of capital accumulation, if they continue in the current direction, are likely to militate against the overly long stay of the Soviet Union in the Horn. In the last analysis, without undiminished Soviet economic and military support, the collapse of the Ethiopian regime seems likely.

The Ungovernability of the Eritrean People

Ethiopia's policy of weakening Eritrea's economy over the decades and the sequential political repressions have had a homogenizing effect on the Eritrean people. Political alienation by the Ethiopian regime contributed to the galvanization of popular support for the nationalists. The disintegration of Ethiopia's feudal order and the promulgation of its attempt at socialism have not changed the basic antagonistic relationship between the two nations.

As Petras and Morley commented, one crucial element that distinguishes Ethiopian colonialism in Eritrea from other advanced forms of capitalist colonialism is the fact that Ethiopia has not resolved the Ethio-Eritrean conflict by installing a neocolonial regime in Eritrea, subservient to Ethiopia's economic and strategic needs. The Ethiopian state lacks the necessary economic conditions to create and control pliant, collaborationist political forces in Eritrea capable of maintaining a neocolonial state.[24]

This analysis suggests that, if Eritrean independence is to be attained, it must be attained on the basis of complete economic and political rupture with Ethiopia, resulting in the Eritrean economy being harnessed to other advanced economies. But this possibility deprives Ethiopia of any incentive to seek an accommodation with the Eritreans on the basis of political dialogue and negotiation. The remaining option will then be for Eritrea to confront Ethiopia with a fait accompli of military victory. At the time of this writing, trends seem to be moving in favor of this option as objective conditions for

Eritrean military victory seem brighter than ever.

Successive Ethiopian campaigns of encirclement and suppression, which began in 1978, have failed to destroy the Eritrean movement. On the contrary, Eritreans have effectively weathered the storm and have regained all the territory they had lost in the 1978–79 Ethiopian offensives. In the last eleven years, Ethiopia has lost 150,000 soldiers in Eritrea, and the material losses it has sustained are even more staggering. The year 1988, in particular, saw a dramatization of Eritrean military resurgence. In March 1988, for example, Eritrea's People's Liberation Army routed the 20,000 strong Ethiopian army at the battle of Af Abet in northern Eritrea. In this stunning victory, the Eritreans captured fifty tanks, sixty multiple rocket launchers, and a large quantity of artillery pieces and ammunition. The British Africanist, Basil Davidson, who was at the scene at the time, described this victory as "one of the biggest ever scored by any liberation movement anywhere since Dien Bien Phu in 1954."[25] Soviet foreign ministry spokesman Gennady Gerassimov for the first time publicly acknowledged that three Soviet colonels were captured by the EPLF and that one was killed at Af Abet.[26]

According to EPLF sources, the People's Liberation Army engaged the Ethiopians in 118 battles in 1988 alone, killing or capturing more than 60,000 Ethiopians, destroying 76 tanks, 20 aircraft, and more than 200 military vehicles, damaging 7 ships, and capturing 55 tanks and 200 trucks in addition to huge quantities of arms and artillery pieces.[27]

The Af Abet victory in March 1988 marked the military reversal in Eritrea. Since then the Eritreans have intensified their counteroffensive against Ethiopia's second army and have scored major victories, highlighted by the capture of the strategic Eritrean port of Massawa on 10 February 1990. Assisted by the newly constituted Eritrean naval unit, the nationalist forces launched an amphibious operation in early February and quickly put the Ethiopian navy at Massawa out of action, sinking most of its fighting vessels. During the operation, in addition to destroying huge quantities of war matériel, the Eritreans captured 80 tanks, over 20,000 light arms, 8 rocket launchers, and several guided anti-tank guns. They also put 35,000 Ethiopian soldiers out of commission.[28]

The capture of Massawa has three important implications. First, it increased Eritrea's international visibility to such an extent that even the two superpowers have been compelled to make some adjustments to the new reality as they have belatedly begun to acknowledge the legitimacy of the Eritrean struggle. Second, it has, for all practical purposes, cut off the 200,000 Ethiopian soldiers in Eritrea from the rest of the empire and has precipitated the rapid deterioration of the military situation in both Eritrea and Ethiopia. As demoralization among Ethiopian soldiers continues, many officers are defecting from the army, seeking refuge either in liberated Eritrea or in neighboring countries. Third, the capture of Massawa has further deepened the crisis within the Ethiopian state, evidenced by the recent execution of twelve senior military officers who had participated in the May 1989 coup against the regime. In mid-1990, another 180 senior officers were still in detention awaiting a similar fate. The military successes have also provided the context for the Ethiopian People's Democratic Revolutionary Front (EPDRF), an umbrella organization of several anticentralist forces, including the TPLF, to make major military advances toward Addis Ababa.

In the context of these developments, Eritrea has once again become a nightmare for Mengistu. The military paradox is that, given the magnitude of modern weapons captured by the Eritreans, Ethiopia is not only losing the war in Eritrea, but also is indirectly subsidizing Eritrea's military operations against Ethiopia.

Taking cognizance of this fact, the Soviets are showing some signs in favor of a political solution to the painful military dilemma. Since 1985, Soviet propaganda warfare against Eritrea has considerably subsided. In fact, one Soviet foreign ministry publication put the blame on Ethiopia for the military situation: "[T]he search for the right ways of solving the national question was adversely affected by political and ideological immaturity and at times incorrect, mechanistic application of some Marxist-Leninist concepts to the specific conditions of Ethiopia."[29]

There are indications that the change of Soviet attitude toward Eritrea has been translated into substantial reductions of Soviet arms delivered to Ethiopia. However, a cautionary note should be inserted here that any change in Soviet attitude is not necessarily a product of its conviction about the just character of the Eritrean insurrection, but rather a result of economic and political considerations and constraints as well as of its perception about the unwinnability of the Eritrean situation by military means.

Furthermore, the objective conditions in Ethiopia itself are not conducive for the Soviet presence any more as the ethnopolitical forces, like the Tigrayan People's Liberation Front, have intensified their assaults on the regime and have scored substantial gains in recent years. Under these conditions, the Soviet Union is very unlikely to continue financing the Ethiopian war effort in Eritrea or elsewhere indefinitely.

Competition from the West

By Western definition, Ethiopia is a full-blown Marxist state. The regime sides with the Soviet Union on every global issue in opposing Western moves and policies. Yet the paradox has been that Ethiopia is the only "Marxist" state exempted from Western economic sanctions and diplomatic isolation. In fact, as we shall see, the West is still the chief source of economic aid to Ethiopia.

Notwithstanding the well-coordinated Ethio-Soviet offensives against Eritrea, sometimes involving up to 200,000 forces, Western support for Eritrean nationalism has been conspicuously absent. The West consciously played down the war by imposing a tacit news blackout on the military activities in Eritrea for fear that the Ethiopian regime might be offended by Eritrea's exposure in the West. Many scholars have been perplexed by the tentative and reflexive posture of the West. James Dougherty, for example, attributes this uncharacteristic Western behavior to the cognitive dissonance and self-induced paralysis of American policymakers: "Through the Watergate and the Carter years, the policy of the U.S. government in the Horn had been essentially that of the hesitant, reactive and uncommitted observer which seemed incapable of understanding what was going on because it lacked a coherent, comprehensive global strategic perspective."[30]

This observation does not, however, fully explain the general policy disposition of the United States and its allies. From the Western standpoint, there are overriding considerations (discussed in Chapter 7) that have restrained the West in general and the United States in particular from openly antagonizing the Ethiopian regime by embracing the Eritreans. Moreover, a traditional hostility exists between the United States and Eritrean nationalists as the former publicly endorses Ethiopia's claim over Eritrea. As the United States continued to train, equip, and advise the Ethiopian army over the decades, Eritrean nationalists singled out the United States as the chief international enemy of the Eritrean resistance. This position was consistently reinforced by the Eritreans' anti-imperialist chanting as Washington continued to buttress Ethiopia militarily and economically. Even after the dramatic change when the Soviets embraced the Dergue in the late 1970s, Eritrean nationalists showed no interest in the United States. In light of this anti-imperialist intransigence, the United States lacked any constituency in Eritrea that might have been used as a countervailing force to the Soviet presence in the area.

More important, however, there has been a consensus among Western powers that the Ethio-Soviet alliance is a result of an aberrant and temporary convergence of interests of the two countries preconditioned by unfavorable Ethiopian internal circumstances that have threatened the "territorial integrity" of the empire. The Western rationale is that the Ethiopian regime has been compelled by circumstances to seek military assistance of a magnitude that the West could not offer, in order to counter the centrifugal forces of discontent. A subsidiary of this argument holds that total cessation of Western economic aid to Ethiopia might propel the Dergue further into the Soviet orbit.

In keeping with this assessment, the United States and its allies have continued pouring economic aid into Ethiopia, irrespective of the regime's unmitigated hostility toward the West. The overarching purpose has been to undermine the Soviet presence in the area by means of a protracted economic competition. According to U.S. sources, between 1976 and 1982, the U.S.-dominated multilateral development banks extended more than $300 million in loans and credits to Ethiopia. With respect to commercial relations, the United States and the European Economic Community absorbed over 50 percent of Ethiopia's international trade in 1978, while the Soviet bloc absorbed a mere 2 percent.[31]

In 1981, the EEC pledged a four-year package of $150 million while Italy made an additional contribution of $44 million. Sweden was providing the regime with $20 million annually. In addition to providing generous humanitarian aid, the United States also continued to be the largest importer of Ethiopian coffee, importing $63 million worth of coffee in 1987 alone.[32]

The economic importance of the West to Ethiopia was revealed
in February 1983 when the regime issued yet another economic edict
opening the Ethiopian economy to foreign entrepreneurs and capital.
The law permitted the transfer of shares, the repatriation of profits
and capital, employment of personnel without government restrictions, and total or partial exemptions from customs duties on items
imported for investment purposes. Mengistu tried to justify these
measures in terms of the economic hardships facing the country, such
as acute food shortages, low industrial production, high unemployment and inflation rates, dwindling export earnings, and insufficient
capital.[33]

Following this economic decree, some Western business firms
began doing business in Ethiopia. In March 1983, for instance, British shipbuilders won a contract to build two general-purpose cargo
ships for Ethiopia at the cost of £25 million.[34] A West German company has also recently agreed to build a pottery factory in Ethiopia
at a cost of $33 million.[35]

But the West viewed state-to-state economic relations as the most
effective vehicle for weakening Soviet influence in the Horn and woo-
ing the Ethiopian regime back to the West. Western politicians frequently stressed the need for patience and flexibility in dealing with
Ethiopia, as they applied the carrot approach. Consequently, the West
continued to extend its generous economic largesse to Ethiopia. Between 1984 and 1988, the multilateral development banks, the EEC,
and its individual members gave or pledged to give Ethiopia a total
of $1.3 billion in development and food aid. For its part, the United
States gave over 692,000 tons of grain, worth $270 million.[36]

The generous economic largesse given to Ethiopia by the West over
the years dramatizes the West's determination to reduce Soviet influence in the area and to bring Ethiopia back to the West. On balance,
the United States and its allies created Ethiopia's economic dependency on the West in significant ways that can be translated into political leverage. This has already posed a painful dilemma to the regime.
Mengistu knows very well that he can save the colonial framework
in Eritrea from disintegration only by the military means that have
made him parasitically dependent on the Soviet Union. By the same
token, he knows that the West will not provide him with arms in
the amount that the Soviets have been offering. Even if the West
provides him with sufficient armaments, it is less likely to provide

combatants as the Soviets and Cubans have done. It has, therefore, become apparent that Mengistu cannot maintain the imperial status quo without active external intervention, which may not be forthcoming from the West. Yet he is aware of the advantages of his economic association with the West and of the growing disaffection of Ethiopians with their economic plight and with Soviet dominance over the country. The excruciating dilemma is then: can he maintain his economic dependency on the West without breaking his military dependency on the East? To put it differently, how can he break with the East without breaking the colonial framework in Eritrea?

From the Soviet perspective, too, the protraction of the Ethio-Eritrean conflict has proven to be an agonizing experience. The Soviets are exhausted from overstretching their human and material resources to a point where they can no longer effectively compete with the West over the Horn and stabilize their presence there. Content analysis of recent Soviet literature and observation of the tentative moves of the present leadership suggest that they are ready to disentangle themselves one way or another from the Brezhnev legacy. Partial evidence is the fact that Vice Premier Anatoly Adanishin took up the Horn for discussion with Assistant Secretary of State for African Affairs Chester Crocker in London in late April 1988, without prior consultation with Ethiopia. Such moves may point to a possible collusion between the two superpowers as an alternative to competition over the region. The current honeymoonlike cordial East-West relations may readily enter into this equation.

As indicated earlier, the rapid deterioration in the military situation in Eritrea has posed a serious dilemma for both superpowers. In January 1990, U.S. Congressional staffers visited liberated Eritrea and evidently received a favorable impression. Their visit was followed by two hearings on the Ethio-Eritrean conflict and the famine, one in the House of Representatives on 28 February and the other in the Senate on 28 March. During both hearings, U.S. Assistant Secretary of State for African Affairs Herman Cohen acknowledged for the first time that the unilateral termination of the federation by Ethiopia in 1962 was illegal and that the Eritrean struggle was legitimate. Although he qualified his recognition of Eritrea's right to self-determination by stating that it should be exercised within the framework of Ethiopian territorial unity, the move was a major departure from the traditional U.S. policy on Eritrea. Cohen further accepted the EPLF position that the United Nations should play a role in the peace process in Eritrea.[37]

In line with the newly evolving regional configuration, Presidents Bush and Gorbachev raised the Ethio-Eritrean conflict during their June 1990 summit. They issued a joint communiqué relating to both the conflict and the famine situation. According to their statement, the United States would provide sorghum and rice and the Soviet Union would divert its Antonov planes, currently used to deploy Ethiopian troops and ammunition, to transport the food aid to areas affected by the famine. The two leaders also agreed on the use of Massawa as a distribution point for relief aid, but to downplay the political significance of this project their statement added that the leaders "believe that such operations will not compromise the unity and territorial integrity of Ethiopia." Finally, the communiqué stated that "the U.S. and U.S.S.R. will support an international conference of governments under the auspices of the U.N. on settlement of conflict situations in the Horn of Africa."[38]

Apart from being ambiguous on the key point, the question of Eritrea's right to self-determination, the communiqué reveals that the two superpowers have not completely abandoned their traditional policy. The insertion of a reference to Ethiopia's "unity and territorial integrity" without making any reference to the recent Ethiopian bombardments of civilian centers in Eritrea—in which internationally banned lethal weapons including napalm and cluster bombs were used—represents duplicity on the part of the two superpowers.

Although how Eritrean nationalists will react to future regional and international realignment remains to be seen, the Ethiopian regime has already begun a new round of diplomatic offensives in the Middle East to undercut regional support for Eritrean nationalism. Worried about the ramifications of possible Soviet backtracking, Ethiopian diplomats have been touring Syria, Algeria, Tunisia, Egypt, Saudi Arabia, North Yemen, and other countries, most of which were until recently regarded as bastions of "international imperialism" and "Arab reaction." This diplomatic activity reveals the extent of Ethiopia's anxiety.

The regime has even applied for membership to the Islamic Conferences, claiming that 20 million of Ethiopia's 42 million people are Moslems. This desperate conversion from socialism to Islam, after fourteen years of a concerted antireligion posture, underlines the political panic facing the ruling elements. Irrespective of her real intentions, Ethiopia has gained some diplomatic successes. She reestablished relations with Tunisia, which were broken in 1975 over Eritrea. Egypt is actively campaigning on Ethiopia's behalf in the region. In 1987, Saudi Arabia, too, pledged $200 million in economic aid to Ethiopia.[39]

Concurrent with these developments, Israel's visibility is also increasing. There has always been a low-keyed Israeli presence, represented by a dozen or so Israeli technicians who maintained Ethiopia's American-supplied fighter planes.[40] In 1983, Israel supplied Ethiopia with $20 million worth of military hardware and spare parts. These arms transactions between the two countries were said to have been handled by a company registered and located in Amsterdam and transferred to a shadowy firm known as Amiran, based in Ethiopia.[41]

Moreover, according to informed sources, Israeli officials have in recent years pleaded with the U.S. government to resume political dialogue with Ethiopia over a wide range of issues including Eritrea. There are also reports that Israel and Ethiopia have concluded several agreements regarding Israeli supply of arms and spare parts. Additionally, a number of Ethiopian officers are said to be receiving military training in Israel itself.[42]

The growing Ethio-Israeli relations were marked by the resumption of full diplomatic ties between the two countries in November 1989. The restoration of diplomatic relations provided the context for the "strategic cooperation accords" signed in the same month. According to this agreement, Israel and Ethiopia would further strengthen their military cooperation. In fact, there have been reports that Israeli experts furnished logistical and strategic support such as surveillance on EPLF troop movements during the February 1990 assault on Massawa.[43]

Israeli Defense Minister Yitzhak Rabin rationalized Israeli involvement in Eritrea in terms of Ethiopia's cooperation in permitting 16,000 black Jews to leave Ethiopia. He further revealed that his government was coordinating its assistance programs to Ethiopia with the United States. Without specifics on the nature of the coordination, he noted, "We, of course, are in direct contact with U.S. officials in regards to what is acceptable to the United States to be done or what is not."[44] This off-hand statement by the Israeli general exposes the Janus-like strategy of the United States, namely its tentative move in favor of Eritrea's self-determination while at the same time seeking to maintain the status quo with Ethiopia.

The dialectic of history is, however, in operation in ways that will ensure the ungovernability of the region short of genuine resolution of the fundamental contradictions that have hitherto plagued the region. The geopolitical configuration will never be the same. A galaxy of statesmen, intellectuals, journalists, and historians have many times commented that the Eritrean insurrection was dead. But to the contrary, the nationalists never resigned themselves to the excruciating odds of humiliation, conspiracy, or betrayal, or to the international oblivion and indifference to their rights and plights inherent in the Ethiopian posture. The endurance and tenacity of the Eritrean people and the discipline, heroism, and determination of the fighters are indeed of epic proportions. If Eritrea's history is a guide to the future, it is certain that the nationalists will continue the armed struggle to realize Eritrea's long quest for national self-determination, for which more than one million Eritreans have shed their blood in this thirty-year-old war.

In summation, in the Horn of Africa things are moving in the direction in which they began before the Ethiopian revolution. The Eritreans control 95 percent of the territory and the anticentralist forces within Ethiopia itself are gathering momentum, threatening seizure of power. Under this state of confusion and paralysis, the Soviet Union seems to be groping in the dark to find its way out without losing face and without losing its influence entirely. Conversely, the West's hopes are brighter than ever as its longstanding pro-Ethiopia policy and patience seem to be vindicated. In short, the metaphysics of international politics is in operation, seemingly to start the cycle anew.

Appendix

United Nations Resolution 390-A(V)

Whereas by paragraph 3 of Annex XI to the Treaty of Peace with Italy, 1947, the Powers concerned have agreed to accept the recommendation of the General Assembly on the disposal of the former Italian colonies in Africa and to take appropriate measures for giving effect to it,

Whereas by paragraph 2 of the aforesaid Annex XI such disposal is to be made in the light of the wishes and welfare of the inhabitants and the interests of peace and security, taking into consideration the views of interested governments,

Now therefore

The General Assembly, in the light of the reports of the United Nations Commission for Eritrea and of the Interim Committee, and

Taking into consideration

(a) The wishes and welfare of the inhabitants of Eritrea, including the views of the various racial, religious and political groups of the provinces of the territory and the capacity of the people for self-government,

(b) The interests of peace and security in East Africa,

(c) The rights and claims of Ethiopia based on geographical, historical, ethnic or economic reasons, including in particular Ethiopia's legitimate need for adequate access to the sea,

Taking into account the importance of assuring the continuing collaboration of the foreign communities in the economic development of Eritrea,

Recognizing that the disposal of Eritrea should be based on its close political and economic association with Ethiopia, and

Desiring that this association assure to the inhabitants of Eritrea the fullest respect and safeguards for their institutions, traditions, religions and languages, as well as the widest possible measure of self-government, while at the same time respecting the Constitution, institutions, traditions and the international status and identity of the Empire of Ethiopia,

A. *Recommends that*:

1. Eritrea shall constitute an autonomous unit federated with Ethiopia under the sovereignty of the Ethiopian Crown.

2. The Eritrean Government shall possess legislative, executive and judicial powers in the field of domestic affairs.

3. The juridsdiction of the Federal Government shall extend to the following matters: defence, foreign affairs, currency and finance, foreign and interstate commerce and external and interstate communications, including ports. The Federal Government shall have the power to maintain the integrity of the Federation, and shall have the right to impose uniform taxes throughout the Federation to meet the expenses of federal functions and services, it being understood that the assessment and the collection of such taxes in Eritrea are to be delegated to the Eritrean Government, and provided that Eritrea shall bear only its just and equitable share of these expenses. The jurisdiction of the Eritrean Government shall extend to all matters not vested in the Federal Government, including the power to maintain the internal police, to levy taxes to meet the expenses of domestic functions and services, and to adopt its own budget.

4. The area of the Federation shall constitute a single area for customs purposes, and there shall be no barriers to the free movement of goods and persons within the area. Customs duties on goods entering or leaving the Federation which have their final destination or origin in Eritrea shall be assigned to Eritrea.

5. An Imperial Federal Council composed of equal numbers of Ethiopian and Eritrean representatives shall meet at least once a year and shall advise upon the common affairs of the Federation referred to in paragraph 3 above. The citizens of Eritrea shall participate in

the executive and judicial branches, and shall be represented in the legislative branch, of the Federal Government, in accordance with law and in the proportion that the population of Eritrea bears to the population of the Federation.

6. A single nationality shall prevail throughout the Federation:

(a) All inhabitants of Eritrea, except persons possessing foreign nationality, shall be nationals of the Federation;

(b) All inhabitants born in Eritrea and having at least one indigenous parent or grandparent shall also be nationals of the Federation. Such persons, if in possession of a foreign nationality, shall, within six months of the coming into force of the Eritrean Constitution, be free to opt to renounce the nationality of the Federation and retain such foreign nationality. In the event that they do not so opt, they shall thereupon lose such foreign nationality;

(c) The qualifications of persons acquiring the nationality of the Federation under sub-paragraphs (a) and (b) above for exercising their rights as citizens of Eritrea shall be determined by the Constitution and laws of Eritrea;

(d) All persons possessing foreign nationality who have resided in Eritrea for ten years prior to the date of the adoption of the present resolution shall have the right, without further requirements of residence, to apply for the nationality of the Federation in accordance with federal laws. Such persons who do not thus acquire the nationality of the Federation shall be permitted to reside in and engage in peaceful and lawful pursuits in Eritrea;

The rights and interests of foreign nationals resident in Eritrea shall be guaranteed in accordance with the provisions of paragraph 7.

7. The Federal Government, as well as Eritrea, shall ensure to residents in Eritrea, without distinction of nationality, race, sex, language or religion, the enjoyment of human rights and fundamental liberties, including the following:

(a) The right to equality before the law. No discrimination shall be made against foreign enterprises in existence in Eritrea engaged in industrial, commercial, agricultural, artisan, educational or charitable activities, nor against banking institutions and insurance companies operating in Eritrea;

(b) The right to life, liberty and security of person;

(c) The right to own and dispose of property. No one shall be deprived of property, including contractual rights, without due process of law and without payment of just and effective compensation;

(d) The right to freedom of opinion and expression and the right of adopting and practising any creed or religion;

(e) The right to education;

(f) The right to freedom of peaceful assembly and association;

(g) The right to inviolability of correspondence and domicile, subject to the requirements of the law;

(h) The right to exercise any profession subject to the requirements of the law;

(i) No one shall be subject to arrest or detention without an order of a competent authority, except in case of flagrant and serious violation of the law in force. No one shall be deported except in accordance with the law;

(j) The right to a fair and equitable trial, the right of petition to the Emperor and the right of appeal to the Emperor for commutation of death sentences;

(k) Retroactivity of penal law shall be excluded;

The respect for the rights and freedoms of others and the requirements of public order and the general welfare alone will justify any limitations to the above rights.

8. Paragraphs 1 to 7 inclusive of the present resolution shall constitute the Federal Act which shall be submitted to the Emperor of Ethiopia for ratification.

9. There shall be a transition period which shall not extend beyond 15 September 1952, during which the Eritrean Government will be organized and the Eritrean Constitution prepared and put into effect.

10. There shall be a United Nations Commissioner in Eritrea appointed by the General Assembly. The Commissioner will be assisted by experts appointed by the Secretary-General of the United Nations.

11. During the transition period, the present Administering Authority shall continue to conduct the affairs of Eritrea. It shall, in consultation with the United Nations Commissioner, prepare as rapidly as possible the organization of an Eritrean administration, induct Eritreans into all levels of the administration, and make arrangements for and convoke a representative assembly of Eritreans chosen by the people. It may, in agreement with the Commissioner, negotiate on behalf of the Eritreans a temporary customs union with Ethiopia to be put into effect as soon as practicable.

12. The United Nations Commissioner shall, in consultation with the Administering Authority, the Government of Ethiopia, and the inhabitants of Eritrea, prepare a draft of the Eritrean Constitution to be submitted to the Eritrean Assembly and shall advise and assist the Eritrean Assembly in its consideration of the Constitution. The Constitution of Eritrea shall be based on the principles of democratic government, shall include the guarantees contained in paragraph 7 of the Federal Act, shall be consistent with the provisions of the Federal Act and shall contain provisions adopting and ratifying the Federal Act on behalf of the people of Eritrea.

13. The Federal Act and the Constitution of Eritrea shall enter into effect following ratification of the Federal Act by the Emperor of Ethiopia, and following approval by the Commissioner, adoption by the Eritrean Assembly and ratification by the Emperor of Ethiopia of the Eritrean Constitution.

14. Arrangements shall be made by the Government of the United Kingdom of Great Britain and Northern Ireland as the Administering Authority for the transfer of power to the appropriate authorities. The transfer of power shall take place as soon as the Eritrean Constitution and the Federal Act enter into effect, in accordance with the provisions of paragraph 13 above.

15. The United Nations Commissioner shall maintain his headquarters in Eritrea until the transfer of power has been completed, and shall make appropriate reports to the General Assembly of the United Nations concerning the discharge of his functions. The Commissioner may consult with the Interim Committee of the General Assembly with respect to the discharge of his functions in the light of developments and within the terms of the present resolution. When the transfer of authority has been completed, he shall so report to the General Assembly and submit to it the text of the Eritrean Consitution;

B. *Authorizes* the Secretary-General, in accordance with establish practice:

1. To arrange for the payment of an appropriate remuneration to the United Nations Commissioner;

2. To provide the United Nations Commissioner with such experts, staff and facilities as the Secretary-General may consider necessary to carry out the terms of the present resolution.

Notes

Chapter 1

1. Patrick Chabal, *Amilcar Cabral: Revolutionary Leadership and People's War*, p. 11.

2. For various definitions of nationalism, see Boyd C. Shafer, *Faces of Nationalism: New Realities and Old Myths*, p. 1.

3. Shafer, pp. 17–20.

4. Ibid., p. 7.

5. From Ernest Renan, *Discours et Conferences*, reprinted in Hans Kohn, *Nationalism: Its Meaning and History*, p. 139.

6. Hans Kohn, *The Idea of Nationalism: A Study in Its Origins and Background*, p. 6.

7. Kohn, 1955, p. 10.

8. Shafer, chap. 10, esp. pp. 275–77.

9. "An official translation of the decisions of the Moslem League of Eritrea as received by B.M.A., Eritrea, January 1947."

10. FO 371/73846, Paddock's Preliminary Report in Eritrea, Enclosure to Mason to Stewart, 9 September 1949.

11. WO 230/246, Political Adviser [Mason] to Scott-Fox, 19 June 1948.

12. Marvin L. Bender, "Introduction," in *Non-Semitic Languages of Ethiopia*, edited by Marvin L. Bender, p. 12.

13. E. David Thompson, "Languages of Northern Eritrea," ibid., p. 598.

14. Richard A. Hudson, "Beja," ibid., p. 97.

15. Thompson, ibid., p. 597.

16. Ibid., p. 599.

17. Ibid.

18. Yemane Mesghenna, *Italian Colonialism: A Case Study of Eritrea, 1869–1934—Motive, Praxis and Result*, pp. 54–64.

19. Tekeste Negash, *Italian Colonialism in Eritrea, 1882–1941: Policies, Praxis and Impact*, chap. 2.

20. Tekeste Negash, p. 34; Yemane Mesghenna, pp. 100–106; Richard Leonard, "European Colonization and the Socio-Economic Integration of Eritrea," Permanent Peoples Tribunal of the International League for the Rights and Liberation of Peoples, *The Eritrean Case: Proceedings of the Permanent Peoples Tribunal of the International League for the Rights and Liberations of Peoples*, Session on Eritrea, Milan, Italy, 24–26 May 1980, p. 62.

21. Ibid., p. 63; Eritreans for Liberation in North America (EFLNA), *In Defense of the Eritrean Revolution*, pp. 40, 154–55; Tekeste Negash, p. 36; Yemane Mesghenna, pp. 112–14.

22. R. A. Caulk, "'Black Snake, White Snake': Bahta Hagos and His Revolt against Italian Overrule in Eritrea, 1894."

23. Yemane Mesghenna, pp. 117–18; Tekeste Negash, p. 124; Caulk, pp. 20–29; Harold G. Marcus, *The Life and Times of Menelik II: Ethiopia, 1844–1913*, pp. 154–55.

24. Caulk, p. 23.

25. Yemane Mesghenna, p. 160.

26. Leonard, *The Eritrean Case*, p. 63.

27. Ibid., p. 73.

28. Tekeste Negash, p. 48.

29. Timothy Fernyhough, "Social Mobility and Dissident Elites in Northern Ethiopia: The Role of Banditry, 1900–1969," p. 9.

30. Tekeste Negash, p. 49.

31. Leonard, p. 68.

32. G. K. N. Trevaskis, *Eritrea: A Colony in Transition, 1941–52*, p. 36.

33. Leonard, *The Eritrean Case*, p. 68.

34. Jordan Gabre-Medhin, "Eritrea: The Roots of War," p. 50.

35. Trevaskis, p. 46.

36. Leonard, *The Eritrean Case*, p. 68.

37. EFLNA, p. 41.

38. Guido Bimbi, "The National Liberation Struggle and the Liberation Fronts," *The Eritrean Case*, p. 171.

39. EFLNA, p. 41.

40. Ibid.

41. Leonard, *The Eritrean Case*, pp. 81–82.

Chapter 2

1. Faadia Touval, *Somali Nationalism: International Politics and the Drive for Unity in the Horn of Africa*, p. 51.

2. Statement of Ethiopian government to the Council of Foreign Ministers, cited in Permanent Peoples Tribunal of the International League for the Rights and Liberation of Peoples, *The Eritrean Case*, p. 25.

3. Cited in David Pool, *Eritrea: Africa's Longest War*, p. 13.

4. Cited in Harold G. Marcus, *Ethiopia, Great Britain, and the United States, 1941–1974: The Politics of Empire*, p. 51.

5. Ethiopian Parliament, cited in Haggai Erlich, *The Struggle over Eritrea, 1962–1978: War and Revolution in the Horn of Africa*, pp. 34–35.

6. See "Introduction" in M. L. Bender et al., eds., *Language in Ethiopia*, and "Introduction" in M. L. Bender, ed., *Non-Semitic Languages of Ethiopia*.

7. Ethiopian government, "The Ethiopian Revolution and the Problem in Eritrea," official document, Addis Ababa, July 1977.

8. From a speech of Mengistu Haile Mariam delivered on Ethiopian radio and television, 7 June 1978.

9. Richard Leonard, "European Colonization and the Socio-Economic Integration of Eritrea," *The Eritrean Case*, p. 57.

10. Permanent Peoples Tribunal, "Advisory Opinion on Eritrea October 3, 1980," *The Eritrean Case*, pp. 369–70.

11. Eritreans for Liberation in North America (EFLNA), *In Defense of the Eritrean Revolution*, p. 32.

12. Ibid.

13. "Joint Declaration of the Eritrean Liberation Front and the Eritrean People's Liberation Front," *The Eritrean Case*, pp. 25–26.

14. George Lipski et al., *Ethiopia: Its People, Its Society, Its Culture*, p. 7; see also Richard Sherman, *Eritrea: The Unfinished Revolution*, p. 5; and J. Spencer Trimmingham, *Islam in Ethiopia*, pp. 5–7.

15. Yuri M. Kobishchanov, *Axum*, p. 35; Sherman, p. 5.

16. Kobishchanov, p. 35.

17. Trimmingham, p. 35.

18. Richard Greenfield, "Pre-colonial and Colonial History," in *Behind the War in Eritrea*, edited by Basil Davidson et al., p. 19.

19. Ibid.

20. Ibid.

21. See Kobishchanov, p. 43.

22. Ibid., p. 83.

23. Ibid., p. 84.

24. Ibid., pp. 80–81.

25. Sherman, p. 5ff; Trimmingham, p. 47.

26. Kobishchanov, pp. 83–84; EFLNA, p. 30.

27. Trimmingham, pp. 46–47; Tadesse Tamrat, *Church and State in Ethiopia: 1270–1527*, pp. 31–32.

28. Trimmingham, p. 22; Tadesse Tamrat, p. 37.

29. Edward Ullendorff, *The Ethiopians: An Introduction to Country and People*, p. 56; Trimmingham, pp. 50–51.

30. Lipski et al., p. 8; Ullendorff, p. 57; Trimmingham, p. 52.

31. Lipski et al., p. 8; Trimmingham, p. 55.

32. Lipski et al., p. 9; Ullendorff, p. 61; Robert L. Hess, *Ethiopia: The Modernization of Autocracy*, p. 35.

33. Trimmingham, p. 48; Tadesse Tamrat, p. 37.

34. Ullendorff, p. 36.

35. Ibid., p. 61; Lipski et al., p. 9; Trimmingham, p. 57.

36. Lipski et al., p. 9; Ullendorff, p. 61.

37. Tadesse Tamrat, p. 54.

38. Ullendorff, p. 61; Trimmingham, p. 57.

39. Mordechai Abir, *Ethiopia and the Red Sea: The Rise and Decline of the Solomonic Dynasty and Moslem-European Rivalry in the Region*, p. 20.

40. Ibid.

41. Greenfield, in Davidson et al., p. 22.

42. For consistency I am using the name "Eritrea" when describing historical areas and events. It should be noted that the name "Eritrea" was officially given to the territory by the Italians in 1890.

43. Sherman, p. 9.

44. Trimmingham, p. 92.

45. Sherman, pp. 7–8; Ullendorff, p. 73.

46. Abir, p. 157.

47. Trimmingham, pp. 86–89.

48. Ibid.

49. Ibid., p. 116.

50. Touval, p. 33.

51. Trimmingham, p. 116.

52. Sven Rubenson, *The Survival of Ethiopian Independence*, p. 143.

53. Ibid.

54. Trimmingham, p. 120.

55. Ibid., p. 29.

56. Zewde Gabre-Selassie, *Yohannes IV of Ethiopia: A Political Biography*, p. 37.

57. Ibid.

58. Ibid.

59. Ibid, p. 35.

60. Ibid, p. 41.

61. Rubenson, pp. 317–18.

62. Zewde Gabre-Selassie, pp. 57, 59.

63. Ibid., pp. 60–62; Rubenson, pp. 319–23.

64. Ibid., pp. 324–25; Zewde Gabre-Selassie, pp. 64–65.

65. Rubenson, pp. 327–28; Zewde Gabre-Selassie, pp. 67, 70–74.

66. Rubenson, p. 330; Zewde Gabre-Selassie, p. 81.

67. Rubenson, p. 334; Zewde Gabre-Selassie, p. 81.

68. Rubenson, p. 335; Zewde Gabre-Selassie, pp. 82–83.

69. Rubenson, p. 337; Zewde Gabre-Selassie, p. 111.

70. FO 407/11 #13, Enclosure, "Notes on the Soudan," to Mr. Lascelles to the Marquis of Salisbury, Cairo, 26 August 1879.

71. Zewde Gabre-Selassie, p. 110.

72. Rubenson, p. 338; Zewde Gabre-Selassie, p. 110.

73. Rubenson, p. 340.

74. FO 407/11 #46, Mr. A. B. Wylde Confidential to the Marquis of Salisbury, Massowah, 20 October 1879.

75. FO 407/11 #46, Inclosure 2, "Gordon Pasha to Her Majesty's Consul-General for Jeddah," Massowah, 12 September 1879.

76. FO 407/11 #46, A. B. Wylde to the Marquis of Salisbury.

77. FO 407/11 #12, "The King of Abyssinia to Her Majesty the Queen," Enclosure to Mr. Lascelles to the Marquis of Salisbury, Cairo, 26 August 1879.

78. FO 407/11 #12, Minute by Mr. Wylde, 16 September 1879, Enclosure to Mr. Lascelles to the Marquis of Salisbury, Cairo, 26 August 1879.

79. FO 407/11 #46, ibid.

80. Ibid.

81. Zewde Gabre-Selassie, p. 115; Rubenson, p. 344.

82. Ibid., p. 348.

83. Robert O. Collins and Robert L. Tignor, *Egypt and the Sudan*, pp. 61–62.

84. D. K. Fieldhouse, *The Colonial Empires: A Comparative Survey*, p. 183.

85. Ibid., p. 184; Collins and Tignor, pp. 81–87.

86. Marcus, 1975, p. 77.

87. Rubenson, p. 356; Zewde Gabre-Selassie, p. 139.

88. Haggai Erlich, *Ethiopia and the Challenge of Independence*, p. 46.

89. Ibid., p. 47.

90. Ibid., p. 56; Zewde Gabre-Selassie, p. 177.

91. Erlich, 1986, pp. 62–64; Zewde Gabre-Selassie, p. 178.

92. Marcus, 1975, pp. 85–86.

93. Zewde Gabre-Selassie, p. 225.

94. Marcus, 1975, p. 96.

95. Fieldhouse, p. 214; Richard Greenfield, *Ethiopia: A New Political History*, p. 92; Thomas Moon, *Imperialism and World Politics*, p. 144.

96. Marcus, 1975, p. 82.

97. Ibid., pp. 61–63.

98. Ibid., pp. 73–74.

99. Ibid., p. 102; Rubenson, p. 382.

100. Marcus, 1975, p. 100; Zewde Gabre-Selassie, pp. 236–38.

101. Chris Prouty, *Empress Taytu and Menilek II: Ethiopia 1883–1910*, p. 60.

102. Trimmingham, p. 125; Marcus, 1975, p. 111.

Chapter 3

1. For an analysis of the Hague convention, see McDougal and Foliano in *International Law in Contemporary Perspective: The Public Order of the World Community—Cases and Materials*, edited by M. F. McDougal and M. W. Reisman, p. 160.

2. David Pool, *Eritrea: Africa's Longest War*, p. 22.

3. Ibid., p. 21.

4. Tom J. Farer, *War Clouds on the Horn of Africa: A Crisis for Detente*, p. 23.

5. From a British memorandum cited by Richard Greenfield in *Behind the War in Eritrea*, ed. Davidson et al., p. 26.

6. Cited in ibid., pp. 26–27.

7. G. K. N. Trevaskis, *Eritrea: A Colony in Transition, 1941–52*, p. 51.

8. Haggai Erlich, *The Struggle over Eritrea 1962–1978: War and Revolution in the Horn of Africa*, p. 4.

9. Ibid.

10. John H. Spencer, *Ethiopia at Bay: A Personal Account of the Haile Selassie Years*, p. 247.

11. G. A. O. R., Third Session, Part II, First Committee, 5 April–13 May 1949 (hereafter referred to as First Committee), p. 115.

12. "Report of the United Nations Commission for Eritrea," G. A. O. R. Fifth Session, supp. 8, 1950, A/1285 (hereafter referred to as UNC Report), pp. 32–35.

13. Tekeste Negash, *Italian Colonialism in Eritrea*, pp. 68–70.

14. Confidential direction to Italian headmasters by Signor Festa, Director of Education in Eritrea, in 1938, cited in Trevaskis, p. 33.

15. Ibid., p. 79.

16. Ibid.

17. FO 371/69362, *Report of the Four Power Commission of Investigation, Former Italian Colonies*, vol. 1, Report on Eritrea, 1948 (hereafter referred to as Four Power Commission).

18. Trevaskis, p. 60.

19. Abuna Marcos, Epiphany address in 1942, cited in ibid.

20. Jordan Gabre-Medhin, ed., "Eritrea: The Roots of War," pp. 55–57.

21. Trevaskis, pp. 60–61.

22. Harold G. Marcus, *Ethiopia, Great Britain, and the United States, 1941–1974: The Politics of Empire*, p. 80.

23. Spencer, 1984, p. 196.

24. Trevaskis, p. 67.

25. Ibid., p. 68.

26. Leonard, "European Colonization and the Socio-Economic Integration of Eritrea, Permanent Peoples Tribunal, *The Eritrean Case*, p. 87.

27. Four Power Commission, p. 84.

28. Ibid., p. 83.

29. Ibid., pp. 84–85.

30. William Roger Louis, *Imperialism at Bay: The United States and the Decolonization of the British Empire, 1941–1945*, p. 5.

31. FO 371/35633, R. V. Howe to Anthony Eden, 4 March 1943.

32. FO 371/35658, "Eritrea and Her Neighbours," Enclosure to Chief Civil Affairs Officer to War Office, 14 September 1943, p. 184.

33. Ibid., p. 187.

34. Ibid., pp. 192–93.

35. FO 371/35658, S. Longrigg, "Future Disposal of Eritrea," 12 August 1943.

36. Ibid.

37. British Committee on Ethiopia in Cairo, in Marcus, 1983, p. 22.

38. FO 371/40601, Memorandum from FO Research Department, 2 March 1944.

39. Ibid.

40. FO 371/35414, Memorandum from FO Research Department, "Disposal of Eritrea," 26 June 1943.

41. Ibid.

42. Ibid.

43. Touval, *Somali Nationalism*, p. 170.

44. Louis, p. 5.

45. Harry Magdoff in Paul M. Sweezy and Harry Magdoff, comp., *The Dynamics of U.S. Capitalism: Corporate Structure, Inflation, Credit, Gold, and the Dollar*, p. 96.

46. Seymour Melman, *The War Economy of the United States: American Capitalism in Decline*, p. 15.

47. Thomas G. Paterson, *On Every Front: The Making of the Cold War*, p. 15.

48. Sidney Lens, *The Forging of the American Empire*, p. 6.

49. Dean Acheson, cited in ibid.

50. Minute by Eastwood, 21 April 1943, CO 323/1858/9057B, cited in Louis, p. 247.

51. Spencer, 1984, pp. 104, 165.

52. Marcus, 1983, p. 15.

53. Marcus, 1983, p. 12.

54. Harry Magdoff, *The Age of Imperialism: The Economics of U.S. Foreign Policy*, p. 40.

55. Ibid.

56. See Paterson, p. 146.

57. For an in-depth analysis of the evolution of Soviet foreign policy see Herbert Marcuse, *Soviet Marxism: A Critical Analysis*, pp. 35–36.

58. For Zhdanov's analysis, see ibid., pp. 40–41.

59. Zhdanov, report at the Cominform conference, Sept., 1947 in *The Strategy and Tactics of World Communism*, House document no. 619, supp. 1, p. 219, cited in ibid., pp. 47–48.

60. Benjamin Rivlin, *The United Nations and the Italian Colonies*, p. 11.

61. Ibid., p. 12.

62. FO 371/31608, Note from Ethiopian Government Respecting Eritrea, enclosure no. 1 to telegram from Robert Howe to Eden, 29 May 1942.

63. FO 371/31608, E. H. Chapman-Andrews, "Memorandum on Eritrea," Enclosure no. 2 to telegram from Howe to Eden, 29 May 1942.

64. See in Berhane Kahasai, "Political and Legal Analysis of the Eritrean Question," 7:25.

65. FO 371/35414, "Disposal of Eritrea," 26 June 1943.

66. FO 371/31608, Chapman-Andrews, "Memorandum on Eritrea."

67. Memorandum of Imperial Ethiopian Government, submitted to the Council of Foreign Ministers, London, 1945.

68. Spencer, 1984, p. 175.

69. Memorandum, Imperial Ethiopian Government, 1945.

70. Spencer, 1984, pp. 237–38.

71. Memorandum of the Government of Egypt, submitted to the Paris Peace Conference, 1946.

72. Ibid.

73. FO 371/73841, Mason to Wall, telegram no. 19, 25 March 1949.

74. Ibid.

75. Background paper, UN Department of Public Information, 1948.

76. James F. Byrnes, *Speaking Frankly*, pp. 93–94, cited in Rivlin, p. 10.

77. Byrnes, cited ibid., p. 11; for Molotov's arguments, see ibid., p. 11.

78. Spencer, 1984, p. 177.

79. Marcus, 1983, p. 69.

80. Spencer, 1984, pp. 176–77.

81. Rivlin, p. 12.

82. Ibid.

83. FO 371/63175, Stafford to Scott-Fox, "Fortnightly Report," 21 December 1946.

84. Ibid.

85. Ibid.

86. Four Power Commission, p. 96.

87. Ibid.

88. Ibid., p. 97.

89. Ibid.

90. Ibid., pp. 103, 108.

91. Ibid., pp. 104, 106.

92. Ibid., p. 105.

93. FO 371/69197, Four Power Commission in Eritrea, Minutes, Scott-Fox to Stafford, 5 January 1948.

94. Ibid.

95. FO 371/63186, Lawson to Scrivener, 25 January 1947.

96. FO 371/69333, Memorandum from the Former Italian Colonies Committee, "Disposal of the Former Italian Colonies: International Considerations," 27 April 1947.

97. FO 371/69353, Drew to the War Office, "Ethiopia's Claims to Eritrea and Somaliland," 30 March 1948.

98. WO 230/246, Mitchell to Secretary of State, telegram no. 236, 2 April 1948.

99. FO 371/69333, FO Minute by Scott-Fox, "Ex-Italian Colonies," 15 April 1948.

100. Ibid.

101. FO 371/69344, "Recommendations to the Council of Foreign Ministers of the Deputies of the Foreign Ministers of the United Kingdom, the United States of America, the French Republic, and the Union of Soviet Socialist Republics Appointed to Consider the Question of the Disposal of the Former Italian Colonies," 31 August 1948.

Chapter 4

1. Spencer, *Ethiopia at Bay*, p. 201.

2. Marcus, *Ethiopia, Great Britain, and the United States*, p. 84.

3. Ibid.

4. Ibid., p. 87.

5. Haile Sellassie to Truman, Addis Ababa, 4 April 1946, File 85E, Truman Library, cited in ibid., pp. 79–80.

6. Ibid., p. 58.

7. Ibid., p. 5.

8. Felix Cole to Secretary of State, Addis Ababa, 12 March 1947, SD 884.143/3–1247, cited in ibid., p. 53.

9. Control 8528, telegram no. 171, Merrell to Secretary of State, 19 August 1949.

10. Ibid.

11. Ibid.

12. Memorandum of conversation between Ethiopian Vice Minister of Foreign Affairs and Secretary Dean Acheson, 30 March 1949.

13. John H. Spencer, *Ethiopia: The Horn of Africa and U.S. Policy*, p. 25.

14. Ibid., p. 22.

15. William D. Leahy to Secretary of Defense, "Disposition of the Former Italian Colonies," a report to the National Security Council, no. 19/3, 5 August 1948.

16. Ibid.

17. Letter from James Forrestal to the Secretary of State, 13 December 1948.

18. Ibid.

19. The following is a summarization of a secret document, U.S. Department of State to U.S. delegation to the UN, "Disposition of the Former Italian Colonies," 27 September 1948.

20. WO 230/246, U.K. delegation of General Assembly to FO, telegram no. 53, 29 September 1948.

21. FO 371/73846, UN U.K. Delegation to FO, telegram no. 213, 22 October 1948.

22. FO 371/73847, Wright to Mallet, 2 November 1948.

23. WO 230/246, "U.K. Draft Resolution on the Disposal of Eritrea," 7 December 1948.

24. FO 371/73841, House of Lords, from the Lord Chancellor to Bevin, 22 January 1949.

25. FO 371/73841, Clutton, FO Minute, "Eritrea," 2 February 1949.

26. Ibid.

27. G. A. O. R., First Committee, Third Session, Part II, 5 April–13 May 1949 (hereafter referred to as First Committee), p. 6.

28. Ibid., p. 7.

29. Ibid.

30. Ibid., p. 9.

31. Ibid., p. 30.

32. Ibid., p. 31.

33. Ibid., p. 32.

34. Ibid., p. 18.

35. Ibid., p. 19.

36. Ibid., p. 22.

37. Ibid., pp. 23–24.

38. Ibid., pp. 13–14.

39. Ibid., p. 14.

40. Ibid., pp. 14–15.

41. G. A. O. R. Fifth Session, Ad Hoc Political Committee, Summary Records of Meetings, 30 September–14 December 1950 (hereafter referred to as Ad Hoc Political Committee), p. 224.

42. First Committee, pp. 29–30.

43. Ibid., p. 33.

44. Ibid., pp. 33–34.

45. Ibid., p. 34.

46. Ibid.

47. Ibid., p. 57.

48. Ibid., p. 92.

49. Ibid.

50. Ibid., p. 93.

51. Ibid., p. 94.

52. Ibid., p. 129.

53. Ibid., p. 147.

54. Ibid., p. 148.

55. Ibid., pp. 82–83.

56. Ibid., p. 90.

57. Ibid., p. 152.

58. Ibid.

59. Ibid., p. 59.

60. Ibid., p. 60.

61. Ibid., p. 61.

62. Ibid., p. 73.

63. Ibid., pp. 155–59.

64. Ibid., p. 168.

65. Ibid., p. 182.

66. Ibid., p. 161.

67. Ibid., pp. 166–67.

68. Ibid., pp. 119–20.

69. Ibid., pp. 169–70.

70. Ibid., p. 262.

71. Ibid., p. 180.

72. Ibid., p. 259.

73. Ibid., p. 184.

74. Ibid., p. 332.

75. Ibid., p. 325.

76. Ibid., pp. 336–37.

77. Ibid., p. 331.

78. Ibid., p. 334.

Chapter 5

1. FO 371/69345, Mason to Clutton, 29 July 1949.

2. Ibid.

3. FO 371/73846, Paddock's Second Report to London, 29 August 1949, Enclosure to Mason to Stewart, 9 September 1949.

4. Ibid.

5. FO 371/73846, Drew to FO, telegram no. 120, 10 August 1949.

6. Ibid.

7. FO 371/69345, Mallet to Strang, 27 July 1949.

8. Ibid.

9. FO 371/73846, Lascelles to FO, telegram no. 7, 26 August 1949.

10. Ibid.

11. FO 371/73844, Lascelles to Wright, 8 July 1949.

12. FO 371/73844, Strang to Mallet, 19 July 1949.

13. FO 371/73846, Paddock's Preliminary Report in Eritrea, Enclosure to Mason to Stewart, 9 September 1949.

14. Ibid.

15. Paddock's second report, enclosure to ibid.

16. G. A. O. R. Document A/1089 and Corr. .1, Report of the First Committee, Fourth Session of the General Assembly, Annexes to the Summary Records of Meetings, 1949, p. 56.

17. G. A. O. R., Fourth Session, Plenary Meetings of the General Assembly, Summary Records. 20 September–10 December 1949, p. 298.

18. Ibid.

19. Ibid., p. 299.

20. G. A. O. R., Fifth Session of the General Assembly, Plenary Meetings of the General Assembly, Annexes to the Summary Records of Meetings, 1949, p. 55.

21. FO 371/73788, Drew to Bevin, 8 October 1949.

22. Ibid.

23. FO 371/73789, FO to Addis Ababa, telegram no. 536, 19 November 1949.

24. FO 371/73790, FO Minute, Stewart, "Internal Security in Eritrea," 7 December 1949.

25. Trevaskis, *Eritrea*, p. 96.

26. G. A. O. R., Fifth Session, United Nations Commission for Eritrea, supp. no. 8, "Report of the United Nations Commission for Eritrea," 1950, A/1285 (hereafter referred to as UNC Report), p. 29.

27. Ibid., p. 29.

28. FO 371/80984, Drew to FO, telegram no. 239, 16 March 1950.

29. FO 371/80986, Drew to FO, 3 April 1950.

30. Ibid.

31. Trevaskis, p. 96.

32. UNC Report, p. 30.

33. FO 371/80984, Stafford, "Note of an Interview with H.I.M., the Emperor of Ethiopia on the 27 January 1950."

34. Ibid.

35. Ibid.

36. FO 371/80984, Stafford to Clutton, 16 February 1950.

37. Ibid.

38. Ibid.

39. Ibid.

40. Ibid.

41. FO 371/80984, Stafford to Smith, 12 March 1950.

42. Ibid.

43. Ibid.

44. FO 371/80985, Stafford to Allen, 16 March 1950.

45. FO 371/80984, Stafford, "The United Nations Commission in Eritrea: A Summary of Its Activities, February 12th–19th [1950]."

46. FO 371/80985, Drew, memorandum, "The Future of Eritrea," 14 March 1950, Enclosure to Drew to FO, 14 March 1950.

47. FO 371/80985, Drew to Allen, 7 March 1950.

48. FO 371/80985, Drew, "The Future of Eritrea," 14 March 1950.

49. FO 371/80985, Scrivener, FO Minute, "Eritrea," 17 March 1950.

50. Ibid.

51. Ibid.

52. Ibid.

53. Ibid.

54. FO 371/80985, Stafford to Allen, 16 March 1950.

55. FO 371/80986, Stafford to Allen, 23 March 1950.

56. Ibid.

57. FO 371/80985, Lascelles to Drew, 17 March 1950.

58. Ibid.

59. FO 371/80985, Lascelles to Allen, 9 March 1950.

60. Ibid.

61. Ibid.

62. Ibid.

63. FO 371/80986, FO to Lascelles, 22 March 1950.

64. FO 371/80986, Lascelles to FO, telegram no. 112, 12 April 1950.

65. FO 371/80984, FO to Mallet, 15 January 1950; Department of State, *Foreign Relations of the United States* 5 (1950):1641 (hereafter referred to as Foreign Relations, 1950).

66. FO 371/80984, Clutton, FO Minute, "Eritrea," 26 January 1950.

67. Paper from Italian embassy, enclosure to ibid.

68. Foreign Relations, 1950, p. 1642; FO 371/80986, FO to Mallet, 28 January 1950.

69. Foreign Relations, 1950, pp. 1647–68.

70. Ibid., p. 1650.

71. Ibid., pp. 1651–52.

72. FO 371/80990, Meade to Allen, 1 June 1950.

73. Ibid.

74. Foreign Relations, 1950, p. 1656.

75. Ibid., p. 1657.

76. Ibid.

77. FO 371/80991, "Eritrea: Record of Meetings in the Foreign Office on 30 June, 1st and 3rd July between Representatives of Italy, the United States and the United Kingdom," 3 July 1950.

78. Ibid.

79. Ibid.

80. Ibid.

81. Ibid.

82. Ibid.

83. Ibid.

84. FO 371/80993, "Record of Meeting held at the United Kingdom Delegation Office on 17 July 1950."

85. FO 371/80991, FO Minute, "United Kingdom Delegation Brief for the Interim Committee on Eritrea," 29 June 1950.

86. Ibid.

87. Foreign Relations, 1950, p. 1662.

88. UNC Report, p. 12.

89. Ibid., p. 23.

90. Ibid., p. 21.

91. G.A.O.R., Fifth Session, Ad Hoc Political Committee, Summary Records of Meetings, 30 September–14 December 1950 (hereafter referred to as Ad Hoc Political Committee), p. 231.

92. UNC Report, p. 24.

93. Ibid.

94. Ibid., pp. 24–25.

95. Ibid., p. 25.

96. Ibid., p. 26.

97. Ibid.

98. Ibid.

99. Ibid., p. 27.

100. Ibid.
101. Ibid.
102. Ibid., p. 30.
103. Ibid., p. 31.
104. FO 371/80992, Stafford to Allen, 13 July 1950.
105. Ad Hoc Political Committee, p. 26.
106. Ad Hoc Political Committee, p. 228.
107. Foreign Relations, 1950, p. 1667.
108. Spencer, *Ethiopia at Bay*, p. 234.
109. Ibid., pp. 234–35.
110. Ibid., p. 235.
111. Ibid.
112. Foreign Relations, 1950, pp. 1667–68.
113. Ibid., pp. 1672–73.
114. Ibid.
115. FO 371/80994, Drew to Wright, 25 July 1950.
116. Ibid.
117. Ibid.
118. FO 371/80996, Stafford to Stewart, 10 August 1950.
119. Ibid.
120. Ibid.
121. Department of State. *Foreign Relations of the United States* 5 (1951): 1241 (hereafter referred to as Foreign Relations, 1951).
122. Foreign Relations, 1950, p. 1698.
123. Ibid., p. 1700.
124. Ibid.
125. Foreign Relations, 1951, pp. 1241–42.
126. FO 371/80998, Allen, "Eritrea," 18 September 1950.
127. Foreign Relations, 1950, p. 1679.
128. Ibid.
129. Ibid.
130. Ibid., p. 1680.
131. Ibid.
132. Ibid., pp. 1681–84.
133. Ibid., p. 1683.
134. For a full account of the proceedings on Eritrea at the Ad Hoc Political Committee, see Ad Hoc Political Committee, pp. 221–47 and 309–55.
135. G. A. O. R., Excerpts from 316th Plenary Meeting of the General Assembly, Sixth Session, 2 December 1950, (hereafter referred to as G. A. O. R. 6th Session), pp. 539–40.
136. Ibid., p. 541.

137. Ibid.
138. Ibid., p. 540.
139. Ibid., p. 546.

Chapter 6

1. The Federal Act is reproduced in its entirety in the appendix.

2. G.A.O.R. A/1959. Progress Report of the United Nations Commissioner for Eritrea during the Year 1951. 16 November 1951, (hereafter referred to as Progress Report), p. 16.

3. Ibid., p. 21.

4. Ibid., p. 37.

5. Aklilou's arguments are constructed from G.A.O.R., A/A/C/.44/S.1 and A/A/C/.44/SR.4, Summary Records of Meetings between Aklilou and Matienzo.

6. For Matienzo's reply see G.A.O.R. A/A/C.44/SR.5, UN Commissioner for Eritrea, Summary Records, from which the following material is summarized.

7. Fernyhough, "Social Mobility and Dissident Elites in Northern Ethiopia," pp. 9–14.

8. Trevaskis, *Eritrea*, p. 112.

9. Progress Report, p. 59.

10. Progress Report, Annex 10.

11. Progress Report, Annex 11.

12. British Proclamation of 19 June 1951, Progress Report, Annex 13.

13. Progress Report, pp. 67–68.

14. Ibid., p. 71.

15. Ibid., pp. 45, 57.

16. Ibid., pp. 54–55.

17. Pool, *Eritrea*, p. 38.

18. Hess, *Ethiopia*, p. 88.

19. Spencer, *Ethiopia at Bay*, p. 304.

20. Bereket Habte-Selassie, in Davidson et al., eds., *Behind the War in Eritrea*, p. 43.

21. Spencer, 1984, p. 303.

22. Ibid., p. 304.

23. Bereket Habte-Selassie, *Conflict and Intervention in the Horn of Africa*, p. 60ff.

24. Andargachew Messay, cited in Erlich, *The Struggle over Eritrea*, p. 9.

25. Spencer, 1984, p. 303.

26. Ibid., p. 305.

27. Sherman, *Eritrea*, p. 28.

28. Memorandum cited in "Joint Declaration of the Eritrean Liberation Front and the Eritrean People's Liberation Front," in Permanent Peoples Tribunal, *The Eritrean Case*, p. 19.

29. Hess, pp. 184–85.

30. Letter to Dag Hammarskjöld, UN Secretary General, from Ibrahim Sultan Ali, Idris Muhammed Adem, and Woldemariam, Cairo, 30 June 1959.

31. See Hess, p. 214.

32. Eritrean Liberation Front, *Eritrea and the Federal Act* (presented to the Afro-Arab Summit Conference in Cairo on 7 March 1977), p. 105.

33. G.A.O.R., Fifth Session, Ad Hoc Political Committee, Summary Records of Meetings, 30 September–14 December 1950 (hereafter referred to as Ad Hoc Political Committee), pp. 310–11.

34. Trevaskis, p. 131.

35. Erlich, 1983, p. 9.

36. Pool, p. 46.

37. Farer, *War Clouds on the Horn of Africa*, p. 29.

38. Pool, p. 46.

39. Patrick Gilkes, *The Dying Lion: Feudalism and Modernization in Ethiopia*, p. 197.

40. Hess, p. 190.

41. Farer, p. 31.

42. Cited in Erlich, 1983, p. 58.

43. Gilkes, p. 200.

44. Sherman, p. 79.

45. Erlich, 1983, p. 48.

46. Sherman, p. 84.

47. Mary Dines, "Ethiopian Repression in Eritrea," in *The Eritrean Case*, p. 309.

48. Erlich, 1983, p. 75.

49. Dines, p. 310.

50. Amnesty International Report of 15 December 1977, cited in Dines, pp. 310–11.

51. Marcus, *The Life and Times of Menelik II*, p. 64.

52. Ibid.

53. Prouty, *Empress Taytu and Menilek II*, p. 115.

54. Jason W. Clay and Bonnie K. Holcomb, *Politics in the Ethiopian Famine: 1984–1985*, p. 12.

55. Marcus, 1975, pp. 66, 185.

56. Robin Lockham and Dawit Bekele, "Foreign Powers and Militarism in the Horn of Africa," p. 11.

57. Rubenson, *The Survival of Ethiopian Independence*, p. 398.

58. C. W. McClellan, "Perspectives on the Neftanya-Gabbar System: The Derasa Ethiopia," p. 435.

59. Timothy Derrick Fernyhough, *Serfs, Slaves, and Shifta: Modes of Production in Southern Ethiopia from the Late Nineteenth Century to 1941*, pp. 186–87, 192–93.

60. Ibid., pp. 233, 240; G. C. Baravelli, *The Last Stronghold of Slavery: What Abyssinia Is*, p. 36.

61. Peter P. Garretson, "Vicious Cycle: Ivory, Slaves, and Arms on the New Maji Frontier," in *The Southern Marches of Imperial Ethiopia: Essays in History and Social Anthropology*, edited by Donald Donham and W. James, p. 205.

62. Fernyhough, 1986, pp. 238–39.

63. Baravelli, p. 38.

64. Fernyhough, 1986, p. 297.

65. Lipski et al., *Ethiopia*, p. 277.

66. Fernyhough, 1986, pp. 78–79; Gilkes, p. 111; Marcus, 1975, pp. 192–93; McClellan, pp. 432–35; John Markakis, *Ethiopia: Anatomy of a Traditional Polity*, pp. 111–14.

67. Hess, pp. 107–14; John M. Cohen and Dov Weintraub, *Land and Peasant in Imperial Ethiopia: The Social Background to a Revolution*, pp. 13–14.

68. Gilkes, p. 51.

69. Donham and James, eds., p. 27; Gilkes, p. 49; René Lefort, *Ethiopia: A Heretical Revolution?*, pp. 18, 35.

70. Gilkes, pp. 55–57; Hess, pp. 109, 111, 147, 149; Cohen and Weintraub, p. 43.

71. Fred Halliday and Maxine Molyneux, *The Ethiopian Revolution*, p. 71.

72. Gilkes, pp. 186–91; Gebru Tareke, "Peasant Resistance in Ethiopia: The Case of *Weyane*."

73. Lefort, pp. 8–9; Cohen and Weintraub, p. 61.

74. Gilkes, pp. 112–13; Cohen and Weintraub, p. 61.

75. Gilkes, p. 115; Cohen and Weintraub, pp. 50–52; Halliday and Molyneux, p. 62; D. Crummey, "State and Society: Nineteenth Century Ethiopia," in *Modes of Production in Africa: The Pre-Colonial Era*, edited by Donald Crummey and C. C. Steward, pp. 242–43.

76. Marcus, *Ethiopia, Great Britain, and the United States*, pp. 42–43, 46; Gilkes, pp. 138, 152–53.

77. Lipski et al., pp. 234, 250.

78. Marina Ottaway and David Ottaway, *Ethiopia: Empire in Revolution*, p. 18.

79. Cohen and Weintraub, p. 8.

80. Ottaway and Ottaway, p. 19; Gilkes, p. 124.

81. Gilkes, p. 128; Cohen and Weintraub, p. 17; John Markakis and Nega Ayele, *Class and Revolution in Ethiopia*, p. 58; Ottaway and Ottaway, p. 16.

Chapter 7

1. FO 371/69345, Mason to Bevin, 23 October 1948.
2. Ibid.
3. Ibid.
4. U.S. Department of State, *Foreign Relations of the United States* 5 1950):1705 (hereafter referred to as Foreign Relations, 1950).
5. U.S. Department of State, *Foreign Relations of the United States* 5 1951):1252 (hereafter referred to as Foreign Relations, 1951).
6. Foreign Relations, 1950, pp. 1695–96.
7. Ibid., p. 1699.
8. Ibid., p. 1700.
9. Ibid., pp. 1701–2.
10. Foreign Relations, 1951, p. 1237.
11. Ibid., p. 1238.
12. Hess, *Ethiopia*, p. 199.
13. Foreign Relations, 1951, p. 1247.
14. Ibid., p. 1255.
15. Ibid.
16. Ibid., p. 1259.
17. Ibid., pp. 1264–65.
18. U.S. Department of State, *Foreign Relations of the United States, 1952–1954: Africa and South Asia*, 11:418 (hereafter referred to as Foreign Relations 1952–54).
19. Ibid., pp. 429–30.
20. Ibid., pp. 439–41.
21. Ibid., p. 441.
22. Marcus, *Ethiopia, Great Britain, and the United States*, pp. 57–58, 77.
23. Foreign Relations, 1952–54, p. 443.
24. Ibid., p. 444.
25. Ibid., p. 449.
26. Ibid., pp. 449–50.
27. "Utilization of Defense Installations within Empire of Ethiopia," 23 May 1953, in *U.S. Trade and Other International Agreements* 5, part 1 (1954): 750–58.
28. Sherman, *Eritrea*, pp. 134, 143; Halliday and Molyneux, *The Ethiopian Revolution*, pp. 217–18.
29. Foreign Relations, 1952–54, pp. 457–58.
30. Ibid., p. 459.

31. Ibid., pp. 462–63.

32. Ibid., p. 464.

33. Ibid., pp. 472–77.

34. Ibid., p. 477.

35. Ibid.

36. Ibid., p. 481.

37. "Mutual Defense Assistance: Facilities Assistance Program," 26 Decem 1957, in *U.S. Trade and Other International Agreements* 8, part 2 (1957):2483.

38. Sherman, p. 144; Halliday and Molyneux, p. 216.

39. Hess, pp. 118, 202; Pool, *Eritrea*, p. 43.

40. Halliday and Molyneux, p. 217.

41. Erlich, *The Struggle over Eritrea*, p. 57.

42. Ibid., pp. 58–59; Pool, p. 42.

43. Pool, p. 43; Farer, *War Clouds on the Horn of Africa*, p. 125.

44. Farer, pp. 126–32.

45. Halliday and Molyneux, p. 215; Pool, p. 42; Sherman, p. 145; Lefort, *Ethiopia*, pp. 182–83.

46. "U.S. Policy and Request for Sale of Arms to Ethiopia," hearing before the Subcommittee on International Political and Military Affairs of the Committee on Foreign Affairs, U.S. House of Representatives, First Session, 5 March 1975 (hereafter referred to as U.S. Sale of Arms to Ethiopia), p. 17.

47. U.S. Sale of Arms to Ethiopia, p. 9; Farer, pp. 138–39.

48. U.S. Sale of Arms to Ethiopia, p. 15.

49. Halliday and Molyneux, pp. 218–19.

50. Mulcahy's testimony, U.S. Sale of Arms to Ethiopia, pp. 5, 13.

51. Ibid., p. 4.

52. U.S. Department of State, "United States Policy toward Ethiopia," doc. 662, *American Foreign Policy Basic Documents, 1977–1980*, p. 1233.

53. Ibid.

54. Halliday and Molyneux, p. 222.

55. Marina Ottaway, *Soviet and American Influence in the Horn of Africa*, pp. 101–102; Halliday and Molyneux, pp. 223–24; Steven David, "Realignment in the Horn: The Soviet Advantage," p. 74.

56. Ottaway, p. 117; Henry Bienen, "Perspectives on Soviet Intervention in Africa."

57. Cyrus Vance, *Hard Choices: Critical Years in Managing America's Foreign Policy*, p. 75.

58. Ibid., p. 86.

59. Zbigniew Brzezinski, *Power and Principle: Memoirs of the National Security Adviser, 1977–1981*, p. 186.

60. Vance, pp. 72–74, 83–87, 91–93.

61. "Free Africa Pledged by Mr. Carter."

62. "Ethiopian Ambassador Has Meeting with Dr. Owen."

63. "Dr. Owen Is Accused by Cubans of 'Arrogance'."

64. Ibid.

65. Gary Sacore, "The Persian Gulf," in *Energy and Security: A Report of the Harvard Energy and Security Research Project*, edited by David A. Deefe and Joseph S. Naye, p. 53.

66. Joseph S. Naye, "Energy and Security," in Deefe and Naye, eds., pp. 3–4.

67. Testimony and Prepared Statement by the Acting Assistant Secretary of State for African Affairs (Walker) before a Subcommittee of the House Foreign Affairs Committee, 2 April 1981, doc. 648, in U.S. Department of State, *American Foreign Policy, Current Documents, 1981* (hereafter referred to as Walker's Testimony), p. 1157.

68. Ibid., p. 1158.

69. Ottaway, p. 126.

70. Walker's Testimony, pp. 1159–60.

71. Ibid., p. 1161.

72. Prepared Statement by the Assistant Secretary of State for African Affairs (Crocker) before a Subcommittee of the House Appropriations Committee, 27 April 1983, doc. 591, in U.S. Department of State, *American Foreign Policy Current Documents, 1983*, pp. 1225–26.

Chapter 8

1. Michael A. Samuels et al. *Implications of Soviet and Cuban Activities in Africa for U.S. Policy*, p. 8.

2. Ibid.

3. Ibid., pp. 12–21.

4. David E. Albright, "The Soviet Policy," pp. 35–36.

5. James F. Petras and Morris H. Morley, "The Ethiopian Military State and Soviet-U.S. Involvement in the Horn of Africa."

· 6. Colin Legum, "The USSR and Africa: The African Environment."

7. Ibid., pp. 1–2; Samuels et al., pp. 35–37.

8. Roberto Aliboni, *The Red Sea Region*, pp. 9–11.

9. Marshall I. Goldman, "The Role of Communist Countries," in *Energy and Security: A Report of the Harvard Energy and Security Research Project*, edited by David A. Deefe and Joseph S. Naye, pp. 112–17.

10. Marshall I. Goldman, "Soviet East-West Trade: Have the Means Become an End?," in *Soviet Foreign Policy in the 1980's*, edited by Roger E. Kanet, pp. 255–56.

11. Bill Keller, "Kremlin Blames Budget Deficit on Subsidies."

12. Goldman, in Kanet, ed., pp. 253–54.

13. PBS, *MacNeil-Lehrer News Hour*. 16 January 1989.

14. Goldman, in Kanet, ed., p. 257.

15. David, "Realignment in the Horn," pp. 83–84.

16. Ibid., p. 86.

17. David E. Albright, "The Middle East and Africa," in Kanet, ed., pp. 285–86.

18. Cited by Lars Bondestam, in "External Involvement in Ethiopia and Eritrea," in *Behind the War in Eritrea*, edited by Basil Davidson et al., p. 67.

19. Farer, *War Clouds on the Horn of Africa*, p. 108.

20. Ibid., p. 109.

21. Ottaway, *Soviet and American Influence in the Horn of Africa*, pp. 67, 76–78; David, pp. 72–73; James E. Dougherty, *The Horn of Africa: A Map of Political-Strategic Conflict*, p. 25.

22. David, p. 74.

23. Erlich, *The Struggle over Eritrea*, p. 112.

24. Ottaway, p. 113.

25. *LeMonde*, 6 May 1977.

26. "Soviet Arms for Ethiopia Jam Sea Lanes."

27. Ibid.

28. Edward Walsh, "Cubans in Ethiopia Put above 10,000."

29. Ibid.

30. "Horn of Africa: Everybody's War."

31. "Russian Troops Said to Be Fighting in Eritrea."

32. R. Wilkinson, "Bombing in Eritrea Described."

33. "Moscow Comes Out in Support of Ethiopia against the Eritreans."

34. "Soviet War Planes Sent to Ethiopia."

35. Dan Connell, "Changing Situation in Eritrea," in Davidson et al., p. 56.

36. "100,000 in an Eritrean Retreat."

37. Jay Ross, "Ethiopia Leans Uneasily on Soviets as Reliable Source of Arms."

38. "South Yemen–Soviet Talks on Horn of Africa War."

39. Nelson P. Valdez, "Cuba's Involvement in the Horn of Africa: The Ethiopian-Somali War and the End of the Eritrean Conflict," in *Cuba in Africa*, edited by Carmelo Mesa-Lago and June S. Belkin, p. 79.

40. Cited in ibid., p. 66.

41. Ibid., pp. 71–72.

42. Ibid., p. 80.

43. William M. LeoGrande, *Cuba's Policy in Africa: 1959–1980*, p. 40.

44. "Cuban Forces Likely to Intervene in Wars against Eritreans"; Dan Connell, "Cubans Move in to Eritrea Battle Front."

45. Sherman, *Eritrea*, pp. 150–51.

46. "Ethiopians Say Eritrea Is Beaten."

47. Carmelo Mesa-Lago, "Cuban Foreign Policy in Africa: A General Framework," in Mesa-Lago and Belkin, eds., p. 7.

48. Merrick Robbins, "The Soviet-Cuban Relationship," in Kanet, ed., p. 149.

49. Mesa-Lago, in Mesa-Lago and Belkin, eds., p. 4.

50. Robbins, in Kanet, ed., p. 148.

51. Ibid., p. 149; Mesa-Lago, in Mesa-Lago and Belkin, eds., p. 4.

52. Serjo Roca, "Economic Aspects of Cuban Involvement in Africa," ibid., p. 165.

53. Edward Gonzalez, "Operational Goals of Cuban Policy in Africa," in ibid., pp. 57–58; Roca, p. 166.

54. Ibid., p. 167; Mesa-Lago, p. 64; Robbins, p. 149; Joseph B. Treaster, "Enemity between U.S. and Cuba May Be Relaxing."

55. Roca, p. 172; Samuels et al., p. 50.

56. Ibid., pp. 50–51.

57. PBS, "Background Report on Angola," *MacNeil-Lehrer News Hour*, 22 December 1988.

58. Roca, p. 180; LeoGrande, p. 47.

Chapter 9

1. Halliday and Molyneux, *The Ethiopian Revolution*, p. 109; Clay and Holcomb, *Politics in the Ethiopian Famine*, p. 19; "Ethiopia: Birth of the Republic."

2. Halliday and Molyneux, p. 109.

3. "Ethiopia Accused of Slave Labour."

4. "Ethiopia: Italy and the Tana Beles Project."

5. Halliday and Molyneux, p. 103.

6. Paul Valley, "How Mengistu Hammers the Peasants."

7. Ibid.

8. Valley, 1985–a.

9. Halliday and Molyneux, p. 108.

10. "Ethiopia: New Appeal for Aid."

11. Ibid.

12. "Ethiopia: Agricultural Prices Rise."

13. Halliday and Molyneux, p. 103.

14. Ibid., p. 104.

15. "Ethiopia: The Last Tangle in Addis."

16. Lockham and Bekele, "Foreign Powers and Militarism," p. 17.

17. Halliday and Molyneux, pp. 101, 109.

18. "Communism Tries to Root in Ethiopian Terrain."

19. "West's Aid Fails to Sway Ethiopia from East Orbit."

20. Valley, 1985–a.

21. "West's Aid Fails to Sway Ethiopia."

22. "Ethiopia: Gorbachev's Policy."

23. Ibid.

24. Petras and Morley, "The Ethiopian Military State," pp. 30–31.

25. Cited in "Ethiopia: The Army Routed."

26. Ibid.

27. "EPLF Military Activities in 1988," EPLF press release, 12 January 1988.

28. "Interview [with EPLF Secretary General, Issaias Afewerki]: We see No Correlation between Peace and Military Might," p. 6.

29. "Ethiopia: Gorbachev's Policy."

30. Dougherty, *The Horn of Africa*, p. 2.

31. Petras and Morley, p. 24.

32. Ross, "Ethiopia Leans Uneasily"; "Ethiopia: Confusion over the ICRC."

33. "Ethiopia Seeks Investors."

34. "25 Million Pounds Order."

35. "Ethiopia: West German Investment."

36. Paul Valley, "Famine: Russia and the US on Collision Course"; "Ethiopia: EEC Aid Sought"; "Ethiopia: Reagan Goes on the Attack"; "Ethiopia: World Bank Provides 70 Million"; "Ethiopia: Italy and the Tana Beles Project."

37. "US Congress Holds Hearing on War and Famine."

38. U.S.-U.S.S.R. Joint Statement on Ethiopia, 2 June 1990.

39. "Ethiopia: Cooperation with Algeria."

40. "Ethiopia: The Red Terror."

41. "Israel Selling Arms to Ethiopia."

42. "Ethiopia: Israeli Aid."

43. Alfonso Chardy, "Israel Aiding Ethiopia in Port Battle."

44. Ibid.

Appendix

Source: G.A.O.R. A/2188. Seventh Session, *Final Report of the United Nations Commissioner in Eritrea*, supp. no. 15, pp. 74–75.

Bibliography

Books, Monographs, and Journals

Abir, Mordechai. *Ethiopia and the Red Sea: The Rise and Decline of the Solomonic Dynasty and Moslem-European Rivalry in the Region.* Jerusalem: Institute of Asian and African Studies, 1980.

Albright, David E. "The Soviet Policy." *Problems of Communism* 24 (January-February, 1978): 20–39.

Aliboni, Roberto. *The Red Sea Region.* New York: Syracuse University Press, 1985.

Baravelli, G. C. *The Last Stronghold of Slavery: What Abyssinia Is.* N.p., 1935

Bender, Marvin L., ed. *Non-Semitic Languages of Ethiopia.* Monograph no. 5. Carbondale: Southern Illinois University, 1976.

———. et al., eds. *Language in Ethiopia.* London: Oxford University Press, 1971.

Bereket Habte-Selassie. *Conflict and Intervention in the Horn of Africa.* New York: Monthly Review Press, 1980.

Bienen, Henry. "Perspectives on Soviet Intervention in Africa." *Political Science Quarterly* 95, no. 1 (Spring 1980): 29–42.

Brzezinski, Zbigniew. *Power and Principle: Memoirs of the National Security Adviser, 1977–1981.* New York: Farrar, Straus, Giroux, 1983.

Chabal, Patrick. *Amilcar Cabral: Revolutionary Leadership and People's War.* Cambridge: Cambridge University Press, 1983.

Chardy, Alfonso. "Israel Aiding Ethiopia in Port Battle." *Miami Herald,* 25 February 1990.

Clay, Jason W., and Bonnie K. Holcomb. *Politics in the Ethiopian Famine: 1984–1985*. Cambridge, Mass.: Cultural Survival, Inc., 1985.

Cohen, John M., and Dov Weintraub. *Land and Peasant in Imperial Ethiopia: The Social Background to a Revolution*. The Netherlands: Gorkin and Co., 1975.

Collins, Robert O., and Robert L. Tignor. *Egypt and the Sudan*. Englewood Cliffs, N.J.: Prentice-Hall, 1967.

"Communism Tries to Root in Ethiopian Terrain." *The Washington Post*, 4 December 1980.

Connell, Dan. "Cubans Move in to Eritrea Battle Front." *The Nation* 226, (April 1978): 530–33.

Connor, Walker. *The National Question in Marxist-Leninist Theory and Strategy*. Princeton, N.J.: Princeton University Press, 1984.

Crummey, Donald, and C. C. Steward, eds. *Modes of Production in Africa: The Pre-Colonial Era*. London: Sage Publications, 1981.

"Cuban Forces Likely to Intervene in Wars against Eritreans." *The Times* (London). 17 March 1978, 8A.

David, Steven. "Realignment in the Horn: The Soviet Advantage." *International Security* 4, no. 2 (Fall 1979): 69–90.

Davidson, Basil, et al., eds. *Behind the War in Eritrea*. Nottingham, England: Spokesman Press, 1980.

Deefe, David A., and Joseph S. Naye, eds. *Energy and Security: A Report of the Harvard Energy and Security Research Project*. Cambridge, Mass.: Bollinger, 1981.

Donham, Donald, and W. James, eds., *The Southern Marches of Imperial Ethiopia: Essays in History and Social Anthropology*. Cambridge: Cambridge University Press, 1986.

Dougherty, James E. *The Horn of Africa: A Map of Political-Strategic Conflict*. Cambridge, Mass.: Institute for Foreign Policy Analysis, Inc., 1982.

"Dr. Owen Is Accused by Cubans of 'Arrogance'." *The Times* (London), 8 April 1978, 4C.

Eritrean Liberation Front. *Eritrea and the Federal Act*. N.p., 1977.

Eritreans for Liberation in North America (EFLNA). *In Defense of the Eritrean Revolution*. N.p., 1978.

Erlich, Haggai. *Ethiopia and the Challenge of Independence*. Boulder, Co.: Lynne Rienner Pub., 1986.

———. *The Struggle over Eritrea, 1962–1978: War and Revolution in the Horn of Africa*. Stanford: Hoover Institution Press, 1983.

"Ethiopia: Agricultural Prices Rise." *The Indian Ocean Newsletter* 316 (23 January 1988): 7.

"Ethiopia: The Army Routed." *The Indian Ocean Newsletter* 325 (26 March 1988).

"Ethiopia: Birth of the Republic." *The Indian Ocean Newsletter* 297 (12 September 1987): 2.

"Ethiopia: Confusion over the ICRC." *The Indian Ocean Newsletter* 332 (14 May 1988): 2.

"Ethiopia: Cooperation with Algeria." *The Indian Ocean Newsletter* 351 (8 October 1988): 2.

"Ethiopia: EEC Aid Sought." *The Indian Ocean Newsletter* 299 (26 September 1987): 7.

"Ethiopia: Gorbachev's Policy." *The Indian Ocean Newsletter* 346 (3 September 1988): 3.

"Ethiopia: Israeli Aid." *The Indian Ocean Newsletter* 353, (22 October 1988): 2.

"Ethiopia: Italy and the Tana Beles Project." *The Indian Ocean Newsletter* 350 (1 October 1988): 6.

"Ethiopia: The Last Tangle in Addis." *Africa Confidential* 25, no. 19 (19 September 1984).

"Ethiopia: New Appeal for Aid." *The Indian Ocean Newsletter* 307 (14 November 1987): 6.

"Ethiopia: Reagan Goes on the Attack." *The Indian Ocean Newsletter* 301 (10 October 1987): 2.

"Ethiopia: The Red Terror." *Newsweek* 9140 (20 February 1978).

"Ethiopia: West German Investment." *The Indian Ocean Newsletter* 353 (22 October 1988): 7.

"Ethiopia: World Bank Provides 70 Million." *The Indian Ocean Newsletter* 319 (13 February 1988): 8.

"Ethiopia Accused of Slave Labour." *The Times* (London), 15 August 1981.

"Ethiopia Seeks Investors." *The Times* (London), 15 February 1983.

"Ethiopian Ambassador Has Meeting with Dr. Owen." *The Times* (London), 5 April 1978, 6H.

"Ethiopians Say Eritrea Is Beaten." *The Times* (London), 19 January 1982.

Farer, Tom J. *War Clouds on the Horn of Africa: A Crisis for Detente.* New York: Carnegie Endowment for International Peace, 1976.

Fernyhough, Timothy Derrick. *Serfs, Slaves, and Shifta: Modes of Production in Southern Ethiopia from the Late Nineteenth Century to 1941.* Ph. D. diss., University of Illinois, 1986.

———. "Social Mobility and the Dissident Elites in Northern Ethiopia: The Role of Banditry, 1900–1969." Symposium on Rebellion and Social Protest in Africa, University of Illinois, April 22–24, 1982.

Fieldhouse, D. K. *The Colonial Empires: A Comparative Survey.* New York: Delacorte Press, 1966.

"Free Africa Pledged by Mr. Carter." *The Times* (London), 3 April 1978, 6G.

Gebru Tareke. "Peasant Resistance in Ethiopia: The Case of *Weyane*." *Journal of African History* 25 (1984): 77–92.

Gilkes, Patrick. *The Dying Lion: Feudalism and Modernization in Ethiopia*. New York: St. Martin's Press, 1975.

Greenfield, Richard. *Ethiopia: A New Political History*. New York: Praeger, 1965.

Halliday, Fred, and Maxine Molyneux. *The Ethiopian Revolution*. New York: Schocken Books, 1981.

Hess, Robert L. *Ethiopia: The Modernization of Autocracy*. Ithaca, N.Y.: Cornell University Press, 1970.

"Horn of Africa: Everybody's War." *The Economist*, 4 February 1978.

"Interview [with EPLF Secretary General, Issaias Afewerki]: We See no correlation between Peace and Military Might" *Adulis* 7, no. 4 (April 1990): 6–8

"Israel Selling Arms to Ethiopia." *The Times* (London), 7 January 1985, 1B.

Jordan Gabre-Medhin. "Eritrea: The Roots of War." *Horn of Africa Journal* 6, no. 2 (1983).

Kahasai, Berhane. "Political and Legal Analysis of the Eritrean Question." Vol. 7 in *African Publications Project* Trenton, N.J.: Red Sea Press, n.d.

Kanet, Roger E., ed. *Soviet Foreign Policy in the 1980's*. New York: Praeger, 1982.

Keller, Bill. "Kremlin Blames Budget Deficit on Subsidies." *The New York Times Weekly*, 31 October 1988.

Kirkland, Richard I. "Why Russia Is Still in the Red." *Fortune*, 30 January 1989, 73–78.

Kobishchanov, Yuri M. *Axum*. Translated by Lorraine T. Kapitanoff. Edited by Joseph W. Michels. University Park, Pa.: Pennsylvania State University Press, 1979.

Kohn, Hans. *The Idea of Nationalism: A Study in Its Origins and Background*. New York: Macmillan, 1944.

———. *Nationalism: Its Meaning and History*. Princeton, N.J.: D. Van Nostrand Co., 1955.

Lefort, Reńe. *Ethiopia: A Heretical Revolution?* Translated by A. M. Berrett. London: Zed Press, 1981.

Legum, Colin. "The USSR and Africa: The African Environment." *Problems of Communism* 27 (January-February 1978): 1–19.

LeMonde, 6 May 1977.

Lens, Sidney. *The Forging of the American Empire*. New York: Thomas Y. Crowell, 1971.

LeoGrande, William M. *Cuba's Policy in Africa; 1959–1980*. Berkeley: University of California Press, 1980.

Lipski, George, et al. *Ethiopia: Its People, Its Society, Its Culture.* New Haven: HRAF Press, 1962.

Lockham, Robin, and Dawit Bekele. "Foreign Powers and Militarism in the Horn of Africa." *Review of African Political Economy* 30 (September 1984).

Louis, William Roger. *Imperialism at Bay: The United States and the Decolonization of the British Empire, 1941–1945.* New York: Oxford University Press, 1978.

McClellan, C. W. "Perspectives on the Neftanya-Gabbar System: The Derasa Ethiopia." *Africa-Roma* 33 (1978).

McDougal, M. G., and M. W. Reisman, eds. *International Law in Contemporary Perspective: The Public Order of the World Community—Cases and Materials.* New York: Foundation Press, 1981.

Magdoff, Harry. *The Age of Imperialism: The Economics of U.S. Foreign Policy.* New York: Monthly Review Press, 1969.

Marcus, Harold G. *Ethiopia, Great Britain, and the United States, 1941–1974: The Politics of Empire.* Berkeley: University of California Press, 1983.

———. *The Life and Times of Menelik II: Ethiopia 1844-1913.* Oxford: Clarendon Press, 1975.

Marcuse, Herbert. *Soviet Marxism: A Critical Analysis.* New York: Random House, 1961.

Markakis, John. *Ethiopia: Anatomy of a Traditional Polity.* Oxford: Clarendon Press, 1974.

Markakis, John, and Nega Ayele. *Class and Revolution in Ethiopia.* Trenton, N.J.: Red Sea Press, 1986.

Melman, Seymour. *The War Economy of the United States: American Capitalism in Decline.* New York: Simon and Schuster, 1974.

Mesa-Lago, Carmelo, and June S. Belkin, eds. *Cuba in Africa.* Pittsburgh: University of Pittsburgh Center for Latin American Studies, 1982.

Moon, Thomas. *Imperialism and World Politics.* New York: Macmillan, 1926.

"Moscow Comes Out in Support of Ethiopia against the Eritreans." *The Times* (London), 16 March 1978, 9A.

"The National Question in Ethiopia: Proletarian Internationalism or Bourgeois Nationalism?" *Combat* 5, no. 2 (1976, special issue).

"100,000 in an Eritrean Retreat." *The Daily Telegraph* (London), 12 December 1978, 5A.

Ottaway, Marina. *Soviet and American Influence in the Horn of Africa.* New York: Praeger, 1982.

Ottaway, Marina, and David Ottaway. *Ethiopia: Empire in Revolution.* New York: Africana Publishing Co., 1978.

Paterson, Thomas G. *On Every Front: The Making of the Cold War.* New York: W. W. Norton Co., 1979.

Permanent Peoples Tribunal of the International League for the Rights and Liberation of Peoples. *The Eritrean Case: Proceedings of the Permanent Peoples Tribunal of the International League for the Rights and Liberation of Peoples.* Session on Eritrea, Milan, Italy. 24–26 May 1980.

Petras, James F., and Morris H. Morley. "The Ethiopian Military State and Soviet-U.S. Involvement in the Horn of Africa." *Review of African Political Economy* 30 (September 1984): 20–31.

Pool, David. *Eritrea: Africa's Longest War.* London: Antislavery Society, 1979.

Prouty, Chris. *Empress Taytu and Menilek II: Ethiopia 1883–1910.* Trenton, N.J.: Red Sea Press, 1986.

Rivlin, Benjamin. *The United Nations and the Italian Colonies.* New York: Carnegie Endowment for International Peace, 1950.

Ross, Jay. "Ethiopia Leans Uneasily on Soviets as Reliable Source of Arms." *Washington Post,* 31 December 1981, A12.

Rubenson, Sven. *The Survival of Ethiopian Independence.* New York: Africana Publishing Co., 1976.

"Russian Troops Said to Be Fighting in Eritrea." *The Times* (London). 2 February 1978, 7G.

Samuels, Michael A., et al. *Implications of Soviet and Cuban Activities in Africa for U.S. Policy.* Washington, D.C.: Georgetown University, 1979.

Sanders, Jerry. *Peddlers in Crisis: The Committee on the Present Danger and the Politics of Containment.* Boston: South End Press, 1983.

Shafer, Boyd C. *Faces of Nationalism: New Realities and Old Myths.* New York: Harcourt Brace Jovanovich, 1972.

Sherman, Richard. *Eritrea: The Unfinished Revolution.* New York: Praeger, 1980.

"South Yemen–Soviet Talks on Horn of Africa War." *The Times* (London), 4 February 1978, 5C.

"Soviet Arms for Ethiopia Jam Sea Lanes." *Washington Post,* 20 January 1978.

"Soviet War Planes Sent to Ethiopia." *The Sunday Times* (London), 23 April 1978, 10H.

Spencer, John H. *Ethiopia at Bay: A Personal Account of the Haile Selassie Years.* Algonac, Mich.: Reference Publications, Inc., 1984.

———. *Ethiopia: The Horn of Africa and U.S. Policy.* Cambridge, Mass.: The Institute of Foreign Policy Analysis, 1977.

Sweezy, Paul M., and Harry Magdoff, comps. *The Dynamics of U.S. Capitalism: Corporate Structure, Inflation, Credit, Gold, and the Dollar.* New York: Monthly Review Press, 1972.

Tadesse Tamrat. *Church and State in Ethiopia: 1270–1527.* Oxford: Clarendon Press, 1972.

Tekeste Negash. *Italian Colonialism in Eritrea, 1882–1941: Policies, Praxis and Impact.* Uppsala, Sweden: Uppsala University, 1987.

Touval, Faadia. *Somali Nationalism: International Politics and the Drive for Unity in the Horn of Africa*. Cambridge: Harvard University Press, 1963.

Treaster, Joseph B. "Enmity between U.S. and Cuba May Be Relaxing." *The New York Times Weekly*, 9 January 1989.

Trevaskis, G. K. N. *Eritrea: A Colony in Transition: 1941–52*. London: Oxford University Press, 1960.

Trimmingham, J. Spencer. *Islam in Ethiopia*. Oxford: Oxford University Press, 1952.

"25 Million Pounds Order." *The Times* (London), 25 March 1983, p. 21A.

Ullendorff, Edward. *The Ethiopians: An Introduction to Country and People*. 3d ed. London: Oxford University Press, 1973.

U.S.-U.S.S.R. Joint Statement on Ethiopia, 2 June 1990.

"US Congress Holds Hearing on War and Famine." *Adulis* 7, no. 4, p. 9.

Valley, Paul. "Famine: Russia and the US on Collision Course." *The Times* (London), 4 June 1985, 12B.

———. "How Mengistu Hammers the Peasants." *The Times* (London), 1 March 1985–a, 15B.

Vance, Cyrus. *Hard Choices: Critical Years in Managing America's Foreign Policy*. New York: Simon and Schuster, 1983.

Walsh, Edward. "Cubans in Ethiopia Put above 10,000." *Washington Post*, 25 February 1978.

"West's Aid Fails to Sway Ethiopia from East Orbit." *U.S. News and World Report*. 29 July 1985, 25–29.

Wilkinson, R. "Bombing in Eritrea Described." *Washington Post*, 17 January 1978.

Yemane Mesghenna. *Italian Colonialism: A Case Study of Eritrea, 1869–1934—Motive, Praxis and Result*. Maryland: International Graphics, 1989.

Zewde Gabre-Selassie. *Yohannes IV of Ethiopia: A Political Biography*. Oxford: Clarendon Press, 1975.

Public Documents

British Public Record Office

FO 371/31608. Note from Ethiopian Government Respecting Eritrea, Enclosure no. 1 to telegram from Robert Howe to Eden, 29 May 1942.

———. E. H. Chapman-Andrews, "Memorandum on Eritrea," Enclosure no. 2 to telegram from Howe to Eden, 29 May 1942.

FO 371/35414. Memorandum from FO Research Department. "Disposal of Eritrea," 26 June 1943.

FO 371/35633. R. V. Howe to Anthony Eden, 4 March 1943.

FO 371/35658. S. Longrigg, "Future Disposal of Eritrea," 12 August 1943.

———. "Eritrea and Her Neighbours," Enclosure to Chief Civil Affairs Officer to War Office, 14 September 1943.

FO 371/40601. Memorandum from FO Research Department, 2 March 1944.

FO 371/63175. Stafford to Scott-Fox, "Fortnightly Report," 21 December 1946.

FO 371/63186. Lawson to Scrivener, 25 January 1947.

FO 371/69197. Four Power Commission in Eritrea, Minutes, Scott-Fox to Stafford, 5 January 1948.

FO 371/69333. Memorandum from the Former Italian Colonies Committee, "Disposal of the Former Italian Colonies: International Considerations," 27 April 1947.

———. FO Minute by Scott-Fox, "Ex-Italian Colonies," 15 April 1948.

FO 371/69344. "Recommendations to the Council of Foreign Ministers of the Deputies of Foreign Ministers of the United Kingdom, the United States of America, the French Republic, and the Union of Soviet Socialist Republics Appointed to Consider the Question of the Disposal of the Former Italian Colonies," 31 August 1948.

FO 371/69345. Mallet to Strang, 27 July 1949.

———. Mason to Clutton, 29 July 1949.

———. Mason to Bevin, 23 October 1948.

FO 371/69353. Drew to the War Office, "Ethiopia's Claims to Eritrea and Somaliland," 30 March 1948.

FO 371/69362. *Report of the Four Power Commission of Investigation, Former Italian Colonies*, vol. 1, Report on Eritrea, 1948.

FO 371/73788. Drew to Bevin. 8 October 1949.

FO 371/73789. FO to Addis Ababa, telegram no. 536, 19 November 1949.

FO 371/73790. FO Minute. Stewart, "Internal Security in Eritrea," 7 December 1949.

FO 371/73841. House of Lords to Bevin, 22 January 1949.

———. Clutton, FO Minute, "Eritrea," 2 February 1949.

———. Mason to Wall, telegram no. 19, 25 March 1949.

FO 371/73844. Lascelles to Wright, 8 July 1949.

———. Strang to Mallet, 19 July 1949.

FO 371/73846. Drew to FO, telegram no. 120, 10 August 1949.

———. Lascelles to FO, telegram no. 7, 26 August 1949.

———. Paddock's Preliminary Report in Eritrea, Enclosure to Mason to Stewart, 9 September 1949.

———. Mr. Paddock's Second Report to London, 29 August 1949, Enclosure to Mason to Stewart, 9 September 1949.

———. UN UK Delegation to FO, telegram no. 213, 22 October 1948.

FO 371/73847. Wright to Mallet, 2 November 1948.

FO 371/80984. FO to Mallet, 15 January 1950.

———. Clutton, FO Minute, "Eritrea," 26 January 1950.

———. Paper from Italian Embassy, Enclosure to FO Minute, "Eritrea," 26–27 January 1950

———. Stafford, "Note of an Interview with H.I.M., The Emperor of Ethiopia on the 27 January 1950."

———. Stafford to Clutton, 16 February 1950.

———. Stafford, "The United Nations Commission in Eritrea: A Summary of its Activities. February 12th–19th [1950]."

———. Stafford to Smith, 12 March 1950.

———. Drew to FO, telegram no. 239, 16 March 1950.

FO 371/80985. Drew to Allen, 7 March 1950.

———. Lascelles to Allen, 9 March 1950.

———. Drew, Memorandum, "The Future of Eritrea," 14 March 1950, Enclosure to Drew to FO, 14 March 1950.

———. Stafford to Allen, 16 March 1950.

———. Scrivener, FO Minute, "Eritrea," 17 March 1950.

———. Lascelles to Drew, 17 March 1950.

FO 371/80986. FO to Mallet, 28 January 1950.

———. FO to Lascelles, 22 March 1950.

———. Stafford to Allen, 23 March 1950.

———. Drew to FO, 3 April 1950.

———. Lascelles to FO, telegram no. 112, 12 April 1950.

FO 371/80990. Meade to Allen, 1 June 1950.

FO 371/80991. FO Minute, "United Kingdom Delegation Brief for the Interim Committee on Eritrea," 29 June 1950.

———. "Eritrea: Record of Meetings in the Foreign Office on 30 June, 1st and 3rd July between Representatives of Italy, the United States and the United Kingdom," 3 July 1950.

FO 371/80992. Stafford to Allen, 13 July 1950.

FO 371/80993. "Record of Meeting held at the United Kingdom Delegation Offices on 17 July, 1950."

FO 371/80994. Drew to Wright, 25 July 1950.

FO 371/80996. Stafford to Stewart, 10 August 1950.

FO 371/80998. Allen, "Eritrea," 18 September 1950.

FO 407/11. No. 12, "The King of Abyssinia to Her Majesty the Queen," Enclosure to Mr. Lascelles to the Marquis of Salisbury, Cairo, 26 August 1879.

———. No. 12, Minute by Mr. Wylde, 16 September 1879, Enclosure to Mr. Lascelles to the Marquis of Salisbury, Cairo, 26 August 1879.

———. No. 13, Enclosure, "Notes on the Soudan," to Mr. Lascelles to the Marquis of Salisbury, Cairo, 26 August 1879.

———. No. 46, Mr. A. B. Wylde, Confidential to the Marquis of Salisbury, Massowah, 20 October 1879.

———. No. 46, Enclosure 2, "Gordon Pasha to Her Majesty's Consul-General for Jeddah," Massowah, 12 September 1879.

WO 230/246. Mitchell to Secretary of State, telegram no. 236, 2 April 1948.

———. Political Adviser [Mason] to Scott-Fox, 19 June 1948.

———. U.K. Delegation of General Assembly to FO, telegram no. 53, 29 September 1948.

———. "U.K. Draft Resolution on the Disposal of Eritrea," 7 December 1948.

United Nations General Assembly

Background Paper, UN Department of Public Information, 1948.

G.A.O.R. Fifth Session, Ad Hoc Political Committee, Summary Records of Meetings, 30 September–14 December 1950.

G.A.O.R. Third Session, Part II, First Committee, 5 April–13 May 1949.

G.A.O.R. Fourth Session, Plenary Meetings of the General Assembly, Summary Records, 20 September–10 December 1949.

G.A.O.R. Fourth Session, Report of the First Committee. Annexes to the Summary Records of Meetings, 1949. A/1089 and Corr. .1.

G.A.O.R. Fifth Session, Plenary Meetings of the General Assembly, Annexes to the Summary Records of Meetings, 1949.

G.A.O.R. Fifth Session, United Nations Commission for Eritrea. Supplement no. 8, "Report of the United Nations Commission for Eritrea," 1950. A/1285.

G.A.O.R. Sixth Session, Excerpts from 316th Plenary Meeting of the General Assembly, 2 December 1950.

G.A.O.R. Seventh Session, *Final Report of the United Nations Commissioner in Eritrea*, supp. no. 15, 1952. A/2188.

G.A.O.R. Progress Report of the United Nations Commissioner for Eritrea during the year 1951. A/1959.

G.A.O.R. Summary Records of Meetings between Aklilou and Matienzo. A/A/C.44/S.1 and A/A/C.44/SR.4.

G.A.O.R. Summary Records, U.N. Commission for Eritrea. A/A/C.44/SR. 5.

United States Government

Department of State. *American Foreign Policy Basic Documents, 1977–1980*. Washington, D.C.: Government Printing Office, 1983.

———. *American Foreign Policy, Current Documents, 1981*. Washington, D.C.: Government Printing Office, 1984.

———. *American Foreign Policy Current Documents, 1983*. Washington, D.C.: Government Printing Office, 1985.

———. Control 8528, telegram 171, Merrell to Secretary of State, 19 August 1949.

———. "Disposition of the Former Italian Colonies." Secret, to U.S. Delegation to the United Nations. 27 September 1948.

———. *Foreign Relations of the United States*, 1950. Vol. 5, *The Near East, South Asia, and Africa*. Washington, D.C.: Government Printing House, 1978.

———. *Foreign Relations of the United States*, 1951. Vol. 5, *The Near East and Africa*. Washington, D.C.: Government Printing House, 1982.

———. *Foreign Relations of the United States*, 1952–1954. Vol. 11, *Africa and South Asia*. Washington, D.C.: Government Printing House, 1983.

———. Letter from James Forrestal to the Secretary of State, 13 December 1948.

———. Memorandum of conversation between Ethiopian Vice Minister of Foreign Affairs and Secretary Dean Acheson, 30 March 1949.

———. *U.S. Trade and Other International Agreements*. Vol. 5, part 1, 1954. Washington, D.C.: Government Printing Office, 1955.

———. *U.S. Trade and Other International Agreements*. Vol. 8, part 2, 1957. Washington, D.C.: Government Printing Office, 1958.

Leahy, William D., to Secretary of Defense. "Disposition of the Former Italian Colonies." A Report to the National Security Council, no. 19/3, 5 August 1948.

U.S. Congress. House of Representatives, 1st sess. *U.S. Policy and Request for Sale of Arms to Ethiopia*. Hearing before the Subcommittee on International Political and Military Affairs of the Committee on Foreign Affairs, 5 March 1975.

Other

"EPLF Military Activities in 1988." EPLF press release, 12 January 1988.

"The Ethiopian Revolution and the Problem in Eritrea." Addis Ababa, July 1977.

Letter to Dag Hammarskjöld, UN Secretary General, from Ibrahim Sultan Ali, Idris Muhammed Adem, and Woldemariam, Cairo, 30 June 1959.

Memorandum of the Government of Egypt, submitted to the Paris Peace Conference, 1946.

Memorandum of Imperial Ethiopian Government, submitted to the Council of Foreign Ministers, London, 1945.

Other Sources

Caulk, R. A. "'Black Snake, White Snake': Bahta Hagos and His Revolt against Italian Overrule in Eritrea, 1894." Symposium on Rebellion and Social Protest in Africa, African Studies Program, University of Illinois at Urbana, 22–24 April 1982.

Ethiopian Radio and Television. Speech by Mengistu Haile Mariam, 7 June 1978.

Fernyhough, Timothy. "Social Mobility and Dissident Elites in Northern Ethiopia: The Role of Banditry, 1900–1969." Symposium on Rebellion and Social Protest in Africa, African Studies Program, University of Illinois at Urbana, 22–24 April 1982.

"An official translation of the decisions of the MOSLEM LEAGUE OF ERITREA as received by B.M.A., ERITREA, January 1947." Reprinted in *Journal of Eritrean Studies* 3, no. 2 (Winter 1989): 65-66.

Public Broadcasting System. "Background Report on Angola." "MacNeil-Lehrer News Hour," 22 December 1988.

PBS. "MacNeil-Lehrer News Hour," 16 January 1989.

Index